CITIZENSHIP AND ITS DISCONTENTS

CITIZENSHIP AND ITS DISCONTENTS

An Indian History

Niraja Gopal Jayal

HARVARD UNIVERSITY PRESS
Cambridge, Massachusetts
London, England
2013

Library of Congress Cataloging-in-Publication Data
Jayal, Niraja Gopal.
Citizenship and its discontents: an Indian history / Niraja Gopal Jayal.
p. cm.
Includes bibliographical references and index.
ISBN 978-0-674-06684-7 (alk. paper)
1. Citizenship—India—History.   2. India—Politics and government—1947–
3. Civics, East Indian. I. Title.
JQ283.J39 2013
323.60954—dc23
2012018084

For
Rakesh
exemplary citizen of the local
and
Gayatri
global citizen extraordinary

Contents

PART THREE

Identity

CITIZENSHIP AND ITS DISCONTENTS

Introduction

The twenty-five-year-old daughter of refugee parents petitions a court to become the first Tibetan to obtain Indian citizenship. Laborers in the countryside agitate to secure their newly legislated right to manual work at a minimum wage for a hundred days a year. A Dalit woman wrests the right to hoist the national flag at the office of the panchayat she heads on Independence Day. On Facebook and Twitter, a few hundred thousand people "Like" or "Follow" the anticorruption campaign led by a seventy-four-year-old activist. These are just a few of the many ways in which citizenship is claimed and performed every day across the Republic of India.

On an equally quotidian basis, even as middle-class Indians bask in the warmth of the global celebration of the world's largest democracy, there are many citizenly aspirations that are routinely thwarted. Squatters periodically evicted from their makeshift homes; young men conveyed to police stations for minor offenses and there flogged and tortured; day laborers harassed in their quest for a Below Poverty Line certificate; low-caste women raped by upper-caste men and prevented from filing a police report; a victim of a communal riot restrained from seeking justice; tribals displaced by an infrastructure project; elderly pensioners bullied by clerks. For all the different ways in which they experience the state, these are all nominally citizens of India.

This book documents the evolution of the Indian idea of the citizen across the twentieth century, primarily as a relation between the individual and the state, but also as a relation between citizens. It explores some of the myriad ways in which citizenship in India is perceived and understood, claimed and asserted, surrendered and abrogated, abridged and violated. It traverses just a few of the many sites on which citizenship is enacted, from the Constituent Assembly and the courts to panchayats and refugee camps. It also surveys the different aspects of citizenship to which claims are made, from the right not to be discriminated against on the basis of caste or religion to the right to food or education.

Every single dimension of the concept of citizenship is contested in contemporary India: citizenship as legal status, citizenship as a bundle of rights and entitlements, and citizenship as a sense of identity and belonging. Such contestations are not a peculiarly Indian phenomenon. All over the world, the idea of citizenship finds expression in states' engagement with both their own citizens as well as those pressing on their borders. When governments adopt or renounce policies of multiculturalism, or cut back subsidies on public education, or enact laws to prosecute and deport immigrants, they redefine citizenship. As policy issues, these are familiar even to the politically disinterested though their association with citizenship may not always be self-evident. Academic thinking about citizenship has kept pace with, and in some cases even anticipated, these concerns. In the pages that follow, I provide an outline of the broad contours of the book, its structure and form of argument. This is prefaced by, first, a brief survey of the important theoretical and conceptual questions in recent scholarship on citizenship, and second, an account, in a comparative context, of how citizenship has come to acquire significance in politics and policy in recent times.

Why Citizenship?

It is hard to find, in contemporary political theory, a concept so enveloped in the glow of moral virtue as citizenship. Paradoxically, it is equally hard to find a category more promiscuously deployed. On the one hand, the idea of citizenship has acquired the status of a universal desideratum; on the other, its very capaciousness often renders it vacuous.

Concealed beneath the placid surface of this apparently consensual concept, lie a multitude of tensions, ambivalences, and disagreements.[1] The tensions are frequently expressed in the form of morally loaded binaries. The malodorousness of subjecthood and the fragrance of citizenship, for instance, permeate and even obscure the fundamental distinction—freedom—which must form the logical premise of such a discussion. Forms of citizenship are in turn expressed through highly normativized binaries, such as good citizenship[2] and bad citizenship; active and passive citizenship; thin and thick citizenship; top-down and bottom-up citizenship,[3] and so forth. The concept of a good citizen expresses our normative preference for citizens who possess and display civic virtue over those who do not. The distinction between "thin" citizenship as legal status and "thick" citizenship as a role or a desirable activity suggests the greater value we attach to the latter. This moral judgment is also reflected in the way we applaud active civic engagement and express disquietude about the passivity of those who are disengaged from politics. Finally, there is the binary between citizenship obtained through struggle and citizenship as a gift of the state. This binary admittedly bears a burden that is more ideological than moral, as adversarial forms of citizenship—such as insurgent citizenship[4]—tend to be valorized in contrast to its more acquiescent quotidian forms.

The ambivalences of citizenship beget equally fierce disagreements though they are less reductively oppositional, and not all of them involve normative principles or judgments. There is for instance no easy resolution of the contention between principles of universal and group-differentiated citizenship. If the first holds fast to the liberal ideal of equal citizenship, the second insists that the principle of difference-blind equality ignores the specific quality of disadvantage experienced by those who belong to social groups that are defined by their "comprehensive identities and ways of life" (Young, [1989] 1995: 195). A recognition of such disadvantage requires us to provide for group-differentiated citizenship through instruments such as affirmative action policies. This ambivalence begets another: how may loyalty to one's cultural community be reconciled with one's civic loyalties and obligations? Is it possible for individuals to be primarily members of an ascriptive community and still profess adherence to the idea of a civic community?

There is some ambivalence also over the expression of citizenship in collective forms of civic action relative to a more individualized conception emphasizing the private enjoyment of rights. The individual enjoyment of citizenship rights may be valuable and necessary, but the very idea of citizenship recalls not only individual entitlements but also the performance of civic duties. This has been the burden of republican critiques of liberalism and also a dominant theme of the social capital literature that has tended to attribute to collective civic initiative many good things, especially effective democracy.[5]

There is finally a long history of ambivalence about the question of determining the proper site for the performance of citizenship which, for Tocqueville as for Mill, was emphatically the local. The recent proliferation in levels of governance confronts the citizen of the twenty-first century with the challenge of citizenship at multiple levels: not merely the local, the regional, and the national state, but defying national boundaries, the supranational and the global. A French citizen thus may take seriously her European citizenship, and when she participates in the World Social Forum, or in protests against the WTO, also partake of global citizenship. In recent years, theories of cosmopolitanism make just such demands on citizens, encouraging them to a better understanding of cultural difference and reminding them that the boundaries of citizenship do not stop at the local but must encompass their duties towards the world, especially its disadvantaged inhabitants.

Despite these ambivalences, there is a widespread though not always well-founded presumption that citizenship and democracy belong together, being naturally compatible and mutually complementary. The origins of this book lie in an earlier work, *Democracy and the State: Welfare, Secularism and Development in Contemporary India* (1999), in which I had proposed that Indian democracy be judged, not by measures of voter turnout or macrolevel generalizations about political participation, but through an evaluation of its ability to provide the conditions for the meaningful exercise of citizenship rights. Needless to say, despite its admirable strengths in creating a reasonably robust electoral democracy, India has made less than significant progress in consolidating democracy in the substantive sense. There is no doubt that the conditions of substantive democracy are considerably more demanding than those of formal procedural democracy, rendering the former always a work-in-progress. Procedural democracy is concerned with the efficacy and integrity of political processes and institutions, with creating and upholding a fair set of rules that structure opportunities for political participation, and with enhancing actual participation in these. Substantive democracy however asks us to consider outcomes such as equity, and in particular to ask whether the formal provisions of equal citizenship do in fact make possible even a reasonably satisfactory realization of the equal opportunities and entitlements of citizenship. It enjoins us also to explore the possible role of structural inequalities in making equality of citizenship a mirage.

It was his attention to structural inequalities that led the young Marx to highlight the discrepancy between the political equality enjoyed by the citizen of capitalist democracy despite the manifest inequality of his position in the class structure[6] (Marx, 1963: 12). It was moreover this deficit that T. H. Marshall, almost exactly a century after Marx, powerfully addressed through the question of whether "basic equality, when enriched in substance and embodied in the formal rights of citizenship, is consistent with the inequalities of social class" (Marshall, [1950] 1992: 7). It was assumed, in mid-twentieth-century British society, that the two were compatible, "so much so that citizenship has itself become, in certain respects, the architect of legitimate social inequality" (ibid.). Marshall famously distinguished between three elements of citizenship: the civil element (the rights necessary for individual freedom), the political element (the right to participate in the exercise of political power) and the social element, which he defined as "the whole range from the right to a modicum of economic welfare and security to the right to share to the full in the social heritage and to live the life of a civilised being according to the standards prevailing in the society" (ibid.: 8). These encompassed not only rights to public education and healthcare but also to housing and legal aid. (ibid.: 27–38). To the present day, this remains the lineage of the idea of social citizenship.

There are diverse opinions about whether citizenship in this fuller sense is a necessary and/or sufficient condition of democracy. We have examples of states which provided, and in some cases continue to provide, the rights of social citizenship within a nondemocratic framework. In the 1920s and '30s, Stalin's Soviet Union universalized access, for its citizens, to education, employment, housing, medical care, and food, even as it denied them elementary political rights and freedoms. What is less well known is that it also *legally* disenfranchised as many as four million people—identified on the basis of their prerevolutionary social position as members of the bourgeoisie—who enjoyed none of these rights, not even the sham voting rights that legal citizens formally enjoyed (Alexopoulos, 2003: 3). In rather similar vein, the Constitution of Kazakhstan today provides "a precarious sort of citizenship" while altogether depriving its people of the elementary civil and political rights and liberties that are associated with democracy (Tilly, 1999: 257).

Social citizenship thus may be at least partially realized outside of democratic contexts. Equally, democracy does not invariably result in the creation of conditions for the meaningful exercise of citizenship. If democracy and citizenship do not necessarily entail each other, under what conditions can democracy be an instrument for the realization of citizenship? The merit of asking such a question lies not only in its explanatory value for political scientists, or even in its exemplary value for citizens striving for more effective democratic citizenship, but especially in its role as a reminder of the ineluctable particularity of the challenges of citizenship.

This empirical specificity of citizenship consistently undermines its normative claim of universality. It encourages us to acknowledge, first, that there are countless ways of being citizens and practicing citizenship, arguably reflecting the countless ways in which states relate to the members of the populations over which they govern. To presume that the concept of citizenship speaks to a common reality across time and space requires us to furnish a robust account of the essence of state power and a theory of how it *invariably* relates to those whom it governs. Most accounts of citizenship—those that pledge allegiance to Foucault no less than to Marx—assume such a similarity, but it would be wise to be cautious about such claims because of the ineluctable specificity of citizenship issues in every society. Context matters.

Contestations over citizenship are also tied to social and political context. Citizenship claims are multiple, varied in content, and never settled in perpetuity. Even liberal and well-provisioned citizens of democratic states are sometimes discomfited when challenged by claims to recognition from immigrants belonging to different cultures. How do particular citizens and groups of citizens perceive, articulate, and negotiate their citizenship claims? What are the aspects of citizenship that they consider to be meaningful to their lived experiences and their civic and political futures? How, in other words, do they define the problematic of citizenship? While Indian negotiations of the idea of citizenship are specifically Indian, they resonate in important ways with the renewal of interest in questions of citizenship in the rest of the world.

Citizenship Redux

The revitalization of the idea of citizenship in recent times has three interrelated sources. First, the return of citizenship to political discourse in the 1980s saw it riding in on the crest of the wave of the resurgence of civil society. The idea of civil society—also uncritically valorized because of its role in bringing down the edifice of totalitarian rule in Eastern Europe—showed individuals their visage in the mirror of citizenship. It demonstrated to them who they could be as members of the political community, as participants in political endeavors that frequently placed them in adversarial positions vis-à-vis the state. Civil society thus offered citizens a space in which they could realize their political selfhood through the exercise of a long-forgotten political efficacy.

Second, the reassertion of civil society in Eastern Europe was also the moment of ascendant neoliberalism in the United Kingdom and the United States, where this loss of political efficacy was attributed to the welfare state. It triggered a questioning of the welfare state on the grounds that it had encouraged a lazy parasitism and discouraged civic sentiments. Redistributive policies were viewed as having induced passivity in citizens who, having become dependent on state provisioning by a gigantic bureaucratic leviathan, were all but parasites upon the state, insensitive to their own duties and civic obligations. Indeed, contra Marshall, welfare was perceived to have diminished, rather than augmented, social solidarity.

That economic turn delegitimized social citizenship and was accompanied, thirdly, by a curiously celebratory rediscovery of the virtues of civic republicanism, which proved to be remarkably adaptable to the needs of a conservative political agenda, showing once again that citizenship can be and has been suborned to all manner of political projects. The convergence between this critique of the big state and that of the cheerleaders of civil society was unmistakable. Both valued active citizen participation, with the minor difference that the conservative version of this did not posit the individual in an interrogative and invariably adversarial role in relation to the state.

In his disquisition on citizenship, T. H. Marshall had in 1949–1950[7] argued that the duties of citizenship entailed not the sacrifice of one's individual liberty or unquestioning obedience to government but certainly demanded that the acts of individuals "should be inspired by a lively sense of responsibility towards the welfare of the community" (1992: 41). The irony is that the rebirth of the civic ideal came at least partly as a response to the perceived solidarity deficit of the welfare state, though the free-market policies of its New Right critics could hardly be said to enhance solidarity.

It is in cosmopolitanism that we encounter not just civic belonging but a globalized moral solidarity which, drawing inspiration from Kant, exhorts every individual to see herself as a citizen of the world, as belonging to a moral community of human beings that transcends national borders (Linklater, 1999). Cosmopolitan thinkers make a case for two types of cosmopolitan citizenship—cosmopolitanism about culture and cosmopolitanism about justice. Cosmopolitanism about culture would have citizens see themselves as constituted not by the particular cultures or communities into which they were born but forming their identities and developing their capacities to flourish by drawing upon cultural resources from almost anywhere (Scheffler, 2001: 114). Cosmopolitanism of justice, similarly, encourages individuals to acknowledge that norms of justice are not restricted to their fellow members of the particular societies to which they happen to belong, but must govern the relations of all individuals to each other. These norms "accrue to individuals as moral and legal persons in a worldwide civil society" (Benhabib, 2006: 16). This is justified at least partially by recourse to the historical phenomena of colonialism, slavery, and genocide to which the contemporary affluence of the global North and the poverty of the global South are attributed (Pogge, 2001: 15).

Even as scholars and philosophers contemplate a postnational and post-statist world of cosmopolitan citizens, however, the idea of citizenship in the western world has been dramatically transformed in a way that is scarcely compatible with the attractive image proffered by the votaries of cosmopolitanism. In the post-9/11 world, the conditions of citizenship have become more demanding. Historically mature states, confident of their place in the world, have been observed searching frenetically for ways of defining their national identities and "national values" to better cement ties between citizens,[8] as also to ensure that new citizens adduce sufficient proof of subscribing to the shared values of the nation. Others have sought to devise ways of monitoring and controlling existing citizens more closely through databases that are scarcely respectful of individual privacy.

These worries have contributed to the intertwining of the three dimensions of citizenship—status, rights, and identity—in new (and globalized) ways. The intersection between legal and cultural citizenship may be illustrated by the citizenship tests that have been instituted (between 2005 and 2008) in the United Kingdom, the United States of America, Australia, and the Netherlands. These affirm popular misgivings about the discriminatory effect of these tests against immigrants who are poor and have not had much education. The US government's attempt to make the citizenship test for immigrants more "meaningful" took the form of a pilot citizenship examination designed to focus on questions about American civic ideals rather than history and politics; and about democracy and freedom in place of the earlier questions about the number and color of the stars on the American flag.[9] Many of these new testing procedures strive to convey the idea, increasingly popular across Europe, that subscribing to a set of shared national values is an essential component of citizenship. The new citizenship test in the United Kingdom, based on the book *Life in the UK*,[10] has attracted the criticism that since very few born Britons could answer all the test questions—such as those about the Geordie, Cockney, and Scouse dialects—the test would create two classes of citizens, those who did not need to know their country's history because they were born there, and those who did simply because they were born elsewhere.[11] In Australia, just a few months after the new test was introduced,[12] concerns about a high "failure" rate—one-fifth of those who took the new test failed to obtain the 60 percent mark needed for citizenship—led to a government review of the test. The review committee, in its report of August 2008, confirmed that the new test had been "flawed, intimidating to some and discriminatory."[13]

The tests introduced in the Netherlands and in two states of Germany (Hesse and Baden-Württemberg) were openly anti-Muslim in nature. They asked applicants loaded questions about women's duties to obey their husbands, the rights of husbands to beat disobedient wives, and whether women should be allowed to go out unescorted by a man. Both these also asked questions about homosexuality, a theme that is part of the citizenship test in the Netherlands where prospective citizens are shown video films of gay men and of nude bathers to show that these are accepted and legal practices in that society.[14] Describing this as "Discrimination in the Name of Integration,"[15] Human Rights Watch claimed that the exemption provided to people of some nationalities while others were compelled to take an expensive and unfair test was clearly discriminatory.

While the examples we have just surveyed are relevant to new and potential citizens, there are also examples of governments seeking to render existing citizens more civic. Braving an opposition boycott and strong criticism from liberals, the Japanese Diet approved a bill requiring schools to instill patriotism in children by teaching them ways of "respecting tradition and culture and loving the nation and homeland." The opposition feared in this appeal to tradition and obedience a resurgence of the expansionist militarist nationalism of prewar imperial Japan.[16] While the Japanese law is about abstractions such as patriotism, a recent British proposal for "compulsory civic service"[17] suggests that this could mitigate unemployment in a recessionary economy rather like President Roosevelt's Civilian Conservation Corps,[18] and simultaneously help people meet social needs that are currently unmet either by public services or the market.

This essentially conservative turn in citizenship practices is unmistakably related to the debacle of multiculturalism in western societies, and in particular its inability to cope with the challenges of immigrants' claims to cultural rights. Rethinking the impact of multiculturalism, theorists have argued that, while seeking to promote tolerance and inclusion, multicultural policies may have unwittingly created institutional structures within communities that become easy prey for capture by fundamentalist groups who use these to undermine the liberal-democratic order (Banting and Kymlicka, 2006: 3). The imperiled project of multiculturalism, and the renewed contentiousness of legal aspects of citizenship, suggests a rethinking of the normative theory of citizenship.

Another disquieting consequence of the failure of multiculturalism is its post-9/11 convergence with security, taking the form of heightened anxieties about the documentation and identification of citizens. In many societies, these have come to be seen as two faces of the same, frequently unnamed, phenomenon of immigration. The documentation of citizens in a national registry has been undertaken in many countries of the global North; the presumed connection between immigration and terrorism has created a further impetus for identification through ID cards of various types, containing a range of personal, including biometric, data. The British Identity Cards Act of 2006, which provided for National Identity Cards for citizens linked to a National Identity Register, was opposed by human rights lawyers and activists, and repealed in January 2011. Misgivings about state surveillance and invasion of citizens' rights to privacy are not persuasively allayed by state-constructed anxieties about terror.

In India, Aadhar,[19] the new initiative to provide a Unique Identification (UID) in the form of a Unique Number, seeks to give a numerical identity to Indian residents and not only citizens. The stated objective is that of targeting welfare-recipients more effectively, and addressing the rampant malpractices in public service delivery, such as the corruption in state-sponsored employment programs where payments are customarily made to nonexistent individuals certified by labor contractors. The official purpose of the UID is therefore to give every individual an official acknowledgment of her existence, such that the rural and urban poor, who remain faceless and invisible in the eyes of the state, can have a numerical identity that validates their existence, thereby protecting them from arbitrary state action and giving them access to various forms of public provisioning.[20] Residual concerns however remain, especially those arising out of the possible abuse of biometric information.

Many of these recent transformations in the practices and projects of citizenship in the North—from neoliberal and multicultural citizenship, on the one hand, to citizenship tests and documentation, on the other—have resonance in the South. Practices of citizenship remain abidingly contentious, bound up as they are with claims to legal citizenship that have become more intense given the scale of global migration; tensions between subnational cultural affiliations and membership of a civic community; and finally, the attribution of social and economic rights to citizens. However, the Indian trajectory of these questions does not mirror their career in the North; these have been unresolved questions in Indian society for the better part of the twentieth century.

The Quest for Indian Citizenship

"At the stroke of the midnight hour," declaimed Jawaharlal Nehru on August 14, 1947, "India will awake to life and freedom." However, 365 million subjects of King George VI were not magically turned into citizens as that midnight hour struck. Many millions were fleeing their homes and crossing newly demarcated borders, motivated by the quest for physical safety more than the search for citizenship; there remained several million more in the Native States whose incorporation was yet to be accomplished; and there were even a million or so who were still governed from France and Portugal. Much as at the beginning of the twentieth century, the residents of the subcontinent were divided chiefly between subjects of the British Empire and subjects of the numerous principalities.

Can subjecthood, on the one hand, and unresponsive domination, on the other, offer a plausible preface to a history of citizenship? This book affirms the appropriateness of exploring the moral and intellectual resources that came to define citizenship in independent India, not least because many of the tensions and contradictions that have found political expression in recent decades have their wellsprings in the contention between ideas in the first half of that century. The history of citizenship in twentieth-century India is a history of a new way of thinking about the relationship of individuals to the state. It is a history of colonial, constitutional, and postcolonial modes of thinking about the relationship of individuals to the state; about how these relationships are, should, or should not be mediated by community; about the relationship between the social and the political; about citizenship given by the state and citizenship wrested from it; about the enactment of citizenship in different prosceniums; about the constitution of individuals and groups as political agents; and about principles of political obligation and legitimacy. The twentieth century in India represents new beginnings in all of these.

Some histories of citizenship are original while others are imitative. But most histories of citizenship encompass popular struggles against political authority, variously constituted. In India, the transition from subject to citizen was the culmination of a distinctive and prolonged struggle for national self-determination, even if the conception of the citizen that informed it was a more or less faithful reproduction of that found in several liberal-democratic constitutions of the western world. The idea of citizenship was moreover forged simultaneously with the idea of the nation. Unlike the struggle of the working classes and of women for the franchise in Britain, or the civil rights movement in the United States, sections of the Indian people did not have to struggle specifically to achieve citizenship. They won it when they won independence; to be free from colonial rule was also to have exchanged the oppressive status of an imperial subject for the liberating one of citizen of a sovereign state. The idea of equality was both the premise and the promise of this conception of citizenship. Its embodiment in the form of constitutionally recognized rights carried the unique ethical mandate of the movement for freedom from colonial rule.

If the inclusionary attributes of the formal structure of Indian citizenship are traceable to the civic ideals forged in the movement for freedom, the contemporary contentions over citizenship can with equal confidence be traced back to the ideological conflicts and uneasy political compromises of this period. Citizenship does not, as Judith Shklar (1991) reminded us, reside in an unchanging and static space, and an account of Indian citizenship in the present persistently recalls historical challenges. Contestation is central to the defining of citizenship in each of the three core dimensions of citizenship: as legal status, as a bundle of rights and entitlements, and as a form of identity. Each of these, the book demonstrates, has a pre-independence and a post-independence life, and though these lives were, in and through the Constitution of 1950, intended to be discontinuous, there are in fact remarkable continuities between them. In the broadest terms, therefore, this is a history of ideas and ideational contests about what constitutes the Indian citizen. These contests—apart from many others that do not find a place in this book—have been in the Indian public domain for over a century now. Many of the arguments that made their appearance in the early twentieth century continue to resonate despite the passage of several decades. These are therefore resilient and ongoing negotiations in the public sphere.

The organizational structure of the book is as follows. It is divided into three parts, each housing one core aspect of the citizenship question, viz. citizenship as legal status, citizenship as rights and entitlements, and citizenship as a form of identity and belonging. The career of each of the three aspects is illustrated in three phases, with a chapter devoted to each period: first, in late colonial India; second, in the constitutional attempt to authoritatively and conclusively embed a citizenship regime for independent India; and finally, in independent India where the constitutional settlement is challenged by political contestation, sometimes opening up new spaces of citizenship, at other times provoking more restrictive redefinitions of citizenship by the state.

The first section of the book then is about the legal status of citizenship, which it is customary to think about as determined by one of two rival principles: birth *(jus soli)* and blood-based descent *(jus sanguinis)*. Jus soli is typically regarded as more inclusive than jus sanguinis which, as a generic principle, excludes all those who do not belong to the nation as an ethnocultural entity. Regardless of which criterion is favored in a particular state, it is fundamentally this principle that determines how citizenship may be acquired and therefore who can (and cannot) be a citizen. In practice, however, the pure type of either principle is rare, with the rules governing citizenship by marriage or naturalization complicating this neat delineation. France and Germany, for instance, were once regarded as stereotypical of jus soli and jus sanguinis respectively.[21] But recent scholarship has shown that although French nationality law has remained relatively stable since 1889, there have been periods in French history before and after that date when more exclusionary policies have been attempted and even for a time prevailed (Weil, 2008). Similarly, Germany has, since 1998, been pursuing a more inclusive nationality law by combining elements of jus sanguinis and jus soli. Large-scale immigration, especially second-generation, has been a particularly important factor in bringing jus soli and jus sanguinis regimes closer. However, though the trend toward hybridization has served to render obsolete the pure form of either, the dominance of one or other principle in different states says something significant about their foundational identities.

The primary differentiators of subject-citizenship in colonial India were race and class. That Australians and Canadians could be imperial citizens in ways that they could not be was a provocation for Indians protesting against the racial criteria by which citizenship in the white and the colored colonies was distinguished. However, even as they campaigned for the citizenship rights of subaltern Indians in the British Dominions, these articulate Indians accepted without question their own privileged class position within India. As chapter 1 suggests, their self-perception as putative citizens was encouraged by the colonial state whose recognition of particular classes of subjects as de facto citizens surely aided its quest for legitimacy.

At independence, India's choice of jus soli as the formal principle of citizenship was only partly a function of its legal inheritance, for jus sanguinis would clearly have been an implausible basis for citizenship in a vastly plural society. Over time, legal citizenship has shifted imperceptibly closer to a jus sanguinis regime, with changes in the laws and rules reflecting the advances made by exclusionary tendencies in Indian society and politics since independence. Chapter 2 argues that the tension between these two conceptions of citizenship was present from the founding moment of the republic, and, with the passage of time, citizenship laws are increasingly rather than decreasingly informed by the divisive legacy of the Partition. Through a survey of the evolution of laws on citizenship, and of the jurisprudence on the subject, the book argues that this bias is most visible in the manner in which law and policy have negotiated the question of Bangladeshi (Muslim) immigrants, as also in the manner in which the claims of wealthy diasporic Indians (mostly Hindus) have been sought to be accommodated. The move from jus soli to jus sanguinis renders legally plausible that which is socially implausible and civically repugnant, eroding India's foundational commitment to pluralism. However, the ethnographic study in chapter 3 of poor, largely Dalit and Adivasi, migrants from Pakistan into the border districts of Rajasthan, shows how their marginal social status and political unbankability render them undeserving objects of such solicitation as other coreligionists may muster.

It is scarcely surprising then that, for these denizens of India who have been awaiting citizenship for decades, legal citizenship is understood only as an instrument to obtain social and economic entitlements.

Social citizenship is the substantive focus of the second section of the book, which traces the evolution of rights in modern India. Chapter 4 shows that early twentieth-century writings in the civics genre invariably conceived of the qualities of "good" citizenship as duties rather than rights. This was less surprising than the fact that both writers of colonial textbooks and of nationalist tracts listed a very similar set of citizenly attributes albeit turned to very different purposes: the duty of obedience in the one case and the duty of resistance in the other. The emerging language of civil and political rights and of the social contract yielded a new way of thinking about political obligation, in which the right to resist, for instance, was born of the duty to disobey. If the colonialist posited citizenship as virtuous moral conduct in opposition to the perfidious political, the nationalist lexicon posited the moral as a resource for political subversion which, mediated by the legal, would fundamentally interrogate the legitimacy of the colonial state.

In the international context of the time, the discursive move from civil and political rights to social and economic rights in early twentieth-century India was astonishingly precocious. Equality is the premise of citizenship, but equal civil and political rights in and of themselves are poor guarantors of substantive equality, their egalitarian promise constantly undermined by the social inequalities that obtain in society. Social and economic rights are widely acknowledged as the principal means by which citizenship's promise of equality and the difficulty of its attainment may be mediated. In the familiar form given to social citizenship by the welfare states of Europe, access to state-provided goods such as public health and education, social security, old-age pensions, and so on, was universalized, though not always expressed in the language of rights. Two aspects of social citizenship are fundamental. First, to the extent that public provisioning requires redistributive taxation, it demands also a broad-based social consensus and sentiments of civic solidarity. Second, anything less than universalization is demeaning to those who need such public provisioning, or else services provided by the state are likely to be stigmatized as inferior. Both these are difficult conditions to meet, which explains why social and economic rights have been profoundly contentious, both within states as well as in the drafting of international covenants on rights.

In India too, despite their impressively early articulation, the rights of social citizenship have, from the 1930s to the present, been deeply contested. Chapter 5 shows how social citizenship has throughout remained a site of contention, inevitably ending in political compromise. However, despite intense debates in the Constituent Assembly, and despite support for these in the alternative constitutional imaginings of the time, what was ultimately yielded was a precarious political compromise in the shape of the nonjusticiable Directive Principles of State Policy. After independence too this remained an embattled project, with the conflict between the Fundamental Rights and the Directive Principles pitting the legislature against the judiciary, or the executive and civil society against each other.

The recent salience of social and economic rights presents a curious paradox, given their appearance in a policy environment in which the withdrawal of the state from public provisioning enjoys great legitimacy. Through an account of the enactment of the right to education, and the impending enactment of a law on food security, chapter 6 examines the hurdles to the fruition of a regime of social citizenship in contemporary India. The inadequacies of the new laws draw our attention to the danger of rights-talk masking strategies of what T. H. Marshall called class abatement. In India, this typically occurs through the construction of official categories of "beneficiaries." The book argues that such markers of citizenship (e.g., Below Poverty Line), ostensibly intended to facilitate targeted inclusions, actually end up entrenching exclusion, as also undermining the social solidarity that must underwrite any egalitarian project.

The distribution of symbolic power and symbolic resources is also an important aspect of the content of citizenship, and this is the theme of the third section of the book. While the principle of universal citizenship provides guarantees of equality, that of group-differentiated citizenship reassures minorities and other identity-based groups that the application of difference-blind principles of equality will not be allowed to operate in a way that is unmindful of their special needs, that these needs arising out of cultural difference or minority status will receive due attention in policy, and that the polity will be truly inclusive in its embrace. In both theory and policy, multicultural polities have in the last two decades recognized the claims of group-differentiated citizenship for groups that have experienced oppression, exploitation, or marginalization on grounds of gender, race, religious identity, sexual orientation, and disability.

The third section of the book interprets Indian political argument across the twentieth century in terms of a contest between the powerful rival claims of universalist and group-differentiated citizenship. Chapter 7 distinguishes between forms of universalist argument in the late colonial period: the substantive-inclusionary universalism of Gandhi and Nehru is contrasted to the descriptive-exclusionary universalism of Hindu nationalist thinking, and both these are counterposed to the impeccable universalism of the women's movement. The group-differentiated citizenship claims of this period likewise come from diverse sources and are presented as antidotes to biases that are alleged to be intrinsic to universalism even as it conceals and denies them: majoritarianism, discrimination, and backwardness.

As a justification for group-differentiated citizenship, "backwardness" is a peculiarly Indian addition to the criteria typically employed to defend the need for departures from difference-blind citizenship. Chapter 8 essays an interpretation of the concept of backwardness, its fuzziness and ambiguities, as a prelude to examining two quite distinct claims to citizenship based on it: those of tribal populations and of the Other Backward Classes. Chapter 9 surveys the thickly populated landscape of group-differentiated citizenship in the present, encompassing both the claims and the policy responses to them. The Indian experience, it argues, instantiates many of the normative complexities that theorists of group-differentiated citizenship have identified, in particular its implications for the construction of a civic community; the prospects of weakening social cohesion; and the difficulties of properly determining which groups are deserving of differentiated citizenship rights. It nevertheless offers an argument against positing universalist and group-differentiated citizenship in mutual opposition, a false dichotomy in a complex and diverse world.

Across the twentieth century and traversing all three domains of citizenship aspects—who can be a citizen, on what terms, and what the content of citizenship is—a persistent tension is manifest between the tendencies of inclusion and exclusion. The structural inequalities of Indian society are reflected in the fragility of the constitutional settlement as well as in the official strategies adopted to address exclusions of both a material and a symbolic nature.

The progressive principles embodied in the Constitution, first, are often presumed to be hegemonic ideas on which there was substantial consensus. Many of these political ideas were supremely well intentioned but less than robust; they signified uneasy compromises that spoke to the particularity of their context rather than to the more general normative principles to which they laid claims of lineage. Further, the tensions that characterize the constitutional settlement are not merely tensions within it, but also between the Constitution on the one hand and social, political, and administrative practices on the other.

On each of the three dimensions of citizenship, thus, this book shows how in the Constituent Assembly, uncomfortable questions were either papered over to achieve political compromises or were deferred for elected governments to figure out at a later date. The shadow cast by the Partition on the constitution-making process resulted in the enactment of the citizenship law being deferred till five years later, with constitutional intentions being repeatedly undermined in the administrative and political domains. Similarly, though social and economic rights lay at the heart of the normative commitment of the political leadership, they came to be intensely contested in the Constituent Assembly and eventually relegated to a nonjusticiable section of the Constitution. Finally, the constitutional ambivalence about "backwardness," a category inherited from the colonial state, meant that it was left undefined except in the most general terms, resulting in an enormous volume of legislation and adjudication that has still not conclusively settled the matter. These unfinished projects and unresolved controversies testify to the enduring quality of the zones of contention in Indian society.

Second, the paradox in the strategies of inclusion adopted by the Indian state is that these were dependent upon the creation of new categories of exception, on the credible assumption that such exceptions to equality (as sameness of treatment) would be more effective in tackling inequality. The naming of the inequality and the identification of those who were victims of it was an important precursor to addressing it, and therefore some had to be labeled as especially unequal before they could be rendered equal. The sociological existence of multiple forms of inequality implied that they had to be distinguished with different labels so that people who were eligible for Below Poverty Line classifications may also be Scheduled Caste, but these were treated as discrete categories attracting different policy provisions. The second and third parts of the book show how the very act of naming these categories for special provisioning ended up entrenching exclusions instead of the inclusions they were ostensibly created to foster. They contrast the privileges of the unmarked citizen with the reproduction of disadvantage for variously marked citizens. To become a citizen required being marked, but paradoxically the very act of getting marked meant the entrenchment of one's exclusion from substantive citizenship. Official categories of secular disadvantage serve to attenuate rather than facilitate the access to public services of those who are only nominally citizens. Thus, the official and sociopolitical categories which have been imposed upon citizens, supposedly to enhance the quality of their citizenship, invariably result in a diminution of it and in the continuing inability of even enfranchised citizens to represent themselves to the state.

Historically antecedent to the official markers of secular disadvantage were the sociopolitical markers of various forms of identity, whose salience is expressed in an abiding and fundamental ambivalence on the question of mediated citizenship. Early twentieth-century Indian liberalism was surely remarkable for its anticipative recognition of what are today called group rights, but were then seen as legitimate mediations of the citizen–state relation by community. Even the socialist project in India in the 1930s and 1940s was strongly inflected by citizenship claims based on caste, at the same time as and in contrast to the tortuous deliberations of the Communist International on the question of nationalities. However, unlike in the West where differentiated citizenship rights emerged in consolidated civic communities, the Indian recognition of rights accruing to collectivities rather than individuals occurred in a society which lacked the prior foundations of a civic community. It is not clear as to whether and to what extent community-mediated rights are compatible with a civic community if they precede the construction of the latter. Ideological tensions in the domesticated forms of liberalism and socialism have informed and complicated the construction of Indian citizenship in no small measure. Caste and community are not merely a part of the grammar of democratic politics, but the appropriateness of community as a quotidian form of mediation between citizen and state possesses legitimacy in rendering citizenship in the conventional western sense a fiction. The absence of alternative indigenous models of constructing citizenship in an egalitarian manner is suggestive of a normative vacuum on this question.

A brief digression on the concept of a citizenship regime is in order. The particular elements that make up a citizenship regime (Jenson and Phillips, 1996; Yashar, 2005)[22] in a given society at a given point in time will differ from those in other societies and even in the same society across time. As a bundle of features, citizenship regimes indicate who is a citizen and what the terms of inclusion and exclusion are; the nature of the identification of citizenship with nationality or cultural identity; what the recognized unit of citizenship is—individuals or groups—especially for the articulation of effective citizenship claims; the substance of citizenship rights, including and especially the rights of social citizenship; the role of the state and its policy strategies in stabilizing or undermining a particular citizenship regime; and how state and societal discourses and policies—of recognition or redistribution—shape citizenship. Despite the singularity suggested by the name, a citizenship regime may often accommodate multiple modes of relating to the state, even different levels and categories of citizenship. The idea of multiplicity itself may, in this context, be interpreted in different ways. Charles Tilly, for instance, would have us recognize the multiple categories of relationship of citizens to the state, in ways that resemble the different types of contracts by which corporations relate to their employees (1999: 255). Ornit Shani, by contrast, would characterize these as multiple citizenship regimes adopted by the state to manage different social groups (2010: 150).[23]

Despite the fragile unities of citizenship regimes, there is some stability and coherence to the architecture of citizenship at any given point in time. The citizenship regime provides the reference point for the contestations that position themselves against it. The presence of contradictory elements does not disprove the unity that may be rendered occasionally inchoate but not incoherent. Because the unity—however contradictory—represents that which is accepted, if not sponsored, by the state, it is, as the word regime suggests, the unity of the dominant consensus. Contestations represent resistance to this dominant consensus, even if they are sometimes managed. There may be, at any given point in time, a multiplicity of contestations of the citizenship regime, and these may occur simultaneously, and without orchestration, in different domains. Thus, the claims of the disadvantaged to the substantive rights of social citizenship; the claims of minorities to differentiated citizenship; and the claims of illegal immigrants to legal citizenship are all challenges to different aspects of the citizenship regime that may be simultaneously present but not acting in concert. As so many contestations of the citizenship regime, they stand in relation and often in opposition to the singularity represented by the dominant framework of the citizenship regime.

Confining ourselves to a restrictive conception of the citizenship regime, comprising only the three dimensions covered in this study, the colonial citizenship regime appears to have been a composite of instrumental ambivalence about who was or could be a citizen; of a limited, fungible, and selectively applicable set of civil and political rights; and of an artful manipulation of identities through institutional strategies of differentiating between groups of citizens. In a sea of subjects, a miniscule percentage of educated, propertied, and enfranchised classes comprised the de facto citizens of colonial India. Though motivated by a search for legitimacy, the state's kid-gloved treatment of these social groups indulged their self-perception as putative citizens. Their claims to civil and political rights however were not always sustained if only because these represented potential threats to the architecture of colonial rule held up by a scaffold in which force played a larger role than legitimacy. Finally, differentiated citizenship—its institutional forms ranging from special electorates and quotas to the symbolic recognition of cultural difference—appeared on the Indian political firmament well before independence. Citing the division of Indian society into multiple communities, the colonial state deployed arguments of political immaturity to deny citizenship rights, all the while remaining keenly attentive and even responsive to the representational claims being made by precisely such groups.

Even as the constitutional regime of 1950 remained surprisingly attuned to the colonial template in designing institutions of governance, it expanded the idea of citizenship beyond recognition. The constitutional provisions relating to the technical and legal aspects of citizenship took two years to be finalized, chiefly because the jus soli principle was intensely contested by votaries of jus sanguinis. Though many favored prescribing an educational or literacy qualification for political rights, the long-standing commitment of the nationalist leadership to universal adult franchise found realization in universally guaranteed civil and political rights. By contrast, the social rights that had been rhetorically pledged from the 1930s onward were quartered in a part of the Constitution that neither guaranteed these rights nor provided for any judicial recourse, but only enunciated these principles as intended *to guide* state policy in a welfarist direction. Economic and social rights became the eternal desiderata, forever compromised by considerations of what was legally feasible, politically expedient, and financially viable. Finally, though universal citizenship was tied to the idea of the nation as a civic community, two important exceptions of group-differentiated citizenship were introduced: the provision of cultural rights for religious minorities and of positive discrimination for historically disadvantaged and "backward" caste and tribal groups.

Many of these unfinished aspects of the architecture of constitutional citizenship have remained enduringly antinomic.

In independent India, as we have observed, all three spheres of citizenship have been contested. Since the mid-1980s, the law on citizenship has been repeatedly amended moving it irrevocably in the direction of a more restrictive jus sanguinis principle of citizenship. On the one hand, the policy imperative to control illegal immigration from Bangladesh led to the contraction of citizenship law into an increasingly descent-based principle; on the other, the descent-based principle permitted the incorporation of prosperous members of the Indian diaspora into the charmed circle of tacit citizenship. As we shall see, there remain communities of migrants who fall into neither of these categories, but whose claims to legal citizenship have nevertheless remained unaddressed by law and policy. Theirs are often encoded claims to social rights, as legal citizenship becomes the only instrument through which basic public services may be accessed. Even for citizens by birth, social and economic rights have only recently begun to be legislated or constitutionalized, often in the face of formidable odds. Perhaps the most fractious of all has been the contest between universal and group-differentiated conceptions of citizenship. The colonial state's recognition of the legitimacy of mediated citizenship has permanently marked the idea of citizenship as a relation between individual and state, as communities have come to be the preeminent repositories of political agency. Even as the Indian polity has been expansive in encompassing new claims to group-differentiated citizenship, this very capaciousness gives rise to legitimate anxieties about whether the possibility of a civic community has not been irretrievably compromised.

If the statist imperative of managing populations has dominated the determination of legal citizenship, social and political struggle have played a preeminent role in the negotiation of questions of rights and identity. The book addresses questions such as which forms of citizenship are claimed and at what juncture, who makes these claims, and where citizens meet the state in the pursuit of their rights. Claims to legal status, it shows, are generally negotiated in the judicial space, claim-making for rights tends to occur on the terrain of civil society, while claimants of differentiated citizenship typically use the sphere of partisan politics to advance their demands. In some cases, such as the campaign for the right to education, these forms of claim-making may lead to an expansion of citizenship; in others, such as claims to differentiated citizenship, they may represent the fragmentation of citizenship; in still others, such as the claims of immigrant groups, they may lead to a constriction of citizenship and a tightening of the legal provisions in the direction of greater exclusion rather than inclusion.

The possibilities of citizenship in contemporary India are the product of a century of disagreement. This book is centrally about how this many-faceted and multiply contested idea of citizenship was forged and continues to be fashioned through contestation. Such an enterprise must necessarily range widely in terms of time as well as the domains in which the idea and its practices find articulation. As the book grapples with multiplicity at various levels, it confronts the challenge of spanning a century by a selection of historical moments that are relevant and salient, avoiding revisiting those we already know much about. For example, the third part of the book on citizenship-as-identity focuses on backwardness as the basis of group-differentiated citizenship rather than the more obvious candidate of minority identity, which has received much scholarly attention. The significance of the minority question is however affirmed by re-siting it, in the first section, as an originary formative influence on India's citizenship law and jurisprudence. As for the many domains in which the impulse to citizenship is expressed, the book draws on existing scholarship in a wide range of disciplines, from politics and political theory to law and policy, history and sociology. Beyond these, it travels from the archive to the field, encompassing journeys from colonial pedagogy to contemporary ethnography.

The diversity of sources is indispensable for a hitherto unattempted account of a concept that is immensely fashionable but so variously interpreted that the opportunities for dialogue between, for instance, those who adopt a legal perspective on citizenship and those who adopt anthropological or philosophical perspectives have diminished. The objective of this book is not to construct a synthesis that facilitates a consensus on the meaning of citizenship, or even Indian citizenship. Its purpose is to tell a story that is historically situated and to open up a scholarly space where this larger narrative about the many contending meanings of citizenship in India, articulated in several domains simultaneously, can be the subject of a multi-dimensional conversation that engages with their inter-relationships, as different facets of a complex whole.

In this respect, the book echoes the architectonic civic ideal immanent in the Indian Constitution which was, it argues, the aspiration that nourished not only a liberal regime for determining the legal status of membership, but also the principles of social citizenship and group-differentiated citizenship, as conditions that would facilitate the fullest realization of a unique civic community in a diverse society marked by multiple and deep inequalities. Intended to be instrumental in the realization of a civic community, these principles have been variously compromised, undermined, or become ends unto themselves.

Unlike in countries such as the United States or the United Kingdom, where histories of citizenship had entailed struggles for institutionalizing inclusion, the Indian Republic started life already equipped with it. Incorporated into this architecture of institutionalized inclusion, a radical notion of citizenship held out the promise of transforming a deeply hierarchical society into a civic community of equals. A strikingly progressive constitution in 1950 defined the political principles that would govern the Indian future, and in particular three core aspects of the lives of its citizens: their equal legal status of membership; their enjoyment of not merely equal civil and political rights but also the social and economic rights necessary for their material well-being; and the nesting of their particular and diverse identities on terms of equality within a larger national-civic identity.

The second half of the twentieth century, the book argues, has demonstrated the fragility of that constitutional consensus and a steady erosion of the civic ideal that animated it. The powerful and potentially transformative project of a civic community, in terms of both the status of citizenship and its performance, and in terms of citizens' relationships to each other as well as to the state, now appears enervated and depleted. The project of a national-civic identity appears to be overwhelmed by a plurality of narrowly circumscribed identities, often in uneasy tension with each other and with the national-civic; the citizenly solidarity that must underwrite policies to reduce inequality is weak and tenuous; the social intolerance of difference compromises the neutrality of the law; and there remains little that is recognizably civic about Indian citizenship. Why and how this unraveling of a progressive founding civic ideal occurred is the subject of this book.

PART ONE

Status

1

The Subject-Citizen

A Colonial Anomaly

In 1906, the Rev. John Morrison of the Church of Scotland in Calcutta made the startling claim that citizenship was one of the most important political ideas to emerge in India in the nineteenth century, adding cautiously that it was still far from achieving the stage reached by British opinion in 1832.

On the face of it, to speak of citizenship in an empire is conceptually implausible, legally dubious, and historically anachronistic. Subjects of an empire can scarcely be properly described as citizens, for a political community of free individuals would appear to be a necessary precondition for citizenship. This chapter attempts a legal and discursive genealogy of the "subject-citizen" of empire. The hyphenated category is a conceptual artifact that attempts to capture the anomaly of citizenship in the colony, as well as the easy elision between the usages of subject and citizen in the discourse of the time. If the one denotes actual legal status, the other represents a claim, even the presumption, of another status. Every usage of the term citizen is not however subversive. It is little more than an unselfconsciously imitative impertinence, an expression of the desire of the small elite of western-educated Indians to be treated on par with other British subjects, and especially with members of the white Dominions.[1]

Morrison himself attributed this new idea of citizenship to three influences in particular: ideas of Christian philanthropy producing a sense of brotherhood and thereby a "civil society"; the free and democratic spirit of English literature; and the English and vernacular newspapers that made people familiar with political life in Britain. As befitted a lecture series[2] devoted to the defense of the Christian faith, it was to the preeminent influence of Christianity that Morrison attributed the assumption, implicit even in criticisms of colonial rule, that "government exists for the good of the governed, and indeed is responsible for the welfare of the masses" (Morrison, 1906: 73). Notwithstanding the social and religious differences in Indian society, he remarked somewhat optimistically, "politically, all India is already *one;* her educated men have drunk at *one* well of political ideas; citizenship and its rights are attractive and destroy no cherished customs" (ibid.: 80–81; emphasis in original). British imperialism was thus crucial to this "consciousness of being a political unit" (ibid.: 72), and indeed the very name *Indian* being used in the politics of the day was a concept that could not be conveyed by any Indian language. It came from Britain and the English language (ibid.: 78–79).

In recent years, the term "imperial citizenship" (Karatani, 2003; Gorman, 2006; S. Banerjee, 2010) has come to enjoy a certain popularity, but the usage obscures an analytical distinction that is fundamental to the understanding of this phenomenon in colonial India. This is the distinction between the external and internal aspects of the citizenship question. I propose the use of the term *imperial citizenship* for the first, external dimension, and *colonial citizenship* for the second, internal dimension. The difference between imperial and colonial citizenship lies in the three primary differences of the addressee of the claim; the bearer(s) of citizenship; and the content of the citizenship claim.

Imperial citizenship here refers to the status of Indians as members of the British Empire , and as such remains close to the original fin de siècle use of the term. This was the site on which claims were made for an equality of status for Indian subjects with other subjects in Great Britain, but also and especially with British subjects in the Dominions and other colonies. It was persistently invoked in claims on behalf of overseas Indians spread across the British Empire, including those by the Imperial Indian Citizenship Association, founded in Bombay in 1915 to advance the cause of Indians in Kenya, Fiji, South Africa, and Canada, among others.[3] The term *colonial citizenship* denotes the more direct relationship between the colonial state in

India (including the office of the Secretary of State for India and the Colonial Office in Whitehall) and its subjects within India. This was the site of claims to civil liberties and political rights including claims to political representation, whether in Indian legislative councils or in the House of Commons.

These twin dimensions of citizenship, it will be seen, subsisted in separate silos, though both reflected and reproduced hierarchies of race and class, with varying emphases: in the case of imperial citizenship, predominantly the racial hierarchy that characterized the structure of the British Empire; in the case of colonial citizenship, predominantly the class hierarchy of colonial society, subsisting within a broader racial hierarchy. In Britain, technically, all imperial subjects including Indians had the same rights. While there was sympathy in some quarters of the British establishment for the unfair denial of equal rights to Indian residents of the Dominions, there was little or no recognition of the denial of rights to Indians *in* India. That the rights available to Indians in Great Britain were not available to Indians within India[4] did not strike the leaders of British public opinion as paradoxical or inconsistent. Again, in arguments for imperial citizenship, the putative bearers of citizenship included subaltern Indians abroad, but subaltern Indians within India were rarely part of the discursive realm of colonial citizenship claims.

Imperial Citizenship: "A Plan of Geographical Morality"

Despite its oxymoronic appearance, imperial citizenship is not a phenomenon unknown to history.[5] Indeed, the architecture of citizenship proffered by the British Empire is strikingly reminiscent of the Roman empire,[6] in particular the 212 CE edict of Caracalla that granted citizenship to all the male residents (excluding the lowest, largely rural, classes) of territories conquered by Rome, estimated at about six million men (Walzer, 1989: 214). In his Roman Oration of 143 CE, the second-century rhetorician Aelius Aristides eulogized this "magnificent citizenship with its grand conception, because there is nothing like it in the records of all mankind. . . . Neither sea nor intervening continent are bars to citizenship, nor are Asia and Europe divided in their treatment here. In your empire, all paths are open to all" (quoted in Nicolet, 1980: 18).

Scholars have interpreted this expansive grant of citizenship status variously as a tool for the incorporation of subject peoples, as a mode of the strategic inclusion of provincial elites in the distribution of public office (Purcell, 1986: 569), and a strategy for raising taxes to pay for wars (Nicolet, 1980: 20).

From the perspective of a comparison with the British Empire, it is notable that, despite its generous embrace of geographically scattered and ethnically diverse populations, there were several classes of Roman citizenship, arranged in a complex hierarchy accompanied by a graduated scale of rights: to vote, to stand for public office, to make legal contracts and hold property, to marry a Roman citizen, and so on. At the heart of the empire, the free citizens of Republican Rome constituted only a minority of the population, with the civic mass being ruled by an oligarchical political class whose privileges stemmed from ownership of property and nobility of birth (Nicolet, 1980: 3–4).

British imperial citizenship was not unlike that of imperial Rome:[7] similarly inclusive in the formal sense, and similarly stratified in reality. In legal terms, the principle of jus soli—birth on the soil of the country—was the normal mode of acquiring citizenship, so all those born within the British Empire shared the common status of being subjects of the king-emperor. This however was pretty much all that was shared or common. Commonality—consisting of common subjection to the sovereign—rather than equality was the defining principle of British imperial citizenship. The symbolic basis of imperial citizenship was the doctrine of natural allegiance to the sovereign, with fealty and loyalty being what subjects offered the monarch in return for his protection.[8] In point of fact, of course, such rights as subjects enjoyed lay in the custody of Parliament, rather than the monarch, and varied enormously. Within Britain alone, there were four subcategories of citizens with differential rights: natural-born, naturalized (whose citizenship was effective across the empire), naturalized (whose citizenship had only local effect), and denizens (Karatani, 2003: 52).[9]

The differential access to rights was even more pronounced across the empire, echoing and reinforcing the inequality between its different constituent units. From 1870 onward, the self-governing Dominions could confer the rights of a naturalized British subject within the territorial limits of the colony. This meant that while a Frenchman naturalized in New Zealand could be a British subject in that country, when he came to England, he lapsed back to being a Frenchman (ibid.: 56). In response to the insistence of Dominion governments in a series of Imperial Conferences, the British Nationality and Status of Aliens (BNSA) Act of 1914 inaugurated a new split regime of legal citizenship that had the effect of further consolidating the difference between the Dominions and colonies. It entrenched the power of the Dominions to make laws of immigration and naturalization in their own territories, and also empowered them to treat different classes of British subjects differently.

From this date onward, the colonies continued to be governed by the older common-law regime of citizenship, while the Dominions came to be governed, from 1914 till the enactment of the Canadian Citizenship Act in 1946, by the so-called common code, which explicitly recognized a form of "local citizenship," sanctifying the divide between Great Britain and its Dominions, on the one hand, and the rest of the empire, on the other.

The Dominions thus wrested from Great Britain the right to enact immigration policies that were deliberately framed to exclude particular racial groups, mostly Asians and especially Chinese and Indians. The British government did not itself adopt this openly discriminatory and invidious practice, offering only the curious justification that the Asians and Africans who might seek naturalization would be the merest drop in the ocean of the enormous number of such subjects. It also pledged—and honored this pledge of—noninterference, allowing the Dominions unfettered freedom to practice race discrimination in immigration policies. The common code thus cemented the ties between Britain and its White Dominions, which were now more starkly separated from the lesser (and nonwhite) colonies of the British Empire. An unintended, even ironical, consequence of this devolution was that, by the time the common code ended in 1946, the national identities of subjects of the Dominions—such as a Canadian or Australian identity—had also crystallized, in ways that could be seen as undermining the "mother" identity of British imperial citizenship.

In British dependencies such as India, there were two categories of subjects. Those who were born on territory controlled by the British government were designated as "non-European, natural-born British subjects" and enjoyed fewer rights than British subjects elsewhere. Those who belonged to the principalities, controlled but not directly administered by the British, were described as British Protected Persons. A third category, of European society in India, included not just colonial administrators, businessmen, and army officers, secure in their identity as British citizens, but also a range of other classes of "poor Europeans" and Eurasians—from skilled and semiskilled workers to orphans, vagrants, prostitutes, and convicts (Arnold, 1979)—thus yielding a complex and stratified picture of subjecthood within India, but also across the British Empire with its varied categories of territorial control.[10]

Neither non-European British subjects nor British Protected Persons (BPPs) could become fully naturalized members of the British Empire, and political equality with other white subjects of the empire was by definition precluded (Gorman, 2006: 164). Till the passage of the Act of 1914, a passport issued in India, as indeed in any of the Dominions, was proof of British subjecthood *within that particular territory.* British nationality in a form that was coextensive with the British Empire was available only to subjects resident in the United Kingdom. Even after the Act of 1914 was enacted, Indians could enter most British colonies, but their entry into the Dominions became subject to the immigration policies of the latter countries. They could still enter Britain with a British passport, although *The Round Table* expressed a complacent optimism that the climate of the United Kingdom would more effectively "keep coloured races away . . . than the most drastic of immigration *restrictions*" (Tinker, 1976: 37).

The nonwhite colonial possessions of Britain had remained marginal to the largely bilateral consultations between Britain and its Dominions that resulted in the BNSA Act of 1914. India was often mentioned, always as an anomalous case because its people formed the large majority of British subjects (Sargant, 1912: 7, 57–58). In 1912, following the Imperial Conference of 1911 at which the premiers of the Dominions had reiterated their demand of the right to frame their own laws of immigration, *United Empire,* the journal of the Royal Colonial Institute, invited contributions from a range of public figures on the meaning of British citizenship: could women in Britain, who had only the municipal franchise, be considered citizens? Should subjects of non-European descent have an inferior political status? Did white men in the Dominions have the right to work and reside in Britain, and would they have the same political rights as other British citizens? Like many of the other contributors, E. B. Sargant sought to define citizenship in terms of voting rights, clarifying the hierarchies collapsed into the term British citizen:

We should . . . have to speak of a descending scale, first of parliamentary electors within the United Kingdom as alone possessed of British citizenship, then of those in the self-governing Dominions overseas as Canadian citizens, Australian citizens, etc. Next would follow various classes of Crown colonists, distinguished as citizens of Jamaica, etc., then a group of British Indian citizens *(since the word "citizenship" is used in the Indian proclamation of the late King-Emperor),* and, lastly, women electors who would be merely citizens of London, Montreal, etc, unless they were domiciled in Australia or New Zealand, when they would rise in the foregoing scale. Finally would come the class of unenfranchised (and disfranchised) persons and minors, who, if not aliens, would, like all the classes already mentioned, be British subjects. Such would be the result of not recognizing that British citizenship is multiform in character. On the other hand, if we agree to include more than one status of citizen in our definition of the term, at what point are we to stop? (Sargant, 1912: 4–5; emphasis added)

What was common to all the different categories of British subjects was the principle that, even if denied equal political rights, they were accorded equal protection under British common law, both at home and abroad. However, the idea of British protection appeared largely fictional as Indian indentured labor—known as "coolies" and in effect not very different from slaves—was moved across the empire with not the merest pretence of consent. The first shipload of indentured labor from India reached the Natal in 1860 followed by Indian traders who participated in the slave trade, dealing in both Indians and blacks. Many of the indentured laborers acquired freedom after five years, and settled in the Transvaal, the Free State, and the Cape Colony. Local European resentment against the free Indians and Indian traders led to the imposition of a poll tax on Indians, and a proposal to disenfranchise even already enfranchised Indians. A brief victory was won when, in response to a petition signed by ten thousand Indians, Lord Ripon quashed the proposed law on the grounds that the British Empire could not endorse a color bar *in law*. Other measures to restrict the activities of Indians were however devised, including the requirement of a license for trading and the requirement to pass an education test in a European language.[11] In the Cape Colony, Indian children were not allowed to attend even public schools; in the Transvaal, Indians were given permission to reside only in unsanitary places far removed from the town. The Indian National Congress's championing of these grievances (in the form of a resolution in 1901) with the government did not produce any results. Gandhi's very first *satyagraha* in 1907–1909 was to affirm the rights of imperial citizens to move from Natal to the Transvaal. It was Gandhi's campaigns that created widespread awareness of discriminatory practices, even as they caused the South Africans and the British to more strongly entrench the bar on the permanent settlement of Indians.

The case of Indians in South Africa is a telling illustration of the distortions introduced into the common law of citizenship in Great Britain, ostensibly unmarked by any racial referent. Nevertheless, the empowering of the Dominions to make their own discriminatory policies, as well as to introduce criteria such as an English language test or a poll tax, confirmed the creation of distinct classes and statuses of citizenship, essentially based on race and suggesting the existence of two empires, one white and the other colored. Notwithstanding the assertion of a common British subjecthood, the common code in effect treated British subjects of Asian origin as uncommon, and undeserving of the bilateralism that characterized agreement among the British government and its White Dominions. In an indignant comment on behalf of the Sikhs who arrived in Canada aboard the *Kamagata Maru* "in exercise of their rights of British citizenship," Lala Lajpat Rai wrote in 1914:

> The fact is that the British Government in India is on the horns of a dilemma. They want the Indians to believe that they are the equal subjects of the King, but when the former claim their rights as such, they behave as if they have neither the power nor the desire to secure the same for them. Perhaps it is not so much the fault of the Government in India as of those statesmen who have to reconcile their professions and principles of Liberalism with their policy of subjection. . . . The desire, the ambition, and the necessity of claiming the rights of British citizenship is no longer confined to educated Indians, but is permeating through the uneducated classes and even the masses. (reproduced in Besant, 1914: 90)

The racial divide, fracturing an ostensibly equal imperial citizenship, was repeatedly interrogated by India at the Imperial Conferences, and accompanied by demands of equal treatment for Indians, especially in Africa. At the 1921 Conference, V. S. Srinivasa Sastri[12] expressed the Indian view that all people be allowed to move freely across the empire, which, he said, stood "for equality, for absolute justice" (Tinker, 1976: 47). At the 1923 Imperial Conference, the demand for political rights for Kenyan Indians advanced by Sastri encountered formidable opposition from the powerful General Smuts who feared that acceding to the claim of civic equality by giving Indian communities in Kenya the franchise would create a dangerous precedent, encouraging Indian penetration into other parts of the empire, including South Africa, "under the guise of the principle of equality which does not even apply among the Indians in India" (ibid.: 65).

The Resolutions of the Indian National Congress annual sessions from 1894 onward made regular and repeated references to the disenfranchisement and other disabilities borne by Indians in South Africa as also in other colonies. They protested the "invidious and humiliating distinctions made between them and European settlers" (Indian National Congress, 1910, 3: 70); the treatment of Indians by these colonies as "backward and uncivilized races" (ibid.: 137); and the fact that "Indian Settlers—subjects of His Majesty the King-Emperor—should continue to be subjected to harassing restrictions and denied the ordinary rights of British citizenship in His Majesty's Colonies" (ibid.: 146). Sir Tej Bahadur Sapru pointed to the reprehensible creation of classes of citizenship based on race and color.

> If, however, Imperial citizenship is not a mere shadow but consists of something substantial then I cannot see how it is possible to divide that citizenship into two grades, a higher and a lower. You may raise your franchise as high as you like, but I do maintain, and maintain very strongly, that notwithstanding any measure of internal autonomy that you may possess you cannot bar out any section of His Majesty's subjects merely on racial grounds. (quoted in Waiz, 1927: 552)

One Imperial Conference after another failed to provide a satisfactory answer to the question posed by the Imperial Indian Citizenship Association, "What part have I as an Indian in an Empire which rejects me even in the Tropics, when I try to land, and gives me no citizen rights?" (Waiz, 1927: 178). This signaling of the state's unreasonable claim to the obedience of its subjects was more explicitly echoed in Annie Besant's statement that "England must live up to her old traditions and share her birthright with 300,000,000 Indians, for the price of Indian loyalty is the gift of freedom" (Besant, 1914: 102).

While citizenship was widely interpreted as implying voting rights and the right to own and inherit property, claims to citizenship were also occasionally based on arguments of military service, seen as not just a duty but a right of the citizen. Indians frequently demanded the right to perform military service, and in a speech in the Imperial Legislative Council in 1903, Gopal Krishna Gokhale claimed that India was "about the only country in the civilized world where the people are debarred from the privileges of citizen soldiership and from all voluntary participation in the responsibilities of national defence" (Gokhale, 1908: 60). The continued refusal of Indian claims to citizenship in the Dominions was the source of some embarrassment for those, such as British prime minister Lloyd George, who recalled India's contribution of a million and a quarter soldiers to WWI (Tinker, 1976: 51). In 1928, the Statutory (Simon) Commission's recommendation of an Indian National Army was presented as a response to the inability of Indians to defend their own country and as such a prerequisite for self-government. Sir Francis Younghusband described this inability as being the product of "unintentional emasculation."

Emasculation has come about through the very sincerity of our desire to maintain order in India and preserve it from outside attack. None the less, it is the fact. Through taking too exclusively upon our own shoulders the burden of defending India and maintaining internal peace we have atrophied the muscles of the Indians. They are soft and flabby. (Younghusband, 1931: 191)

On the question of imperial citizenship, the gulf between Indian aspirations and imperial concession was vast and unbridgeable as only an immutable racial divide could be.[13] In the arena of colonial citizenship by contrast—particularly on the question of who could be recognized as a de facto citizen—the distance between the official position and the articulate sections of Indian society was much smaller, despite the intersection of race and class. In the Indian perspective, moreover, until at least the early twentieth century, these dimensions—the external and the internal, the imperial and the colonial—were not entirely delinked. For many, the highest conceivable form of citizenship was that of full and equal participation *in* the British Empire. This is reflected not only in early claims to citizenship but also in the declared aspiration of the Congress (and other organizations) to the model of the British settler colonies. Indeed, India's appetite for Commonwealth citizenship, even at the highly symbolic and nationalistically charged moment of freedom, reflects its inability to altogether break free from the hold of this conception.

Colonial Citizenship: The Men Who Would Be Citizens

Ostensibly inclusive, British imperial citizenship was, as we have seen, deeply hierarchical in reality. By contrast, colonial citizenship evinced no pretence at inclusiveness, though rhetorical inclusion was an inevitable, if occasional, repercussion of the management of empire.

Colonial citizenship had primarily three features. First, in formal terms, all had the uniform legal status of *subjects* in relation to the government of British India, though different rights—such as the right to vote—could and did attach to some sections of subjects. Second, these differential rights—implicit identifiers of particular classes of subjects—contributed to the self-perception of members of these groups of rights-holders as *putative citizens,* a perception often also encouraged by the state. These classes of protocitizens would include the enfranchised, the property holders, and the educated, reproducing the conventional association of citizenship with modern education, property, and enfranchisement. Finally, such citizens demanded civil liberties and conveyed *political expectations* of representation in the House of Commons as well as in the emergent Indian representative institutions. Also implicit in the content of civic status were expectations of the right and the duty to defend their country as free citizens of the empire, and "in the discharge of their civic and imperial obligation" (Satyamurthy, 1919: 76).

The source of the common legal status of subject-citizen in the British Empire was the Queen's Proclamation of 1858, following the revolt of 1857. Responses to this Proclamation provide a view of how subjecthood and citizenship were perceived and appraised. In 1858, the monarch had declared her government's resolve not to interfere with either the faith or customs of its Indian subjects, and to impartially admit them to the service of the government—without regard to race or creed, keeping in view only their education, integrity, and ability. Finally, she said:

> We hold ourselves bound to the natives of our Indian territories by *the same obligations of duty which bind us to all our other subjects,* and those obligations, by the blessing of Almighty God, we shall faithfully and conscientiously fill. (Keith, 1922, 1: 384; emphasis added)

This imperial proclamation was hailed by some as the Magna Carta of Indian liberties. Close to a century later, it was still being eulogized as being as dear to the hearts of Indians as the Sermon on the Mount was to that of orthodox Christians (Buch, 1938: 191). Dadabhai Naoroji, an adherent of the Magna Carta view, traced the rights of his compatriots even further back to 1669, the year of the earliest grant of territorial rights to the East India Company in the form of Bombay. The grant document had stated that "all persons being His Majesty's subjects inhabiting within the said Island and their children and their posterity born within the limits thereof, shall be deemed *free denizens and natural subjects, as if living and born in England*" (Indian National Congress, 1910. 1: 857; emphasis added). For Naoroji, the claim of every British Indian to the right of self-government, to vote, and even to become a member of Parliament originated in this commitment, given two and a half centuries earlier, at the time of "the very first political connection with England" (ibid.) In his presidential address to the Twenty-Second Session of the Congress in 1906, he claimed that "we are British citizens and are entitled to and claim all British citizens' rights" (ibid.: 856).

The myth of inclusion was beguiling enough to lead a section of educated middle-class Indians to believe that equal citizenship was a sacred pledge whose redemption depended only on the claim being powerfully enough articulated. The assumption by the Queen in 1877 of the title *Kaiser-i-Hind,* Empress of India, was construed by the more optimistic of her Indian subjects as a derivative elevation in their own status inasmuch as they now became citizens of the British Empire, and subjects of an Empress rather than a mere Queen. A rival view was fired by the resentment around Lord Lytton's ostentatious Imperial Assemblage of the same year—held at a time when the country was ravaged by famine and cyclone, when salt duties were controversially equalized across India even as all duties on imported cotton goods were simultaneously withdrawn, and when a draconian law clamped down on the vernacular press—provoking a contemporary description of Indian society in the Lytton viceroyalty as "bordering upon revolution."[14] All this certainly conveyed to the more voluble Indian subjects of the monarch that their status, far from being elevated, had in fact diminished. Bipin Chandra Pal commented that educated India did not appreciate what this title really signified—"not a constitutional monarch but something like an "Oriental" despot" (Pal, 1932: 275).

King Edward VII's 1908 Proclamation signified a weary recognition of both these positions. Even as he endorsed his mother's Proclamation of forty years earlier, and affirmed that steps were being taken to effect it, he rather churlishly reminded his Indian subjects that their claims were a product of ideas introduced by British rule into a subject population largely insensible of these.

> Important classes among you, representing ideas that have been fostered and encouraged by British rule, claim equality of citizenship, and a greater share in legislation and Government. The politic satisfaction of such a claim will strengthen, not impair, existing authority and power. (reproduced in A. K. Ghose, 1921: 238)

Apart from this sullen acknowledgment of the claim to equal citizenship, Edward's proclamation also signaled the imperial recognition of particular classes of subjects as "important." The self-perception of these classes of subjects was in turn both informed by and echoed in this implicit recognition of them. The list of invitees to the Assemblage of 1877 may be read as a list of these classes, already officially apprehended as constitutive of the body of putative citizens. The invitees included, on Cohn's account, not just the princes and aristocrats of the feudal order, but also "other categories of Indians, 'native gentlemen,' 'landlords,' 'editors and journalists' and 'representative men' of various kinds" (Cohn, 1996: 658). For Cohn, this attested to the existence of contradictory perceptions of Indian society among British ruling groups on which were based prescriptions about modes of ruling. Those who perceived India as an essentially feudal society thus believed that it should be ruled through the cultivation of loyal feudatories to the British monarch. On the other hand, those who saw India as a society composed of disparate communities distinguished by religion, region, caste, and education, thought about ruling it in a modernist representational mode, in which individuals could represent these diverse communities (ibid.: 633).

This mapping of significant interests in Indian society yielded a presumptive identification of de facto citizens worthy of recognition, because able to articulate indigenous opinion and to represent the different sections of Indian interests. However, it also encompassed landlords and merchants who were not the typical educated and articulate leaders of middle-class opinion. Thus, in late nineteenth- and early twentieth-century India, there appears to have been a consensual ambivalence on the question of who was or could be, and who was not or could not be, a citizen; a tacit agreement between the colonizer and the colonized on a subtle differentiation between Indian subjects who are citizens or putative citizens, and those that are neither.

The presumption of property ownership or wealth or a modern education in the English language as defining characteristics of such citizens was strong.[15] On such an interpretation, putative citizens, invariably male, would include not just the propertied classes, but also educated professionals such as civil servants, lawyers, and doctors. By the middle of the nineteenth century, each of the three presidencies had its own university, training lawyers, engineers, and lower-level bureaucrats.[16] The universities were producing an increasing number of graduates with uncertain prospects of being absorbed into the administration, the lack of opportunity eventually leading them into nationalist politics.

The two most precarious categories of putative citizens were civil servants and journalists, victims of race discrimination and repression respectively. Viceroy Lytton's proposals to reduce the numbers (and thereby numbers of Indians) admitted to the covenanted civil service, and to establish a "close native civil service" to which appointments would be made by nomination rather than competition, clearly indicated that the British had reneged on the imperial promise of 1858. Even as Indians were agitating for the simultaneous conduct of the civil service examination in India, Lytton was working toward their exclusion. The lowering of the maximum age for taking the examination—from twenty-one to nineteen—only confirmed this interpretation, as it made it even more difficult for Indians to compete. If he recognized at all the necessity of employing more natives in the civil service, it was for the financial advantage that would accrue from employing the cheapest available person.[17] This affirmation of the monopoly of Europeans over higher positions in the Imperial service based on the superior qualities of their race was roundly denounced by Surendranath Banerjea (Banerjea, 1909: 114–115).[18] The Bengal paper *Sadharanee* editorialized:

> It was declared in 1858 that, if the natives of the country proved themselves equal, all appointments so far as practicable would be given to them. But now we are told that all high executive offices are to be given to Englishmen only. If these two declarations are not contradictory, then henceforward there will be no difference in colour between black and white. (quoted in Buch, 1938: 154)

The press had acquired some importance in the first half of the nineteenth century; by the second half, the English language press enjoyed an undisputed supremacy as the voice of the English-educated citizenry. By 1905, there were two million Indians subscribing to 1,359 newspapers and journals, of which 285 were in English and another 82 in English as well as a vernacular.[19] Rammohun Roy's attachment to the values of the French Revolution and his enthusiastic support of the Reform Bill of 1832 led an early biographer to describe Roy's dream for India thus: "an *English-speaking India;* . . . moreover, a *Christian* India . . . a *generally Anglicised India*" (Collet, 1914: 208. Emphasis in original).[20] Almost a third of the founders of the Congress in 1885 were journalists, and the press—viewed as public service—was the main organ of publicity for nationalist ideas, and most prominent nationalist leaders, in different parts of India, ran a paper (Chandra, 1989: 102–103). Throughout the nineteenth century and beyond, the issue of press freedom became a rallying cry of Indian liberals and nationalists. Lytton's Vernacular Press Act (1878) led to widespread protest, and was repealed by his successor four years later. Nationalist leaders who were also newspaper owners found themselves routinely charged with sedition[21] and equally routinely adopting clever strategies to avoid attracting legal provisions. At least one vernacular paper, the *Amrita Bazar Patrika* in Bengali, turned itself into an English paper overnight to avoid attracting the provisions of the Vernacular Press Act.

Thus, notwithstanding the limited quality of de jure membership in the British Empire, and the precarious quality of de facto membership, John Morrison was surely right in claiming that the idea of citizenship was already in currency within India. It was implicit in the negotiations of the British rulers with sections of local society. It was implicit in the rules of membership of the British Indian Association founded in 1853, which professed to be open to all but charged a membership fee that precluded the entry of the lower middle class.[22] It was implicit also in the writings of nineteenth-century Indian liberals and political pamphleteers who, ignoring the infirmities of de jure Indian citizenship in the empire, deployed the terms citizen and subject interchangeably, as in this statement by the Rev. Lalbehari De (1824–1894), an advocate of the spread of education as a means of reducing crime: "If we spend 60 lakhs every year for catching rogues and thieves, I submit, it is not too much to spend that sum in teaching *Her Majesty's subjects* to be honest and useful *citizens*" (quoted in B. Majumdar, 1967: 103; emphasis added).

This bias was reflected also in the predisposition of Indian liberals to view the citizenry as comprising little more than their own social class. In 1873, Sisirkumar Ghosh's explicit championship of middle-class democracy rested on the argument that the dissolute and selfish landed aristocracy could not be trusted to represent the masses, nor could the Ryots (peasants) be entrusted with a voice in public affairs, because of their deep ignorance. Albeit unrecognized by the government, the middle class was the obvious custodian of democracy.

> The gentry class is the most important of all, but unfortunately the existence of such a class is not even so much as acknowledged by Government. They have, in fact, no legal existence in Bengal. Amongst all civilized countries the gentry or middle class carries the greatest influence in all matters, and so it is in Bengal. But Government purposely ignores the existence of this class. (quoted in B. Majumdar, 1967: 133–134)

The consensus among nineteenth-century Indian liberals on the shared objective of a legitimate and representative government did not preclude a fierce debate about whether political reform should precede social reform or vice versa.[23] Notwithstanding its conviction that all the elements of a nation had been achieved—"a common political citizenship, a common loyalty to the Queen Empress, a community of interests . . . and a common language or literature which binds us morally and spiritually together" (Buch, 1938: 260)—Indian political liberalism clung to the ideal of the greater achievement of citizenship *within* the framework of British rule and, even when it aspired to Swaraj, *within* the empire. In reminders to the colonial state of its obligation to provide the conditions of equal citizenship, the classical association of citizenship with martial service to the state was repeatedly recalled in nineteenth-century political argument.

The Indian liberal's aspiration for citizenship within the empire need not be read as an inconsistency or contradiction in Indian liberalism, for there was, even in Britain, a fundamental ambivalence in the relationship between liberalism and imperialism. As Jennifer Pitts has shown, liberals have been both the strongest defenders of imperialism as well as its strongest critics (Pitts, 2005: 4). Liberalism may thus be seen as inherently imperializing, as it seeks to export—in ways reminiscent of the political agenda of democracy promotion in the present—liberal ideas of progress and the rule of law to the colonies. Equally, however, liberal critics of empire were troubled by the smuggling in of illiberal principles into a political doctrine that they interpreted as inherently anti-imperialist, given its commitment to human equality and self-government. Preeminent among the Indian adherents of this view was Dadabhai Naoroji who attempted to speak the liberal truth to an avowedly liberal, but actually insufficiently and inconsistently liberal, imperial power.

The content of citizenship appears, in the writings of a number of social and political commentators across the nineteenth century, as a function of assumptions about the proper relationship between the citizen and the state, the preparedness of Indian society for such a modern political relationship, and the basis of the state's claim to obedience. In these writings, citizenship largely denoted membership, which was more often associated with a sense of public purpose than rights, and an awareness of the greater good and the ability to articulate it. Belonging to various schools of early Indian liberalism,[24] these writers offered rather elementary arguments about political obligation and legitimacy, ranging from considerations of how to judge the benefits provided by a government to why representation was necessary. In 1835, Dwarkanath Tagore had specified the elementary rights of citizens as the protection of life and property (B. Majumdar, 1967: 81). Only a decade later, Govindachandra Dutta asserted that a particular form of government should be judged by the degree of protection it afforded its citizens (ibid.: 1967: 90). By 1870, Sisirkumar Ghosh was demanding a parliament for India as well as civil liberties and the impartial administration of justice (ibid.: 131–137). Even as they sought the fullest reconstruction of Hindu society, these reformers appealed to the modern principle of reason, rather than the medieval principle of authority, and to contract, rather than custom.

By the beginning of the twentieth century, a partial form of de jure membership had begun to evolve, mediated by the franchise. In 1906, John Morrison identified those who enjoyed this new political citizenship of India as the electors, including "men of learning, the burgesses of the chief towns, the British traders, and the landowners and country gentlemen" (1906: 85–86) Property and modern education remained as central to this as to the earlier regime of purely de facto membership, and even though there was an additional element of representation here, the categories used to disaggregate the composition of the Legislative Councils in the 1920s clearly confirmed and formalized the earlier pattern of de facto citizenship. About half the seats in the Provincial Legislative Councils[25] were designated as General seats with the remaining half indicating the *interests* that the colonial state recognized as being worthy of representation: Communal; Landholders; University; Commerce, Industry and Planting; Representatives by Nomination; and Officials (Archbold, [1926] 1973: 188). Commerce in turn was differentiated by race, yielding separate categories of European and Indian commerce.

The shift in principles of representation that occurs at this time is important for two reasons. First, neither the expansion of the franchise nor the entry of more Indians into the legislative councils led to a diminution of the elitist quality of citizenship, serving rather to reproduce and entrench the already privileged nature of representation. Second, this is the period that saw the recognition of the principle of collective or group representation and its introduction into a protodemocratic politics, however limited by its colonial provenance.

The expansion of the franchise may have led to the term citizen being interpreted in India, as it was in Britain at this time, as encompassing those entitled to vote (Sargant, 1912: 13). If franchise is a plausible proxy for citizenship, property also acquires significance, since the franchise was substantially based in property ownership. Indeed, there had long been widespread support in Indian society for making the franchise dependent upon property and education. Nabagopal Mitra, a nineteenth-century Bengali intellectual nicknamed "National Nabagopal"[26] was among those who asked for Indian representation in the British Parliament. However, realizing that the size of the

Indian population might lead to the swamping of the House of Commons, he proposed limiting the franchise to those with wealth or education or both (B. Majumdar, 1967: 115–117). He even opposed educating the peasantry lest it develop distaste for agriculture (ibid.).

The population that could conceivably be considered as falling within the category of the citizen so defined was obviously miniscule. It was in the first constitutional document of the twentieth century that the principle of election was recognized, in however limited a fashion, for the Central Legislative Council.[27] Under the Act of 1919, while 70 percent of the members of the Central Legislative Council and Provincial Councils were to be elected, barely 3 percent of the adult population (over the age of 21) was entitled to vote. Unsurprisingly, this included one in ten men, and one in two hundred women (Chiriyankandath, 2001: 60). Even in 1925, after the expansion of the electorate by the Government of India Act of 1919, only 2.8 percent of the population was enfranchised. The Indian Franchise Committee of 1932 proposed extending the size of the electorate to 36 million or 14.1 percent of the population. In the last set of constitutional reforms before independence (Government of India Act of 1935), the franchise was extended to about a fifth of the adult population.

The link with property remained strong, as both government documents and successive Congress resolutions acknowledged and accepted.[28] In rural areas, evidence of eligibility was based on the payment of land revenue, rent, or local rates: and in urban areas, by the payment of income tax and municipal rates. Even in an electorate so stringently defined, there were concerns about the relatively high levels of illiteracy. The Bengal Presidency conducted three enquiries, in 1925–1926, into the literacy levels of the electorate, the first of which showed that 41 percent of the non-Muslim electors (to the Provincial Legislative Council) and 55 percent of the Muslim electors were illiterate (Government of India, 1928: 187). In Madras, the fact that street corner oratory was the main form of electoral canvassing "among an electorate of such low average educational development and consequent poor capacity for intelligent criticism" generated worries about civic competence (ibid.: 96). Regardless of official concern about the "poor capacity for intelligent criticism," there would however have been a substantial overlap between this "small loquacious section of the people" (Alston, 1910: 194) and the social classes mentioned earlier. The Indian Franchise Committee acknowledged this explicitly by stating that property has from the outset been the main foundation of the franchise. It is a system which is well understood in India, where it has been in force for local bodies for nearly two generations . . . all the evidence we have received shows that it is now well established and commands general approval. (Government of India, 1932: 33)

The social background of those nominated or elected to the various Provincial Councils in India between 1893 and 1906 is revealing: 36 percent were lawyers and 22 percent were landholders (B. Majumdar, 1965: 358). The predominance of lawyers was enhanced and entrenched in subsequent years, with close to half the Provincial Councils being composed of lawyers by 1916 (ibid.: 399). This was a phenomenon that official reports recognized, albeit with patronizing concern.

The large proportion of professional lawyers and of members of local boards show the extent to which membership of that profession or of such bodies assists in getting a candidate known and in furnishing opportunities for canvassing and persuasion. (Government of India, 1928: 96)

This was also of course far from being unusual, whether in Europe or Latin America in the nineteenth and early twentieth century. In Hungary and Uruguay, for instance, specified occupational groups were excluded from voting rights to preserve class dominance (Keyssar, 2000: 297). In many other countries, the literacy test performed the same function.

The Franchise Committee made some provision for members of the depressed classes and industrial labor, but found it "difficult to provide" for agricultural laborers and artisans on the grounds that they had no property and no education, and would find some representation under the depressed classes category (Government of India, 1932: 34). Women, in late colonial India, were therefore the only group to be treated as an exception to the property and literacy rule, for purposes of representation in the provincial legislatures, with Muthulakshmi Reddi, the first woman representative, entering the Madras Legislative Council in 1926.

The second important aspect of the shift that took place in the early twentieth century was the official recognition that not merely individuals, but also groups and collectivities, could proffer legitimate claims to political representation. The Viceroy Lord Minto's sympathetic response to the Muslim League's demand for separate electorates found institutional expression in the Government of India Act of 1909 that provided for such electorates for

Muslims. In an early echo of what is today described as the "politics of presence" (Phillips, 1995) this argument was taken forward by the Indian Franchise Committee, which justified community representation thus.

> . . . no important section of the community should be deprived of the opportunity of making its needs and opinions felt in the legislatures, because under all democratic systems it is the interests of those who are represented which tend to receive consideration, while the interests of those who are not represented are liable to be ignored, both at election time and afterwards. (Lothian, 1932: 596)

The idea here was that there were classes and groups who were capable of representing special interests, and this was underpinned by an implicit recognition of which sections of Indian interests were deserving of such forms of representation in legislative bodies. A split was now introduced into the category of hitherto de facto citizens, which was the product of two conflicting principles. The first was the principle of the representation of collective group interests of various types, whether those of special interests such as landholders or commerce or of religious groups such as the Muslims or Sikhs, designated as Communal. The second, more modern principle of undifferentiated representation was captured by the category of General seats, mostly based on education and drawing into the legislative councils occupational groups like lawyers. The tension between these two principles of representation, between group interests and individualized representation, has continued to inflect citizenship well into the present, and is the subject of the last section of this volume.

Representation mediated by community was evidently not seen as contradicted by an emphasis on liberal political values such as rights as individual entitlements, the rule of law, and democracy. Indeed, the emphasis on community notwithstanding, the content of colonial citizenship in the early twentieth century was largely envisioned in terms of civil liberties and political rights attached to individuals, rather than groups. In a tract titled *Rights of Citizens*, S. Satyamurthy made the individuation of citizenship an imperative arising out of the recognition of law as an artifact of human creation:

> Ordinarily the average Indian citizen, at least till very recently, took the law enacted for him as dispensations of providence. Thanks, however, to the political awakening in the country, a different attitude is beginning to be assumed towards these man-made laws. In order that this attitude

should become the normal attitude of the Indian citizen towards the laws, it is necessary that he should have a clear conception of his rights as an *individual citizen* of the state. (Satyamurthy, 1919: 1; emphasis added)

Satyamurthy's catalog of rights encompassed rights to personal freedom and public meeting; freedoms of the press and of judicial trial; as well as the freedom to enter the public services, to bear arms, and to serve in the Army and the Navy. Such a consciousness had consequential implications for the idea of political obligation. From customary obedience to the rulers (arising out of fear or habits of subservience) we now encounter a shift to a seventeenth-century idea of contract, in which government represents a constraint upon freedom that individuals have voluntarily combined to accept for the greater good of their collective freedom.

> The State is no longer a sovereign power which commands; it is a group of individuals having in their control forces which they must employ to create and to manage public service. (ibid.: 1)

Elaborating on the components of the Rule of Law as the purpose of all legislation, Satyamurthy also lamented the absence of a public law in India and quoted C. Vijairaghavachariar[29] to say that the collection of Acts, Regulations, and Ordinances by which India is governed are only products of a bureaucracy for which "the whole of British India is one Schedule District, one backward tract without the name" (ibid.: 2). Here then is a claim to a national selfhood that is openly resentful at being infantilized, and insists on being accorded the respect implicit in a government of laws rather than executive discretion.

From a government of laws, it was but a short step to the claim of participation in the making of such laws. Among the liberals of the late nineteenth and early twentieth century, representation in the House of Commons was widely perceived as the only way in which the promise of equal citizenship contained in the Queen's Proclamation could be realized. The claim to representative government as a form of colonial citizenship was justified by a claim to equality with the white Dominions, just as the claim to equality among all subjects of the empire, within the framework of imperial citizenship, had been based in the assertion of parity between India and the Dominions. If, the argument went, Britain had granted or conceded representative institutions to Australia, Canada, and the Cape, why not to India? Reference was also made to the representation of regions of India colonized by other European nations. By 1904, invoking the example of France's Third Republic, which had allowed French Overseas Territories—such as Pondicherry—to elect representatives to the Chamber of Deputies and the Senate (B. Majumdar, 1965: 367), and the fact that Goa elected members to the Portuguese Parliament, the Indian National Congress made the audacious claim that every province or presidency in India should be allowed to elect at least two members to the House of Commons in Britain.

The Marquess of Lothian, who had been the chairman of the Indian Franchise Committee, summed up the benefits of the gradual extension of "responsible government" in terms of the virtues of democratic citizenship that it enabled.

> Democracy tended to develop a new and better type of citizen. Obedience was a good virtue but responsibility was a greater virtue, and democracy did tend to develop in the people the power to think for themselves and not merely do as they were told. That was precisely was India needed and what her noblest citizens, from the extreme Left to the extreme Right, wanted to develop—an emancipated type of Indian citizen capable of taking decisions on his own responsibility and of standing in a position of equality alongside the rest of the world. (Lothian, 1932: 616)

Conclusion

This synoptic survey of the colonial period has attempted to show how the apparently common subjecthood of approximately two million Indian subjects of the British monarch, and the many thousands in British colonies and Dominions overseas, concealed a complex set of gradations. Both forms of imperial and colonial citizenship were enormously stratified. Though the grand all-encompassing master narrative of imperial citizenship affected not to recognize the essentially racial hierarchy within the empire, the idea of imperial citizenship and the debates on it were strongly inflected by both race and class. In late Victorian and Edwardian Britain, debates on imperial citizenship occurred within a fairly restricted circle of aristocratic elites, and the implications of imperial citizenship for intra-imperial immigration and the racial ideal of whiteness were clearly matters of anxiety in Britain.[30]

While race was indeed the primary signifier of what Partha Chatterjee has called "the rule of colonial difference" (1993: 16)—qualifying the universality of modern institutions of self-government either on grounds of its

unsuitability for particular cultures of the world, or else by the need to educate and prepare the natives for such institutions—it is clear that class and
assumptions about community[31] were equally important. Indeed, it is arguable that the rule of colonial difference was also modified over time. Until the
late nineteenth century, there were only social rather than legal spaces for the
recognition of particular classes of subjects. The Imperial Assemblages are an
example of such an incorporation of the feudal sections of Indian society into
the very restricted social space of imperium. In this phase, the relationship
between the monarch and the Indian nobility represents little more than an
inversion of the relationship of two centuries previously between the Mughal
emperor and the British trader. In the following years, the rule of colonial difference appears to have been substantively modified, with "the construction of
a legally instituted space where legally defined subjects could exercise rights,
however limited those might have been" (Scott, 1995: 208). The defining of
social categories—such as Landholder or Commerce—worthy of representation in the legislative councils is an example of this. The other side of this
specification of the categories eligible for representation is a repudiation of the
representational aspirations of the Indian National Congress. Visiting India
in 1912, Beatrice and Sidney Webb wrote that the members of the Congress,
"these five hundred highly educated, widely cultured and usually travelled
gentlemen—predominantly lawyers and editors, with a sprinkling of landlords and business capitalists" were "not 'representative' of the 250,000,000 of
peasant cultivators, petty retailers, jobbing craftsmen, artisans and laborers of
India" (Webb and Webb, 1987: 7).

   Premodern states typically entertain fewer anxieties about or desires for
legitimacy; they rarely seek to justify their rule, whether to themselves or
to those they govern. But it is axiomatic that all modern states, arguably
including colonial ones, need to build alliances with the societies they control, for stability and order, if not legitimacy. The British had weathered the
revolt of 1857 but not forgotten its lessons, and the transfer of control from
the Company to the Crown reflected the concern for maintaining order and
preventing rebellion. By the 1880s, Disraeli's aspiration to found the British
raj on sentimental loyalty to Queen Victoria had registered a shift as Dufferin
strove for popular support through the reform of the legislative councils so
that the government of India would not be "an isolated rock in the middle
of a tempestuous sea" (Gopal, 1965: 162). This was echoed in Kimberley's[32]
acknowledgment that while the British could not, as foreigners, expect to be

really loved, they could "do much to secure acquiescence in our supremacy as the best system possible in the circumstances" (ibid.: 166). Similarly, Lytton's preference for the princes and landlords belonging to the feudal classes gave way, in Ripon's viceroyalty, to an embrace of the educated middle classes. The colonial state thus moved from working to keep rebellion at bay to seeking willing acquiescence and local collaborators. Underlying this was the official recognition of financial considerations as much as moral ones (Brown, 1985: 100) and the rationale for local self-government as a means of some political education. Even as officials spoke in terms of entire communities, government policy preferred elite groups within them.[33]

Based on class as much as on race, colonial citizenship thus allowed for the recognition of particular classes of subject-citizens. The recognition of de facto citizens was a perfectly tolerable and useful arrangement, with its movement in the direction of even a partial de jure citizenship being carefully controlled, as the slow expansion of voting rights affirmed. The discourse of colonial citizenship, in which both the colonial state and Indian elites participated, disguised the class hierarchy within the colony. All were equally subjects, but some subjects were allowed the delusion that they were citizens.

If imperial citizenship was the more intractable of the two dimensions, it was obviously because race distinctions were harder to transcend than those of class. As we have seen, the British government failed to persuade the white Dominions to make concessions, disregarding race, to immigrants from its colored colonies. For themselves, the British were convinced that their cold climate was a sufficient deterrent to colored subjects coming in from the colonies. It was only after WWII that large-scale immigration from the colonies began, mostly to meet labor shortages in Britain; and it was only a couple of decades later that the politics of race became combustible.

Meanwhile, race, class, and gender together served to define the subject-citizen in colonial India and the Indian subject overseas. Independence made the racial divide irrelevant, and while the formal marking of citizenship by class and gender was decisively eroded by universal adult suffrage, the practice of citizenship and indeed political participation itself continues to be marked in significant ways by class, caste, and gender. The next chapter shows how, in the years following independence, even the formal equality of legal citizenship came to be attenuated by subtle markers of religious difference.

2

Legal Citizenship and the Long Shadow of the Partition

In the summer of 2004, following a decisive electoral victory, there was a very real possibility of the Congress Party President Sonia Gandhi—the Italian-born widow of the former prime minister Rajiv Gandhi—being sworn in as prime minister of India. However, as the nation held its collective breath, Gandhi announced that she would not join the government, much less lead it, but would continue as president of the party and an ordinary member of Parliament. The backdrop to this decision was an ongoing hostile campaign against her "foreign origin" led by the Hindu nationalist party, the BJP, but resonating also within the Congress, three of whose most venerable politicians had, only five years earlier, walked out of the party protesting against her becoming the president of the Congress Party. Though Sonia Gandhi was already a naturalized Indian citizen, there were cases filed in courts challenging her citizenship status, and her eligibility for public office.[1] The Indian Constitution, unlike many others,[2] only requires citizenship as a condition of holding public office, and is silent on the question of whether a naturalized citizen qualifies. This silence is only one source of ambiguity, among the many more profound tensions and ambivalences in Indian constitutional and legal provisions on citizenship.

India's choice of jus soli as the basis of citizenship is unsurprising, not only because this was the principle inherited from Britain, but also because jus sanguinis would have been an implausible principle on which to base citizenship in a multiethnic society. In the absence of a singular ethnocultural basis for nationhood, the Indian nation was substantially a political entity under construction. In a territorially defined political community, the Indian choice of jus soli could not but be premised on a delinking of citizenship from nationality. In the late colonial period (as we note in chapter 4) Indians had been repeatedly reminded that their claims to citizenship were dubious because they did not fulfill the preliminary condition of being a nation. At independence, India affirmed the possibility of citizenship as a political identity without an anchorage in culture.

The consensus in a rather sparsely populated field of scholarship suggests that the Indian republic started life with an inclusive jus soli regime: and, since the 1980s, in response to the vast numbers of illegal migrants from Bangladesh on the eastern border, has moved towards a more exclusionary jus sanguinis conception of citizenship (Rodrigues, 2008; Sadiq, 2009; A. Roy, 2010). While this is not incorrect, the history of Indian citizenship as legal status is considerably more complicated. This chapter questions the standard linear narrative of citizenship traveling from virtuous jus soli to less virtuous jus sanguinis, with the moment of rupture occurring in the 1980s. It argues that the tension between these two conceptions was present from the founding moment of the republic and is reflected in the constitutional settlement of the question. The subsequent move from jus soli to jus sanguinis occurs gradually over time, with a relatively concise specification giving way to a comprehensive and increasingly detailed account of Indian citizenship, constantly refined with more qualifications yielding new classifications and exceptions, each of these reflecting the primary fault line of religious difference in India, that between the Hindus and the Muslims. Even as the lapse of time between Partition and the present increases, this is a move that is increasingly—rather than decreasingly—informed by that divisive legacy.

This chapter charts the trajectory of the construction of Indian citizenship as legal status. It begins with a discussion of the first citizenship claim to be disavowed, that of Indians who had been living and working abroad, thus narrowing the universe of claims to the resident population of the territory of undivided India and effecting a severance between the principle of citizenship and nationality. The second section of the chapter is about the two most important citizenship claims to emanate from within this universe, those of the groups vulnerable to violence on either side of the border: Hindu refugees fleeing Pakistan, and a sizeable number of Muslims who initially fled from India to Pakistan later choosing to return. Despite some hostility to the claims of returning Muslims, the constitutional definition of citizenship provided for both. The ways in which questions of religious identity and property were negotiated in the constitutional settlement bears the lasting imprint of the Partition on the definition of Indian citizenship. The Indian Constitution adopted a secular jus soli conception of citizenship, but the idea of the "natural" citizen, usually Hindu and male, strongly inflected the debate on it. In later years, this bias increasingly found expression and even entrenchment in statutory law through a modification of the jus soli principle following large-scale illegal immigration from Bangladesh in the east, as well as modest immigration from Pakistan in the west. The third section of this chapter flags the major milestones on this legal and political journey from jus soli to a regime visibly marked by elements of jus sanguinis.

This is reflected also in the adjudication of the citizenship claims of Muslims moving from Pakistan to India in the first few decades after independence. This yielded an extensive body of case law dealing with questions of their volition and intent, of loyalty and allegiance, and of the evidentiary value of the documents that were furnished to buttress their claims. Claims to legal citizenship thus came to bear many affective burdens of identity and self-identification including though not only through documentations of identity. The fourth section of the chapter is about such adjudications of citizenship claims, and in particular four significant issues arising out of these: the considerations that played a part in determining the citizenship claims of those who crossed the border after the specified date; the equivocation on the evidentiary value of documents as forms of identification; the question of the inheritance of property; and the question of determining the "natural" citizenship of women. In the fifth and final section, the chapter discusses briefly the claims of two categories of peripheral citizens, the Chakmas and the people of the Chitmahals, the settlement (or not) of whose claims echo and reinforce the overarching argument of this chapter.

The Delinking of Citizenship and Nationality

At midnight on August 15, 1947, all the erstwhile Indian subjects of King George VI did not, as we might expect, automatically become citizens of the new Indian nation. Several factors contributed to making this a far more

complicated story, with multiple claimants and diverse sources of claims to
citizenship. The Partition of the subcontinent was preeminent among these.
There was the migratory (mainly Hindu) population flowing in from the territories in both Punjab and Bengal that had become part of the new state of
Pakistan. There were also Muslim families fleeing Partition violence, migrating from India to Pakistan, and occasionally migrating back to reclaim their
homes and lives. Then there were the subjects of the erstwhile princely states,
which were gradually being assimilated into India, and of the French and
Portuguese possessions, and also Europeans who had been long settled in
India. Finally, there were the Indians based in many countries in East and
South Africa, as also in—as they were then known—Burma, Malaya, Ceylon, and many other countries, who were thrown into confusion. Were they
now British or Indian or indeed Kenyan or Malaysian? While the substantive
focus of this chapter is on the first two categories of claimants to citizenship,
the fact that the earliest exclusions were those of overseas Indians is notable,
not least because this marks the first contest between the jus soli and jus
sanguinis notions of citizenship. From the early twentieth century onward,
Indian leaders had been active in supporting the citizenship claims of overseas Indians in the British Commonwealth as *citizens of the Empire*.[3] Gandhi
worked tirelessly, for a decade, for the rights of Indians in South Africa. Others campaigned against indentured labor in Fiji and discriminatory policies
against Indian traders in Zanzibar and Burma, and in support of miners and
plantation workers in South Africa, Malaya, Ceylon, and Australia. Even as
nationalist leaders expressed concern for Indian communities overseas, the
first foreign policy document produced for the Congress by Jawaharlal Nehru
in 1927 encouraged overseas Indians to identify with the countries of their
adoption (J. Nehru, 1972b: 362).

In 1947, it is estimated that there were four million Indians in the British Commonwealth, about half of whom were living in Ceylon, Burma, and
Malaya, and most of whom were descendants of people who had emigrated
as indentured labor in the nineteenth century. Only the previous year, Nehru
had visited Singapore and promised a crowd of ten thousand Indians that
India would soon be in a position to protect its children overseas, and that
they would be Indian nationals unless they chose otherwise (Kudaisya, 2006:
84). This rhetorical embrace of Indians abroad, in an expression of a jus sanguinis conception of citizenship, was odd considering the unambiguously
jus soli based British law of nationality. It was especially odd because it had

been the consistent position of Nehru, Gandhi, and other nationalists that overseas Indians should reserve their loyalty for the country of their adoption, instead of maintaining divided loyalties. Indeed, this had formed the basis of the nationalists' support for the integration of overseas Indians in their host societies on terms of equal citizenship.

After the Partition, however, the territorial criterion acquired greater importance so that, despite the memoranda submitted by overseas Indian communities, their claims to membership were initially viewed as inadmissible by the Constituent Assembly, on the grounds that they were not ordinarily resident or domiciled in India. But Indians abroad pleaded that they encountered difficulties in the countries where they lived and worked, even in places other than the Dominions. In Ceylon, for instance, the proposed Indian Residents Citizenship Bill would at best give Indians a second-class citizenship as it placed stringent conditions of residence, personal law, and even a discriminatory means test on Indians seeking citizenship. Indians in Malaya likewise emphasized that what they were being offered in that country was "federal citizenship," with few or no civil and political rights, but that this truncated form of Malayan citizenship would deprive them of the possibility of being able to seek Indian citizenship.

In a memorandum on behalf of Indians in Malaysia, the advocate B. Ramani referred to the effective statelessness produced by "resting a definition of nationality on permanent abode or domicile" (Rao, 1968, 4: 522) and made a strong plea for "dual nationality," such that even if an individual was born outside India, in Burma, Ceylon, or Malaya, but had not become a national of a foreign state, he[4] should be able to qualify for Indian citizenship, if either of his grandparents was born in India. Ramani's case was that just as people of all nationalities—Indian, Chinese, or Malay—could be Malayan citizens and still retain their nationality, India too should not debar those who had taken such citizenship because they were after all Indian nationals.

The Indian government, however, repudiated this separation, arguing that taking *citizenship* of a foreign state was tantamount to giving up Indian *nationality*. The delinking of citizenship from nationality was consistent: it applied as much to the members of India's multiethnic society as to diasporic Indians abroad. Since the Indian nation was not defined in terms of any ethnocultural identity, nationality could not form the basis of claims to citizenship from either. Nehru was not averse to offering Indian citizenship to such people living in the countries of the British Commonwealth (the Dominions and Colonies), so long as this choice was not offered to people in Pakistan. Sir B. N. Rau also eventually acknowledged that people could acquire Indian citizenship through birth or domicile or descent.[5] By this token, a citizen of India who was also a subject of the British Commonwealth would not lose his citizenship; and an Indian voter in Singapore should not, by virtue of registering himself for purposes of voting, be considered as having acquired the citizenship of a foreign state (ibid.: 532). Ultimately, though there was some disappointment among overseas Indians that more was not yielded, the Constituent Assembly enacted Article 8 by which persons of Indian origin living outside India, with no domicile in India, could become citizens if they were not citizens of other countries. An unhappy consequence of the new rules was that those whose grandparents had emigrated from the princely states were disqualified by these provisions, rendering them potentially stateless persons (Sutton, 2007: 286). Dual citizenship was in any case ruled out, acquiring some purchase only in recent years, in response to the demands of a newer, economically stronger and politically vociferous diaspora. Dual citizenship within India was also ruled out, so that there would be no citizenship at the state level (as, for instance, in the United States), and the freedom to move or reside anywhere in the country was guaranteed by Article 19 (1) of the Constitution. Such internal migration in search of livelihood opportunities has intermittently spawned nativist movements in the states of Maharashtra and Assam, challenging the idea of a unified singular citizenship.

Having substantively excluded Indians abroad, the Constituent Assembly was now faced with a bigger challenge: that of producing a definitive settlement of the question of legal citizenship in the context of the massive exchange of population entailed by the Partition.

The Partition and the Constitutional Settlement of Citizenship

The Partition caused approximately fourteen million people to cross the newly created border, about half of this transfer occurring on the Indian and Pakistani sides of the western province of Punjab, and the other half between the two sides of the eastern province of Bengal after its division into the Indian state of West Bengal and East Pakistan. The Constituent Assembly, which had begun its deliberations six months before the announcement of Partition and Independence, was suddenly confronted with the importance of arbitrating the various claims to citizenship that would arise as a consequence of these large-scale movements of people, who were coping with fear and violence and even some confusion about their presumed and attributed identities. A topic that was barely significant earlier now became contentious and divisive, leading Jawaharlal Nehru to declare that the articles relating to citizenship had "probably received far more thought and consideration . . . than any other article contained in this Constitution" (CAD 9: 398).

There was little disagreement on the basic principle of jus soli, not least because of its lineage in both the antecedent British law[6] as well as a range of protoconstitutional documents drafted by the nationalist leadership. The Motilal Nehru Committee Report of 1928,[7] for instance, had included, within the ambit of citizenship, anyone born or naturalized, or the child of a *father* born or naturalized, within the territorial limits of the "Commonwealth of India," with citizens of foreign countries being eligible only if they renounced their citizenship of the other country. The Sub-Committee on Fundamental Rights of the Constituent Assembly also started out with a reiteration of this basic principle that any person domiciled in India, and born or naturalized in the country, would be a citizen. All manner of exceptional possibilities—from traveling foreigners giving birth to children on Indian soil to Indian women marrying foreigners to the rights of children of foreign expatriates—were identified and discussed and indicate the variety of challenges that could arise in determining entitlements to citizenship.

The choice of jus soli was justified by its presumed "enlightened modern civilized" (CAD 1: 424) character, contrasted with a racial conception such as jus sanguinis. The advocates of jus sanguinis were reminded that it would be inconsistent for India, which had been supporting the rights of Indians settled in South Africa, to adopt a narrow principle of nationality itself. The jus soli regime inaugurated by Article 5 of the Indian Constitution was tempered by domicile and descent-based considerations arguably meant to complement, rather than to undermine or qualify, the primary form of citizenship based on birth.[8] While jus soli was fairly easily accepted as the basis for citizenship, the zone of contention around returning (impliedly Muslim) migrants from Pakistan was marked by arguments that persistently recalled jus sanguinis principles. Constitutionally, jus soli remains the defining doctrine of Indian citizenship. The infiltration of a jus sanguinis regime is more visible in statutory law, in particular in recent amendments to the Citizenship Act.[9]

The markers of religious difference were not explicitly displayed, but are easily recognizable in the debates on what eventually became Articles 6 and 7 of the Constitution, which introduced qualifying provisions to help manage the massive population migration occasioned by the violence that accompanied the Partition of the subcontinent. They referred to, respectively, those moving from what had now become Pakistan into India, and those who had moved from India to Pakistan and were now seeking to return and once again resettle in India. Thus, Article 6 was about citizenship for those who migrated to India from what became Pakistan before July 1948. Those migrating after July 1948 (i.e., more than one year after the Partition) would need to be registered with the government. This was a largely uncontroversial clause because it pertained to "refugees"—the euphemism used, in the Constituent Assembly, to denote Hindu migrants fleeing communal violence and their homes in what was now Pakistan. What eventually became Article 7, on the other hand, was about citizenship for those who had fled in the opposite direction *to* the newly constituted state of Pakistan—i.e., Muslims escaping from communal violence and abandoning their homes in Indian territory—but returned to India under a permit of resettlement or permanent return issued by an Indian government official. These people were euphemistically described as "migrants," and this was the most intensely contested article on citizenship in the Constituent Assembly. The nomenclature of refugee and migrant is not used in the Constitution but was very much a part of both discussions in the Constituent Assembly, and of the official and nonofficial vocabulary outside the Assembly. In a shared universe of meaning, the use of the terms refugee and migrant served to conceal the religious identities they encoded.[10] The fragility and tenuousness of the disguise is however laid bare in the tenor of the debate.

In the Assembly, Article 7 was frequently referred to, by its detractors, as "the obnoxious clause." The debate on it was extremely combative, with arguments for a more inclusive interpretation clashing repeatedly with arguments for a more restrictive one. Those in favor of more inclusive provisions argued that the returning migrants were people who had fled on account of riots and disturbances: that they should be welcomed back, and their properties restored to them. Those in favor of more restrictive provisions claimed that Indian citizenship was being sold too cheaply:[11] that those who had migrated had done so deliberately and intentionally and that their desire to return was definitely suspect. Who then could legitimately be entitled to Indian citizenship? A few vocal participants in the debate suggested that every Hindu or Sikh (who was not a citizen of any other state) should be entitled to Indian citizenship. Jaspat Roy Kapoor, the Punjabi Hindu author of the phrase "obnoxious clause," explained his opposition to it thus:

It is a serious matter of principle. Once a person has migrated to Pakistan and transferred his loyalty from India to Pakistan, his migration is complete. He has definitely made up his mind at that time to kick this country and let it go to its own fate, and he went away to the newly created Pakistan, where he would put in his best efforts to make it a free progressive and prosperous state. (CAD 9: 366)

Claims about volition were central to the debate: the supporters of the "obnoxious clause" emphasized the circumstances—communal violence and riots—under which the returning migrants had fled to Pakistan, while its opponents insisted on the deliberate and voluntary nature of their migration from India to Pakistan.[12] This emphasis on the volitional aspect of agency—defining the act of seeking refuge as involuntary and of migrating as voluntary—is echoed in contemporary international refugee law, with the difference that here migrants always migrate, voluntarily, for *economic* reasons, while refugees are forced, hence involuntarily, to flee for *political* reasons. In the Partition discourse, on the other hand, refugees flee because of religious insecurity, but Muslims fleeing India in the postpartition riots and later returning to their homes in India are labeled migrants who migrated *voluntarily* to Pakistan because of their attachment to the idea of a Pakistani nation. When they return,[13] the stigma of their presumptively declared attachment to Pakistan is not easily erased—their loyalty remains doubtful, they may have come back as spies or fifth columnists to sabotage Indian independence (CAD 9: 354) or for base material motives such as selling off their properties, or simply because they thought that Pakistan was a happier country but found it to not be so. The term migrant conveys the opprobrium of that first act of disloyalty, migration from India to Pakistan. The imputed transfer of allegiance established, some argued, that returnees had "forfeited their right to become citizens of this country" (CAD 9: 381). The suspicion was frequently articulated that, since the acquisition of a permit did not entail an oath of allegiance, "migrants" who had secured permits were returning only temporarily to dispose of their properties and that there was no guarantee that they would stay on, much less that they were likely to be loyal citizens of India. This assumption was disputed by Alladi Krishnaswamy Aiyar, one of the most powerful liberal voices in the Constituent Assembly, who insisted that a secular state could distinguish between those who had "voluntarily and deliberately chosen another country" (CAD 9: 404), but could not make a distinction on racial or religious grounds. But, even in faraway East Africa,

the registration of aspiring citizens was heavily inflected by religious difference, as the presumed "divided and uncertain loyalties" of Muslim applicants
were put to the test of allegiance and loyalty to the new Constitution (Sutton,
2007: 283).

The question of property was an important aspect of this hostility. For the
critics of Article 7, there was simply no question of evacuee properties being
restored to such people, because these properties had already been allotted
to Hindu refugees from the Punjab and were needed for their rehabilitation. The "obnoxious clause," it was frequently argued, had important financial implications. Since the properties evacuated by departing migrants were
being used to rehabilitate (Hindu) refugees, returning them to the (Muslim)
migrants, if they chose to return, would mean that "our refugee brethren"
(CAD 9: 367) would have to bear the cost. A further anomaly would arise
if some migrants secured a valid permit and succeeded in returning, as they
would be admitted to citizenship but without the right to their property. The
concern about property was curiously shared even by some of those arguing
for a more liberal interpretation. A Zoroastrian member, R. K. Sidhwa, strenuously defended the right of all to the equal status of citizenship, and felt the
"obnoxious clause" was important for other minorities such as Zoroastrians
and Christians in Pakistan who may wish to move to India. However, even
he perceived "genuine danger" and grounds for apprehension in the matter
of evacuee property and was in favor of introducing safeguards against the
cynical misuse of such provisions.

These claims were countered by Jawaharlal Nehru, whose argument not
only invoked the principle of justice, but also emphasized the small numbers of such migrants and the insignificance of the size and number of such
properties.

> To argue against that amendment is to argue definitely for injustice, defi-
> nitely for discrimination, for not doing something which after full enquiry
> has been found to be rightly done, and for doing something which from
> the practical point of view of numbers or property, has no consequence. It
> is just dust in the pan. In order to satisfy yourself about that little thing,
> because your sense of property is so keen, because your vested interest is
> so keen that you do not wish one-millionth part of certain aggression of
> property to go outside the pool . . . you wish to upset the rule which we
> have tried to base on certain principles, on a certain sense of equity or
> justice. (CAD 9: 401)

Invoking and echoing Gandhi's invitation to all Muslims to return,[14] Brajeshwar Prasad argued that moral principles were more important than economic ones; and that India was not "a nation of shopkeepers; we cannot dethrone God and worship Mammon" (CAD 9: 405).

Notwithstanding these denials, the question of citizenship remained deeply imbricated in religion, and closely linked to property. On both sides of the border, as murder and mayhem prevailed, millions of people left their homes and belongings in mortal fear of violence. The properties so abandoned were, in both countries, taken over by a government agency, the Custodian of Evacuee Property.[15] The Indian legislation that made this possible was a response to the occupation of Muslim properties by Hindus, and was initially intended to protect the rights of the "evacuees" when they returned to their homes. In the interim, such properties could be "allotted" to Hindu and Sikh refugees in immediate need of shelter; and these people could be evicted only when alternative accommodation was provided to them (Zamindar, 2007: 28–29). The Custodian was also instituted in both countries to make intergovernmental compensation possible though this objective was eventually abandoned.[16] Meanwhile, India even toyed with the concept of the "intending evacuee," and it was only the forceful opposition of the minister for rehabilitation, on grounds that making such a provision in the law would be openly discriminatory toward Muslims, that prevented it from being enacted (ibid.: 131–132).

Discouraging the putative (Muslim) citizen from returning was thus a dominant theme in the formulation of Article 7 of the Constitution, as well as in the negotiations around evacuee property. Preceding the constitutional provision, in July 1948, the Indian government promulgated the Influx from Pakistan (Control) Ordinance, requiring a permit to enter India from its western border. The requirement of a permit was introduced to filter and screen migrations taking place one year after the Partition, which was announced in June and took effect in the middle of August 1947. The massive and unprecedented movement of people continued well into 1948. Article 6 (b) provided that those who migrated from Pakistan into India (impliedly Hindus) after July 19, 1948, would have to register themselves as citizens with a government official. Article 7 required those who had migrated from India to Pakistan after March 1947 and now desired to return (impliedly Muslims) to obtain a permit for resettlement or permanent return from the Indian High Commission in Pakistan. The High Commission claimed that it received a thousand applications from Muslim refugees every day (Zamindar, 2007: 86), and though the actual figures remain uncertain, this was clearly a much larger influx than in the opposite direction. Joya Chatterji shows that by the end of 1948 and through 1949, serious concerns about permits being faked or otherwise inadequate led to stern instructions from the Rehabilitation Secretary to stop issuing the permits for permanent resettlement that were the substance of Article 7.[17] Similar restrictions were being placed by the Ministry of Rehabilitation on Muslims visiting India to dispose of their properties, and the grant of permits came to be informed by this suspicion. Questions about property found a place on the application form for a permit, and counterfoils of the permits were required to be sent to the office of the Custodian of Evacuee Property.

Notwithstanding the provisions being written into the Constitution, officials were already engaged in scripting exclusions, suggesting a contrast between the conception of legal citizenship—in its pristine borrowed form— in the constitutional citadel, with another demotic version being enacted outside, by official agencies and civil society. This resonates with a distinction proposed by Upendra Baxi, between "the constitutional State (the normative and aspirational framework enunciating the desired social order) and the political State (as framework of competition for political power, or even the struggle to capture the constitutional State)" (U. Baxi, 2010).

Thus, while the Indian Constitution did make provision for citizenship for both the Hindu "refugees" and the Muslim "migrants," the accommodation of the claims of returning Muslims was a hard-won battle in the constitution-making process. It was intensely contested, and these disagreements within the Assembly were echoed outside it not just in civil society but also in the practices of official agencies, especially in the exercise of their discretionary powers and grant of permits, and in the sizeable body of case law that emerged over the next few decades. Framed in this way, the incipient conception of legal citizenship in the Constitution conceals a deep tension, suggesting different ways in which even straightforward doctrinal conceptions of citizenship—such as the principle of jus soli—may be appropriated, transformed, and translated in the rules, practices, and discourses of official agencies, courts of law, and civil society. Both the case law on citizenship in the following years, as well as the story of evacuee (later enemy) property bear testimony to this, suggesting that there were already discernible elements of jus sanguinis in official and judicial decisions. Only the explicit shift in the law was manifested a few decades later.

There was of course another site of Partition—the eastern border dividing India from what became East Pakistan and, in 1971, Bangladesh. The eastern border was hardly discussed in the Constituent Assembly, apparently on the assumption that few Hindus would leave East Pakistan for West Bengal. Despite the same laws of citizenship being in operation, this was a theatre playing to a slightly different script.[18] The government did not expect—and Nehru in fact dismissed as baseless rumor—the in-migration of Hindu refugees from East Pakistan, let alone the influx that by the end of 1951 had touched two and one half million refugees (Chatterji, 2008: 130n72). However, as Chatterji shows, the central government continued to insist that the rehabilitation of refugees from East Bengal was unnecessary and even to be discouraged, and compensation and expenditure on rehabilitation was accordingly much lower than on the western border (ibid.: 129–130). Unlike on the western border, the property of Muslim evacuees from Bengal was not allotted to incoming Hindu refugees, as the state government endeavored to hold on to these till their original owners returned to reclaim them. Migration continued unabated, first from East Pakistan and then, following the conflict of 1971, from the new state of Bangladesh. But it wasn't all Hindu migration, and it was only when the scale of this immigration began to upset the demographic-religious balance in the eastern state of Assam, and became politically volatile, that the government moved toward a more restrictive citizenship regime.

Legislating Citizenship

It was a full five years after the creation of the republic that the Citizenship Act of 1955 was enacted, specifying the broad framework enunciated in the Constitution. It classified the various sources of claims to citizenship: by birth, descent, registration, naturalization, and incorporation of territory. A significant feature of the Act was to reserve to the executive the power to determine and certify the citizenship of persons whose citizenship of India is in doubt. This had important implications for cases in which judges were called upon to make pronouncements on citizenship. There was also a potential inconsistency with the provisions of the Foreigners' Act, 1946, which placed on the individual in question the burden of proving that s/he was not a foreigner.

The most consequential amendment to the statute was enacted in 1985 to cope with the in-migration from Bangladesh. An open-ended process of migration from 1947 onward, peaking in 1971, and continuing steadily thereafter, had resulted in large numbers of refugees/migrants, regardless of religion, getting enfranchised.[19] This became politically contentious in Assam in the early 1980s, when a powerful nativist student movement led the protest against the swamping of Assam with "foreigners." This mobilization between 1979–1985 resulted in a political agreement (the Assam Accord) with the central government according to which (a) all those who had migrated before 1966 would be treated as citizens; (b) those who had migrated between 1966 and 1971 could stay provided they put themselves through an official process of registration as foreigners; and (c) all those who migrated thereafter were simply illegal immigrants.

It was no secret that many of these illegal immigrants—numbering around ten million—had already, through what Kamal Sadiq has called "networks of complicity" and "networks of profit," acquired forms of "documentary citizenship" including ration cards and election cards, which had enabled them to vote in elections. The Citizenship Act was accordingly amended to ensure that the names of those in the last two categories (i.e., those who came in after 1966) would be deleted from the electoral roll. After the lapse of ten years from an individual's "detection" as a foreigner, the person would become a full citizen with political rights.

The vulnerability of these people made them eager voters and the avowedly secular Congress the natural party of choice for them. This encouraged the Congress government at the Centre to pass The Illegal Migrants (Determination by Tribunals) Act (IMDT) 1983, ostensibly assuaging nativist Assamese sentiments by providing for tribunals to detect and expel foreigners, and cannily banking on local networks of ethnic solidarity to render such complaints largely irrelevant. The Act created an Assam-specific exception to India's law on foreigners, which ordinarily places the burden of proving citizenship status on the individual in question. The IMDT Act removed this burden from individuals suspected of being illegal immigrants and placed it on their neighbors, who could file a complaint to report illegal immigrants in their area. These complaints would, under the Act, be adjudicated by a tribunal that would determine conclusively as to whether the person was indeed an illegal migrant and, if so, order his/her deportation.

One of the leaders of the students' movement that had led the agitation against immigrants now filed a writ petition in the Supreme Court claiming that the Act was *ultra vires* the Constitution, because it made it "impossible for citizens who are resident in Assam to secure the detection and deportation of foreigners from Indian soil" (*Sarbananda Sonowal*, 2005: 4). The petition also claimed that non-Indians who had surreptitiously entered Assam after 1971 had changed the "whole character, cultural and ethnic composition of the area" (ibid.). There was support for the petition from both the state and the central governments. The latter, a coalition headed by the Hindu nationalist Bharatiya Janata Party (BJP), assured the Supreme Court that it was contemplating the repeal of the Act because its application to only one state (Assam) was discriminatory, and also because the scale of the influx had implications for internal security (ibid.: 5). Also making a case for its repeal, the Asom Gana Parishad (AGP)[20] state government in August 2000 attributed the small numbers of foreigners detected and deported to the provisions of the IMDT Act which, it claimed, actually protected them.[21]

The politics of religious nationalism played no small part in these positions. In May 2001, in a political reversal of the earlier situation, the newly elected Congress government in the state claimed that the Act was entirely constitutional and declared its commitment to its preservation. In 2004, the Congress Party came to power at the Centre, and the Court was informed that the Union Government had now reconsidered its position and decided to retain the IMDT Act in its present form, applicable to the state of Assam. The politics of the contrasting interpretation of numbers deported/not deported are notable. For the AGP and the BJP, the small numbers actually deported—1,481 persons of the 10,015 declared to be illegal immigrants—showed that the Act was designed to protect illegal immigrants. For the Congress, the fact that such a small number had been deported showed that the Act worked well in ensuring judicial scrutiny and so protecting Indians from being wrongfully deported.

In 2005, the Supreme Court struck down the Act as *ultra vires* the Constitution, pointing out that citizens were unlikely to initiate proceedings for the deportation of illegal migrants, and that the Act itself was the biggest impediment to the identification and deportation of illegal migrants, as it had resulted in expulsions in less than half of one per cent of all cases initiated.

> A deep analysis of the IMDT Act and the Rules made thereunder would reveal that they have been purposely so enacted or made so as to give shelter or protection to illegal migrants who came to Assam from Bangladesh on or after 25th March 1971 rather than to identify and deport them. (ibid.: 30)

Indeed, the question of illegal migration from Bangladesh triggered the most egregious xenophobia and not only from political parties. A report of 1998 by the governor of the state, cited by the Court, asserted that the illegal migrants coming into Assam from Bangladesh were "almost exclusively Muslims" (ibid.: 14).

> The silent and invidious demographic invasion of Assam may result in the loss of the geostrategically vital districts of lower Assam. The influx of these illegal migrants is turning these districts into a Muslim majority region. It will then only be a matter of time when a demand for their merger with Bangladesh may be made. The rapid growth of international Islamic fundamentalism may provide for [sic] driving force for this demand. (ibid.)

The Supreme Court endorsed the view that the illegal migrants had reduced the people of Assam to a minority in their own state, and represented a threat of "external aggression and internal disturbance" (ibid.: 35–36). Though the IMDT Act was eventually struck down, the law on citizenship continues to reflect the issue of illegal migrants from Bangladesh, and the exclusions enacted by some of its provisions remain, in particular the 2004 amendment to the Citizenship Act, *modifying the provision of citizenship by birth to exclude from it such persons born in India as have one parent who is an illegal migrant at the time of their birth* (Article 3(c) (ii)).

Meanwhile, the western border has witnessed periodic waves of immigration into Rajasthan and Gujarat during the wars between India and Pakistan in 1965 and 1971, and most recently in the wake of the demolition of the Babri Masjid in 1992. Of the 17,000 migrants who came in after 1992, mostly on Pakistani passports and valid Indian visas, which they overstayed, about 3,000—almost entirely Dalits and Adivasis—still await the realization of their citizenship claims (the subject of the next chapter). Those who obtained citizenship were legalized in Citizenship Camps. This was accomplished through a delegation of powers to District Collectors, powers that, on account of the Assam agitation in the 1980s, had earlier reverted to the Central Government, following charges of the manipulation of citizenship in that state. In 2004, through an amendment to the Citizenship Rules 1956, these powers were once again—and as a region-specific exception—delegated to District Collectors in Rajasthan and Gujarat. This amendment makes an open declaration of the religious identity of the immigrants. It does not even describe them as migrants, much less as illegal migrants, the label used for the immigrants from Bangladesh.

Section 3 (2) (ii) of the Amendment to the Rules states:

> In respect of *minority Hindus with Pakistan citizenship* who have migrated
> to India more than five years back with *the intention of permanently settling
> down in India* and have applied for Indian citizenship, the authority to
> register a person as a citizen of India . . . shall be the concerned Collector
> of the district where the applicant is normally resident. (emphasis added)

The comparison with what was once "the obnoxious clause," Article 7 of the
Constitution, is instructive.

> Notwithstanding anything in articles 5 and 6, a person who has after the
> first day of March, 1947, migrated from the territory of India to the terri-
> tory now included in Pakistan shall not be deemed to be a citizen of India:

> Provided that nothing in this article shall apply to *a person who, after hav-
> ing so migrated to the territory now included in Pakistan, has returned to the
> territory of India under a permit for resettlement or permanent return* issued
> by or under the authority of any law and every such person shall for the
> purposes of clause *(b)* of article 6 be deemed to have migrated to the terri-
> tory of India after the nineteenth day of July, 1948. (emphasis added)

Two points of contrast are worth noting. First, Article 7 (adopted in 1950)
made no mention of the religious identity of those covered by this article,
even though the history of the Partition and the debates in the Constituent
Assembly made it amply clear that this clause was used to describe returning Muslims who had migrated to Pakistan. By 2004, as the amendment
to the Citizenship Rules shows, religious identity was no longer a matter of
covert signaling: the Rules explicitly refer to "minority Hindus with Pakistan
citizenship."

Second, not only do the Hindu migrants not require any permit for resettlement, their *intention to permanently settle in India*—expressed through
residence of at least five years—is adequate. By contrast, the *intention* of
returning Muslims was repeatedly questioned in the Constituent Assembly
and subsequently in judicial decisions. Some of them had to wait ten years to
seek citizenship by naturalization.

Both elements of jus sanguinis that have infiltrated the jus soli constitutional regime—the ineligibility of persons born in India but with one
parent who is an illegal migrant at the time of their birth, and the special
dispensation made for "minority Hindus with Pakistan citizenship" through
the exceptional delegation of citizenship-conferring powers on District

Magistrates—draw our attention to the salience of religious identity in the construction of legal citizenship.

Such a reading is reinforced by an examination of how citizenship has been adjudicated, through a focus on four key issues: the factors that went into deciding the citizenship claims of those crossing the border after the Cinderella hour; the judicial interpretation of the documents they furnished to bolster their claims, and the implications of such documents both for the identity of the individual claimant and the state itself; the question of property and citizenship; and the issue of the natural citizenship of women.

Adjudicating Citizenship

A survey of thirty-eight High Court and Supreme Court judgments in citizenship-related cases decided from 1951 to 2009 shows that approximately half of these are direct offshoots of the legal fact of partition between India and Pakistan, and only six cases are completely unrelated to migration within South Asia. The cases that the Partition spawned were generally about people who found themselves on the wrong side of the border or of a date after which their movement from one country to the other caused their citizenship to become marked, and eventually settled, in particular ways. Ironically, though judicial pronouncements decided cases by imputing intentionality and agency to people, the decisions were seldom in consonance with their stated intentions.

The act of crossing the border in the twilight zone between the Partition, on the one hand, and the enactment of either the Constitution or the Citizenship Act of 1955, on the other, gave rise to a considerable body of litigation. The claims to legal citizenship of such individuals came to be imbued with meaning at many levels and were often arbitrated by resort to affect. Did the person intend to migrate (to Pakistan) and then change his[22] mind, or did he find himself inadvertently on the wrong side of the border? Did his possession of a Pakistani passport indicate compulsion or voluntary agency? Was the passport a sign of shifting loyalties or was it simply a necessary instrumentality that he had been compelled to acquire to enable the return to his preferred homeland? The answers to these questions rested, more than occasionally, on the religious identity of the individual in question. The often innocent act of crossing the border was thus invested with the multiple burdens of identity and self-identification. Similarly, the possession of official documents from the hostile Other, as well as the questions of property and women, were variously interpreted in terms of such identities and intentions.

Citizenship and the Judicial Determination of Home

Many individuals who had migrated from India to Pakistan at the time of the Partition returned to India on Pakistani passports and valid visas, often overstaying their visas from anywhere between three days to nine years (*State of Assam v. Jilkadar Ali,* 1972) before being detected. On detection, they would typically be arrested or convicted or served notices of deportation, which they would appeal in court. In some cases, the question of determining the "other" of a citizen—viz., a foreigner—became important.[23] In its judgment in a habeas corpus petition in *Shabbir Hussain v. State of Uttar Pradesh* (1951) the Supreme Court commented sympathetically on how the constitutional prescription of a date had the power to change the lives of ordinary people, who may not even have been aware of what was a transitional and constantly changing legislative scenario. The plaintiff in this particular case was a merchant from Uttar Pradesh, who happened to be on a two-month business visit to Lahore when the Influx from Pakistan (Control) Ordinance was promulgated. He could not return without a permit, but the permit given to him by the Indian High Commission was temporary. He returned home, "overstayed" his permit, and was arrested on grounds that he had migrated to Pakistan and had been permitted to return only temporarily. The judgment discussed the meaning of "migration" in some detail, and argued that it was scarcely likely to be a word that could be used interchangeably with the word "gone." Such "casual or fortuitous departure" (*Shabbir Hussain,* 1951: 16), said the Court, did not constitute migration, and this was all that Shabbir Hussain and large numbers of others had done, getting caught in a legal no-man's land when, in their absence, the laws were altered.

> The mere visits of persons residing in the territories of India to those now included in Pakistan between the 1st March and 15th August 1947 could not have been considered sufficient to take away citizenship rights. (ibid.: 7)

There were many cases in which individuals had acquired Pakistani passports in order, they said, to return to India. In some of these, the Court chose to disregard their possession of the passport, taking the view that other factors were more important in determining Indian citizenship. In others, the courts sought to ascertain the intentionality of individuals who held such passports. The date on which people (often unaware of these technicalities) left, or the fact that they changed their minds and returned, was not covered by the jus soli principle, as it was overridden by a judicial attribution of voluntariness and agency having been exercised in deciding to migrate, and deciding to obtain a Pakistani passport. Thus, the Supreme Court Constitution Bench decided, in *Izhar Ahmad Khan v. Union of India* (1962), that Izhar Ahmed's possession of such a passport was conclusive proof of his having voluntarily acquired the citizenship of that country. Only the previous year, in *State of Andhra Pradesh v. Abdul Khader,* the Supreme Court had ruled that Abdul Khader could not be convicted as a foreigner even though he had returned from Pakistan with a passport of that country, because he had not renounced his Indian nationality. Again, in *State of Gujarat and Anr. v. Saiyad Aga Mohmed Saiyedm Ohmed* (1978), the government was restrained from deporting the plaintiff, and his being in possession of a Pakistani passport was not considered adequate proof of Pakistani nationality because, the Supreme Court ruled,

> If a plea is raised by the citizen that he had not voluntarily obtained the passport, the citizen must be afforded an opportunity to prove that fact. Cases may be visualized in which on account of force a person may be compelled or on account of fraud or misrepresentation he may be induced, without any intention of renunciation of his Indian citizenship to obtain a passport from a foreign country. (ibid.: 7–8)

The courts were thus frequently called upon to decide on the evidentiary value of official documents such as passports and, as time went on, electoral rolls and ration cards. As we have seen, in the early years, the possession of a Pakistani passport did not contradict an individual's claim to Indian citizenship (*State of Andhra Pradesh v. Abdul Khader*, 1961); over time, even the possession of an Indian passport (by an individual presumed to be an illegal migrant from Bangladesh) became insufficient proof of Indian citizenship. In *Razia Begum and Ors. v. State and Ors*, for instance, the Court ruled that Razia Begum had obtained an Indian passport in a third attempt, "on the basis of forged and fabricated documents and in collusion with the passport officials." Her ration card, election identity card, and nationality certificate were similarly obtained through false documents (*Razia Begum and Ors. v. Union of India*, 2008).

Citizenship, Identity, and Identification

As the previous section suggests, the relationship between documents and citizenship in post-Partition India inverts the standard expectation that it is the possession of citizenship that enables the acquisition of documents certifying it. Here, we have many cases in which the documents themselves are proffered as certifying and authenticating claims to citizenship. These include passports as well as other forms of official documentation, with the courts deciding the value of these as proofs of Indian (or Pakistani) citizenship. In general, passports perform two functions: those of identification and of the facilitation of movement across national borders.[24] In undivided colonial India, the passport was a document that certified subjecthood of the British Empire, and as such enabled travel. In the aftermath of the Partition, movement came to be mediated by the permit system, and indeed the first passports issued by the new states of India and Pakistan—labeled the "India-Pakistan Passport"—were only intended as documents for travel between the two countries. There was some suspicion of passports and their potential to freeze citizenship. There was in fact no law governing the grant of Indian passports till 1967 when the Indian Passport Act was passed.[25]

The idea of a passport in the western sense had not, the case law shows, been institutionalized or internalized, so that people acquired passports quite casually without realizing the implications of such an act for nationality and citizenship. On their part, the courts interpreted the possession of a passport quite cynically: it could have been acquired inadvertently or involuntarily or under duress; equally, it could have been acquired through the use of devious means. If there were cases (such as *T. A. Mahomed Usman v. State of Madras*, 1959) in which even an unlettered person's application to the Pakistan High Commissioner for a passport was interpreted as voluntary and intentional, there were also other cases (such as *State of Andhra Pradesh v. Mohd. Khan*, 1962) in which the mere acquisition of the passport of another country did not mean the cessation of Indian citizenship.

It was only in the context of illegal migration from Bangladesh that the courts began to exhibit a more consistent cynicism about passports, arguing that an Indian passport may have been acquired by misrepresentation and fraud (*Motimiya, Rahim Miya and Ors. v. The State of Maharashtra*, 2003; *Razia Begum and Ors. v. State and Ors*, 2008). This was a period in which "documentary citizenship" (Sadiq, 2009)—in contrast to "undocumented" illegal immigrants in the western world[26]—became a common mode of acquiring citizenship by illegal immigrants. Ration cards and election identity cards were certainly more frequently, and therefore perhaps more easily, acquired than passports. The courts repeatedly ruled that registration on a voters' list is no proof of citizenship *(Bhanwaroo Khan and Ors.* v. *Union of India and Ors,* 2002). Prior to independence, franchise had conferred a citizenship-like status. By the 1980s, however, proof of appearing on the electoral rolls became highly suspect as a claim to citizenship, not least because similar names were routinely picked off the existing rolls to get local officials to issue Voter Identity Cards.

In most cases, it was the mode of acquisition of these documents that rendered them suspect. The benign interpretation was that these were merely indications of "continued residence," even though "mere residence, howsoever long, does not confer any citizenship" *(Motimiya, Rahim Miya and Ors.* v. *The State of Maharashtra,* 2003). A more strident ruling did not hesitate to echo the discourse of the "political state," making gratuitous predictions about the implications of such documents.

> Thus, the petitioners and such other large number of Bangladeshis present in the State of Assam have a major role in electing the representatives both to the Legislative Assembly and the Parliament and consequently, in the decision making process towards building the nation. They have become the kingmakers. The dangerous effect of the cancerous growth of Bangladeshis finds mention in the report of the then Governor of Assam. . . . If this phenomenon continues, the day is not far off, when the indigenous people of Assam, both Hindus and Muslims and other religious groups will be reduced to minorities in its own land and the Bangladeshis who are freely and merrily moving around the fertile land of Assam, will intrude upon the corridors of power. *(Mustt Sarabari Begum and Syera Begum and 2 Ors.* v. *State of Assam and Ors,* 2008)

Judicial recognition of the ways in which such documentation of citizenship is acquired thus led the courts to deliver rulings in which, ironically, the validity of practically all forms of official documentation was impugned. When the entire edifice of state documents, their verisimilitude, their integrity, and their sanctity, is called into question, the implications of such a complete erosion of the credibility of official documents are arguably of enormous significance. What, if anything, can state documents testify to any longer?

Citizenship and Property

Official documents are of course key to the possession of property, a right historically attached to citizenship. The link between property and citizenship can be broken when an individual changes citizenship or when a transfer of sovereignty takes place. In an early example from western India, the ownership of lands granted by the erstwhile ruler to some of his subjects was permanently lost as the territory of the principality of Junagadh was incorporated into India, and the subjects became citizens of the Indian state.[27] Even governmental suspicion of an intention to switch citizenship could have the same effect, as in the case of a Muslim woman, Kumar Rani, married to an Indian Hindu, whose property was declared Evacuee Property as she traveled frequently to Pakistan. This case is especially striking because the Supreme Court, in an unusual decision, chose to determine her citizenship independently of that of her husband;[28] otherwise, for the most part, the citizenship of women (and children/minors) was a simple projection of their husband's citizenship.

Most significantly, the legacy of the Partition continues to endure in the contentiousness of the more than two thousand properties, spread across India, which have since 1968 been called "enemy property."[29] Initially called "evacuee properties," these were placed in the charge of a Custodian of Evacuee Property when their original owners left for Pakistan. Following the India-Pakistan war of 1965, both countries agreed (in the Tashkent Declaration of 1966) to discuss the return of property seized by the other side. All that occurred instead was a change in nomenclature, as evacuee property came to be redesignated as enemy property. While Pakistan sold off all enemy properties left by departing Indians at Partition during 1965–1976 (when the countries had broken off diplomatic relations) the Custodian in India continues to hold properties estimated to be worth Rs. 1300 crores (US$300 million). These are governed by the Enemy Property Act of 1968, which gives the central government the sole power to divest them to the lawful heirs of the owner.

In 2005, the most high-profile legatee of all, Mohammed Amir Mohammed "Suleiman" Khan, the Raja of Mahmudabad in Uttar Pradesh, won a prolonged legal battle lasting 32 years the culmination of which was a Supreme Court verdict giving him the right to take over his late father's many and very valuable properties. M. A. M. Khan's properties account for almost half of all (1,100 of 2,100) enemy properties in the country. His father, the previous Raja of Mahmudabad, had migrated to Pakistan in 1957,[30] but his wife and son stayed on as Indian citizens. M. A. M. Khan was twice elected to the Uttar Pradesh Legislative Assembly and even once contested a parliamentary election. His public response to the Supreme Court judgment interpreted the order as a vindication of his loyalty as an Indian citizen, privileging the removal of the stigma of "enemy" over the obvious gains of property. "I petitioned everyone, saying my mother and I are Indians, not enemies. I wanted the stigma of enemy of state on my family to be removed and I am happy that I have won this battle" (*The Indian Express,* August 26, 2010).

Following the Supreme Court judgment in the Mahmudabad case, there was a spate of court orders that cited this verdict to give ownership to other such claimants, some of them on the basis of oral gifts or unregistered wills and even adoption certificates. This led the government to propose an amendment to the Enemy Property Act of 1968 that sought to empower the government to prevent the indiscriminate purchase and sale of "enemy property," to debar courts from passing more such orders giving away enemy property worth huge sums of money, but simultaneously to allow rightful legal heirs to reclaim their property, so long as they are Indian citizens and can prove their claims. Meanwhile, in a curious development, the government on July 2, 2010, promulgated the Enemy Property (Amendment and Validation) Ordinance, 2010. While the Bill (since withdrawn) enabled lawful heirs to claim their property, the Ordinance sought to undo the effect of such claims by vesting all rights in the Custodian and the central government.[31] This was interpreted as an attempt, on behalf of tenants and others with an interest in these properties, to undo the effect of the Supreme Court verdict of 2005, and prevent the Raja of Mahmudabad from claiming his property. Muslim Members of Parliament, cutting across party lines, mobilized and urged the prime minister to consider this matter as an important guarantee of minority rights, since most of the claimants in enemy property cases are Muslims. The Raja of Mahmudabad also asked: "Are they being punished for choosing to stay back in India even though the SC has upheld their rights as Indian citizens?" (*The Hindustan Times,* August 25, 2010).

The Enemy Property issue is an important manifestation of the enduring legacy of Partition on the defining of citizenship and the property rights that it entails. The Raja's family history—with his father taking Pakistani citizenship while he and his mother remained Indian citizens—highlights the

incomplete and contingent quality of the Partition.[32] Indian citizenship is one
of the primary requirements to sustain a claim to the inheritance of "enemy"
property.[33] M. A. M. Khan's implicit claim is that what was at stake in the
Court was not so much property, but the ignominy of being designated an
enemy. While a cynical view might hold that this is less an affective and more
an instrumental view of citizenship, in which wealth has a central place,[34] the
fate of enemy properties hangs in the balance, its resolution encumbered by
the fact of its being strongly inflected by religious identity and a presumptive
association with a hostile neighbor, Pakistan.[35]

The Female Citizen

The citizenship of Kumar Rani, as we saw in the previous section, was determined independently of her husband's, though she lost her property on suspicion of having gone to reside permanently in Pakistan. The legal and social
predicament of most women and minors in the context of the Partition was
quite different.[36] In the brutal violence of those times and on both sides of
the border, thousands of women were variously separated from their families, raped and sometimes killed, abducted, or through a variety of circumstances came to live with men of the other religious community. There were
a sizeable number[37] of abducted Muslim women and children in India, just
as there were abducted Hindu and Sikh women and children in Pakistan.
The Constituent Assembly debated the issue, some interventions betraying
strong Hindu patriarchal sentiment for the restoration of abducted women
and minors, and in December 1949 it passed the Abducted Persons (Recovery
and Restoration) Act.

The Act had laid down a date after which all mixed unions—i.e., unions
between men and women belonging to different religions—would be treated
as cases where women had been abducted and forcibly married and/or converted; and in all such cases, a procedure was provided for rescuing such
women, establishing their original identity, and restoring them to their kin.
There was an intergovernmental agreement, between India and Pakistan, for
the restoration of such Hindu women found in Pakistan, and Muslim women
in India. These arrangements not only denied women any agency in determining where they chose to live, or who they chose to marry, but also ignored
the contingent nature of individual predicaments and the diverse and complex tapestries of human relationships. Thus, there were cases where women

had married their "abductors," had children, and preferred to live with these men instead of being sent back to their families. There were Hindu families who were reluctant to accept women who had had sex with, or been impregnated or worse still had children by, men of the other religion. Chastity and purity were considerations that surfaced frequently, so pregnant women were more likely to be shunned, while women who had children would be taken back only on condition that they gave up these children of mixed unions to orphanages. Older women were vulnerable in other ways. If they owned property, younger men would force these women to "adopt" them, in order to inherit their property. A curious complication was that any woman living with a man of the other religion after March 1, 1947, was presumed to be an abducted person, so that even women in voluntary mixed marriages would be viewed, by both governments, as having been taken by force (Butalia, 1998: 109). Since the official date was quite arbitrarily determined, women who had married these men by choice now became victims of the new law.

The Act was implemented through an intergovernmental mechanism of tribunals, which had representatives from both countries, and in which many well-intentioned women social workers were involved. Difficulties arose when women were "recovered" but did not wish to be "restored" as also when women were willing to be restored but were not accepted by their families. The paradigm of the "recovery" and "restoration" of women was a form of biological citizenship,[38] as it entailed not only determining the religion (at birth) of a woman, almost as if it were a biological characteristic, but also her biological status as a woman whose body had been violated, impregnated, or otherwise defiled by union with a male of another religious community. A powerful patriarchal nationalism informed such interpretations of the abducted woman's body as a metaphor for national purity, honor, and morality. Women's citizenship was thus produced by three concentric circles: the citizenship of her father or husband, religious identity, and—on the basis of the first two—her imputed national identity. This mapping of religious difference onto citizenship of the nation meant that not only could abducted women not choose their citizenship, as men theoretically could, the assumption was that India was the natural home for Hindu and Sikh women, while Muslim women were naturally Pakistani. By the time the Abducted Persons Act was repealed in 1957, approximately 20,000 women[39] had been so "recovered" and "restored" to the biological citizenship of their respective "natural" nations.

Peripheral Citizens

A similar assumption of a natural nation, and of religious identity defining citizenship of it, has informed, till very recently, the characterization of citizens in the Chitmahals, geographically discontinuous enclaves of India in Bangladeshi territory and of Bangladesh in Indian territory. There are 111 Indian Chitmahals (formerly of Cooch Behar state) and 51 Bangladeshi Chitmahals (formerly of Rangpur) in India. Their populations (50,000 persons) are technically nationals of a country from which they are geographically separated, but foreigners in the country on whose territory they actually reside. Their livelihoods are necessarily conducted in zones of illegality, as even going to market can entail as many as four border crossings for them. Despite being technically Indian citizens, however, they are not enrolled in the electoral lists, have no access to schools and colleges, or to hospitals and medical facilities. After 1947, new citizenship identities were thrust upon them by the governments of India and Pakistan, alienating them from family and friends outside the enclave. Some of them were encouraged to privilege their proxy citizenship (Hindus in Pakistan as proxy citizens of India, and Muslims in India as proxy citizens of Pakistan) over their formal citizenship, further distancing them from their neighbors and relatives within the enclave. Over time, realizing that their proxy citizenship brought them into conflict with their immediate neighbors, these identities have been abandoned and superseded, as van Schendel argues, by a new transterritorial community identity that they have forged and defined for themselves as "enclave people" with shared experiences of insecurity, vulnerability and exclusion (van Schendel, 2002: 132). In September 2011, India and Bangladesh signed an agreement by which they decided to "define more accurately . . . the demarcation of the land boundary" between the two countries, and to exchange the "adversely possessed" enclaves.[40] This is expected to lead to formal citizenship of their choice being given to the residents of the enclaves, thus potentially subverting the idea of the natural citizen of India being Hindu and that of Bangladesh being Muslim.

While the final settlement of the Chitmahals has an instrumental importance for bilateral relations between India and Bangladesh, possibly the most compelling groups of aspiring citizens whose predicament raises issues of citizenship and peripherality are the Chakmas and Hajongs in Arunachal Pradesh in northeastern India, on the border of Bangladesh in the east and China in the north. These are tribal groups that, displaced by the construction of the Kaptai Hydel Power Project in 1964, fled from what is now Bangladesh into the states of Assam and Tripura in India. Most of them became Indian citizens over time. About 4,000 Chakmas however were relocated from Assam to Arunachal Pradesh (then called the North East Frontier Agency or NEFA), and given some monetary assistance for rehabilitation by the central government, as well as land, in consultation with local tribals. Land remains at the heart of the problem as the passage of close to half a century has not resulted in their claims to citizenship being met even as their numbers have naturally increased, to approximately 65,000 persons today. Human rights and civil liberties organizations have mobilized to support and advocate their claims, and the Chakmas have themselves formed the Committee for Citizenship Rights of the Chakmas (CCRC). Even as their citizenship claims have been supported by a range of judicial and executive agencies—specifically by rulings and orders from the Supreme Court, the National Human Rights Commission, the Parliamentary Committee on Petitions (Rajya Sabha), and the Government of India—the Chakmas and Hajongs continue to be denied all citizenship rights by the state government of Arunachal Pradesh. Economic blockades have prevented food, medicines, and other essential items from entering their refugee camps, and also prevented the Chakmas from selling their wares in the market. They have been effectively excluded from access to public education and employment. The Chakmas remain largely unenfranchised; they do not have access to the public distribution system; they have suffered political persecution and human rights violations; and they have been victims of violence, often justified by labeling them as criminals.

All these forms of persecution have been made possible by a defiant state government refusing to heed the directives of the federal government, parliament, and courts to grant them the status of citizenship under a nationally applicable law. The state government claimed in the Supreme Court that the settlement of Chakmas would "disturb its ethnic balance and destroy its culture and identity" (*NHRC v. State of Arunachal Pradesh & Anr,* 1996). A local students' organization, the All Arunachal Pradesh Students Union (AAPSU), issued "quit Arunachal Pradesh" notices to the Chakmas, on pain of violent eviction. The indigenous people of Arunachal are opposed not so much to the Chakmas' claims to citizenship, as their competing claims to the land (Singh, 2010: 254).

Technically, the Chakmas who have been resident for over forty-five years in Arunachal Pradesh are fully eligible for citizenship under the Constitution as well as the Citizenship Act. Though the central government is the sole authority that can grant citizenship, it has been ineffectual in doing so, because the procedure specified by the law makes it necessary for the application for citizenship to be scrutinized, verified, and approved by the local administration before being sent to the centre. The Supreme Court therefore directed the state government, in 1996, to ensure the safety and security of the Chakmas, to protect them from forced eviction, and to send their applications for citizenship to the centre with a minimal role for the local administrators. While there has been little progress on this front, about 1,500 young Chakmas and Hajongs born in Arunachal Pradesh were, through the intervention of the Election Commission of India, enabled to vote in the 2004 parliamentary election. In a curious inversion of the traditional relationship between citizenship and private property, the denial of any and all economic rights follows the denial of political citizenship to the Chakmas of Arunachal Pradesh.

The peripherality of the Chakmas is not merely a function of territorial or ethnic marginality. They are peripheral, most of all, to the identities of Hindu and Muslim being gradually encoded in the law as the core identities of Indian citizens.

Conclusion

This chapter has questioned the narrative of a linear move from jus soli to jus sanguinis by arguing that there have been contending elements of jus sanguinis present from the founding moment of the republic, discernible in the debates of the Constituent Assembly as well as in early official practices, such as the instructions to restrict the issuance of permits. It has also argued that exceptions to the laws of citizenship—including the IMDT Act in Assam, the withdrawal of powers to grant citizenship from District Collectors in an area of "Muslim" migration, and the delegation of these powers to District Collectors in Rajasthan and Gujarat for "Hindu" migrants—have generally been made in the "political state" reflected in the ordinary law and rules. Above all, it has shown that the politics of religious identity remain central to the framing of citizenship in the political state, even if distanced from the constitutional state. As such, attributions of affect have played a significant role in determining the veracity of citizenship claims as well as the valuation of documents of identification and claims to property.

As the next chapter will show, aspiring citizens on the western border define citizenship not in terms of affective ties of blood, belonging, or religion, but in terms of access to social goods like subsidized food, public education, and healthcare.[41] Citizenship is more an instrumental than an affective notion also for the newly created category of the diasporic Overseas Citizens of India, to which all members of the Indian diaspora can aspire except those who are or have ever been Pakistani or Bangladeshi citizens. Even in its thinnest legal sense, therefore, the concept of citizenship apparently holds different meanings in different institutional arenas as well as for diverse social groups.

Nevertheless, state responses to such claims tend to filter them through the prism of a citizenship identity mediated by religion, whether ignoring the religious identity of some for votes (as in the east) or treating claimants as legitimate on the basis of their religious identity (as in the west). Property is also frequently intertwined with religion, particularly in the case of the unfortunately named Enemy Property. Above all, there is no doubt that the legacy of Partition endures, as religious difference continues to inform the construction of at least the formal status of Indian citizenship.

Nowhere is this more evident than in the discourse on allegiance and loyalty as conditions of citizenship. Fifty years earlier, allegiance was critical to arbitrating the claims of Indian Muslims resident in Kenya who were asked to prove their allegiance and loyalty to the ideals of the Indian Constitution. Even the claim to citizenship of Indians in Malaya—though devoid of any religious element—sought to counter domicile as the defining principle of nationality, by proposing a definition of nationality in terms of allegiance. In the Constituent Assembly, returning (Muslim) migrants after Partition were suspiciously regarded as fifth columnists and saboteurs who had shown disloyalty by first migrating to Pakistan. This suspicion—again linked to religious identity—was heightened in the case of the "illegal migrants" from Bangladesh, who have been officially pronounced as potentially aligned with "international Islamic fundamentalism."

At the time when the Indian conception of citizenship in its foundational legal form was being articulated, the principle of political obligation was also, like the new nation, in a moment of transition. The older principle of political obligation—from the Proclamation of Queen Victoria onward, albeit contested through the first half of the twentieth century—was essentially a feudatory notion, in which loyalty was the basis of imperial protection, attached more to duties than rights. The transition to a more critical conception of political obligation, tied to rights rather than duties, moved through a transitory phase in which allegiance and loyalty to the Constitution were sought to be privileged over domicile in determining eligibility for citizenship. That this could as easily be turned into "tests" of loyalty, administered only to citizens belonging to religious minorities, is a problem that India continues to live with even in the present.

The story of how Indian citizenship came to be defined in the law also calls into question the smug shibboleths that have characterized the standard view of the foundational values of the Indian Constitution—robustly inclusionary, multicultural before the word was invented, and a model for diverse and plural societies. This chapter has explicated the contests, since independence, between the doctrines of jus soli and jus sanguinis as rival principles for embedding legal citizenship. It has indicated that the roots of the shift from the first to the second lie in the early debates on citizenship in the Constituent Assembly, where an ultimately progressive settlement in favor of jus soli could not eliminate the ever-present threat of encroachment from jus sanguinis.

The debates on citizenship and cultural rights demonstrate how the authors of the Constitution wrestled with questions of identity and territorial boundaries in determining citizenship. Partition was only the first tectonic movement that occasioned such uneasy, conflicted, and even tortuous negotiations around citizenship. Subsequent events—especially the creation of Bangladesh, and the continuing movement of people across both the eastern and western borders of India—saw the sedimentation of the discourse of legal citizenship in an increasingly exclusionary direction. Controlling the definition of citizenship in this manner arguably became a proxy for the state's imperfect control over its own borders, as well as its ability to exact a secular loyalty from its citizens.

3

Aspirational Citizenship

Migrants and Emigrants

The defining of citizenship is inevitably an act preceded by a circumscribing of borders. In the process of delineating the territorial boundaries of the political community of citizens, every state implicitly creates a default category of those who live outside these boundaries and are by definition beyond the pale of membership. The unprecedented scale of global migration in recent times—including skilled and unskilled economic migrants but also refugees fleeing political or ethnic persecution—has threatened this congruence between membership and borders by bringing many such outsiders into the territorial space of the nation. Over time, as refugees and migrants become candidates for legal citizenship, societies are confronted with the challenge of deciding whether or not they should be conferred the legal status of full members or limited rights, or neither. The legal aspect of this challenge may appear to be intractable, but it is more easily apprehended than its moral dimension. When and under what conditions does the moral personhood of a refugee or migrant generate a right to legal or juridical personhood in the form of citizenship? Are, as Hannah Arendt famously argued, the so-called universal rights of man utterly meaningless in the absence of citizenship? What, in the end, is citizenship for?

The previous chapter highlighted the importance of the borders created by the Partition in the construction of legal citizenship, the uncomfortable convergence they effect between territory and religious identity, and their enduring impact on the vexed question of legal citizenship in India. This chapter takes forward these issues through a consideration of the citizenship claims of a particular group of denizens who are neither migrants nor refugees in the standard sense in which these terms are defined in international law. They are rather a hybrid, and more, of these categories—part refugee, part migrant, but also part indigene, exemplifying the peculiar character of migration in the South. In the North, illegal immigrants are often ethnically distinguishable from the host population, especially when they are from the countries of the South. By contrast, migration in the southern hemisphere is generally between and across developing countries, and immigrants are frequently not ethnically distinct from those in the host society. The ethnic diversity of India, and the fact that different parts of the country attract ethnically kindred immigrants from the neighboring regions of the countries of the South Asian subcontinent, makes it a unique example of this phenomenon, though it is a characteristic of immigration in Pakistan and Malaysia as well.

This chapter discusses the citizenship claims of a few thousand effectively stateless people who came to India from Pakistan and now live in the border districts of the state of Rajasthan in western India, and on the periphery of citizenship. These are people of uncertain nomenclature, and none of the many labels that have been used to describe them—refugees, migrants, displaced persons, oustees—captures, accurately or adequately, their condition, though the politics of naming do appear to inform state response to their claims. These are the very people for whom the rules were amended, as discussed in the last chapter, to provide for an exceptional delegation of the administrative power to grant citizenship. For the sake of convenience, I will refer to them as migrants. Two types of citizenship claims are at issue here: first, the claims of those who have been denizens of the country for several years and are awaiting the grant of legal citizenship, and second, the claims of those among them who *have* been granted legal citizenship but remain disappointed with its inability to afford them access to the more substantive rights that citizenship is presumed to entail.

The central question addressed here is: how do citizens or those who aspire to be citizens understand the meaning of citizenship? The question is explored ethnographically to yield an account of how those who aspire to it understand the promise of citizenship, the privileges it affords, and its potential for providing rights. Does the value of political membership lie in political rights or rights of cultural recognition or economic opportunities, or in all of these in greater or lesser measure? Canvassing and simultaneously interrogating the resources of recent political theory, we negotiate the ethics of these claims, seeking to defend and ground them in a normative framework that can address them meaningfully in a context-sensitive manner. The chapter also examines state responses to these claims, contrasting them with the state response to another category of claims to citizenship, from members of the Indian diaspora. Both claims appeal to the doctrine of jus sanguinis based on blood and descent, though this is more strongly invoked by the deterritorialized diasporic aspirants to citizenship than by the denizens of western India.

The Moral Basis of a Legal Claim

There is a curious disjuncture between the ways in which citizenship as legal status is treated in the worlds of theory and of policy. In many countries, including the United States, legal citizenship has lately acquired a policy importance; attempts have been made to "revalorize" the legal status of citizenship by making it harder to obtain but also to count for more (Bosniak, 1998: 30). This contrasts oddly with the neglect of thin citizenship in political theory on the assumption that citizenship-as-legal-status is a settled issue, and an overwhelming preoccupation with thick citizenship.[1] Our case provides an empirical challenge to the compartmentalization between thin and thick citizenship. In line with recent scholarship, it also questions the normative nationalism that typically frames the understanding of citizenship and the propensity of citizenship theory to construct the citizen as a natural member of a territorially defined national polity, ignoring the fact that most nation-states today have "others"—aliens, migrants, refugees, asylees—who also live within these bounded communities, but are not legally citizens.[2] It seeks to show that for its claimants, the question of legal status holds meaning that cannot be captured by the simple distinction between thin and thick citizenship.

The long shadow of normative nationalism is visible in two dominant strands of citizenship theory, both of which are in different ways inspired by the search for thick citizenship as practice and performance. Multiculturalism first presumes that questions of identity and belonging lie at the core of thick citizenship, and seeks to reconcile the tension between cultural particularism and civic universalism. Its animating question is: how do we give adequate recognition to the diversity of the cultural attachments of citizens and simultaneously secure their common loyalty to the political community? A second important strand of citizenship theory that is informed by normative nationalism emphasizes the performance of thick citizenship in an active republican mode.[3] The claim here is that the welfare-state has induced passivity in the practice of citizenship and has created apathetic voters and welfare-dependent citizens, wholly unmindful of their civic obligations and duties; the idea of civic engagement is offered as a powerful counter to this.[4] The case presented here interrogates the sequestration of thin and thick citizenship, suggests that these are closely linked, and points to the difficulties of sustaining arguments of normative nationalism.

Since a focus on thick citizenship implies an exclusive focus on those who *are* already citizens, neither of these otherwise powerful debates on citizenship has questioned the realist framework of international law, which affirms the right of sovereign nation-states to determine for themselves the rules of admittance or immigration and the terms of naturalization. Refugees are *not* citizens. Such rights as they are granted are a result of the humanitarian provisions of international law, and if they claim citizenship, it is on terms specified by the state. International refugee law makes a distinction between migrants and refugees, depending on whether the cross-border movement in question was voluntary or involuntary—categories that are seen as congruent with economic and political imperatives. This, as the previous chapter noted, is a binary in which migrants always migrate, voluntarily, for economic reasons, while refugees are forced, hence involuntarily, to flee for political reasons. The aspiring citizens of Rajasthan do not fit neatly into either of the two categories of migrant or refugee. Indeed, the case questions this simplistic binary by introducing us to people who migrated more voluntarily than involuntarily, but not for economic reasons, and are today refugees and applicants for citizenship. Their official description—"Pak oustees"—places the burden of the description on where they came from without conveying anything at all about where they are or have, so to speak, "been ousted to," thus effectively freeing state authority from the responsibility of redress.

Further, India does not have a national policy or law, not just on apparently anomalous cases such as the one discussed here, but even more generally on the status of refugees. Like all other South Asian countries, India has neither ratified the 1951 Convention on the Status of Refugees nor the Protocol of 1967. The former defined a refugee as someone who, "As a result of events occurring before 1 January 1951, and owing to a well-founded fear of being persecuted for reasons of race, religion, nationality, *membership of a particular social group* or political opinion, is outside the country of his nationality."[5] This provision for "membership of a particular social group" (MPSG) in international refugee law has, in signatory states, increasingly been interpreted in ways that admit of the recognition of social and economic rights for refugees (Foster, 2007). For instance, a Canadian court in October 1996 ruled that a married couple belonging to a Dalit caste were persecuted because of the unchangeable character of their membership in this caste, which is therefore a particular social group (ibid.: 304). India's ratification of the International Covenant on Civil and Political Rights (ICCPR), as well as the Covenant on Economic, Social and Cultural Rights does, however, place the country under an obligation to accord equal treatment to citizens and noncitizens wherever possible, although India has put in a reservation to the ICCPR, reserving its right to implement its law on foreigners. In any case, Articles 14 (right to equality before the law and equal protection of the law), 21 (protection of life and personal liberty), and 25 (freedom of conscience and religion) of the Indian Constitution apply to all persons within the territory of India, even if they are technically "aliens" (Chimni, 2005: 300).

As neither domestic nor international law regimes provide a way of negotiating the citizenship claims of our migrants, we can only ask if aliens have any *moral* rights in the countries where they live, and if so on what basis. Does the length of their stay strengthen their claim to citizenship rights? Are they entitled to become full citizens, or should they only be given rights to some programs of social welfare? The claim that immigrants, guest-workers, and noncitizens must have political rights and political membership may be justified by the argument that they are already participants in the economy and are governed by laws in the making of which they do not have a voice. However, these rights generally follow upon admittance, which is governed by rules that the sovereign state has the exclusive power to make (Walzer, 1983: 52–61). Even Joseph Carens has recently revised his famous injunction to strive for open borders.[6] Now, explicitly presupposing the right of the state to control immigration, he asks that we recognize, as the determining criterion for rights of citizenship, the "moral importance of the length of stay, even if unauthorized," and proposes a period of five to seven years (Carens,

2008: 35).[7] Curiously, for a supporter of free immigration, Carens is willing to countenance restrictions on the rights of aliens to access redistributive social programs (ibid.).

By accepting the nation-state as its normative boundary and operative framework, citizenship theory has laid itself open to the charge of reproducing the tension between, on the one hand, upholding universal human rights principles and, on the other, simultaneously confining their application to national boundaries. Ultimately, perhaps the only way to consistently uphold universal principles of human rights—including for refugees—is by invoking cosmopolitanism. Seyla Benhabib's (2004) assertion of the moral right of refugees to first admittance seeks to fill the hiatus in theories of global justice, which have been largely concerned with issues of just distribution rather than just membership. Though this is an admirable ideal, and though the gradual emergence of an international human rights regime in some arenas bodes well, the problem articulated by cosmopolitan theorists is ultimately trapped in the terms suggested by Hannah Arendt in her discussion of statelessness:

> . . . *the right to have rights,* or the right of every individual to belong to humanity, *should be guaranteed by humanity itself. It is by no means certain whether this is possible.* (Arendt (1951) 1962: 298; emphasis added)

The *moral* claims of refugees are addressed to humanity in general, but it is not very clear to whom the *legal* claims might be addressed in the absence of a new international legal regime. A global citizenship regime alone can transcend and extirpate the fundamental tension between universal principles of human rights and the acceptance of nation-states as the normative framework for citizenship. But in the less than ideal and far from cosmopolitan real world of nation-states, and of multiple inequalities both between and within these states, how should we think about the very real predicament of statelessness?

Even as theories of alienage and cosmopolitanism repudiate national boundaries and uphold universal principles of membership, their foundational understanding of the problem of alienage is deeply embedded in their own empirical context, limiting its usefulness as an aid to thinking about the ways in which alienage is experienced in the global South in at least three ways. First, the particularities of history and of affect, and of the claims that we encounter in the field, invoke genealogies, cultural affinities, and even old geographical ties to the land that the migrants now, ironically, inhabit illegally. These are not customarily a part of the experience of alienage in the North.

Second, like many aliens in Europe and North America, our migrants are unauthorized, having mostly overstayed their visas, and do not therefore meet the criterion of first admittance in accordance with the laws of the state.[8] However, unlike in North America—where the rights available to aliens include the right of children to attend public school, property-related rights, the right to have a driving license, etc.—our migrants do not enjoy even basic rights of personal mobility let alone other types of social rights. Even where they fulfill the test of length-of-stay, and this is accepted by the law and the government, they are generally too poor to be able to afford the citizenship fee. Finally, for the political theorist, it is the *political* rights of membership that are most consequential. But, as we shall see, political rights and political membership hold little meaning for the migrants in Rajasthan. Citizenship is for them a mechanism for gaining access to entitlements to redistributive social programs. This has been an intractable question in the United States;[9] in India, it is an even more embattled claim because the absence of substantive rights of citizenship for comparably poor or disadvantaged local groups makes it morally and practically difficult to insist upon their prior fulfillment for immigrants.

While our focus is on migrants on the western border, it bears mentioning that there are many different refugee communities in India. Apart from those from Bangladesh (which we encountered in the last chapter), there are also refugees from Sri Lanka in the southern state of Tamil Nadu, and Tibetan refugees living in many different parts of India.[10] Of the more than 100,000 Sri Lankan refugees in India, approximately 73,000 remain stateless persons living in camps in Tamil Nadu. About 60 percent of these have been born in India but, due to the 2003 amendment which denies citizenship to any individual one of whose parents was an illegal migrant at the time of his/her birth, are ineligible for legal status. Small numbers have begun to return to Sri Lanka since August 2010.

India is also home to approximately 120,000 Tibetan refugees since the first exodus from Tibet, led by the Dalai Lama half a century ago. Tibetans are eligible for registration and identity certificates from the government, which has however applied greater stringency with respect to recent entrants.[11] It was only in December 2010 that a young Tibetan girl won the right to citizenship by appealing to the law courts against the government's rejection of her application for an Indian passport. Namgyal Dolkar was born in 1986, just a few months before the Citizenship Act was amended (in response to the in-migration from Bangladesh) to take prospective effect. Unlike many Tibetans who seldom apply for Indian citizenship, whether because they feel this amounts to a betrayal of their homeland or because that would render them ineligible for getting political asylum in western countries, Dolkar asserted her right to be treated as an Indian citizen by birth. In court, her claim was contested by the government on the grounds that she already had an identity certificate. In an expedient coupling of nationality and citizenship, the government also claimed that since she had stated her nationality as Tibetan, it clearly meant that she could not be an Indian citizen. However, the High Court of Delhi ruled in her favor, upholding her right to Indian citizenship (*Namgyal Dolkar vs. Government of India, Ministry of External Affairs,* 2010).

Stateless in Rajasthan

The western border of the state of Rajasthan is also part of the international border between India and Pakistan. Rajasthan has witnessed in-migration on a substantial scale from the districts on the Pakistani side of this border, and this research is based on interviews with people living in three districts of the state of Rajasthan: Barmer, Jaisalmer, and Jodhpur, with most of the people interviewed having come from Sindh and southern Punjab in Pakistan.[12] The first wave of migration occurred at the time of Partition, and comprised mainly well-off Sindhi Hindus who were comfortably settled several decades ago. Following Partition, and till the fencing of the border in the early 1990s, there was considerable seasonal migration of agricultural labor— especially in drought years, and in the opposite direction—from Rajasthan into Sindh and southern Punjab in Pakistan. Sindh and Punjab are areas of irrigated agriculture, while the study districts of Rajasthan are essentially desert regions. There was also, in all caste and social groups, frequent movement across the border for marriages and family occasions.

A large wave of migration occurred in the wake of the 1965 war, when over 8,000 people crossed over from the district of Thar Parkar in Sindh. This region had a substantial Hindu population that included Rajputs as well as Dalit and Adivasi groups.[13] Thar Parkar is one of the four districts of Sindh that has a high concentration of scheduled castes. It is also the only district of Pakistan that dropped on the Human Development Index between 1998 and 2005 (Z. Shah, 2007: 63). In the 1971 war, India occupied a large part of Thar Parkar, bringing in 90,000 Hindus who decided not to return when the territory was restored to Pakistan as a result of the Shimla agreement of 1972. In the 1980s, migration remained at low levels, and it was only after 1992, following the demolition of the Babri Masjid, that it began to occur at an accelerated pace. The increased vulnerability of Indian Muslims in the backdrop of Hindutva was matched, on the other side of the border, by the increased insecurity of Hindus in a climate of rising religious fundamentalism, religious persecution and conversion, and violence against women.[14] Most of the people interviewed in this study are those who came to Rajasthan during the 1990s, chiefly from Sindh and Punjab. Following the out-migration, the Hindu population of Sindh has declined, though this province remains home to 95 percent of Pakistan's Hindu population, which numbers 2.5 million, of which 2.1 million are upper caste, some of them successful businessmen or Rajput landlords. The remainder belong to the scheduled castes and are invariably poor, and subject to "discrimination on the basis of caste, descent and occupation. They are in [sic] dual disadvantageous position as they are Hindu (minorities in a Muslim majority country) and also of lower caste within the Hindu population. They are called 'achoots' or 'untouchables' (Z. Shah, 2007: 14).

The migrants from these groups are largely people who came to India as visitors with valid travel documents—Pakistani passports and Indian visas—but simply stayed on and applied for citizenship. The 8.000 refugees who came in 1965 and the 90,000 who came in 1971 came largely from Thar Parkar district and have, for the most part, been granted citizenship. These refugees were from all castes: though Rajputs and Meghwals (a Dalit caste) together accounted for 50 percent of the migrants, there were also other caste groups such as *maheshwaris* (traders), *malis* (gardeners), *nais* (barbers), and the Adivasi Bhils. Of the 17,000 migrants who came after 1992, approximately 95 percent are Dalits (Meghwals) and Adivasis (Bhils)—which means that, if they were Indian citizens, they would belong to the officially designated Scheduled Caste and Scheduled Tribe groups.[15] They mobilized for the grant of citizenship, under the leadership of the Pak Visthapit Sangh (PVS), resulting in the granting of citizenship to about 13,000 people, most of which was accomplished between January and February 2005 at citizenship camps organized in several districts.[16] There are now about 3,000 persons in Jodhpur division, still awaiting citizenship.[17]

State response to the migrants' predicament has varied over time. In 1972, twenty-five refugee camps for these migrants were set up in Barmer district, accommodating close to 60,000 people. There were a limited number of tents that were assigned to joint families, sometimes to two or three such families. Ration cards (to access the public distribution system) were issued to the head of the family, and this formed the basis for land allotment in later years, creating difficulties for the larger families as only the head would be allotted land, and more so for those families who were arbitrarily clubbed together with them. The refugees had to report daily for attendance and had no permission to travel or to visit relatives anywhere. The Jana Sangh government in Rajasthan granted citizenship rights to 54,000 people in the camps at Barmer. While these refugees did get citizenship, the rehabilitation package they were given was poor. The stated policy was to give each family either twenty-five bighas of land (in canal-irrigated areas) or 50–75 bighas (in barren desert areas). In reality, most got only a part of this, whether on account of bureaucratic corruption, or because it fell within the region of the Desert National Park, or because of its prior occupation by the local population. For every unit—or *murba*—the Rajasthan government charged an additional sum of Rs. 30,000 to be paid over twenty years at 18% interest.

With the exception of this state initiative for citizenship in the 1970s, these migrants have been curiously uninteresting to political parties, including the Bharatiya Janata Party, whose leadership has not, in either Rajasthan or the neighboring state of Gujarat, been conspicuously vocal on this issue. In Gujarat, the Kachch region in 1971 received a large number[18] of Meghwal families from Thar Parkar, who were given citizenship as well as land, money to buy cattle with, and, as scheduled castes, reservations in public employment (Ibrahim, 2008: 94). These migrants were staunch supporters of the Congress Party, though some of them did make a feeble attempt to switch loyalties to the BJP in 2002 (in response, they claimed, to a fatwa asking Muslims to vote Congress). Notwithstanding this, it is notable that Kachch was the one region where the BJP was defeated, even as it came back to power in the state of Gujarat (ibid.: 100). Ibrahim's work, however, suggests that these Dalit citizens may be willing collaborators with the Hindu right's attempts to co-opt them, for this would cohere with their already quite successful strategy to construct their own identity in ways that repudiate their Dalit origins.

In Rajasthan, by comparison, neither the Congress nor the BJP have shown great political interest in these migrant groups, though governments of both parties have shown initiative in the granting of citizenship. In 2001, Congress Chief Minister Gehlot set up a review committee[19] that gave an impetus to the citizenship camps of 2005. Subsequently, BJP Chief Minister Vasundhara Raje set up a permanent cell, which recommended to the government of India an extension of the delegated powers of district collectors in Rajasthan and Gujarat to confer citizenship. These were the powers possessed by district collectors that had reverted back to the central government during the Assam agitation in the 1980s, amid charges of manipulation of citizenship. In 2004, through an amendment to the Citizenship Rules, 1956, and possibly as a result of pressure from the state government and the PVS, the Centre delegated these powers to district collectors in Rajasthan and Gujarat for a limited period of one year, enabling citizenship to be given to 13,000 people. Subsequently, BJP Chief Minister Raje also urged a reduction in the fees and the inclusion of those refugee families who had been given Indian citizenship in the next survey to identify below-poverty-line households. Her successor (Ashok Gehlot, who was also her predecessor) repeated this request, and got the Union Home Minister to give an assurance, in the course of the 2009 election campaign, to work out a solution to the citizenship issue. This attracted the ire of the Election Commission, though it is not entirely clear how the promise of citizenship to a large group of *nonvoters* should constitute an unfair electoral practice. While political parties have been largely disinterested in these migrants, the Rajasthan administration–irrespective of which party is in power[20]—has been reasonably active.

But how do the migrants themselves perceive citizenship and their relationship to the state that does not recognize them? What are their expectations of this relationship, and how do they view its meaning and significance? The next section presents some narratives from the field.

The Meanings of Citizenship

In Jaisalmer and Jodhpur districts, the migrants lead a precarious existence. They are visibly poor and dependent upon daily wage labor. They wistfully compare their work in the fields across the border with the hard labor of breaking and carrying stones that they now have to do.[21] Why then did they migrate? The answer is usually presented in terms of an escape from the insecurities of minority status, though there is a difference between the experiences of those who migrated from Sindh and the Punjab. Sindh has historically witnessed little communal violence, a fact that has been attributed variously to Sufi tradition and a shared desert culture. In fact, the migrants themselves speak of the contrast between Sindh and the Punjab: in Sindh, they say, "mullah culture" was not pervasive, as it was in the Punjab; in Sindh, the landlords gave protection to their Hindu tenant farmers, while in the Punjab, both urbanization and the growth of religious fundamentalism contributed to the vulnerability of religious minorities.

In either case, it is hard to discern, in their narratives, a strong sense of the idea of India, or of belonging to it. To the extent that there is a sense of belonging, it is often defined in terms of the Hindu faith, but preeminently in terms of family roots and ties to the land. The facts that their grandfathers and great-grandfathers lived in Jaisalmer or other parts of Rajasthan, that many of them once owned land here, and almost all have had extended families on both sides of the border are frequently invoked. It appears that while minority identity is a significant factor in the decision to leave Pakistan, it becomes rather less important on arrival as a refugee. Denying the equivalence between state, territory, and religious identity, one respondent said that the issue of citizenship is "not an issue of Hindus. It is an issue of nation, of country."

There are two crucial aspects of quotidian life that have to be confronted on arrival: first, the fulfillment of basic needs and livelihoods; and second, the hostility of the host population. Religious identity obviously has little purchase in an environment populated by coreligionists, and hence becomes less relevant. It is the markers of difference that count for more, and there is dismay that they are penalized for their identity on both sides of the border.

> In Pakistan, they say we are Indians (Bharatiya) because we are Hindus, here we are called Pakistanis and all our actions are suspect.

Nevertheless, comparisons are inevitably offered between the quality of life in Pakistan and India. Physical insecurity, especially the vulnerability of women to rape and abduction, appears to be of paramount importance. Some speak of how family members would take turns staying awake at night in order to guard their homes against burglars and dacoits; others claim that such crimes are common regardless of religious identity. Religious persecution and efforts at religious conversion are also frequently mentioned, as is the destruction of temples in the period following the destruction of the Babri Masjid in Ayodhya. The present is preferred in terms of better conditions of law and order and freedom from religious persecution, but in terms of livelihood, almost all compare their lives as agricultural labor working in the fields favorably with their current insecurity and the back-breaking nature of the work they now have to do. In Jaisalmer, an elderly Bhil man whose life is more or less devoted to religious performances explains the original move to Pakistan as a response to the drought conditions and food insecurity in Rajasthan. Even livestock, he says, would run away to Pakistan where there were productive fields, a place to stay, and agricultural labor to be done. But now, he says, "Indira Mai" (a reference to Indira Gandhi and the Rajasthan canal named after her) has changed all this. The canal brings water to the fields and all is well. Now, even if there is hunger, it is possible to sleep well, secure in the knowledge that you are in your own country.

The legal status of residence and eventually citizenship is a challenge that has to be negotiated on arrival. Almost every individual—regardless of caste, tribe, and gender—defines citizenship in terms of the *suvidha* it is or was expected to provide. *Suvidha* is a Hindi word that loosely translates as "facilities." In this context, it suggests a meaning closer to the fulfillment of basic needs, which are spelled out as land, livelihood, government school, water, and electricity. It also implies a range of official documentation, such as ration cards, caste certificates, and BPL cards, which entitles their holders to various governmental poverty-reduction programs. In the rather florid account of an applicant for citizenship,

> Citizenship is a piece of paper. But for us, it is a jewel. We left Pakistan to come here, but now we belong neither to Pakistan nor to India, we are torn into two pieces. What is the third way before us? If we get citizenship, at least we can be called Indians, travel anywhere in India to earn a living, to meet relatives and to build a future for our children. . . . If we could get citizenship, the jewel of citizenship, the fields of freedom will be seen blossoming. But for now, we are tied in chains. We cannot travel anywhere, we cannot do the work we want to do. We do not have domicile so our children cannot get admission to, for instance, medical school. (Teacher of Arabic)

Both for those who do not yet have it, as well as for those who do, citizenship remains the architectonic aspiration under which all their dreams and hopes for greater security and a better quality of life are subsumed. Many of those who have obtained citizenship have laminated and framed their certificates of citizenship, and now complain about being deprived of the usual accoutrements of official poverty—the Below Poverty Line (BPL) card, the caste certificate, and the *patta* signifying ownership of a small fragment of land. For those who do not have it yet, the magic key to all these goods is citizenship. For those who do, there is acute disappointment at the promise of citizenship remaining unfulfilled. This explains why many people speak of citizenship as an *instrument*. Comments such as the following are legion:

- "We have got citizenship, but have not yet got its full fruit. We have no place to stay, no fields to till. The citizenship is lying there, but it is of no use."
- "We have got citizenship, but it is just a piece of paper. We have not got one rupee of gain so far."
- "We have come on to the road of citizenship, but we are still to reach our destination. Earlier, everything seemed like a maze, now citizenship shows the way out of the maze."
- "Citizenship is the key to everything. Even to apply for a water or electricity connection, you need citizenship."

Only rarely, in these conversations, is the vote spontaneously mentioned. One elderly woman in Jodhpur, who had obtained citizenship after a wait of over ten years, said she looked forward to getting the vote, because "if we give them votes, the politicians will give us *suvidhas*." And if, she added rebelliously, they are not going to give us these *suvidhas*, including the BPL card, they should give us back our papers so we can go back to Hyderabad (Sindh). The lack of interest on the part of political parties in their plight is remarked upon and vouched for by all. In Jaisalmer, the young schoolteacher Peera Ram explains the BJP's disinterest in terms of the migrants being Adivasis, a population group that has traditionally been a Congress vote bank. However, he adds, "if these people were asked whom they would vote for, they would surely vote for the BJP, the party of Hindutva, because of what they suffered in Pakistan on account of being Hindus." In Jodhpur, a range of alternate explanations are offered for the disinterest of political parties. Some argue that political parties are not interested in them because they do not have the vote. The Vishwa Hindu Parishad and the RSS, argued one young man, claim to be the stewards and custodians of the Hindu faith worldwide. But, "not only do they not raise their voice against the atrocities on the Hindu minority in Pakistan, not once has any representative of any of these organisations come to see what the condition [*sic*] of the Hindu migrants is, what their problems are. It is clear," he concludes, "that they are only interested in sloganeering; they have nothing to do with Hinduism."

Much less surprising, of course, is the hostility of the host population. Khatu, a migrant from the Rahimyar Khan district of the Punjab, arrived in 1991 in Rajasthan, to an area that her family had left to escape from scarcity and hunger, and tempted by the abundance of food grains in the Punjab. But the host population refuses to view them as returnees, seeing them instead as aliens:

> They say that we have come from Pakistan, so we must have plenty of money. Even if government provides any assistance, they don't like it. They say we should not be given any employment, even on famine relief works—only they should get employment, though the drought affects us as much as it affects them. We buy wheat in the open market while they get subsidised wheat in the ration shop. When we came to a *kacchi basti* and built our huts—the municipality started demolishing them, saying you are Pakistanis, not Indian citizens, so you have no right to be here. Now we have got citizenship so we can assert the right and say that we are also Indians and now our difficulties are becoming less. (Khatu, Ghafoor Bhatta Kachchi Basti, Jaisalmer)

The teacher of Arabic in Jodhpur confirms this: "when we seek admission for our children in the local school, we are told that you are Pakistanis so why are you becoming a burden on India." Every other person speaks of how they carry the stamp or *"thappa"*[22] of their Pakistani origins. People who return after crossing the seven seas, they say, are warmly welcomed. Why are we treated differently? There is of course an obvious economic explanation for this. Where, as in Jaisalmer, there is an abundance of land and a low population density (both characteristic of the desert region), there is no questioning of resettlement policies or the allotment of land to the migrants. Where, on the other hand, the pressure of population on resources is higher, as in Jodhpur, there is resentment and opposition to the refugees being given land. This would be no different if they were internally displaced people, but since they are migrants, describing them as Pakistanis in a way that is abusive and derogatory becomes a more effective expression of local hostility. It is a form of social exclusion underwritten by a perception of economic threat.

Apart from the hostility of local society, the migrants must contend also with quotidian harassment by the Criminal Investigation Department (CID), the police, and the municipal authorities.[23] Since most migrants came to India with a visa that restricted their visit to a certain city, they were not allowed to reside elsewhere, even in the village to which their ancestors belonged. Restrictions of this kind obviously make mobility difficult, and the limited possibility of finding agricultural employment in a dry and arid region makes for livelihood insecurity. Their *kachcha* settlements (mud huts, rather than buildings made of concrete or cement) stand on government land, and municipal authorities regularly threaten demolition and eviction.

The predicament of these people bears a striking similarity to those who migrate, within the country, in times of drought, from Rajasthan to other states—or indeed with the nomads of Rajasthan, who are similarly struggling for ration cards and for poverty alleviation and welfare programs (Pant, 2005: 92–94). But, of course, the quality of interstate relations in the region has an impact on the extent to which such people are, or are not, "owned." Violence against Muslims in India has repercussions visited upon Hindus in Pakistan. The quality of citizenship is not, in this sense, confined to territorial boundaries; it is also shaped by geopolitical and strategic considerations. The migrants cannot find acceptance where they live, nor go back to where they came from. They hang in a state of statelessness. States and host populations tend to perceive the border as porous, but the presence of these stateless migrants suggests the nonexistence of the border as something that is felt and experienced. They need to negotiate two sets of boundaries, both of which are substantively inaccessible to them. The first of these is the "external" boundary of the India–Pakistan border—they live beside it, it is physically proximate to them, but it is a boundary that, once crossed, becomes inaccessible. The second is an "internal" boundary between state and society. To be able to negotiate this boundary, they need to be recognized as members of society, which not even local society, let alone the state, does.

What Is Citizenship For?

At the beginning of this chapter, we noted the distinction between thin and thick conceptions of citizenship, and the common assumption that legal citizenship merely provides the qualifying threshold for reflections on thick conceptions of citizenship.[24] Our case underlines how critical so-called "thin" citizenship can be to the very expression of moral personhood.[25] The claim of a refugee in a modern state is generally a claim to at least "juridical personhood," if not citizenship, and juridical personhood is arguably premised on a prior and more profound claim about moral personhood. Here, in a strong endorsement of Hannah Arendt's argument, we find the claim of juridical personhood taking precedence over, and arguably even viewed as a precondition for, moral personhood.

In the post–T. H. Marshall world of multicultural citizenship, where the demands of recognition have displaced the demands of redistribution, the response of citizenship theory to legitimately admitted immigrant populations is generally couched in terms of cultural rights, seeking to strike a balance between the ideal of universal citizenship and the particular rights of minority cultural groups. Cosmopolitan writings on alienage also share this sense that immigrant groups generally represent the "other" in some cultural/ethnic/religious sense. In our case, however, the migrants manifest strong cultural and even genealogical affinities with the host population—they are racially and ethnically similar, if not identical; practice the same religion(s); have been intermarrying with equivalent caste groups across the border; and even speak variants of the same language.

This is why it is particularly striking that the argument of shared culture does *not* form a prominent part of the citizenship or even recognition claims of these people. If they mention their identity as Hindus, it is in the context of their experiences of religious discrimination in Pakistan. In their claims to citizenship in India, it is defined in terms of *social* citizenship. Even as the deficiencies of citizenship in the Pakistani context are signified by the insecurity engendered by religious difference, the presumed security of religious freedom is not viewed as a satisfactory substitute for the expected *content* of citizenship in India. This content is the substance of citizenship, and the interviews clearly signal the importance of social citizenship.[26] With the political parties keeping their distance, the migrants have mobilized for collective action in terms of hitherto unfamiliar categories. Neither caste nor religion, but displacement and statelessness become their primary identity, the basis for a new collectivity.

The hegemonic idea of citizenship, interpreted purely in terms of identity and belonging, is thus interrogated by alternative narratives of citizens and protocitizens. Identity, or indeed any affective dimension, is irrelevant to these claims, and to the state's response to them. A conception of citizenship that is centered on identity not only precludes the recognition of material inequalities, it also ignores the important overlap between different types of inequality, such as the cultural and the economic. It is no accident that these claimants of citizenship are, for the most part, poor Dalits and Adivasis whose condition is marked by the twinning of social exclusion and economic marginalization. The more prosperous upper-caste groups that migrated are comfortably settled, while those who stayed on enjoy reasonable social relations with Muslims of the same social class as themselves. Unlike the Rajput and Muslim elites who could deal well together, on both sides of the border, Dalits and Adivasis have, also on both sides of the border, suffered marginalization and exclusion.

Finally, the contextual assumption of much theory has been that immigrants have entered a society where public social provisioning is the norm, or which is in a position to provide redistributive social programs through taxation. As such, it becomes easy to argue that if immigrants pay these taxes, they are fully entitled to the benefits of these. In our case, however, the migrants have entered a society that is resource-poor, in which 250 million people already live below the poverty line. This is why the claim of the migrants is not for their basic needs to be met, as a theory of justice might require, but for Below Poverty Line cards to access such welfare programs as are available, and for caste certificates to access quotas in public education and employment. They are so poor that they find it hard to even rustle up the resources to pay the official fee when they become eligible for citizenship.[27]

The claims of these protocitizens seeking to forge a relationship with the state offer arguments not of blood and belonging, or even voting rights, but rather of land, livelihood, and basic services. It is the meager entitlements to subsidized food grains, job quotas, and development schemes that are at stake, along with caste certificates, the public distribution system, and Below Poverty Line cards.[28] As such, citizenship is rendered instrumental—a formal qualification for access to certain material opportunities. Indeed, one could even say that citizenship is the form taken by claims of what are little more than rights to the fulfillment of basic needs, for those who are citizens in no more than juridical terms, but also for those who are not yet citizens even in the minimum juridical sense.

It is perfectly reasonable to defend, in cosmopolitan vein, the position that it should, at least minimally, be their moral right to be political members—and as such legally recognized citizens—of the community that they have entered, if only because they are escaping from a situation of physical and personal insecurity. But it is, in normative terms, much harder to argue that this moral right should encompass social rights, or that migrants should be given privileged access to social rights that similarly disadvantaged—in terms of class, caste, or tribal status—members of the host population do not possess. To argue for social rights requires us to argue for social rights for all, including migrants. In the meantime, for the migrants per se, it is only possible to argue for the prior guarantee of the right of political membership through which—along with locals—they can effectively advance their claims to social rights.

Emigrant Citizenship

The claim to legal (and impliedly social) citizenship of the stateless Rajasthan migrants provides a striking contrast to a radically different category of claims mounted by those who are already citizens of other states but wish to enjoy the *additional* privileges of Indian citizenship. These are less often the descendants of the nineteenth-century emigrants from India, largely indentured labor shipped to Fiji, Mauritius, Trinidad, Guyana, Malaysia, and East and South Africa, and more often the educated professionals who migrated to the United States[29] and other developed countries in search of prosperity and professional opportunities after the mid-1960s.

The attitude of the Indian state toward the older diaspora[30] was summed up, as we saw in the previous chapter, in Jawaharlal Nehru's injunction to these people to maintain their allegiance to their adoptive homelands. This attitude began to undergo a change around 1998 when, at a conference of global Indian entrepreneurs, Vajpayee, then prime minister, announced his government's intention of setting up a committee to go into the issue of dual citizenship for Non-Resident Indians (NRIs).[31] The explicitly stated justification was the need to attract investment as India faced international sanctions for its nuclear tests. The government floated the patriotically named Resurgent India Bonds scheme, which was offered to select NRIs and former citizens in the United States, Canada, and Europe. It was accused of "dollar and pound apartheid" as it explicitly excluded citizens of Pakistan and Bangladesh, and implicitly excluded the poorer groups within the diaspora—those whose ancestors had, in the first wave of migration from India, been shipped as indentured labor to the Caribbean or Fiji or Mauritius. The bonds scheme offered more attractive interest rates than the US bond market, with an option of redemption in American or German currency, as well as exemption from wealth tax and income tax in India. As a result, the scheme was wildly successful, and in two weeks raised twice as much (US$4.2 billion) as had been hoped for, approximately half coming from the Middle East and Southeast Asia, and 20 percent from Europe and North America (Newland and Patrick, 2004: 5). This was followed by the India Millennium Deposit scheme in 2000, which raised another US$5.5 billion.[32] Seeking and securing diasporic investments is by no means an uncommon phenomenon in states whose emigrants have prospered abroad, and the Indian government, impressed by China's success in attracting investments by its diaspora, has been exceedingly solicitous of the interests of emigrant Indian businesses, ostensibly on grounds of their affective attachment to the mother country.

In its report, submitted in 2001, the High-Level Committee on the Indian Diaspora recommended the grant of dual citizenship through an amendment of the Citizenship Act. The 2003 amendment to the Citizenship Act that followed was however cautious: it allowed persons of Indian origin to be registered only as "overseas citizens of India." At the time, this privilege was also restricted to Persons of Indian Origin in sixteen countries, with the restriction being justified by an argument of reciprocity, viz. that these sixteen countries themselves provided for dual citizenship. It was scarcely a coincidence that all these countries were located in the advanced industrial societies of the West, and it was clearly the expectation of investments by the diaspora in these countries that drove this initiative. Over time, this anomaly has been removed, and now it is only the prejudice against those with any prior links to Pakistan or Bangladesh that persists. In a recent case, the Delhi High Court upheld the government's rejection order denying a Person of Indian Origin (PIO) card to a woman holding a British passport, who had once held a Pakistani passport—despite the facts that her parents were born in India, she was the spouse of a PIO, and the parent of two PIOs.[33]

The Congress-led United Progressive Alliance coalition government has continued the practice inaugurated by the previous BJP-led National Democratic Alliance government's policy of holding—in collaboration with the Confederation of Indian Industry—an annual Pravasi Bharatiya Divas (Festival of Overseas Indians). Despite the celebratory rhetoric that marks these occasions, India's policies toward its emigrants over the last decade have been marked by some fluidity and even confusion. Prime ministerial statements routinely promise dual citizenship and latterly even voting rights for overseas Indians,[34] but the policy provides for the status of overseas citizens of India

(OCIs), which confers various benefits including a multipurpose, multiple entry visa for life and other rights, such as to purchase property, as applicable to nonresident Indians. The professionals among them—doctors/dentists, nurses, engineers, advocates, and chartered accountants—have also been permitted to practice their professions in India (Notification by Ministry of Overseas Indian Affairs in the *Gazette of India,* January 6, 2009). OCIs do not thus far have the right to vote (and correspondingly no duty to pay taxes); are ineligible for political office and "normally" ineligible for public employment. A standing committee of the Rajya Sabha is (at the time of writing) contemplating a further amendment that would replace the term "overseas citizen" with the term "overseas Indian cardholder." Close to 650,000 people have already been granted OCI status, with the overwhelming majority being from the United States (269,730) and the United Kingdom (103,587).[35]

Contemporary political rhetoric suggests that India appears to be inching slowly toward granting dual citizenship or at least political rights for emigrants. This is broadly in consonance with international trends, where a visible pluralization of citizenship has been evolving over the last decade, though the correlation between dual citizenship and voting rights presents a mixed picture. Almost a third of the world's countries recognize dual citizenship, but only about half of these give emigrants the right of international absentee voting. Conversely, about half of the 115 countries that do *not* recognize dual citizenship do give voting rights to emigrants (Rhodes and Harutyunyan, 2010: 474). Sometimes, these rights are based on a delinking of nationality from citizenship, with *nationals* being given the right to vote and even to contest elections. Rights may also be attached to duties toward the country of origin, and in the countries of the South, the expectation of investment has tended to loom large in the list of such duties.

The example of Mexico is instructive. Initially, emigration from Mexico was regarded as a sign of disloyalty and even treason. Over time, intensive lobbying by emigrant groups worked to secure a constitutional amendment that allows Mexicans (and their children born overseas) to remain Mexican *nationals*—with the attendant benefit of a Mexican passport and the right to own property and business—without being Mexican *citizens.* This implied an ethnic (or jus sanguinis) definition of the nation that extends beyond the territorial boundaries of the state. In 2005, Mexico passed a law allowing expatriates to use absentee ballots to cast their votes in Mexican elections. Meanwhile, in line with neoliberal policies of structural adjustment, a shift in public discourse reconfigured emigrants from treacherous non-citizens into heroic citizens (Barry, 2006: 34).

The Indian political establishment too was inspired, in the early 2000s, by precisely such a hope that the Indian diaspora would start pouring investments into India and so contribute to rapid economic growth. Today, the West is experiencing recession, and India's industrialists have spread their own wings abroad, with the Tatas being the largest employers in the United Kingdom. Investments can therefore no longer be the impetus for offering incentives to what the Singhvi Committee had effusively described as the "National Reserve of India" and "the National Resource of India" (Government of India, 2001: 526).

However, the substantive argument the Committee made in support of dual citizenship appealed to the nostalgia and emotional bonds of emigrants, and their desire for dual nationality as "a higher form of the acknowledgement of their linkage with Mother India" (ibid.).[36] Their report rejected the argument against dual citizenship arising out of national security concerns, pointing out that existing laws—such as the Foreigners' Act or the IMDT Act (which had not until then been struck down by the Supreme Court)—had failed to check illegal migration into the country. By contrast, people entering the country with dual citizenship would surely be easier to monitor and regulate. In an unselfconscious but formal statement of class bias, it promised that the descendants of the first-wave émigrés (indentured laborers) would be kept out, and the process of granting dual citizenship would be very selective. Implicitly responding to anxieties about divided loyalties and even disloyalty, the report offered the assurance that these emigrant citizens would not be allowed to join the defense forces or the police or the civil service, and that political rights—such as the right to vote or hold public office—for these groups were ruled out (ibid.: 567).

The reiteration of the promise of political rights today provokes the question as to why such rights need to be conferred on members of the Indian diaspora. If the practice of civicness is to be the touchstone of citizenship, it is clearly difficult and even undesirable for people to perform acts of citizenship in two locations. In principle, the loyalty of a citizen to two states may be conflicted especially if the two states went to war against each other, or if their foreign policy interests clashed.

There are only two possible arguments in favor of granting political rights to emigrants, and neither has much purchase in the Indian case. The first argument is a weaker version of the case against statelessness. It emphasizes the *loss of political voice* and the inherent injustice of a state of political deprivation and rightlessness. The claim is that just because citizens emigrate, they should not lose rights of citizenship in their country of origin especially because they will not, at least initially, enjoy any rights of citizenship in the host country, and no human being should be altogether deprived of political rights. From a normative perspective, no section of citizens should be rendered second-class citizens, for reasons only of change of domicile, which it would be unfair to treat as equivalent to an abdication of citizenship (Lopez-Guerra, 2005: 227). The claim to voting rights by the Indian diaspora is typically articulated by its more voluble members, frequently energetic participants in the political life of their adoptive countries, rather than by those sections of the Indian diaspora who are vulnerable to a loss of political voice. The second, which we may call the argument of *recompense*, is the obverse of the "no taxation without representation" argument. Thus, Americans resident abroad enjoy overseas voting rights and are required to pay taxes. This would be a dubious argument in the Indian case, given the enormously class-differentiated Indian diaspora, as it would potentially align political rights with financial status.

However, it is not simply the fact that they do not pay taxes or are ineligible for public service that makes the diaspora less than deserving in the matter of political rights. Political participation is properly the prerogative of those who are members of a political community. Those who have ethnic or other forms of cultural affinity with a country can have and need have ties only of a cultural nature. Their cultural identity does not give them a lien on the civic community, and it is certainly neither strengthened nor diminished by their enjoyment or otherwise of political rights. Ultimately, only those who have a determinate stake in the political process of a country, and are affected by the laws and policies of that state, have a right to participate. The longer their absence from the country, the more compelling the argument for disenfranchising them, on the grounds of what we may, in an inversion of Carens's argument, call the moral importance of the length of absence.[37]

Indian leaders have a propensity to treat citizenship as a gift of hospitality, without following Kant's injunction to be consistently hospitable to all. Instead, provisions for emigrant "citizenship" have, over time, discriminated on the basis of class and even religion. Kantian hospitality would have Indian leaders recognize also the claims of the Bangladeshis, Sri Lankans, and many others who have lived in the country for decades without any rights.

Conclusion

The contrast between how OCIs experience the state and how the Rajasthan migrants experience it—both as apparent "outsiders"—could scarcely be sharper. The denizens of Rajasthan have been living on Indian soil for a decade and a half, but continue, in their camp settlements, to inhabit a miserable and unstable zone of *illegality*. The Indian diaspora, whose primary political affiliations lie elsewhere, lead lives of considerable luxury outside India—some of them feted by queens and presidents—but are *honorary members* of the Indian political community. The migrants do not possess any rights of mobility—they are forbidden from traveling even to the villages to which their ancestors belonged, let alone in search of livelihood. The OCIs are not merely free to travel in and out of India at will, they even have dedicated queues at immigration counters at airports to minimize the inconvenience that ordinary citizens must endure.

The state seeks to inveigle OCIs through the annual ritual of the Pravasi Bharatiya Divas, described as "the largest gathering of the Global Indian Family."[38] At this event, every year, OCIs are reminded of their affective ties to the Indian nation through ceremonies of official recognition and awards, the Pravasi Bharatiya Samman (Honor). The strong familial and affective ties of the Rajasthan migrants to the land and to kinship groups remain unrecognized by the state. Having lost their citizenship of Pakistan, the Rajasthan migrants are effectively stateless people seeking membership of the Indian state. The OCIs would ideally like dual citizenship, or membership of two states—of the state of their adoption, as well as the state of their birth or origin. In the end, of course, the Rajasthan migrants are largely poor and mostly Dalit or Adivasi, while the OCIs do not usually share any of these attributes. What distinguishes them and makes them appealing, in the eyes of the state, is their potential to bring capital and professional skills into the country. Class thus mediates not just relations between states, citizens, and social groups, but also relations between aspiring citizens and the state. To deploy Aihwa Ong's (2007: 57) metaphor, though more literally than in its original usage, the latitudes of citizenship—of Sindh and Jaisalmer, on the one hand, and of London and New York, on the other—bespeak a hierarchy, not only of geography, but also of power. The distinction between the global North and South is here mirrored, with alarmingly perfect symmetry, in state responses to citizenship claims emanating from these quite different latitudes.

The preceding chapter showed how, through subtle changes introduced into the laws of citizenship, exclusion based on religious difference has come to be legally entrenched over time. This chapter has complemented it with an account of how attempts at accommodating the citizenship claims of the diaspora, deploying arguments of jus sanguinis, also indicate a covert Hindu bias. The indifferent response to the citizenship claims of groups on the margins of Hindu society—the Dalit and Adivasi migrants in Rajasthan—does not contradict this assertion; it only reaffirms the social marginality of these groups whose predicament finds expression in the Citizenship Rules, rather than the body of the Act. In a jus sanguinis regime, the claims of both the Rajasthan migrants and the Indian diaspora could easily be admitted. The fact they have so far been accommodated in the interstices of a largely jus soli law signals the discomfort with openly undoing the existing regime of jus soli, instead tinkering with it at the margins to include groups that represent the jus sanguinis impulse.

PART TWO

Rights

4

Pedagogies of Duty, Protestations of Rights

Important as it is, the legal status of citizenship is in itself vacuous and connotes nothing. It is the threshold condition for the enjoyment of the rights and entitlements from which it derives meaning and significance. Indeed, citizenship is uniquely defined and expressed through such rights as well as through the discharge of civic obligations. That claims to legal citizenship frequently have an instrumental quality—whether, as we saw in the previous chapter, in the claims of the migrant communities in Rajasthan or the Overseas Citizens of India [OCI is a designated legal status that comes with a passport-like document] —only confirms this. Conversely, claims to rights are implicitly claims to citizenship, and often to an expanding conception of it.

Conventional taxonomies of rights—civil, political, social and economic, and cultural—have been influentially superimposed onto histories of citizenship, most notably by the British sociologist T. H. Marshall, whose arrangement of the first three categories in a historical sequence fueled the assumption that this is the inexorable sequence of their achievement, not just in Britain, but in a universally valid trajectory of citizenship rights. In the early 1950s, the division in international covenants between civil and political rights, on the one hand, and social and economic rights, on the other, as well as their

arrangement in a hierarchy, was justified in precisely these terms. Civil and
political rights were pronounced as immediately realizable, while social and
economic rights were deferred on the grounds that they could only be progressively realized. The *conceptual* case for their separation provided a *normative* argument for sequencing these different types of rights.[1] As products of a
political and ideological compromise between member-states in the postwar
international order, the twin International Covenants,[2] jointly presented as
an International Bill of Rights, failed to reflect the acute insight of Marshall
that citizenship in a capitalist society is a core element of the architecture of
inequality and its legitimization.

The contingent quality of this division is evident also in the reductionist
and even absurd way in which the socialist world appropriated the exclusive
credit for providing social and economic rights, with the more anemic civil
and political rights being attributed to the capitalist world. Not only did this
cardboard representation overlook the substantial gains made by European
capitalist welfare states, its assumptions of separability and sequence came to
be fundamentally questioned by the civil society movements of the 1980s in
eastern Europe and eventually glasnost, which asserted, among other things,
the significance of political rights and civil liberties.

What rights citizens possess; how equally or unequally these are distributed and enjoyed; when and under what political, economic, and social circumstances they are claimed; who claims them and on whose behalf; the
methods by which they are claimed; and what the substance of these rights
is—all these too are contingent. Notwithstanding the derivative quality of
rights-claims in late colonial India, it must be acknowledged that they were
turned against those they were learned from, and though these were indeed
civil and political rights, the Indian experience does not sustain a straightforward sequence narrative.[3] The reasons for this were quite specific. Since self-
determination was the primary claim, civil rights—such as the right to free
speech and association—were prerequisites for even making that first claim.
Political rights—in the form of claims to representation, and therefore suffrage—were similarly necessary to acquire a voice in the legislative councils
to which entry was initially barred. Explicit references to so-called third-generation rights—social and economic rights—are also found, though what are
today called cultural rights found greater recognition, both by the colonial
state as well as in society. The claims of cultural citizenship (which form the
subject of the third part of this book) were as conspicuous and fundamentally
constitutive as any others in India's history of citizenship claim-making.

The substantive focus of this section of the book is on the troubled career of social citizenship[4] in modern India, both in the constitution-making period as well as in the contemporary. By way of a prelude, this chapter provides an account of the early articulation of citizenship in colonial India, and the manner in which this is, discursively and politically, tethered to claims to rights in a modern sense. These are mostly, but not entirely, civil and political rights; the social and economic rights of citizenship also make a surprisingly early appearance. The obviously subversive implications of making rights-claims in a repressive colonial context are counteracted by the postulation of an almost umbilical relationship between rights and duties. Locating claims to rights within the frame of an argument about civic and political obligation arguably renders them less threatening.

The discursive terrain of citizenship explored in this chapter is defined by two poles—colonial and nationalist[5]—with contestations taking place on three fronts. The first of these is about the fashioning of the modern citizen's self, including inculcating sovereignty of judgment, through citizenship education. The fact that the citizenship discourse in both the metropole and the colony was similarly circumscribed in class terms may account for the intriguing similarities—despite the presumptively antagonistic location of colonizer and colonized—in the delineation of the ideal qualities of citizenship in the account of the British textbook writer, on the one hand, and in contemporary Indian accounts such as those of the Arya Samaj, on the other.

The second contestation is about determining the limits of citizenship in a divided society, and how citizens relate to their "others." The colonial pedagogic enterprise is obsessed with the difficulty of constructing governable subjects given the immutable divisions of Indian society. In response, the nationalist project perseveres to identify a plausible basis for a durable civic order. The third element is about the sites of citizenship, with rival colonial and nationalist prescriptions about the appropriate arena for the performance of citizenship. Colonial intransigence in confining the practice of citizenship to the local is resisted and gradually transcended by the nationalist attempt to forge and claim newer and more expansive spaces for the enactment of citizenship.

Pedagogies of Duty: Lee-Warner's The Citizen of India

It may appear surprising and even ironical that the founding discourse of citizenship in India was colonial, but the turn of the century was a time when civics textbooks were being written in many countries, including British

dominions and colonies such as Australia and Canada.[6] In India, its earliest articulation is arguably to be found in the title of a textbook published
in 1897: *The Citizen of India.* The author of this book was Sir William Lee-
Warner, who entered the Indian Civil Service in 1869, served as private secretary to the Governor of Bombay, as Acting Director of Public Instruction
in Bombay, and as member of the Education Commission of 1882–1883.[7]
Lee-Warner was reputed to despise Indians, and to entertain an obsessive
antagonism toward Maharashtrian Brahmins, in particular. This suspicion
of Brahmins was not atypical of the civil service, but Lee-Warner systematically collected statistics to demonstrate the stranglehold of Brahmins over all
positions in the Covenanted Civil Service, and was among those civil servants
who opposed Lord Ripon's reform of local government on the grounds that
the expansion of participation in the municipalities would only benefit the
Brahmins (Cashman, 1975: 20–23).

In 1902, Lee-Warner became a member of the Council of India where
his influence was, according to Wolpert, "most powerfully anti-Congress
and anti-Hindu" (Wolpert, 1967: 53). Wolpert's biography of Morley depicts
Lee-Warner as a particularly nasty individual who denounced Indians as
lacking "any sense of honour" and in his effort to poison Morley's mind
against Gokhale, claimed he had caught the latter's mentor, Justice Ranade,
in an act of "petty pilfering" (ibid.: 170). Lee-Warner was also involved
twice in legal charges of assault against and by Indians, thirty years apart,
in Bombay and London. In the first instance, he tried to drive his carriage
through a Parsi religious procession. In the second, he racially abused and
falsely accused a young Indian petitioner at the India Office of having physically assaulted him. Lee-Warner's use of racist abuse earned him, Wolpert
tells us, the disapproval of King Edward VII (ibid.: 53–55). This reputation
may explain the reference to "the villain Lee-Warner" in a letter from the
young Jawaharlal Nehru, then a student in Cambridge, to his father in 1911
(Nehru, 1972a: 89).

The apparently innocuous story of how and why Lee-Warner's civics textbook came to be written, and then, following a controversy, partly rewritten,[8]
is in fact a compelling account of how a new narrative of subjecthood masquerading as citizenship and of political obligation was being crafted at the
turn of the century. Despite its rather controversial content, this little book
became the template for every other civics textbook for decades to come,
and this chapter will discuss some of these books, apart from examining

discourses of citizenship emanating from other writings by both Indian and British authors.

In February 1894, the publisher Maurice Macmillan invited Lee-Warner to write a book teaching Indian boys in elementary schools "something about their country and the way it is governed." He also offered the inducement that this could be "a source of some profit" for Lee-Warner, since there was a good chance that his authorship of it would result in an endorsement by the Education Department. Lee-Warner wrote to A. P. MacDonnell in the Home Department submitting a proposal for such a book and asking whether, if in the government's judgment, the book was "sound and good," it would consider getting it introduced into schools. The Home Department wrote back lauding Lee-Warner's "object of promoting a better spirit in society and a common interest in life" through such a book but expressing its reluctance to get involved in the business of promoting the book on several grounds, including the somewhat feeble institutional plea that the selection of textbooks fell within the domain of local governments.[9] The substantive anxiety expressed by MacDonnell however was that the book did not seem to be a "moral text-book" of the type that had been contemplated in a Home Department Resolution of 1889, and hence perhaps was dangerously close to being political. The proposed outline of the book suggested to him that

> . . . however free from polemical matter the book might be, it would still remain a treatise on politics. If it were officially included in the school curriculum, there would be a danger that any schoolmaster might use it as a peg on which to hang lectures on politics to his classes. We have not much control over the oral teaching in our schools, and there are grounds for believing that the teaching of History is sometimes perverted into an instrument of political education, notwithstanding orders to the contrary. The danger would be still greater with a treatise on politics, which, whatever its own scope and spirit, might easily give opportunities to a schoolteacher so disposed for criticizing the actions of Government and disparaging, if not denouncing, its policy. (A. P. MacDonnell to William Lee-Warner, from Simla, August 20, 1894. Private Papers of William Lee-Warner. Mss.Eur. F92/9.)

MacDonnell therefore proposed that if Lee-Warner did undertake this task, he should confine himself to an account of the Bombay Presidency, and definitely omit potentially controversial sections such as the proposed chapter on "The Press and Free Association."

In the coming months, the fate of the book came to hang not so much on the colonial administrator's fear of politics in the public sphere as on politics within the bureaucracy. Disheartened by the idea of a limited provincial remit, Lee-Warner submitted the entire correspondence to the governor, emphasizing the urgent need for a book on the Indian citizen. Lee-Warner's reasoning was tied to the central purposes of empire.

> I need only refer to Mr. Ranade's opening chapters of his Maratha history lately sent me, to explain why. I believe that a book on the Indian citizen drawn up with a desire to unite classes and give pre-eminence to none, and calculated to inspire the Indian youth with higher ideas as to his *social and political duties and a truer sense of what he owes to his present Government,* is urgently needed. The educational out-look in India is to my mind alarming. Education is and must be a mighty power, and that power we are more and more entrusting to non-Government agency with the result that the Brahman recognizes the power in his hands and is using it for his own purposes. (emphasis added)

It is clear that Lee-Warner saw in education a powerful instrument of ideological control, and recognized its potential for exacting obedience to the colonial state. He realized also the need to wrest control over education from the hands of the Brahmin, and though it is not entirely clear what he meant by the latter using it for his own purposes, it is possible he was referring to the upper-caste members of the Indian National Congress, especially his bête noire Ranade. As far as Lee-Warner was concerned, the purpose of a civics textbook was not to inculcate moral values (as MacDonnell wanted) but to persuade young Indians of their duty to obey. This was fully in consonance with the imperatives of empire and so, confronted by MacDonnell's suggestion to write a moral textbook with a limited regional provenance, Lee-Warner grumbled, sulked, and even threatened to walk out of the project till, finally, in June 1895, he received the consent of the government to give it an all-India focus. The Government of Bombay accepted the need for such a book and admitted the possibility of its being officially introduced.

In August 1896, however, Lee-Warner received a rude shock when the task of writing the book was officially assigned to the brother of another civil servant in the Home Department. A civil servant in that department sent Lee-Warner a copy of an office memorandum addressed to J. S. Cotton, asking him to write a book such as had been proposed by Lee-Warner, who—the memorandum stated—had "been obliged to drop the work for want of time." It indicated also that the book "should not be a treatise on politics, but should be mainly an outline or resumé of indisputable facts." As the publisher of the volume, Macmillan was puzzled by the official memorandum and assumed that the arrangement had Lee-Warner's approval. Lee-Warner was furious. He took up the matter with J. P. Hewett in Simla, claiming ownership of the idea of the book and, despite ostensibly offering all assistance to Cotton, asserted clearly his rights over "the scheme" of the book, in his individual rather than official capacity. The correspondence that followed resulted in the Government of India withdrawing its proposal to the hapless Mr. Cotton—who had, in the meanwhile, resigned his editorship of *The Academy*[10]—and imploring Lee-Warner to write the book with the promise that, if approved, it would be recommended to the local governments as well. Having managed to outmaneuver the bureaucrat and have the commission restored to himself, Lee-Warner formally communicated to Simla in January 1897 that he would do his best "to meet the wishes of the Government of India." By the end of that year, the book was ready and Lee-Warner was decorated with the Star of India.

By June 1898, the book was being recommended by the Government of India[11] for use in all government-aided high schools where English was taught, and plans were made for its publication also in Urdu, Marathi, Gujarati, Hindi, and other languages. The controversy over *The Citizen of India* did not however end with its publication. In 1901, in response to the minutes of a meeting of the Syndicate of the Allahabad University, and other communications from local governments about the book being too difficult for the "boys" for whom it had been prescribed, the Government of India sought the opinion of the various local governments. The responses—from headmasters of schools across the country to officials in the education departments of the provinces—were printed in a closely typed document *(Views of Local Governments)*[12] running to thirty-six pages and what they tell us about the reception of the book in the world of pedagogy is also suggestive of the contests, however muted, over citizenship in the world of politics.

While most of these comments emphasized the fact that the language used in the book was too difficult for Indian schoolboys to comprehend, and the concepts possibly alien, there was also discussion of its content, including some discomfort with its unabashed justification of colonial rule. One commentator claimed that "the teaching of civics merely by means of a text-book prescribed for all India . . . is opposed to pedagogic theory . . . if the learner has no basis of experience or of analogous apperceiving concept to rely upon, he is deluding himself with idle words" (*Views of Local Governments:* 22). Its apologist tone was described as "calculated to provoke hostile criticism by its perpetual chorus of praise" (ibid.: 31) and even as "too obvious a case of special pleading to be of any value with astute teachers teaching subtle-minded Hindu boys who have far more pronounced cynical views than English boys" (ibid.: 3–4).

> Frankly, this is not a suitable book for the boys concerned. The Indian view or feeling is not touched. The all-perfect Government of India has come into chaos and altered it into cosmos. That is the feeling left on one's mind from a reading of the book. A little democracy would not do any harm in such a book. (ibid.: 4)

Accepting that the book was politically controversial, the Education Department of the United Provinces of Agra and Oudh expressed its official concern thus:

> The rights of citizens as compared with rights acknowledged by the ruling power in former times are hardly touched on; and the duty of a citizen to his neighbor does not receive the treatment which is foreshadowed in the preface. The book should, in the Lieutenant-Governor's opinion, be *more moral and less political.* (ibid.: 36; emphasis added)

This, of course, was the precise anxiety that the Home Department had expressed in 1894. There seems to have been a widely shared assumption that the moral and the political are quite distinct, and that discussions about rights and duties properly belong to the moral, rather than the political, domain. Many referred to the book's failure to adequately develop the "rights and duties" of Indian citizens, as promised in the preface. This ostensibly "moral" dimension of the book, adjudged to be inadequate, was little more than a few pompous homilies confined to the opening pages. Lee-Warner wrote that he hoped his book would "lead some of the rising generation in India to value their heritage of British citizenship, and to acknowledge the duties which they owe to themselves and their fellow countrymen" (Lee-Warner, 1900: viii). As far as the political obligation of the Indian "citizen" was concerned, Lee-Warner's argument was unabashedly practical—obedience was justified by the benefits of British rule, which vastly exceeded those of precolonial rule.

Possibly embarrassed by the grossly materialist nature of this argument, the bureaucracy desired a more subtle moral justification of colonial rule, and Lee-Warner was asked to revise the book, which had already been reprinted several times.[13] Macmillan even published, in 1900, Rev. A. Tomory's *Authorised Guide to Lee-Warner's Citizen of India,* anticipating and perhaps even confirming the validity of the criticism that the original book was too difficult for schoolboys, and testifying of course to the business acumen of Maurice Macmillan.

The revised edition, published in 1906,[14] had a new introductory chapter titled "Citizens and their Rights." The author began with a discussion of rights and duties in a tone that was, as he had been instructed, moral rather than political. Thus, examples of duty included children learning to honor and obey their parents and shopkeepers dealing honestly with their customers. Examples of rights included the farmer's expectation that his crops would not be stolen or spoiled; and the reciprocity between rights and duties was illustrated by the farmer's restraint in leaving the fields of other farmers well alone. The government, which made its citizens secure through safe roads and armies, and provided hospitals and courts, was thereby performing its duties. Duties were, moreover, not restricted to our "fellow-countrymen" for we also have "duties to our neighbors in foreign countries."

The relationship between state and citizen was expressed, as in much political writing of the time, in terms of the relationship between the whole and its parts. In the "best ordered State," the different "duties" (not functions) performed by citizens are, in relation to the body politic, "similar to those performed by different parts of the body to the whole."[15] The whole generally referred to India, though citizenship was defined in terms of "membership of the whole Indian empire," rephrased in the second edition as "citizens of the British Empire, which extends to all parts of the earth . . ." (Lee-Warner, 1907: 9).

In line with contemporary European ideas, the core constitutive element of citizenship, for Lee-Warner, was territory. He argued that the unity of European countries could be fostered, despite diversity, because of the "national respect for law and a general feeling of patriotism," both of which were conspicuously absent in India. Clearly unaware of older regional patriotisms (Bayly, 2001), Lee-Warner wrote that the word patriotism and the phenomenon of love of country were unknown in India. Nevertheless, India did possess an alternative foundation for what he called "useful citizenship"—traditions of "personal devotion to a chief, obedience to the father of a family, a strong sense of religion, and village communities," and through these customs, the people had already learned "the practical advantages of common action" (Lee-Warner, 1900: 3).

Lee-Warner also described at some length the manifest inconveniences of precolonial rule—especially the lack of protection by earlier governments against invaders and their neglect of the people in times of distress, such as famine. This wanton neglect did however have the unintended good consequence of teaching the people how to provide for their own safety by relying on little more than the "ties of family feeling and common defence" (ibid.: 10). In the circumstances, they could scarcely be expected to have feelings of love and devotion, or even regard, for their rulers and their country. It was only under British rule that a seamless web of memberships—from the family to the village to the province and finally the empire, each merging into the next larger sphere—was wrought. A miniaturized state in precolonial times, the village now became an integral part of province and empire. Its narrow walls—whether of caste or of the prickly pear fencing it—gave way to an enlarged sphere for the exercise of the duties of citizenship (ibid.: 14). Exciting new possibilities now opened up—the freedom to go wherever self-interest takes one in the knowledge that "the hand of government is visible" wherever you go (ibid.: 12). The spirit of mutual help and the common good, previously confined to the village, was now unleashed and made available to the province and the country.

Even as the reader is led to believe that the Indian citizen is finally escaping the narrow parochialism of the village, Lee-Warner quickly and not a little anxiously circumscribes the arena of citizenship, offering an elaborate justification for self-government—in the city.[16] The only arena where the citizen was actually encouraged to participate was the municipality—represented as the ideal terrain for the performance of civicness. Approvingly quoting Lord Ripon[17] on the virtues of municipal government as "instruments of political education," he added:

> If the citizens unite to oppose abuses of authority and suggest improvements, their views are sure to carry the day. . . . The municipal residents find out by degrees that their votes and opinions may become a force which acts upon the local authorities. Each citizen can thus feel that he is a part of the government of his own town. He is raised to a new sense of right and duty, and the prosperity of the town becomes a source of pride to its whole population. (ibid.: 23)

Despite this emphasis on the territoriality of citizenship in British India, Lee-Warner was inconsistent in fixing the site for its performance. The Indian citizen was unshackled from the oppressive environment of the village, and introduced to the province and the district—the latter described as "the centre of life in the Indian empire" (ibid.: 34)—but only as units of administration about which the citizen should have *knowledge,* as opposed to experience.

This emphasis on the local was consistent with British thinking of the time. Sargant's treatise on imperial citizenship, for instance, viewed municipal citizenship as the "original and elementary" basis of citizenship (Sargant, 1912: 44). Restrictive as it seemed, this was also in fact the arena in which many nationalist leaders cut their political teeth. In 1923, Jawaharlal Nehru "reluctantly allowed himself to be pushed forward as the consensus candidate for chairmanship of the Allahabad Municipal Board" (Zachariah, 2004: 53). C. R. Das was the first mayor of Calcutta and Subhas Bose its chief executive officer; the brothers Vithalbhai and Vallabhbhai Patel were presidents of the Bombay and Ahmedabad municipalities respectively; and C. Rajagopalachari was the chairman of the Salem municipality. The shift effected by Lee-Warner was to liberate the practice of citizenship from the village and facilitate its arrival in the city. It remained for the nationalist project to take it beyond, and sometimes through, the municipality to an incipient nation.

Lee-Warner's justification of empire was unabashedly pragmatic. Obedience to the empire was commended to his audience of young "natives" not because of its moral superiority or liberal values but on the grounds that the practical achievements of British rule were visibly greater than those of any of its predecessors. What Lee-Warner offered were not the arguments of moral improvement, but the largely amoral inducements of modernity. The quest for legitimacy was grounded in crude transactional claims that sought to appeal to the rational self-interest of Indians, and demanded their gratitude and loyalty for the material benefits provided by British rule.

Moreover, even as Lee-Warner acknowledged the diversity of Indian society—and the attachment of Indians to family, caste, and religious affinities—he emphasized the importance of creating citizens of the Indian empire by unifying society. Indeed, citizenship was presented as something that grows out of, even as it transcends, these "restrictive" belongings. The rights and obligations of citizenship were tantalizingly offered but only through and conditional upon this overarching identification.

The explicit goals of the imperial actors of late Victorian and Edwardian Britain were, as Gorman writes, "to preserve, to maintain, to solidify, to perpetuate" (Gorman, 2006: 3). To this list could be added "to legitimize." Citizenship education was a response to the challenge to imperial legitimacy expressed by the formation and annual meetings of the Indian National Congress since 1885; the participation of Indians like Dadabhai Naoroji in the House of Commons; and in general the critical voices, both local and metropolitan, against the political excesses and economic exploitation of British imperialism. Even colonial states need legitimacy as an instrument of rule. The very conceding—albeit perfunctory application—of principles such as rights and the rule of law necessitated the creation of obedient political subjects. Citizenship education was one way of mitigating the possibly uncontrollable political consequences of these. From the perspective of a paternalist colonial state, civic education could be part of a carefully guided and managed process of raising an infantile subject population aspiring to political adulthood, but ensuring that these remained loyal and obedient political subjects. From the protonationalist perspective, however, as we shall see in the next section, training in citizenship was in fact critical political education.

Meanwhile, at least part of the Indian response to the colonial project of citizenship was to emphasize its ironies. A year before the publication of Lee-Warner's revised edition, there appeared a book with a very similar title, *The Indian Citizen,* published in Madras and by an author who chose to remain anonymous, signing himself merely as "An Indian Citizen."[18] The book was evidently intended as a riposte to Lee-Warner, whose "sympathetic volume," An Indian Citizen wrote, treats the subject from a rather different point of view.

> The blessings of British rule can be better appreciated, perhaps, by the people themselves and a book representing the point of view of the people can more freely express all the advantages and benefits of British rule without reservation or delicacy. (An Indian Citizen, 1905: i)

Though An Indian Citizen (henceforth AIC) deployed a template that was broadly imitative of Lee-Warner's, the content was redolent of dissent. In an inversion that was the mirror image of Lee-Warner's crass account of the benefits of British rule, AIC emphasized the benefits that Britain had derived from colonialism in India, and argued that if India's gratitude toward Britain was great, "Britain's gratitude to Providence should be greater" (ibid.: 14).

Protestations of Rights

Over the next decade and a half, as the framework of raw paternalist imperialism gave way to a new problematic of citizenship, the citizen came to be discursively relocated—in both colonial and nationalist writings—in relation to the nation in theory as well as in its European manifestations. The European exemplar was repeatedly contrasted with the particularities of Indian society, invariably described as mired in caste and religious identities. The very possibility of citizenship became contingent upon the prior possibility or otherwise of the nation and the characterization of Indian society in terms of social difference therefore came to redefine the core of the contention around citizenship. On the one hand, the multiple sources of disunity in Indian society were viewed as evidence of the implausibility of the Indian nation; on the other, the attachment of Indians to these affiliations of family, caste, and religion were taken as evidence of a serious deficit of individuality (to be forcefully challenged by Gandhi), making the people unfit to be liberal citizens.

In the early decades of the twentieth century, colonial writings on citizenship—with a few exceptions like John Morrison (1905)—were largely preoccupied with arguing the improbability of a national consciousness in India, with the bleak prospect of an Indian citizenship being firmly tied to this assumption. Two years before he assured Indians, in *The Citizen of India,* that the ties that bind them need not be strained by differences of religion or ways of life, Lee-Warner too had expressed discomfort with the application of "political abstractions founded upon English facts . . . being applied to a society which, as Sir Henry Maine observed, belongs, through nine-tenths of its structure, to the thirteenth century of the West" (quoted in Karkaria, 1895: 25). The existence of diverse social and cultural groups, and the affinity of people with these groups, simultaneously negated the possibility of nationhood and of citizenship. The recognition of Indian society as immutably and incorrigibly divided undermined the candidature of its inhabitants for admittance to the world of modernity, nationalism, and liberal citizenship. The heterogeneity of Indian society did not however preclude the recognition of a distinctive sphere of politics that could both transcend and eventually domesticate these differences by molding them into the form required by modernity.

The political as a way of transforming the social has a fairly extended lineage in the Indian political tradition, one that is echoed in the Constitution though by no means invented by it, as Uday Singh Mehta suggests (Mehta, 2010: 23–25). Take for example the writings of Kashinath Trimbak Telang,[19] who proposed a sequencing of political and social reform such that the political would acquire primacy over the social, and would in fact act as an instrument of social change. This was because, in politics, victory could be won *by argument* with a progressive colonial government—"the benign mother of free nations"—while in the social sphere, the traditions and strong *prejudices* of an ancient nation rendered "impotent" all appeal to logic (Telang, 1916: 287–289). The political was thus the home of public reason and argumentation, while the social housed tradition and prejudice.

This separation between the political and the social[20] is also mirrored in the views of many of the early leaders of the Indian National Congress—Pherozeshah Mehta, Dadabhai Naoroji, Mahadev Govind Ranade, and eventually Gandhi. Naoroji asserted the specifically political purpose of the Congress, on the grounds that every community had its own social problems, and none would want outside interference in their social affairs. A National Congress must confine itself to questions in which the entire nation has a direct participation, and it must leave the adjustment of social reforms and other class questions to class congresses (Naoroji, 1917: 8). All the Indian National Congress would deal with, said Naoroji, would be issues of good government and of a "modified type of self-government," and asking why it would not engage with social reform was akin to asking the House of Commons why it did not discuss abstruse problems of metaphysics or mathematics (ibid.: 7).

Between the two extremes of those who denied the possibility of citizenship in a diverse society, and those who sought to use the political (freedom and self-determination) as an instrument to overcome the divisive inadequacies of the social, there were a few who contemplated how citizenship might be acquired under the guidance of British rule. This was the burden of R. N. Gilchrist's case,[21] as he argued that it was only under the conditions of peace and order provided by British rule that the project of "regular, uninterrupted political development" and the attendant "growth of Indian citizenship" became possible (1920: 184). Gilchrist claimed that the people appreciated the civic value of the British raj because of the constitutional system specifying their public and private rights. Under semitheocratic indigenous laws, the Hindu had remained chiefly a citizen of his family or caste, and the private had predominated over public relations. However, the application of English law enabled the Hindu to look "beyond these boundaries to the citizenship of a *patrie*" (1920: 187–188).[22] Lacking "the standard elements of nationality," the Indian people would have to acquire a civic sense and a consciousness of unity, which the "mere existence of a system of rights involving equality before the law" would facilitate (1920: 207).

Such possibilities of citizenship offered by English law were duly appreciated and repeatedly invoked in the legalistic accounts of citizenship encountered in the writings of Indians such as S. V. Puntambekar[23] and V. S. Srinivasa Sastri.[24] Acknowledging the similar "denotations" but different "connotations" of citizen and subject, Sastri clarified that his 1926 lectures, titled *The Rights and Duties of the Citizen,* were using the term citizen "in the ordinary literal meaning of the word, and not in the strict legal sense" ([1926] 1948: 10). His observation that there is "no law which binds the whole Empire together . . . no such thing as British Empire law and British Empire citizen" (ibid.: 50) echoed the prewar consensus on the subject in Britain and the dominions, and discredited the platitudinous assertions of imperial citizenship made by Lee-Warner.[25]

More importantly, the absence of a common legal framework across the British Empire highlighted the difficulties of claiming rights, especially political rights. For Srinivasa Sastri, the distinction between rights and duties was often blurred. There were some rights—such as the right to education or the right to vote—that were simultaneously duties, such that "they may in fact be the same thing looked at from different points of view" (ibid: 16). Then there were rights that ripen into duties, as when we exercise our rights with solicitude for others and the harmony of society (ibid.: 19). Finally, there was the right and simultaneously the duty of resistance. Each citizen must ultimately determine and judge for himself when he can no longer acquiesce in a public wrong. But it is an imperative of citizenship that this right be exercised only after the most careful consideration of the public welfare (ibid.: 76). Of course, the right to resist is not a legal, but only a moral, right that cannot therefore be enforced against the state. As such, it should be viewed as a moral right, which an individual may exercise when he feels he must, but which the state will justly be entitled to punish him for exercising (ibid.: 79).

Both Sastri and Puntambekar were firmly rooted in the English legal tradition, and it was the philosophical and political resources of this tradition that gave force to their critique of the moral deficit of imperial rule. It is interesting that, for both the colonial bureaucracy as well as early nationalist writers, the relationship between the moral and the political was a signifier of their position on the larger question of colonialism and obligation. The colonial bureaucrat's anxiety about Lee-Warner's book being overly political instead of properly moral betrayed nervousness about the implications of a *political* questioning of the legitimacy of colonial rule, but ignored the more radical possibilities of a moral questioning. The conception of the moral was here limited to personal virtue and the expectation of certain patterns of essentially compliant behavior from subjects.

Indian writers, on the other hand, lamented the difficulty of being obedient when political rights were denied, and the most important rights could only be asserted in moral (rather than legal) terms. A moral, but politically significant, questioning of legitimacy was implicit here, but so was the sense of morality as a weak instrument of political action. It was only in Gandhi's hands that this weakness was transformed into strength. In the meantime, by introducing a legal dimension into the colonial framing of the issue as moral versus political, Indian writings skillfully and successfully effected a discursive shift from the duty of obedience to the right to interrogate state legitimacy.

Puntambekar injected a new idea—that of reciprocity and nascently that of the social contract—into his representation of the relationship between the people and their government, and the rights and duties that characterize this relationship. The state, he said, comes into existence for the protection of rights and the provision of welfare (1929: 203), and his classic textbook account of rights and duties meticulously catalogued these welfare rights,[26] including the right to work (and to unemployment benefits when employment is unavailable), to a minimum standard of living, to elementary education, to good housing, and so forth. Unusually, the rights of the state were also specified: they included the right to obedience to all its laws, the right to receive taxes, the right to expect constitutional agitation rather than revolutionary methods of protest, the right to compulsory military service, etc. This surprise had a rhetorical purpose, for having shown how these rights are enshrined in the American and European constitutions, and upheld in those nations through principles such as the rule of law, equality of all citizens before the law, and accountability of the state to the people, Puntambekar proceeded to document the absence of such rights in the Indian context, and the obvious implications of this for reciprocity and therefore legitimacy.

Throughout adopting a measured, legalistic tone, Puntambekar laid bare the stark reality of extraordinary laws, exceptional powers, ordinances, and race-based arbitrariness that characterized executive action in India. His catalogue of denial included the absence of habeas corpus; the fact that government was both prosecutor and judge; racism in public service appointments; restrictions on holding public meetings, limitations on the liberty of speech, free movement, and the right of association; taxation without representation; executive interference in many areas where the judiciary could not intervene; and, above all, the absence of a right of resistance. Each of these was carefully demonstrated in a restrained and dispassionate manner, and it was only on the doctrine of resistance that Puntambekar was forthright.

> The state in India . . . compels complete obedience to its laws whether they are consented to or recognised by the people or not. It rejoices in its foreign character and its superiority and advocates its right to rule India according to its own wishes. In India, political conditions are abnormal. But in normal states the right of the state to obedience to its laws is based on the necessities of social order. (1929: 214–215)

It was India's deviation from the normal that accounted for the denial of the rights that in other, more normal states are the basis of political obligation and state legitimacy. But it was also this deviation from "normality" that undermined any presupposition of a social contract with the obligations that such a contract would usually entail. As a committed constitutionalist, Puntambekar did not directly question the legitimacy of colonial rule, though he did explicitly state that the law does not exhaust morality, and therefore

> Resistance can never be legal but can be only moral. To the resisters the state is not the whole community, and the law is not the whole morality. They are merely parts of them and are likely in many instances to go against the interests of the community and higher morality. (ibid.: 215)

This expectation of resistance was echoed in Lala Lajpat Rai's argument that an interest in politics and the affairs of state is an imperative for the citizen. The essence of politics, for him, was the responsibility placed on each individual as a servant of the nation, for "promoting (or marring) the interests of the nation." It is this responsibility that also generated the right "to meddle in the affairs of the state" or to offer criticisms and suggestions for correcting imperfections in the system ([1920] 2007: 290). The source of the right to resist thus lay, for Lajpat Rai, in the citizen's duty to promote the public good.

In these among other texts, then, the question of political obligation was ultimately to be resolved by reference to the right to resist. This was acknowledged and justified as a moral right though the choice of whether and when to exercise it was largely left to the conscience and judgment of the individual citizen. How then was the individual citizen's judgment to be educated? What were the qualities of the ideal citizen, and how might these be inculcated?

The Citizen's Self: Civic Education for Good Citizenship

The inculcation of the appropriate qualities of citizenship was an ubiquitous concern of the textbooks on citizenship being written in this period, across the world. Their emphasis was on the pedagogy appropriate to the task of producing citizens capable of political activity or at least political reasoning and understanding. In America, the new model of citizenship at the turn of the century has been described as one that "called for a voter more intelligent than loyal" (Schudson, 1998: 182).[27] This conception of citizenship arguably finds greater resonance in the Indian writings of the time than it does in colonial accounts.

Among British writers, Colonel Willatt's book on the responsibilities and privileges of the Indian citizen, first published in 1936, is notable for its recommendation of good citizenship as simultaneously a duty and the only solution for poor governance. "It is no use our complaining that our village is uncomfortable or that our district is badly run. The fault is ours. We are bad citizens. And bad citizens get the discomfort, ill health and bad government that they merit" (1946: 3).

Bad citizenship also placed a greater burden on the public exchequer, and therefore the poorer the country, the greater the need for good citizenship. These sentiments may reflect the considerable momentum acquired by the movement for freedom by the mid-1930s. Only fifteen years earlier, Professor Gilchrist had quoted complacently from a government resolution of 1915 that stated that "there is definite and satisfactory evidence of the growth of a feeling of good citizenship, particularly in the towns" (Gilchrist, 1920: 201) and attributed this improvement to the spread of education.[28] Now, Willatt expostulated that while citizenship is indeed about the duties and *privileges* (not rights) of the citizen, we are wont to overlook the former in favor of the latter.

So what exactly does a good citizen do? The good citizen, said the colonel, discharges his responsibilities toward his family and his neighbors; cooperates with the government so as not to place additional burdens of expenditure upon it; carries out official orders willingly and helpfully; assists officials to perform their functions, keeping in mind that as servants of the government, they are also his servants; pays his taxes; is tolerant and does not perform religious ceremonies without regard to the equal rights of others; and uses the power of the vote intelligently. Finally, he tries to make good citizens of all others who come in contact with him and seeks to influence his neighbors by being an exemplary citizen himself (1946: 144–147). Such were the obligations owed by the Indian citizen to the colonial state.

A comparison with even moderate and anti-Congress Indian opinion suggests a rather different political deployment of rather similar virtues. The qualities of the ideal Indian citizen, for Srinivasa Sastri, included public spiritedness or the willingness to sink one's own purposes in the larger good of the community; practical common sense that enabled an individual to decide between right and wrong without becoming excitable; and, finally, the ability and training to properly appreciate and understand the different elements that make up the welfare of a society ([1926] 1948: 12–13).

In Sastri's writings, these were therefore rather different types of civic virtue—instruments of independent thought and critique rather than of unthinking obedience. "True citizenship," he wrote, "should be informed by the ethical spirit of self-sacrifice for the benefit of the community and the ability to consider issues dispassionately, hearing all sides and deciding without reference to self-interest" (ibid.: 14). He emphasized the importance of cultivating this quality "as a fundamental part of the citizen's equipment" (ibid.: 14) and saw this duty of teaching "patience, reflection and sober study" (ibid.: 15) as devolving upon those who could influence the thinking of India's first generation of enfranchised citizens.

A similar emphasis on study and deliberation is found in Lala Lajpat Rai's reflections on how to train young *men* for the legislative councils. He advocated the sort of training in civics and citizenship that obtained in the United States, making Americans grow "into politics from boyhood to manhood," form reasoned opinions on public affairs, and exercise their franchise in a more informed and intelligent manner ([1920] 2007: 253). In India, by contrast, he lamented, the heads of students were filled with political theories without giving them the ability or the opportunity to form intelligent and practical opinions on the important political issues of the day.[29]

In sharp contrast to Willatt's intention to create citizens who would be docile and acquiescent, Sastri and Rai privileged the creation of independent citizens with the ability to think critically. One way or the other, education was the main instrument for training in citizenship, even if the sites of civic

education were many and varied.[30] Of the educational institutions established in the late nineteenth and early twentieth centuries, and not controlled
by the state, some had an obviously religious character (such as Aligarh or
the Gurukul Kangri), while others were quasi-religious or experimental in
nature—such as the National University at Adyar and the Theosophical Society. Each of these sought to foster, through their curriculum and pedagogy,
their own particular vision of citizenship.

There are striking similarities between some aspects of the colonial "char-
acter-building" project and that of Indian educational and social service
organizations. Consider the Arya Samaj project of creating the ideal citizen,
also bearing the unmistakable imprint of Herbert Spencer—the social whole
envisioned as a body, with each of its parts performing their designated functions.[31] The Gurukul Kangri[32] of the Arya Samaj consciously sought to create
citizens who would defy the stereotype of the weak and effeminate Hindu.
Through training—including discipline, physical exercise, and sport; revulsion for bodily pleasures; intellectual and spiritual development; the repudiation of individualism and the cultivation of the spirit of self-sacrifice for
the community—they would be transformed into manly, virile, and socially
responsible men selflessly devoted to the nation. These "social engineers"
would constitute an elite corps of the nation-in-progress, transmitting their
civic values to the population at large.[33]

Even as they disdained the weak physique and effeminate character of
Indian men, the English were nevertheless nervous about the introduction of
the Boy Scout movement, which had the potential to rectify it. In England,
the Boy Scout movement aimed at producing healthy citizens who, "unre-
flecting and inarticulate" would go out and administer the empire (Baden-
Powell, quoted in Watt, 1999: 41), , but it was far from clear what dangerous
implications such a vision might have in the context of political restiveness in
the colony. With its regimen of physical culture and military training, scout-
ing could potentially encourage and enable seditious activity.

The Citizen's Other:
Limits of Citizenship in a Divided Society

It was not unusual for the question of the desirable qualities of citizenship,
and the civic education that could promote them, to be linked to the nature
of Indian society and the "problem" of an insufficiently individuated social

order. For many writers, mostly but not only British, this was precisely the stumbling block to an Indian citizenship. Lee-Warner had referred to the diversity of race, language, and religion as a "Jarring Concord" (1900: 104). For Gilchrist, the cultivation of the civic spirit that is essential for nationality could not, in just one or two generations, overcome the legacy of centuries of family, caste, and factional and religious politics. The most favorable medium of growth for such an evolution of the civic spirit was a moderating power such as the present government of India. "Indian nationality," he wrote, "is—or will be when completed—a product of British rule," which laid the foundation for a state in which the people could share common interests and common rights (1920: 211–212).

There was of course a burgeoning nationalist historiography—represented by, among others, the works of Sukumar Dutt, Radhakumud Mookerji, and Bipin Chandra Pal—challenging this view, through the assertion of various elements of an Indian nationality. For Mookerji, it was the geographical unity of India, fostered by institutions such as the pilgrimage, which cultivates love of the motherland (1921: 39–45);[34] for Dutt, it was religion, culture, tradition, language, literature, and art (1926: part I). These elements, presented as the bases of an Indian nationality, were the very features of Indian society that British writers cited as the source of disunity and the reason for the implausibility of claims of an Indian nationality. Assertions of an Indian nationality, further, were accompanied by a distinction between western patriotism and an Indianized patriotism whose distinctiveness was attributed to "the idealizing and spiritualizing process of Hindu thought" (Mookerji, 1921: 32). In fact, Bipin Chandra Pal went so far as to argue that Indian patriotism, centered on love of the motherland, was superior to the "narrow, selfish and pathological" patriotism, which, inspired by secular material interests, had repeatedly led European nations into war with each other (Pal, 1958: 102).

From the Indian modernist end, Sastri pricked the British claim of a *naturally* divided society somewhat differently, through his criticism of the deliberately divisive attempts of the colonial state to encourage "smaller loyalties" by placing entities like the community between itself and the citizen (1948: 80). He savaged the practice of state law instructing the citizen to consider himself, for purposes of voting, a member of this or that community, and affirmed the citizen's relationship to the whole rather than to a section of it (ibid.: 81–82).

The Citizen's Place: Sites of Performance

In effect, Sastri was implicating the colonial state in the reproduction of the very subnational cultural identities that, it claimed, were an impediment to citizenship. He was also simultaneously taking the practice of citizenship to the highest legislative body in India. He claimed to have felt personally humiliated by the way in which Indian members of the legislative assembly voted to continue the Bengal Regulation III of 1818 (a preventive detention law allowing no recourse to trial). "This deadly blow at the very basis of citizenship," he complained, would not have received the support of the majority of members had they been familiar with the fundamentals of political action and cherished their legal rights and duties. "If every candidate at an election and every voter had read a declaration of rights half a dozen times, India might be a safe home for democracy. That is a suggestion for the professor and the schoolmaster to consider" ([1926], 1948: 29).

The introduction of this idea of civic competence was informed by the modernist assumption that the boundaries of religion and caste could be overcome by civic training in both understanding and then speaking effectively and convincingly on public issues. In 1920—three years before elections to the Councils but after the enlargement of the electorate by the reforms of 1919—Lala Lajpat Rai proclaimed that there was a need for "enlightened young men with new vision in our Councils and not men of stereotyped, outmoded thinking whose vision has not travelled beyond temples and mosques" ([1920] 2007: 290).

Where precisely might an individual display such newly acquired qualities of citizenship? Lee-Warner would surely have been horrified at Lala Lajpat Rai's idea of political competence as a civic quality displayed in representative legislative institutions. He had approved of the Indian citizen broadening his horizons by acquainting himself with the structure of governance in the district and the country, but this was intended as useful general knowledge rather than actual practice. The optimal site for the performance of citizenship, for Lee-Warner, as indeed for Gilchrist, remained the local.

> In India the self-governing spirit had to be extracted by the central Government. . . . The prospect of an independent legislature in Simla or Delhi is far grander than the efficiency of a *mofussal* district or municipality; but it is to the less showy *mofussal* that we must look for the real success of an independent central legislature . . . it is in the district and division

that the common interests of citizenship can first be recognised, that the elementary lessons of national self-government can be learnt. (Gilchrist, 1920: 206)

To Gilchrist, the existence of a system of rights providing equality before the law was too passive. The active cooperation of the citizen in the community was more desirable, because at this level, the citizen could participate in the making of local laws by voting or even getting elected, and so feel that he was an active agent in determining the destiny of his country (ibid.: 207). Gilchrist evidently saw no irony in the assertion (his own as well as that of many others) of, on the one hand, the inability of Indians to think beyond family, kinship, and caste, and, on the other, the British insistence on confining the practice of citizenship to the local.[35]

The tension between the rural and the urban—and the cultural and intellectual stereotypes associated with them—is also apparent in many of these writings. The "narrowmindedness" of the village is thus a recurrent theme. In fact, Zook (2000) has argued that colonial policy in the early twentieth century conceptualized the education of the rural citizen differently from that of the urban citizen. Rural citizens would be emphatically citizens of the local, educated in the local vernacular, and their training—even that in civic values—would be aligned to their presumed vocation of agriculture.[36] In southern India, cooperatives were seen as playing an important role in this training and indeed in development—these, rather than the abstract nationalism of the towns, were to be the forces contributing to the creation of citizens in the villages.

This is not to suggest that urban citizens were cast as national actors. Studies of urban civil society and citizenship in colonial Bombay, for instance, have shown how class privilege determined rights of participation and political representation that were limited to the local arena.[37] Associational life and a nascent civil society too were the preserve of a small urban elite comprising the English-educated intelligentsia, the propertied, and the merchant aristocracy (Kidambi, 2007: 157–161).

An alternative anticolonial strategy used by many Indian writers was the persistent invocation of internationalism. The very first chapter of AIC's book, titled "Humanity as an Organism," engages in a discussion of international dependence, of how some nations progress rapidly and others slowly, and of how nations should know and understand each other better and so promote the welfare of all. This internationalism, in sharp contrast to Lee-Warner's localism, encouraged the citizen to be "a lover of humanity" first and only then "a patriotic son of his own country" (AIC, 1905: 5). The subversive potential of internationalism was underscored in AIC's admiring references to the press and public opinion as he asserted the power of ideas over that of force. In the absence of an international court of arbitration, he asked, who should be the final authority when there are differences of opinion? He proposed that the press of the whole world be taken as representing "the sum total of the opinions of all nations" (ibid.: 4).

Conclusion

Early twentieth-century contestations over the idea of citizenship reflect and parallel the dramatic developments in the sphere of political action, where the mendicant approach of the late nineteenth century is giving way to a more oppositional, even combative, political discourse. Despite superficial similarities in the way in which the idea of citizenship, and the qualities of the good citizen, were constructed by colonial textbook writers and by their Indian interlocutors, the concept does appear to have been substantively transformed.

At the close of the nineteenth century, as we saw, Lee-Warner was being told by his superiors in the colonial bureaucracy to focus on the moral, and steer clear of the political, in the writing of his textbook. His politics may have been an embarrassingly unsubtle rationalization of imperialism, giving rise to colonial anxiety about the moral vulnerability of an excessively loyalist political argument. What is certain is that the terrain of the argument soon shifted—from the straightforward injunction of obedience to a quest for legitimacy that at least partly depended upon reason and persuasion. Further, the framing of the problem of citizenship in terms of an opposition between the moral and the political was to undergo a radical change when reframed as an opposition between the moral and the legal. For the colonial bureaucracy, an emphasis on the moral signaled a reassuringly apolitical zone. In the writings of Indian protonationalists, the moral acquired a new and subversive efficacy, as it permitted apparently innocent but actually fundamental questions to be asked and colonial power to be potentially delegitimized.

A new political language is clearly coming into being at this time. Citizenship may, at this point, be a misnomer, a futuristic anachronism. Even so, it is clear that the historical subjecthood of the Indian people—to monarchical rule of various types—has given way to a qualitatively different way of being a subject, one through which the aspirations of citizenship can potentially be expressed. Though introduced by an English textbook, with the overt object of exacting obedience, the discourse of citizenship suggests a new—albeit only partially realized—mode of conceptualizing relationships of authority and power, and eventually an opportunity to contest the legitimacy claims of the colonial state.[38] There is a visible groping with unaccustomed questions, and multiple discursive renegotiations of the relationships between individual and state, between the social and the political, and the mediation of both of these by community.

Though animated by quite different political purposes, many of these arguments are underpinned by contractualist assumptions.[39] Arguably the weakest form of contract is that invoked in Lee-Warner's textbook: demanding obedience because British rule has brought greater material benefits than precolonial rule. A much stronger contractual argument is found in Puntambekar's assertion of the reciprocity between rights and obedience, and his insistence that it is the gap in practice between them that permits the claim of the right of resistance. Here, the justification for repudiating political obligation lies in the failure of the imperial government to provide rights in the same spirit and to the extent that they are available elsewhere. Many contemporary Indian accounts validate the moral right to resistance by yoking the idea of citizenship to the state and its law, pointing to inconsistencies between the promise of the law and the actual access of Indian citizens to it, and making resistance not just a moral (as opposed to legal) right, but also a duty. Where Lee-Warner enjoins obedience as a duty, Lajpat Rai asserts the duty to disobey.

The divide is really about the nature of state authority and its claims to legitimacy. In the texts we surveyed, the colonial project seeks a sacralization of the secular authority of the state. The colonial state is presented as a new, secular form of social authority, in contrast to and standing above, the traditional forms of social authority in Indian society, viz., religion, caste, and clan, to which Indians are seen to be ineluctably attached. The superiority of this professedly secular but sacralized authority is already incipient in Lee-Warner's conception of the state as a neutral authority mediating social conflict, though it acquires more sophisticated articulation in Gilchrist's writings. In the writings of Naoroji, as we have seen, the Indian National Congress is cast in the mirror image of such a state: neutral, secular, and standing above "classes."

Arguments about citizenship bear the imprint of this disagreement about whether or not India is, even potentially, a nation: and about whether such a divided (rather than diverse) society can yield a conception of citizenship, much less individuals who can be citizens. We noted varied views on the sequencing of nationhood and citizenship, and on the extent to which, and how, the realization of the one may be dependent on the achievement of the other. The way in which citizenship and nationality come to be linked shows that, despite the confusion about what sort of political community Indians are or can be citizens of, the usual injunction to the colonized is to first learn to become citizens, and only then aspire to nationality. Gilchrist, for instance, makes Indian nationality contingent upon the achievement of citizenship, with practices of civicness presented as the very instrument for the creation of nationhood. The project of good—read obedient—citizenship is apparently a way of fending off for longer the other, and manifestly more dangerous, project of nationalism and the expression of citizenship through resistance that it entails.

There are, as we have seen, at least two distinct and definable Indian positions on this question. For some Indian writers, the basis for the claim of citizenship is the historical fact of Indian nationality and nationhood. On this view, citizenship is the more distant goal, the immediate preoccupation being to justify the idea of a national unity. For others, especially those steeped in the English legal tradition, the reference point for the practice of citizenship, even in the moment of its interrogation, is emphatically the law of the state, rather than an abstract or historical idea of a prior or incipient national unity.

Finally, we noted the superficial similarities in the way in which the qualities of good, even active, citizenship are defined. In colonial accounts, these qualities are seen as serviceable for the legitimacy of colonial rule; in protonationalist writings, however, they appear as the very virtues required to resist it. Similar qualities of citizenship are thus intended to produce very dissimilar types of citizens: compliant, submissive, and obedient, on the one hand, and questioning, insubordinate, and even disobedient, on the other. This divergence in expectations about how citizenship should and will be performed is further underscored by the difference in fixing the site for the performance of citizenship. For colonial writers, the local is inevitably the most appropriate site for the lessons of citizenship to be learned, rehearsed, and practiced. Despite their other ideological differences, nationalist writers are unequivocal that the putative nation is the site of citizenship practices. They do not, of course, acknowledge that the practitioners of such civic virtues would be a miniscule elite. Indeed, in this phase citizenship discourse is both of and for the upper classes. In subsequent years, as the nationalist movement encompasses other social classes as well, it remains a discourse of, but by no means only for, the upper classes.

This elite orientation is occasionally sought to be offset, by the elites themselves, through an emphasis on the social rights that can be the vehicles through which the privileges of civil and political rights may be more fruitfully enjoyed by the vast mass of impoverished Indians. In the 1920s and 1930s, the earlier debate about deploying the political to transform the social for the more efficacious accomplishment of modernity is complemented by a privileging of social rights with a view to making the enjoyment of political rights more effective and meaningful.

5

The Unsocial Compact

The discourse on citizenship in the first two decades of the twentieth century was, as the last chapter showed, largely concerned with demonstrating to colonial power the gap between the promise and the performance of the civil and political rights of subjects. Up until this time the contrast between formal and substantive rights was no more than a contrast between the formal availability and the substantive unavailability of civil and political rights. From the late 1920s onward, this came to be rearticulated as a contrast between the formal, construed as civil and political, and the substantive, interpreted as social and economic,[1] with the former deemed unlikely to be meaningful in the absence of the latter. This sentiment found expression in the speeches and writings of political and intellectual elites but also animated the movements of peasants and workers in this period.

This does not imply that civil liberties and rights became less important. In a highly repressive colonial context, where extraordinary laws were the rule rather than the exception, civil liberties could hardly go out of fashion. Through this period and well into the 1930s, political tracts making the case for civil liberties were legion.[2] In 1936, Jawaharlal Nehru launched the Indian Civil Liberties Union, and Rabindranath Tagore served as one of its presidents. An illiberal law like the Rowlatt Act[3] was not only a raw exercise of colonial power, but arguably also a refutation of and response to these demands. Claims to civil liberties and claims to social rights occasionally converged, as in some of the nationalist reports we shall survey, but as the time to give them constitutional form drew closer, their trajectories increasingly diverged. This chapter traces the genealogy of social and economic rights in the late colonial period and the constitution-making process at independence. It tracks the first hesitant steps toward the articulation of social rights that found expression in three types of documentary forms: first, resolutions in the annual conventions of the Indian National Congress; second, a range of protoconstitutional documents, some sponsored by the Indian National Congress, others conducted under the auspices of all-parties or nonparty conferences and committees; and finally, alternative and competing political imaginings explicitly offered as draft constitutions for a possible future. The substantive focus of the chapter is on the contest over social rights in the Constituent Assembly and their eventual relegation to the Directive Principles of State Policy, which are meant to guide policy but are not enforceable in the courts.

Antecedents

The precise timing of the appearance of social and economic rights on the Indian political and intellectual horizon, as well as the ideological origins in nationalist politics of the impulse to incorporate these, remain uncertain, though a perceptible shift in the Congress's discourse occurs sometime between 1918 and 1925. The Declaration of Rights that emanated from the Bombay session of the Indian National Congress in 1918 asked that the British Parliament pass a statute including a Declaration of the Rights of the People of India as British Citizens, guaranteeing rights to equality before the law; liberty of life, property, and association; the right to bear arms; and freedom of the press (Zaidi, 1979: 322). In 1925, Congress endorsed the Commonwealth of India Bill that had been prepared by a committee chaired by Annie Besant, supported by forty-three Indian political leaders from different political parties, and submitted to the House of Commons.[4] This bill asserted the right to free primary education and gender equality, and proposed that the electorate be comprised of the educated, the propertied, and the taxpayers. Gandhi approved of the Besant Bill, disagreeing only with its proposals regarding the franchise. The crux of his argument was that "there is no provision anywhere for labor. My formula is, no labour, no vote; hence the *spinning franchise*" (*CWMG* 31: 215; emphasis added). Nevertheless, many provisions of the Besant Bill were carried almost verbatim into the Motilal Nehru Committee Report of 1928, which was the product of all-party deliberations and endorsed by an inclusive all-party conference.[5]

The Nehru Report prefigured the Indian Constitution of 1950 in several important ways. Apart from providing for parliamentary government, it also defined who could be a citizen of India and specified the rights that would attach to citizenship. Article 3 of the Report affirmed the jus soli basis of citizenship, such that anyone who was born or naturalized, or was the child of a *father* who was born or naturalized, within the territorial limits of the "Commonwealth of India" would be a citizen. A citizen of a foreign country could not be a citizen of India unless "he" renounced the citizenship of that other country (All Parties Conference, 1928: 101). The more striking aspect of the Nehru Report is its delineation of Fundamental Rights. In addition to the rights to personal liberty, equality before the law, freedom of association, freedom of conscience, freedom of speech, and the separation of the state and religion, it also enunciated a set of social and economic rights. These included equal rights of citizenship for men and women; the right to free elementary education without any distinction of caste or creed, making this right "enforceable as soon as due arrangements shall have been made by competent authority"; and "freedom of combination and association for the maintenance and improvement of labour and economic conditions" for people belonging to all occupations. It also enjoined Parliament to make "suitable laws for the maintenance of health and fitness for work of all citizens, securing of a living wage for every worker, the protection of motherhood, welfare of children, and the economic consequences of old age, infirmity and unemployment" (Rao, 1966, 1: 60). In sum, the right to education and the right to unionize for better conditions of labor were proposed as rights to be guaranteed by the Constitution; while health, employment, and other measures of social security were to be provided for by Parliament through statutory provision. In Austin's inventory, ten of the nineteen subclauses "re-appear materially unchanged" in the Fundamental Rights chapter of the Indian Constitution, while three of the rights in the Nehru Report resurface in the Directive Principles (Austin, 1966: 55). The report also recommended a right to property, despite the opposition of many on the grounds that it was a bourgeois right (Datta, 2000: 278).

Situating the Nehru Report in the context of the international discourse on rights in the late 1920s suggests that this was a rather exceptional document in its early envisioning of social and economic rights. Even the report of the Academie Diplomatique Internationale, which became a resource for the Declaration of the International Rights of Man, was only published in 1929. Charles Beitz's account of the evolution of a transnational human rights regime shows that the Covenant of the League of Nations failed even to endorse a Japanese-sponsored clause guaranteeing nondiscrimination on grounds of race or religion, though the constitution of the International Labour Organization did give recognition to the reduction of poverty, and the setting of standards for the elimination of forced labor (Beitz, 2009: 15–16).

In India, the next major documentary moment in the evolution of a rights regime was the presentation, to the Karachi session of the Congress in 1931, of *The Resolution on Fundamental Rights and Economic Changes*. A footnote in the *Collected Works of Mahatma Gandhi* states that this document was "presumably drafted by Gandhiji" (*CWMG* 51: 327). Nehru's biographer Sarvepalli Gopal claims that the resolution was drafted by Jawaharlal Nehru and revised by Gandhi (Gopal, 1975: 152). Moving the resolution at the session, Gandhi's statement prefigured the divide that was resurrected, two decades later, in the Constituent Assembly, on rights that legislators and jurists could acknowledge and others that would be of interest only to the poor.

> This resolution is meant for those who are no legislators, who are not interested in intricate questions of constitution, who will not take an active part in the administration of the country. It is meant to indicate to the poor, inarticulate Indian the broad features of swaraj or *Ramarajya*. (*CWMG* 51: 329)

The Resolution itself opened with the statement that "in order to end the exploitation of the masses, political freedom must include real economic freedom of the starving millions" (*CWMG* 51: 327). Its twenty points listed the fundamental rights that should be provided in a constitution for a Swaraj government. These included the standard civil rights—personal liberty and freedom of speech, association, conscience; equal rights for all citizens; the protection of minority cultures; and the right to bear arms. It also demanded adult suffrage, state neutrality toward religion, and free primary education. The social vision of the Resolution included an end to bonded labor, the elimination of child labor, the protection of women workers, the right of workers to form unions and, for industrial workers, "a living wage . . . limited hours of labour, healthy conditions of work, protection against the economic consequences of old age, sickness and unemployment" (*CWMG* 51: 328). For the peasantry, the Resolution demanded reduction in rent and revenue, control over usury, and the removal of the salt duty. It also proposed state control over key industries and ownership of mineral resources. Several points in the Resolution hit out quite directly at the colonial state apparatus and its revenues, asking for a 50 percent cut in civil servants' salaries, the reduction of military expenditure, and the protection of indigenous cloth. Many of these had already figured in the Eleven Points that Gandhi had submitted to the viceroy in January 1931, and which, in an interview to *The Bombay Chronicle* a few months later, he had declared to be "as dead as Queen Anne." In the same interview, however, he signaled that the Eleven Points had been "revived in an invigorated form in the Fundamental Rights resolution of the Congress" (*CWMG* 53: 302).

The question of authorial attribution—how much of this Resolution was Gandhi's and how much Nehru's? Did it represent a Gandhian concession to Nehruvian socialist ideas or a Nehruvian concession to Gandhi's Eleven Points?—is important because its ideational pedigree is also a pointer to the genealogy of the Directive Principles two decades later. The extant interpretations range from an unhappy political bargain between Gandhi and Nehru to a collaboration between them.[6] Judith Brown presents this as a genuinely collaborative endeavor between Gandhi and Nehru, one that marked, for Nehru, "a real advance on the socio-economic front" (Brown, 2003: 99). Granville Austin's interpretation of the Resolution as a synthesis of Socialism and Gandhism implicitly endorses a similar interpretation. The Resolution thus brought together the Eleven Points of Gandhi along with the negative rights from the Nehru Report, as well as four new provisions: adult franchise, freedom of movement, the abolition of titles as well as of capital punishment (Austin, 1966: 56).

Other historians interpret this as a political compromise, with Gandhi's sponsorship of the resolution on fundamental rights being seen as a *quid pro quo* for Nehru's reluctant agreement to move a resolution ratifying the Gandhi–Irwin Pact, which had disappointed him (Nehru) and other Congress leaders as it conceded, in their opinion, far too much to the government. In Sarvepalli Gopal's view, the argument of political compromise is not credible, simply because the Resolution encompassed little more than the Eleven

Points of Gandhi, and was far from being the revolutionary charter that the
Congress had accepted as necessary in 1929. The failure of the Resolution to
mention the abolition of landlordism or to demand that land be socialized
and agricultural debt be even partially annulled suggested that this could
scarcely have been a worthwhile political compromise. Sumit Sarkar has also
argued that there was little socialism in this Resolution, only modest promises
to labor, and a very moderate program of agrarian change. Sarkar is critical
of the absence of any mention of rural indebtedness, and no explicit intent of
either eliminating landlordism or redistributing land (Sarkar, 1983: 312–313).
On the accounts of both historians, this insufficiently radical Resolution was
clearly not a prize for which Nehru need have struck a bargain of reciprocity.

Nehru appears to have been fully cognizant of, and even a little dissatisfied
with, the Resolution, which he described as "very mild and prosaic" (J. Nehru
[1936] 1989: 266). Moreover, he acknowledged that he had drafted the resolution incorporating Gandhi's suggestions (ibid.: 267–268). The Congress had,
with its nationalist preoccupations, so far avoided economic issues, Nehru
said, but at Karachi

> it took a step, a very short step, in a socialist direction by advocating
> nationalisation of key industries and services, and various other measures
> to lessen the burden on the poor and increase it on the rich. This was not
> socialism at all, and a capitalist state could easily accept almost everything
> contained in that resolution. (ibid.: 266)

The reception of the document is telling. The social and economic rights
mentioned in the Resolution fueled all sorts of speculation including, in government circles, the suspicion that that the revolutionary politician M. N.
Roy had been involved in its drafting, or that at the very least the document
was intended to be a concession to the communists. This attribution derived
credence from the fact that the industrialist Ambalal Sarabhai attacked it, in
a note to his fellow members in the Federation of Indian Chambers of Commerce and Industry, as designed to effect a government on the Russian model
(Sarkar, 1983: 312–313). Roy himself later "denounced (it) as confused, compromising with foreign imperialism and native feudalism" (Gopal, 1975: 152).
Nehru too repudiated the speculation about Roy having had anything to do
with it (Nehru [1936] 1989: 267–268). However, in 1940, V. B. Karnik, the
trade unionist and close associate of Roy in his League of Radical Congressmen, described the Resolution as "a hesitating step" that was shelved because

it did not find favor with the leadership of the Congress despite visualizing "inadequate and ill conceived reformist measures" (*League of Radical Congressmen's Programme of National Reconstruction, 1940*, reproduced in Panikkar, 2009: 98). The very fact that the Resolution was received with alarm in quarters as diverse as the colonial state and Indian industry suggests that, despite its modest program, it represented a threat to important sections of dominant interests. The significance of these declarations of fundamental rights may lie more in their symbolic announcement of intent, signaled by the title of the Karachi Resolution and its twinning of fundamental rights with economic change.

The development of social and economic rights was unsurprisingly interrupted as the movement for freedom acquired momentum, and as the "communal" problem occupied political center-stage. In 1939, the trade union leader B. T. Ranadive lamented that the Congress saw nothing but communal divisions and, with its economic program confined to hand-spinning and weaving, failed to notice the economic struggles of the masses, which had brought about economic unity (*National Front,* March 12, 1939, reproduced in Hasan, 2008b: 1762). The preoccupation of all political parties with the communal question found reflection in the constitution of a committee headed by Sir Tej Bahadur Sapru (who had also been a member of the Nehru Committee of 1928) to go into issues relating to minorities from a constitutional and political perspective.[7] In its chapter on Fundamental Rights, the Committee dwelt substantially on the civic and political rights—including rights of, and mechanisms for, representation—of the religious minorities, the Scheduled Castes, the Backward Classes, and the "Aboriginal Tribes." While there was some mention of the goal of equality, and even some flag-waving about "vested interests" and "privileged classes," there was only an oblique mention of the problem of social inequality.

> If we are going to have a democratic constitution, we feel strongly that we should provide certain standards of conduct, citizenship, justice and fairplay to all members of the community, when we know that we are making a deliberate and conscious attempt to emerge from a state of society, in which inequality was the rule, to a state of society in which we hope equality will be [*sic*] normal standard. Fundamental Rights, therefore, will not only be a standing warning to the vested interests or to the privileged classes but also a standing invitation to the governments, administrators and guardians of the law that the period of privileges and inequality is over . . . (Sapru Committee Report, 1945: 258)

In what was surely a testimony to prodigious optimism and extraordinary enthusiasm, there were several individuals[8] and political groups who, a year or so before independence, began publishing draft constitutions. These alternative constitutional imaginings included Manabendra Nath Roy's[9] *Constitution of India: A Draft* (1944), the Socialist Party's *Draft Constitution of Indian Republic* (1948), and Shriman Narayan Agarwal's *Gandhian Constitution for Free India* (1946) with a foreword by Gandhi himself. On the rights of citizenship, each of these reflected a different shade of left-wing political opinion. M. N. Roy was the author of by far the most populist and radical of these manifestos of the "New India." As his draft preceded the establishment of the Constituent Assembly, he wrestled with the question of how to vest the sovereign power of the Indian people in such a body, and concluded that once power had been transferred by the British Parliament to the Indian people, there was no need to leave the fate of the people in the hands of parties and leaders. There was enough evidence of massive popular support for these ideas, and therefore the content of the Constitution was more important than the question of how such a constitution could be legitimately arrived at.[10] In Roy's republican constitution, "adequate remunerative employment or relief is a right of citizenship" (M. N. Roy, 1944: 14). There were rights also to the statutory provision of social security for the sick and elderly; to free, compulsory, and secular education for children up to the age of fourteen; and "identical rights and responsibilities of citizenship for men and women" (ibid.: 15).

The Socialist Party's draft addressed the concurrent deliberations in the Constituent Assembly, which, Jayaprakash Narayan said in his foreword, had "failed to enthuse the country" by its "humdrum work . . . inspired not by the revolutionary mood and aspirations of the people, but by the natural conservatism and timidity of worthy *diwans* and legal luminaries" (Socialist Party, 1948: 5). In its discussion of economic rights, the Party exhorted the Assembly to reincorporate its provisions against human trafficking and forced labor. While it broadly endorsed the Directive Principles of State Policy, it urged the Assembly to lay the foundations of a socialist economy alongside those of political democracy. There was no natural right to property; indeed, property was merely a social institution that could hinder social progress and welfare. The state should therefore have "the full right to regulate, limit and expropriate private property by means of law, if [*sic*] common interests of the people require it" (ibid.: 33).

Agarwal, finally, began by referencing the Besant, Nehru, and Sapru attempts at constitution-making, and presented his draft as an alternative "based on indigenous traditions" (1946: 14). His list of Fundamental Rights and Duties included every citizen's right to free basic education in accordance with the *Nai Talim,* the Gandhian educational curriculum; the right to obtain a minimum living wage "through honest work or employment"; the "right to rest, by not being compelled to work for more than eight hours a day"; and the right to "medical freedom," which came with the assurance that "existing rules and regulations regarding compulsory vaccination or inoculation shall be suitably amended" (ibid.: 78). Clearly modern medicine was not part of the Gandhian vision of a right to health. The enjoyment of these rights was contingent upon the performance of duties: to be faithful to the state, to promote public welfare by contributing to it in cash or kind or labor, and to "avoid, check and if necessary, resist exploitation of man by man" (ibid.: 79). In terms of the political arrangements envisaged, the self-styled Gandhian Constitution was predictably keen on self-sufficient and self-governing village panchayats at the base of a pyramidal structure of decentralized governance. Though Gandhi graciously wrote a foreword to it—in which he cautioned the reader against mistaking every detail for his view and underscored Agarwal's own remark that he had only provided a broad idea of "what a constitution of my conception would be" (Agarwal, 1946)—he did not apparently support the Constitution to which his name was so attached. It was Nehru's Objectives Resolution that enjoyed Gandhi's support, as did the leadership of the Constituent Assembly by Ambedkar (Parel, 2006: 66–67).

Social and Economic Rights in the Making of the Constitution

The contention over social and economic rights was most fully played out in the Constituent Assembly where a classification of rights into two distinct categories—those that could be legally enforced and those that could not—was proposed by the Sub-Committee on Fundamental Rights of the Constituent Assembly (SFCR). The Sapru Committee had already, in the context of minority rights rather than social and economic rights, grappled with the British constitutional debate about whether enshrining fundamental rights implied an undermining of parliamentary sovereignty. It had explicitly distanced itself from this view, asserting that in "the peculiar circumstances of India" there was a case for making such a distinction with respect to the rights of minorities, and providing mechanisms of enforcement for both justiciable and non-justiciable rights (Sapru Committee Report, 1945: 256–257). Now, as introduced in the Constituent Assembly by B. N. Rau (Constitutional Adviser to the Assembly), the distinction was influenced by the Irish Constitution of 1937—which had incorporated and placed outside the purview of the courts a set of "directive principles of social policy"—and the International Bill of Rights drafted by the international law expert Sir Hersch Lauterpacht in 1945. Many members of the Assembly were riled by the extent of "foreign" borrowings, which they saw as irrelevant and also indicative of a lack of originality in Indian legal experts.

The international context is consequential because this was a time of intense debate about human rights in international circles. The provocations were many: if the experience of the Holocaust led to thinking about the need for guarantees of the most basic human rights, the postwar economic devastation led to thinking about the state's role in guaranteeing minimum levels of well-being for its citizens. This was, after all, the period in which T. H. Marshall delivered his classic lectures on citizenship and social class at Cambridge (1950). It was also the time when intellectuals like Hannah Arendt began to reflect on the futility of "the rights of man" in situations where statelessness, such as that of the Jewish people in Europe, could deprive humans of all possible rights including and especially "the right to have rights" (Arendt [1951] 1962: ch. 9).

The post-World War I German Constitution, as well as the socialist constitutions of eastern Europe, provided obvious early exemplars that were familiar to Indian leaders. International debates of the late 1940s and early 1950s are especially important not only for the way in which they shaped Indian thinking, but also for the insights they provide into Indian interventions in rights-debates abroad. By the late 1940s, work had begun on the drafting of a Universal Declaration of Human Rights, and in 1947, a committee of distinguished philosophers[11] was set up by UNESCO to enquire into the philosophical bases of human rights. Seeking responses from different "schools of thought" from different cultures and civilizations, the committee sent out a questionnaire to many people, among them Mahatma Gandhi and S. V. Puntambekar. Gandhi's brief response, written on a moving train, may not have been terribly helpful to the committee for it all but dismissed the idea of human rights, first by making all rights derivative of duties and second by implicitly suggesting that rights could be differentiated by gender.

I learnt from my illiterate but wise mother that all rights to be deserved and preserved came from duty well done. Thus the very right to live accrues to us only when we do the duty of citizenship of the world. From this one fundamental statement, perhaps it is easy enough to define the duties of Man and Woman and correlate every right to some corresponding duty to be first performed. Every other right can be shown to be a usurpation hardly worth fighting for. (UNESCO, 1948: 3)

Gandhi's less than enthusiastic defense of rights at this time stemmed from his abhorrence of the rights assertions that culminated in the communal violence of the Partition. Puntambekar's despondent response was similarly influenced by this context. Human rights were no doubt necessary and desirable, he wrote, but hardly possible in the current Indian context where human beings had all but disappeared leaving behind only

> . . . religious men, caste men or group men. Our intelligentsia and masses are mad after racial privileges, religious bigotry and social exclusiveness. In short, we are engaged in a silent war of extermination of opposite groups. Our classes and communities think in terms of conquest and subjugation, not of common association and citizenship. (ibid.: 199)

The incorporation of economic rights in the Universal Declaration of Human Rights was contentious, and challenging the assumption that this represented a "political accommodation" of the USSR, Beitz shows that this initiative enjoyed the support not only of the Soviet bloc but also of the United States, which invoked Roosevelt's "four freedoms," which famously included "freedom from want" (2009: 22–23).[12] The Latin American countries were particularly influential in the inclusion of economic rights, though the inspiration for their emphasis on rights to safeguard freedom, dignity, and social justice appears to have come from the Catholic intellectual tradition rather than Marxism or Communism (Glendon, 2003).

Even a few years later, as the Human Rights Commission debated the issue of whether there should be one all-encompassing convention for all rights or two conventions (one on political and the other on social, economic, and cultural rights), India championed the cause of two conventions, arguing for the primacy of political rights, affirming their superior justiciability and presenting the improvement of social, economic, and cultural conditions as goals to be attained *through* the exercise of the more precisely definable civil and political rights. In a memorandum to the Commission in 1951, it expressed its unyielding opposition to including economic, social, and cultural rights in the convention on the grounds that "financially weak countries where these rights are not justiciable will not be in a position to implement them" (Berkes and Bedi, 1958: 147).[13]

India's worry about being unable to perform obligations made binding by international conventions had its antecedents in an already fractious debate in the deliberations of India's Constituent Assembly. That dispute proceeded in two distinct stages, initially centered on the distinction between social policies and fundamental rights, especially about whether or not it was at all *appropriate* for a constitutional document to include social policies. If, as some members of the Assembly argued, social and economic policies were important enough to be accommodated in the Constitution—as opposed to being left to the legislative wisdom of governments—in what form could they be included? If rights were the chosen instrument, it was important to remember that only civil and political rights could be legally enforceable, as negative guarantees involving state abstinence rather than positive state action. The lawyers were therefore in favor of the separation of civil and political rights from social and economic rights, on the grounds that the latter were not *practical*. Ranged on the other side of the debate were the Gandhians and socialists who felt that the promise of the Constitution would be belied and the poor of India betrayed unless these welfare rights were constitutionally secured.

While both strands of argument—the criterion of appropriateness as well as the criterion of practicability—were reflected in the debates, the latter became the basis of the distinction between justiciable and non-justiciable rights, which were eventually housed in an altogether separate section of the Constitution.[14] Three of the most distinguished members of the Assembly— B. R. Ambedkar, K. M. Munshi, and K. T. Shah[15]—were opposed to such a separation and prepared draft notes for the deliberations of their colleagues in the Sub-Committee on Fundamental Rights (SCFR). Munshi's note proposed the incorporation of several rights of workers (including the rights to work and to social security) and the right to education, while K. T. Shah's note included a section explicitly named "Economic and Social Rights." These rights, he argued, were indispensable because without such rights, civil and political rights would be meaningless: "The right to free elections without a full belly would be a mockery" (Rao, 1967, 2: 46). The list of fifty-nine rights proposed by Shah "to make Swaraj real and lasting for all" (ibid.: 198) included the right to a free education; the right to employment, but also the duty to work as "an inescapable obligation of citizenship"; and the right of social security for those unable to work by virtue of old age, ill health, disability and so on (ibid.: 49–55).

It is however in Ambedkar's famous *Memorandum and Draft Articles on the Rights of States and Minorities* (March 24, 1947, in Rao, 1967. 2: 84-114)) that we find the strongest articulation of social and economic rights.[16] One of the purposes of The United States of India—as Ambedkar proposed to name the new republic—would be, according to his draft preamble, "to remove social, political and economic inequality by providing better opportunities to the submerged classes" (ibid.: 84). This idea was further elaborated in Clause 4, which proposed, among other things, that key industries should be owned and run by the state and that agriculture should be a state industry. Ambedkar argued passionately that a modified form of state socialism in industry was necessary for rapid industrialization, and that collective farming was the only way in which to help the sixty million landless laborers belonging to the untouchable castes. State socialism alone could meet both the objectives of economic productivity and the equitable distribution of wealth combined, in the political domain, with parliamentary democracy. Anticipating the protests of constitutional lawyers that the proposal went beyond the usual understanding of fundamental rights, Ambedkar argued that the purpose of prescribing the economic structure of society was to protect the liberty of the individual from invasion by other individuals, which was surely also the object of fundamental rights. He specified the four premises of political democracy as follows: that the individual is an end in himself, that the individual has inalienable rights guaranteed by the Constitution; that the individual should not have to relinquish any of these rights as a condition of receiving a privilege; and that the state should not delegate its powers to private persons to govern others. The last two premises are endangered, and possibly even violated, in an economy based on private enterprise, leading to many people having no choice but to submit themselves to being governed by private employers (ibid.: 99–100).

> Ask those who are unemployed whether what are called fundamental rights are of any value to them. If a person who is unemployed is offered a choice between a job of some sort, with some sort of wages, with no fixed hours of labour and with an interdict on joining a union and the exercise of his right to freedom of speech, association, religion, etc., can there be any doubt as to what his choice will be? How can it be otherwise? The fear

of starvation, the fear of losing a house, the fear of losing savings, if any, the fear of being compelled to take children away from school, the fear of having to be a burden on public charity, the fear of having to be burned or buried at public cost are factors too strong to permit a man to stand out for his fundamental rights. The unemployed are thus compelled to relinquish their fundamental rights for the sake of securing the privilege to work and to subsist. (ibid.: 100)

If the "soul of democracy is the doctrine of one man, one value" (ibid.: 102), the limited vision of constitutional lawyers has ensured that this principle remains confined to the political structure, but is completely ignored in the economic structure where it is equally essential. Throwing a fundamental challenge to "old time constitutional lawyers"[17] and repudiating the delinking of the political and the economic, Ambedkar stated:

> Time has come to take a bold step and define both the economic structure as well as the political structure of society by the law of the constitution. All countries like India which are late-comers in the field of constitution-making should not copy the faults of other countries. They should profit by the experience of their predecessors. (ibid.: 102)

By its second sitting (within barely a month of its first meeting in February 1947), the Sub-Committee on Fundamental Rights had decided on separation, and having tentatively completed its formulation of justiciable Fundamental Rights, turned its attention to the formulation of the Directive Principles of *Social Policy*. Clauses enjoining the state to promote the welfare of the whole people and "protecting as effectively as it may a social order in which justice, social, economic and political, shall inform all the institutions of national life" were supplemented by imports from a wide variety of sources, including Munshi's draft, the Japanese Constitution, and most significantly Lauterpacht's *International Bill of the Rights of Man*. From the latter, the Sub-Committee took inspiration in prescribing that the union and state governments should "within the limit of their economic capacity and development" provide for the right to work, to education, and assistance in case of unemployment, sickness, and old age. Also from Lauterpacht's bill came a proposal to provide for just and humane conditions of work and maternity relief for workers (ibid.: 136).

At this point, both sets of rights were still viewed as subsets of the broader category of fundamental rights. As two distinct classes of fundamental rights, they were placed in two distinct chapters, with chapter 1 specifying the justiciable rights that could normally be enforced by legal action and chapter 2 the non-justiciable rights that were "not normally either capable of, or suitable for, enforcement by legal action."[18] More nomenclatural quibbling followed, and it was decided that chapter 2 should be renamed "Fundamental Principles of Governance" while chapter 1 should be titled "Fundamental Rights."[19] While the SCFR justified the division citing international practice, its chairman, J. B. Kripalani, invoked the particularity and complexity of Indian conditions, saying that the committee had, by adopting the Irish model, pursued a middle path between the US Constitution and recent European constitutions, "which have mixed up the two sets of rights" (ibid.: 169).

The more searing critique—echoing Ambedkar's dissatisfaction with the legal experts—came from those in the Assembly who tried repeatedly to draw attention to the poverty and vulnerability of ordinary citizens. B. Das of Orissa, an avowed Gandhian, was frustrated by the House being "reduced to the status of children" by a "brick wall of lawyers" (CAD, 5: 339) Dr. P. S. Deshmukh[20] also blamed the legal experts for the "mere platitudes and pious wishes" (ibid.: 341) of the minimalist principles adopted, accusing them of having simply copied out parts of the Constitution—some from the Irish Constitution, and three-fourths from the Government of India Act of 1935 (ibid.: 342). He reminded the Assembly of the impotence of the fundamental rights incorporated in the document, in particular the inadequacy of the right to vote as a way of addressing poverty. Vishwambhar Dayal Tripathi reiterated the inadequacy of the right to vote as a panacea for the poor. "Except for goodwill, no other word is found in the whole constitution. Except for the right to vote, the poor man has not yet got any other right under the constitution . . . this is not enough" (ibid.: 345).

The most substantive and impassioned objections, however, came from K. T. Shah, who insisted that the very drawing of a distinction between justiciable and non-justiciable rights meant that the second category could never be more than "so many pious wishes" (Rao, 1967, 2: 192). The nomenclature—fundamental principles of social policy—made it clear that these were not intended to be *obligations* of the state to the citizen. The committee had itself recognized the right to education, making it enforceable within a period of ten years, keeping in mind the limitations of finance and personnel that made it unfeasible in the short term. Shah pleaded that all these "principles of social policy" be made into "categoric injunctions," not mere directions but "mandates of the community to its organized representative, the State, to be carried into effect at the earliest possible opportunity"; and argued that "by keeping them on the Statute Book without making them imperative obligations of the State towards the citizen, we would be perpetrating a needless fraud, since it would provide an excellent window-dressing without any stock behind that dressing" (ibid.).

In what was arguably a radical recommendation for the time, Shah suggested that the principle of equal pay for equal work between men and women should also encompass the recognition of the housewife's work as useful work, including for purposes of national accounting. Reiterating and elaborating on each of the rights he had originally proposed—such as the right to work and to social security—Shah insisted these were a matter of "the national will to make Swaraj real and lasting for all" (ibid.: 198).

By October 1947, the Drafting Committee of the Constituent Assembly, chaired by B. R. Ambedkar, had decided to include the Directive Principles of *State* Policy (DPSP) in a new part of the Constitution. There was more quibbling over the relative value of the terms Fundamental and Directive. To some, it appeared that Directive was not as strong a word as Fundamental, but to Ambedkar the word Directive summed up better the directing role that these principles would have in relation to state policy. The die was cast: social and economic rights were relegated to a section of the Constitution that was explicitly and intendedly noncognizable in a court of law. Ambedkar had, as we noted earlier, challenged constitutional lawyers to think differently about the possibility of incorporating social and economic rights. He now accepted and even defended their location in the Directive Principles of State Policy. In his landmark speech of November 4, 1948, moving the draft constitution, Ambedkar said that the Directive Principles were a novel feature in a parliamentary democracy, and that there was no merit in the criticism that these were only pious declarations with no binding force. They did not, he acknowledged, have binding force in law, but that did not mean that they are useless and do not have binding force of another kind. Like B. N. Rau,[21] Ambedkar also likened the Directive Principles to the Instruments of Instruction issued to the Governor-General by the British Crown, and claimed that Directive Principles were simply another name for Instruments of Instruction. It is surprising that Ambedkar chose to clothe the DPSP in a garment of legitimacy that had been decisively questioned by the fact of independence itself, invoking a principle of legitimacy derived

from a colonial legislation to justify a feature of a new republican constitution. (CAD 7: 41).

The shift in Ambedkar's position did not go unnoticed. In the debate
that followed, many members commented upon it. Kazi Syed Karimuddin
reminded the Assembly that Dr. Ambedkar had said, "in his own book, that
these principles should be embodied in the Constitution as Fundamental
Rights and that a scheme embodying these principles should be brought into
operation within ten years" (CAD 7: 473). Hussain Imam described these
directives as unnecessary because they were ineffectual and "singularly inop-
erative" (ibid.: 491). The indefatigable K. T. Shah also commented wryly on
how "the course of conversion operates very swiftly with a brain so alert, an
intelligence so sharp, a mind so open to new ideas as that of the learned Doc-
tor" (ibid. 478).

How and why Ambedkar's position on social and economic rights changed
remains a puzzle.[22] In March 1947, he gave strong support to the project of
incorporating such rights in the Constitution. In November 1948, however,
introducing the draft constitution in the Assembly, he provided a reasoned
defense of the eventual outcome without acknowledging that this implied
any sort of withdrawal or retraction. This could be explained, as other such
paradoxes about Ambedkar have been, in terms of the necessity for political compromise, an argument which has derived credence from Ambedkar's
own statement in 1953 that he had drafted the Constitution at the request
of the Congress Party, and was "compelled to incorporate provisions which
I disliked most" (quoted in Rodrigues, 2007: 153). Was this just the political
maneuver of a seasoned politician rather than the undermining of cherished
principles?

This maneuver, if such it was, is suggestive of three tensions at work. The
first of these is the tension between Ambedkar the lawyer and Ambedkar
the pragmatic politician; the second is that between Ambedkar the socialist
and Ambedkar the parliamentary democrat; and the final, perhaps determining, tension is that between Ambedkar's primary cause—Dalit emancipation—and his other constitutional and political concerns. The first tension is
signaled by Ambedkar's challenge, in the initial phase, to the "old lawyers"
to recognize that the constitution-making exercise in India need not merely
borrow from older constitutions but should respond to the new needs of the
time. By time the Assembly's deliberations drew to a close, the pragmatic politician in Ambedkar probably recognized and capitulated to the

intransigent conservatism of the lawyers whose central argument ironically was about the *impracticability* of social rights.

The second tension is reflected in Ambedkar's attempt to synthesize parliamentary democracy with socialism. His memorandum and draft articles on the rights of states and minorities had an entire clause (Clause 4) with seven subclauses spelling out the details of his economic program. These subclauses formed part of a section titled "Remedies Against Invasion of Fundamental Rights" and declared, among other things, that key industries would be state owned and agriculture would be treated as a state industry. In an explanatory note, Ambedkar clarified that the purpose of the clause was to place on the state the obligation of planning for a maximally productive economy; for an equitable distribution of wealth; and for an economy in which, despite state preeminence, every door would not be shut to private enterprise. So important was state socialism that making it constitutional was the only way to secure it against any future alteration by the legislature or the executive. This was therefore an attempt at establishing "State socialism without abrogating Parliamentary democracy *and without leaving its establishment to the will of a Parliamentary democracy*" (Rao, 1967, 2: 101; emphasis added).

As for the third, it is possible that Ambedkar may have had to enter into political compromises, as he simultaneously fought to secure the rights of Dalits and also for social and economic rights for all citizens. On issues relating to the Dalits—especially untouchability and reservations—Ambedkar made impassioned and decisive contributions to the Constituent Assembly's proceedings. It is possible that he may have been compelled to be less inflexible on other issues. What is more than clear is that Ambedkar did not, as Jaffrelot suggests, think of the Directive Principles as a handy dustbin into which to toss Gandhian ideas that he was uncomfortable with[23] (Jaffrelot, 2005: 112–113). This explanation, apart from its unverified attribution of motives, fails to account for the many Articles in this chapter of the constitution. to which Ambedkar's enduring and sincere commitment cannot be doubted, such as the right to livelihood and workers' rights.

Indeed, the story of social and economic rights in India, both before and after independence, may be read as a story of political compromises. In 1931, this appears as a compromise between Gandhi and Nehru: in 1947–1948, as a compromise between Ambedkar and the Congress Party, on the one hand, and the modernizers and the Gandhians on the other. In the early twenty-first century, it reappears as a contest between civil society and state, and between a political agenda of inclusion and an economic agenda of reform. In the Constituent Assembly, the Directive Principles of State Policy emerged as a reliquary, a receptacle to which contentious items were consigned either because they did not meet the exacting standards of legal experts or because they bore a heavy burden of political or religious denomination or because they were matters on which a consensus was practically impossible.[24] The entire list of DPSP was displaced from the chapter on fundamental rights for one or other of these reasons. The provision relating to the Uniform Civil Code, for instance, was clearly a way of writing the long-term goal of such a code into the Constitution to counteract the effect of allowing personal laws but without compromising the constitutional guarantee of religious freedom provided in Article 19 of the Fundamental Rights. The provisions relating to cow protection and prohibition could be read as Gandhian elements but also as modernist embarrassments.[25] If they must be accommodated, this expanding reliquary of good intentions was the only plausible space for them.

In substantive terms, then, the justifications for locating particular provisions in the Directive Principles were fourfold. The first two were arguments about constitutional propriety, while the third and fourth were about practicality. The first characterized these provisions as ideological, and positing ideology in opposition to democracy, suggested that, lacking the necessary political neutrality, these predisposed the polity in a particular ideological direction. As such, giving them the status of rights would undermine the democratic principle by constitutionalizing that which the democratic public should determine for itself. Implicitly suggesting that what could not be settled by consensus should be left to democracy to settle, this argument placed on democracy the burden of too many expectations. This was also a rather expansive conception of the purposes of democracy, given the conditions—of widespread poverty, illiteracy, and underdevelopment—under which it was being instituted.

It is however possible that social citizenship, instead of being conflicted *by* politics, may actually have the potential to transcend politics and enjoy a wide cross-cutting appeal across political boundaries. Recent British experience of the political difficulties that attend the withdrawal of social welfare provision once it has been granted attests to this. As social citizenship came to be viewed as a core element of citizenship, equivalent to the rights to vote and hold property, even the New Right in the United Kingdom found it difficult to reduce the public provision of health and education (King and Waldron,

1988: 417). And yet, the assumption of conflict is pervasive in the debates of the Constituent Assembly. Both the speeches that accompanied the moving of the two most important resolutions at the beginning and conclusion of the Assembly—the Objectives Resolution by Nehru and the Draft Constitution by Ambedkar—implicitly address this prejudice. As he introduced the Objectives Resolution in the Assembly on December 13, 1946, Nehru said:

> We have given the content of democracy in this Resolution and not only the content of democracy but the content, if I may say so, of economic democracy in this Resolution. Others might take objection to this Resolution on the ground that we have not said that it should be a Socialist State. Well, I stand for Socialism and, I hope, India will stand for Socialism and that India will go towards the constitution of a Socialist. . . . But the main thing is that in such a Resolution, if, in accordance with my own desire, I had put in, that we want a Socialist State, we would have put in something which may be agreeable to many and may not be agreeable to some and we wanted this Resolution not to be controversial in regard to such matters. (CAD 1: 62)

The second strand of argument encouraged the making of a distinction between policies and rights. Unlike the first, this was not so much the product of a liberal conscience grappling with socialist predilections, but rather a distinction inspired by a legal and technical understanding of the purposes of a constitutional document. In this understanding, while rights could be constitutionally guaranteed, policies were simply and inherently unsuitable candidates for a constitution. As Ambedkar moved the Draft Constitution on November 4, 1948, his speech brought both these arguments together. Apparently hinting at and repudiating the practice in the Soviet Union, Ambedkar made a formal and legalistic argument, according to which a draft constitution merely provides an institutional framework of governance and should not be invested with any particular ideological or programmatic character. This was nothing if not a contradiction of Ambedkar's own earlier challenge to the lawyers. Following from the first, and suggesting that making programmatic pronouncements would be tantamount to undermining democracy, Ambedkar's second argument rested on the legitimacy of the democratic system.

> The Draft Constitution as framed only provides a machinery for the government of the country. It is not a contrivance to install any particular

party in power as has been done in some countries. Who should be in power is left to be determined by the people, as it must be, if the system is to satisfy the tests of democracy. But whoever captures power will not be free to do what he likes with it. In the exercise of it, he will have to respect these instruments of instructions which are called Directive Principles. He cannot ignore them. He may not have to answer for their breach in a Court of Law. But he will certainly have to answer for them before the electorate at election time. (CAD 7: 41)

The third and fourth arguments—both of a practical nature—centered on the difference between negative and positive state action, suggesting that the protection of the fundamental rights of citizens entailed restraint on the part of the state rather than positive intervention by the state. From this followed the assumption that positive intervention was unaffordable in a resource-poor country and/or unenforceable through the courts. It is now widely acknowledged that the dichotomy between negative and positive rights is a false one, because arguably all rights call for a measure of restraint and some intervention by the state. Even the most classic of negative rights—typically the rights that protect liberty—require an apparatus of policing and courts, instituted and administered by the state, and funded by the taxpayer, to maintain and uphold them. In a sense, then, all rights are positive, and all rights entail costs because the remedies sought against their violation necessarily generate demands upon resources (Holmes and Sunstein, 2000: 43–48). Conversely, even positive rights are sometimes negatively protected, as when the impact of municipal laws of land-use or zoning on the supply or cost-escalation of housing triggers judicial intervention (Michelman, 2007: 24–25). The division between the votaries of negative and positive rights is essentially ideological: frequently expressed as a practical concern about justiciability, it is fundamentally about how much state intervention is acceptable.

In the Constituent Assembly, the Sub-Committee illustrated the distinction between justiciable and non-justiciable rights by arguing that if a citizen's right to liberty was infringed, he could go to a court of law, and the court could determine whether or not the right had in fact been infringed. If, however, a right required "the State to endeavour to secure a decent standard of life for all workers . . . it is as impossible for a worker to prove, as for a court to find, that a general right of this kind has been infringed in a given case" (Rao, 1967, 2: 137).

Other members rejected both the arguments of inadequate resources as well as of enforceability. K. T. Shah disputed the practicability objection, saying that "nothing in practice is practicable until it is tried" (CAD 7: 479). Even the right to compulsory primary education, he said, had been provided for in such a "clumsy, half-hearted and hesitating manner that one wonders whether the framers of this Draft were at all anxious that the curse of ignorance that has rested upon us all these years should be removed at all" (ibid.). He claimed that the same arguments were offered by colonial officials when Gopal Krishna Gokhale had proposed a bill for compulsory primary education. The colonial state refused to bear the burden of spending Rs. 3 crores on education, spread over a ten-year period, but not long after, and without consulting its subjects, spent Rs. 30 crores on the war (CAD 7: 480). Shah also argued that enforceability was a red herring.

> I would lay down that these shall be mandatory, compulsory obligations of the State, which every citizen will have the right to demand should be fulfilled, and if today you think of no sanction . . . then it is up to you to devise something . . . It is either bankruptcy of intelligence if you say that you cannot find a way; or it is really a genuine lack of desire to make good what we have been hoping and striving for. (ibid.)

It remained for Mahboob A. K. Baig Sahib Bahadur to resuscitate the very arguments that had been offered at the beginning of the Assembly's deliberations, viz. that it is inappropriate to include policies in a constitution. By the conclusion of the Assembly's deliberations, Ambedkar's argument—placing the weight of implementation upon the future workings of democracy—was hoist on its own petard. Baig asserted that such principles were undemocratic insofar as they sought to bind political parties of the future to particular political principles. In years to come, he said, political parties with different programs and policies would be seeking election and if one of them got elected on a platform that was antagonistic to the directive principles, what would be the status of the latter? Making a case for the deletion of this chapter on grounds of their incompatibility with parliamentary democracy, he argued:

> I fail to see how this programme can come into the constitution. Either they are fundamental or they are matters of policy. If they are so fundamental that no legislature can interfere with them and have to be placed beyond the purview of the legislature and the executive, they should be

placed somewhere else. In my view, however, these are not fundamental but mere State policy. (ibid.: 489)

Ambedkar responded by clarifying that while the Constitution should contain a vision of economic democracy, it cannot privilege one particular mechanism for accomplishing it. Some people, he said, believed that economic democracy could be brought about through individualism; others through socialism and still others through communism. These differences justified the directive principles remaining open ended, rather than fixed or rigid, in respect of the mechanisms by which economic democracy may be realized within the framework of parliamentary democracy (ibid.: 494).

The decisive criterion in the debate on the Directive Principles was evidently about practicability and enforceability. No member openly contested the value of social and economic rights per se. The disagreements appeared as technical: on the one hand, about whether it is appropriate, in a democracy, to write a programmatic vision into a binding constitutional document; and, on the other, about state capacity to provide these rights on its own or through litigation and court dicta. By the end, it was accepted—with a sense of satisfaction by some and resignation by others—that since these rights were not obligatory, they were unlikely to be implemented. No echo was heard of B. N. Rau's suggestion that in cases where there is a conflict between individual rights and the principles of policy intended to further the general welfare, the latter should prevail.[26]

A Legacy of Conflict

In the years that followed, there was a perpetuation of the construction of the relationship between the fundamental rights and directive principles as inherently adversarial rather than complementary. The Directive Principles, though nonjusticiable, were frequently invoked in judicial opinion, and this was most often the case when some socialist policies of the government, mostly those that conflicted with the fundamental right to property, were challenged in the courts as infringing one fundamental right or another. Some of the earliest confrontations between the executive and the judiciary were in fact about conflicts between the Directive Principles and Fundamental Rights. When the executive essayed policies to further its program of social transformation—such as land reform, the abolition of the *zamindari* (landlordism) system, and even quotas in educational institutions—they invariably ran afoul of the Court. Nehru's premiership witnessed the beginnings of a trend that was further entrenched by his daughter Indira Gandhi: the use of parliamentary powers of constitutional amendment to overturn adverse decisions by the Court. At this time, the executive tended to hold an impatient view of Fundamental Rights as an annoying hindrance in the way of its pursuit of social justice. Nehru famously said:

> If the courts see a contradiction between the Fundamental Rights and the Directive Principles, it is up to Parliament to remove the contradiction and make the Fundamental Rights subserve the Directive Principles of State Policy. (quoted in Austin, 1999: 108)

This trend became increasingly marked in Indira Gandhi's prime ministership, in particular in response to court judgments striking down her "socialist" policies of bank nationalization, the withdrawal of the privy purses, and of course land reform. Once again, this was constructed as a conflict between the judiciary and the Government-in-Parliament. Indira Gandhi sought to overturn the judicial decisions by enacting constitutional amendments, leading to a major confrontation with the judiciary, which, overturning its own earlier judgment,[27] reclaimed supremacy holding that the amending power of Parliament was subject to the Fundamental Rights listed in the Constitution. This was widely interpreted as an affirmation of the supremacy of the Fundamental Rights over the Directive Principles. In another landmark case, *Kesavananda Bharati v. State of Kerala* (1970) the Court held in 1973 that

> ... the fundamental rights themselves have no fixed content, most of them are empty vessels into which each generation must pour its content in the light of its experience ... in building up a just social order it is sometimes imperative that the fundamental rights should be subordinated to directive principles. (para. 1769)

Over time, the battle between the judiciary and the government got embalmed as one between individual rights and the impulse to social justice or equality, with the judicial branch of the state being framed as the conservative champion of the first and the executive branch as the progressive advocate of the second. Even as the hierarchy of rights was being contested, social transformation remained elusive.

If anything defines the National Emergency imposed by Indira Gandhi in 1975, it is the wholly unprecedented suspension of all civil liberties. During this period, a legislative push was given to various constitutional amendments, especially the Forty-Second Amendment, which sought to fundamentally transform the Constitution, ostensibly in a socialist direction. As a prelude to these changes, the Congress Party had instituted a committee under one of its veteran leaders, Dr. Swaran Singh; among the committee's many far-reaching proposals was the recommendation to definitively establish the primacy of the Directive Principles by inserting a new clause into Article 31 (the right to property). By this amendment, no laws intended to implement any of the Directive Principles could be deemed as void on the grounds that they contravened Articles 14, 19, or 31 (the rights to equality, freedom and property, respectively). Other consequential changes included the addition of the word "socialist" to the preamble of the Constitution, and the insertion of a section on Fundamental Duties after the Directive Principles. Much of the elected opposition was in prison at this time, so the debate on the Forty-Second Amendment was joined primarily by members of the Communist Party of India[28] who were vocal in their support of any initiative to give priority to policies furthering the objectives of the Directive Principles.

The duties of citizens had been part of nationalist discourse (as in the writings of Srinivasa Sastri). They had also been emphasized in most of the draft constitutions we have discussed, including and especially the socialist ones. M. N. Roy's ideological origins were reflected in his assertion that "to bear arms for the defence of the commonwealth is a right as well as a responsibility of citizenship" (M. N. Roy, 1944: 1). In keeping with its roots in the tradition of *sarvodaya,* the Socialist Party emphasized the duty of citizens to serve the state and local institutions of governance (Socialist Party, 1948: 30). S. N. Agarwal's Gandhian constitution had likewise made the rights of citizens contingent on the performance of their fundamental duties of faithfulness to the state; the promotion of public welfare through contributing in cash, kind, or labor; and the resisting of exploitation (Agarwal, 1946: 79). In the decades that followed, the discourse of duties had however been largely eclipsed by that of rights.

In the parliamentary debates in the autumn of 1976, few expressed reservations about inverting the conventional hierarchy of rights; those that did, such as V. K. R. V. Rao, essentially spoke on behalf of the individual liberties and rights that might be endangered by allowing policies of social justice the unfettered power to trump these. (Lok Sabha Debates, October 27, 1976: 29) The repudiation of this view took the form of a novel argument of democracy, rather different from the one that had been articulated in the Constituent

Assembly. There, as we saw, many members were averse to including a policy orientation in the Constitution, on the grounds that it was inappropriate for the founders of the Constitution to decide what sorts of policies were in the public interest; being a matter of political negotiation, it was for the democratic public to express its own will. The parliamentary debate of 1976 was an unlikely time and space for democratic argument, for the civil liberties of citizens were in a state of suspension, the people had—in Brechtian vein—been all but dissolved, and all dissidents including many opposition parliamentarians were in prison. Nevertheless, the rationale now offered for privileging the Directive Principles was that these represented the rights of society as a whole, while the Fundamental Rights stood for the rights of individuals. As such, "the larger interests of the masses must take precedence over the narrow individual needs."[29] This was a majoritarian argument that was not dependent on any democratic process for its validation; it was perfectly legitimate for this to be decided, not by the electorate but by an elite that had forsaken the democratic path in the name of the people.

It is only quite recently that the fundamental rights and directive principles have settled into a relationship of complementarity. A spate of judgments, sometimes citing judgments on unenumerated rights from the United States Supreme Court, has generated a substantial body of case law reading several rights—to privacy and legal aid, health care and housing, clean air and water, and so forth—into the right-to-life provisions of Article 21. Courts have even emphasized the complementarity between these two parts of the Constitution saying that they "are not supposed to be exclusionary of each other" (*State of M.P. v. Pramod Bhartiya*, 1992).[30]

The initiatives for social transformation that represented social and economic rights as necessarily violating or at least conflicting with civil and political rights turned out to generate more heat than social justice. The faux socialism of the Emergency did appear to overturn the balance in the name of a progressive social agenda, but its rhetorical power far outpaced any substantive social gains. The suspension of civil liberties during the Emergency created a renewed consciousness about the importance of civil and political rights, the restoration of which has made them pretty much irreversible. The revival of social rights in the twenty-first century has little in common with the hoary battles of the 1960s and 1970s, when the executive—as the champion of the underdog—confronted the judiciary that it sought to represent as the enemy of the people, the defender of privilege. Over time, and through its increasingly interventionist role in public interest litigation, the judiciary has sought and secured an unparalleled popular legitimacy, becoming the ultimate champion of the public interest, even if it is sometimes accused of overreach by the other two branches of the state.

Social and economic rights everywhere—including in India—remain poor cousins of civil and political rights. This hierarchy of rights—civil and political on top, social and economic below—appears invincible, though it continues to be frequently attacked. However, the very fact that the grammar of rights is being constantly reinvented through struggle is in itself a testimony to the power of an idea of citizenship in which the core mainstream rights—civil and political—are simultaneously the weapons of achieving the rights on the margins and of the marginal populations, as well as the object or that which is sought to be undermined.

6

Social Citizenship in Neoliberal Times

What, if anything, can citizenship mean in the presence of deep social inequalities? Even as citizenship professes equality as its foundational essence, we know it to be the deceitful purveyor of a misleading promise, a sentiment famously captured in Anatole France's wry quip about the majestic equality of the law forbidding "rich and poor alike to sleep under bridges, to beg in the streets, and to steal bread."[1] Citizenship appears as either Janus-faced or internally conflicted as it plays these two fundamentally opposing roles: committing to undermine inequality, on the one hand, and presenting inequality as legitimate, on the other. This is the central contradiction that lies at the heart of the theory of citizenship—usually apprehended as formal civic and political equality—and its practice. Full inclusion—civic, political, social, economic, and cultural—is the condition of full citizenship. Anything less diminishes it.

Social citizenship is generally seen as a way of mediating this contradiction. The public provision of welfare—whether through social and economic rights or through progressive and sometimes redistributive policies associated with welfare states[2]—can be a plausible way of bridging this gap. Although the author of the idea, T. H. Marshall, had defined social citizenship in terms of rights,[3] in the canonical welfare states of northern and western Europe in the twentieth century it has been through social policy rather than rights that social citizenship has been achieved. Such policies sought to provide education, healthcare, work, unemployment insurance, and social security.[4] Their negotiation of the usually rough road from norm to policy was skillful, and the globally accepted doctrine of the progressive realization of social and economic rights—which, as the previous chapter showed, resulted in a divorce between civil, political, and cultural rights, on the one hand, and social and economic rights on the other—did not prevent these states from designing and successfully implementing an elaborate institutional architecture to provide for the material conditions that form the basis of social citizenship and the acceptance of people as full members of a society. According constitutional status to social and economic rights, as in Brazil and South Africa, is a relatively new idea.

There has been an enduring presumption—fueled substantially by the commanding role assumed by the state in the 1950s in the governance of the economy and by its professions of socialism—that India is a welfare state, even if a (literally) poor cousin of the European original. The miserable failure of this state in achieving its objective is generally attributed to poor state capacity rather than lack of intent,[5] for the nascent project of social citizenship in independent India was distinguished by a strong rhetorical commitment, even if rather little by way of social policy and—given the constitutional compromise between fundamental rights and directive principles—nothing by way of social rights. Curiously, however, as the Indian economy has over the last two decades moved in a neoliberal direction, albeit with the state actively playing a promotional role in facilitating capitalism, the assertion and legislation of social and economic rights appears to have acquired a new impetus. The paradox is that social citizenship was at its weakest when the socialist rhetoric was at its peak, and has gained momentum in a policy environment that emphasizes state withdrawal from public provisioning. How and why these rights have emerged on the Indian political landscape in a time of ascendant neoliberalism[6] and the increasing commodification of public services, and what their substantive contribution might be to a putative project of social citizenship, is the subject of this chapter.

Even as international pronouncements insist that there is no hierarchy between civil and political rights, on the one hand, and social and economic rights (henceforth SERs) on the other, the latter have remained marginal to the mainstream of human rights discourse and enforcement. This is in no small part due to the vagueness and ambiguity of the idea of "progressive realization" and the difficulty in determining when particular state actions are or are not in conformity with the covenant. The European Social Charter of 1996—essentially a draft agreed upon in 1960, designed to ensure respect for social and economic rights among its members, but drawn up before issues like feminism and racial equality had come to inflect human rights discourse—left considerable choice to member states to choose the obligations they wished to take on. It is only the revised Social Charter that incorporates provisions on the right to housing, freedom from poverty, disability rights, and women's rights (O'Cinneide, 2009: 4–5).

Unlike civil and political rights—regarded as being integral to the civic status and therefore conferred and enjoyed equally by all citizens—SERs are deeply contentious on at least four counts. First, there is the question of how expansive or restrictive the scope of SERs should be and which goods must minimally be provided by the state to give content to social citizenship. Second, there is the vexed question of determining who the proper bearers of these rights are, how universal a social right should be, and whether or not it is appropriate or desirable to limit such rights to those who need them rather than to the entire population in a society. Should, for instance, services like health care be universal in coverage or restricted to the poor, or indeed universally available to all but free only for the poor? Third, there is a debate about whether the state must guarantee equality of income, or confine itself to providing equality of opportunity. Finally, there is the all-important question that the electorate of every democratic polity grapples with periodically— how should social rights be financed? This has an impact on relationships between citizens, especially those who bear the burdens of redistributive taxation and those who benefit from it. A social right that is limited only to those who need it can be stigmatizing, and therefore diminish the solidary aspect of citizenship. There is an abiding tension here: in normative terms, social provision is legitimately seen as a moral imperative of substantive citizenship, which is seriously incomplete in the presence of social inequality. However, in the realization of this normative ideal through policy, the redistributive taxation that is necessary for social rights is presumed to diminish the sense of civic community and solidarity that must form the foundation for the practice of citizenship. Each of these questions is differently addressed in different regimes of social citizenship, and some of them inflect contemporary

Indian debates on social rights. The Indian debate on reservations (quotas/ affirmative action), for instance, is centrally about equality of outcome versus equality of opportunity. The discussions around the right to food, likewise, are enmeshed in an apparently intractable dispute between the advocates of universalism and those of the targeting of public provisioning.

As India moves toward constitutionalizing some social and economic rights, it is important to remember that this is, in comparative constitutionalism, a relatively recent phenomenon. Popularly (and appropriately) called the "Citizen's Constitution," the Brazilian Constitution of 1988 has a most comprehensive listing of social rights, including "education, health, work, leisure, security, social security, protection of motherhood and childhood, and assistance to the destitute" (Article 6).[7] It also includes, among others, guarantees of a national minimum wage, unemployment insurance, labor rights, retirement pensions, no discrimination in hiring and wages for handicapped workers, and rights for domestic servants (Article 7). It declares the "eradication of poverty" to be one of the fundamental objectives of the republic (Article 3). The South African Constitution of 1996[8] also provides for justiciable SERs, though it implicitly creates two categories of these (Pieterse, 2007: 806). The first, which brooks no limitations, provides entitlements to basic nutrition, shelter, health care services, and social services, among others. In respect of the second—which includes the right to have access to adequate housing, health care, sufficient food and water, and social assistance—the state's obligations are limited in ways that are reminiscent of the Indian Constitution's Directive Principles. On many of these, such as housing, the state is tasked only with adopting "reasonable legislative and other measures, within its available resources, to achieve the progressive realization of this right" (Article 26).

In its pronouncements since the 1980s, India's Supreme Court has read a variety of unenumerated[9] rights into the Constitution through an expansive interpretation of Article 21 that guarantees the right to life. These include the right to live with human dignity, the right to livelihood, the right to shelter, the right to a pollution-free environment, the right to privacy, the right not to be subjected to bonded labor, and the right to medical aid. This chapter provides an account of the incomplete—some might say incipient—project of social citizenship in India before and after the economic reforms of the 1990s, presenting these as two distinct regimes of social citizenship in India. It also offers an explanation for the emergence of social and economic rights at the present juncture, focusing on the rights to work, education, and food in particular. Finally, it analyzes the emerging regime of social citizenship, in terms of its substantive content, the prospects for its realization, and the extent to which it does (or not) represent a qualitative departure from older forms of social provisioning, taking (or not) India to the threshold of social citizenship. Does the use of the language of rights imply a substantive rather than rhetorical advance over the older language of state paternalism and official largesse? What are the prospects for social rights helping to advance the project of citizenship by providing a basis for greater social integration and solidarity?

The Illusion of Social Citizenship in the "Socialist Pattern of Society"

The pre-reform regime of social citizenship in India bore the strong imprint of the state, and welfare was cast in the mold of official largesse. Despite the powerful intellectual links between Indian policy makers and Fabian and other socialist circles in Britain[10] at the time, the Indian project of what may loosely be called welfare was untouched by any of the contemporary debates on the subject, whether that between equality of outcome and equality of opportunity, or between selectivity and universalism in social benefits. At its best, it was about relieving absolute poverty, which Indira Gandhi, then prime minister, famously described, at the United Nations Conference on the Human Environment in 1972, as "the worst polluter."

The first feature of this regime of social citizenship was the argument of underdevelopment that it offered as an alibi for the denial of welfare. Welfare was unaffordable for the foreseeable future because India simply lacked the material base of economic development to make this possible. As an infant state, India's primary objective was to increase the national wealth through centralized economic development planning conducted in five-year cycles.[11] The first three plans (covering the formative years from 1951–1966) paid ritual obeisance to the Directive Principles of State Policy. While the first plan merely affirmed the importance of citizen participation in the process of planning, the next two plans enunciated the doctrine of "the socialist pattern of society," the historically specific character of which—neither fixed and rigid, nor dogmatic and doctrinaire[12]—was repeatedly emphasized, possibly to obviate odious comparisons with the Soviet Union.[13] Though the classic welfarist themes of inequality of incomes, employment, health, education,

housing, and social welfare appear recurrently in these plans, there is a palpable ideological distance between the philosophy of the welfare-state in, say
Britain, and that embodied in India's early plans.

For India, then, the fundamental imperative was to increase the social
product and enlarge the national economic pie before a decent standard of
living for all could be accomplished. The overarching objective was economic
development, with welfare goals being largely subsidiary—either subsumed
within it, or made contingent upon it, or simply rendered instruments of it.
An important exception to this was of course the project of land reform, to
which the Congress had long been committed. After independence, though
the first two plans provided for tenancy reform and ceilings on landhold-
ings, the reforms failed due to resistance and patchy implementation by the
states, not least because of the capture of local Congress organizations by
landed interests.[14] The contradiction, as Frankel characterizes it, was between
the twin goals of rapid industrialization and gradual agrarian reform (2006:
113)—and it was the former that won out.

Marshall had viewed education as the prime instrument of mitigating the
inequality of status expressed in differences in manners and he had therefore
defended education both as a social *right* that held the key to equality of opportunity as well as a *duty* for everyone to develop their potential as an individual
and a citizen of a democracy (Marshall, [1950] 1992: 36–39). India's planners,
by contrast, envisioned education purely instrumentally, as "a determining
influence on the rate at which economic progress is achieved and the benefits
which can be derived from it" (Government of India, 1956a: ch. 23, ¶1, with
implications neither for the promotion of equality nor for the self-realization
of citizens. Being contingent on an enlargement of the social product, the distributive project had necessarily to be deferred for a long time to come. In the
shorter run, social services were simply unaffordable. The argument of scarce
resources justified circumscribing social welfare to encompass only especially
vulnerable groups and those in need of special assistance.

The second distinguishing feature of this social citizenship regime was
its unselfconscious adoption of a charity perspective on poverty. Despite the
domination of the state in both the political and economic spheres, there was
a separation in the norms that governed the citizen–state relationship. The
political was constituted as the proper realm of rights, citizenship, and formal
equality. As the social and economic aspects of people's lives fell within the
economic domain, not subject to the rule of formal equality that obtained

in the political and civic spheres, the absence of rights implied the absence of obligations, and the predominance of the language of relief, charity, and alleviation.

Philosophically, needs and rights represent alternate ways of grounding claims to welfare, and the Indian path was a weakly articulated form of the first.[15] Needs may appeal to public authority, invoking the idea of justice and advancing a moral claim to the fulfillment of the absolute minimum required for physical well-being. States, inspired by philanthropic benevolence, may respond to such appeals by assuming altruistic purposes. Needs can equally plausibly form the basis of a plea for charity, which generates no moral requirement to assist (though it would be virtuous to do so) and places no obligation on institutions or governments. Neither as a claim to justice nor as a plea for charity does the idea of needs generate *rights*.[16] Rights carry the mandate of enforceability and thereby demand that the state recognize both the legal obligation and the moral imperative of bearing responsibility for its citizens, or else risk its legitimacy and authority by failing to do so. Notwithstanding its use of an idiom of need-based justice, the limited philosophy of welfare intervention in India has in practice been embedded in ideas of charity and state paternalism. This typically yields reliefs (such as drought relief or poverty relief) that are not normally subject to political negotiation. Even as welfare appears to stand outside the domain of political contestation, electoral populism—from promises of subsidized rice and clothes in the 1970s, to free water and electricity to farmers in the 1980s, to television sets and notebook computers today—is projected and received as a form of welfare, even if it is part of a top-down regime of political incentives in elections, and entrenches further the relationship between the citizen and her elected representatives as one of giver and receiver, benefactor and beneficiary.

If social citizenship is a matter of state largesse, is it citizenship at all or—in its construction of categories of exception for special provision—the opposite? The categories that populated the political sociology of the colonial state—depressed classes, tribes, and minorities—were now supplemented with nonascriptive categories of those whose claims to welfare were particularly compelling and could not be ignored. Such a construction of categories for exceptional provision is surprising in a country where the absolute number of the poor in 1993–1994—320 million, according to official figures—was more or less equivalent to the *entire* population of India in 1950.[17] Reliance on the creation of categories of exception to classify different sections of the population for purposes of delivering welfare goods is the third characteristic of the preliberalization regime of social citizenship. Do such categories make for better targeted welfare interventions, or do they subvert the very idea of citizenship?

The propensity of formal citizenship to legitimize and entrench inequality[18] is reinvented every day in social and political practice, not least through such a severance of welfare entitlements from the status of citizenship. This sentiment inflects the Indian strategy of special rights for special groups, albeit in the name of substantive citizenship. The assumption underlying such special provisioning was that social and economic rights would, by supplementing formal citizenship rights, eventually bridge the gap between the formal and the real. However, not being universal, social and economic provisioning never took the form of rights at all; and did not attach to citizenship in the way in which civil and political rights were integrally linked to it.

In the 1950s, the objects of social welfare were defined as "women and children, family welfare, youth welfare, physical and mental fitness, crime and correctional administration and welfare of the physically and mentally handicapped" (Government of India, 1956a, ch. 29, ¶3). In the late 1970s, they were expanded to encompass special subplans for the scheduled castes and scheduled tribes. In addition, many special programs were devised for small and marginal farmers, agricultural laborers, rural artisans, women, children, and young people in the rural areas, and the elderly. The program content ranged from self-employment or wage employment schemes to schemes providing housing or well-construction subsidies to special area programs such as those for drought-prone regions. The subsequent proliferation in the special categories of entitlement made welfare provisioning administratively complex and politically controversial.

The definition of "social welfare" in terms of defined categories of the population continues to inform the governmental architecture of welfare even into the present. In the mid-1980s, the Ministry of Welfare was bifurcated into a Department of Women and Child Development and a Department of Welfare (encompassing divisions relating to the Scheduled Castes, the Scheduled Tribes, Minorities, and Backward Classes). In 1998, senior citizens and persons with disabilities were added; women and children and tribal affairs were removed to separate ministries; and the nomenclature of the Ministry was changed to the Ministry of Social Justice and Empowerment. Social welfare remains emphatically something to which a citizen can only be entitled if s/he belongs to an officially defined category of disadvantage. From being confined to rather restrictively defined categories at first, the idea of welfare was thus gradually made more extensive, but as its expansion served to make citizenship less rather than more universal, the separation from civic status was only reinforced. Thus, the creation of the Below and Above Poverty Line categories in 1997 were designed precisely to restrict a previously universal (however poorly so) national food security subsidy.

This severance of welfare from civic status entrenched the prior separation between civil and political rights, on the one hand, and social and economic rights, on the other. All citizens are entitled to civil and political rights. Those who possess some additional entitlements to social and economic provisioning are also formal citizens in this sense. However, their enjoyment of such provisioning is derivative of, and conditional upon, their placement in particular categories. The ostensible rationale of these categories is that greater substance will be given to their equal civic status through socioeconomic provisioning. In reality, the creation of such categories of exception with the ostensible objective of facilitating the conditions of substantive citizenship actually works as a strategy of what Marshall called "class abatement," for it suggests the presence of two mutually reinforcing forms of separation: that between *types of rights* (civil/political and social/economic) and that between *social groups* (those that are entitled to social and economic provisioning and those that are not). The irony is that those who are not eligible for special forms of social and economic provisioning are effectively well provided without needing to be placed in special boxes marked "deserving"; and those who hold special entitlements to social and economic goods do not have the minimal conditions for the enjoyment of even their civil and political rights.

The fourth and final characteristic of this social citizenship regime was the construction of the citizen of new India as a duty-bearing rather than a rights-bearing individual. Unlike late colonial India, where the chief duty of the citizen was to resist the state, the citizen of free India must be a productive citizen. In an extremely popular book for young people (which sold half a million copies in the 1940s),[19] Minoo Masani sought to educate the young on the problems of India (poverty, starvation, low agricultural productivity, illiteracy, and unemployment) and the best way in which India's resources could be used to produce more steel, generate more electricity, start cooperative farms, and develop the country. Speaking rhetorically for the reader, he asked:

Do this, do that—and India will be a paradise of plenty. Which is all very well, but who is going to get all this done, you wonder. Yes, *who?* . . .

My answer, in case you'd like to know, is "YOU." Yes, you, Young Sir, and you, Little Lady, you alone can fit together the odd pieces of the puzzle with which this book started. You alone can make a lovely picture out of them. After all, this is *your* country—or it's going to be—and if *you* don't, who d'you think will? (Masani, 1940: 151)[20]

In this period, civic duty is defined as contributing to making the nation strong and economically self-reliant. The chief protagonist of the epic Hindi film of the 1950s, *Mother India,* was Radha, a rural woman who struggles in the face of poverty and indebtedness to bring up her children. In this film, the theme of the land as a nourishing and nurturing mother-force is transposed on to the nation as a whole. Radha persuades an entire village migrating to escape the drought to stay back, by simply admonishing them for abandoning their mother. When there is finally a good harvest, we see an aerial visual of the harvested sheaf forming a map of India. There is an unambiguous equation between Radha (adored by her children), the land and the nation: they are all expressions of the idea of the mother and the motherland.[21]

Radha's struggles are woven into a larger narrative of nation-building and national progress, with an implicit exhortation to work hard to regenerate the land, for even land condemned as fallow can be retrieved by hard work and made productive. Self-sufficiency in foodgrain production being a symbol of national pride, hard work and relentless toil are an obligation to Mother India, not simply a duty to one's own family. As time passes, the symbols of prosperity are not merely an abundance of cattle and green fields, but also the machines—tractors and earthmovers—seen in the opening frame of the film, thus melding the narrative of the parallel progress of agriculture and industry.

In the policy discourse of the time, likewise, the tasks of nation-building and economic development required that all shoulders be put to the wheel, with everyone contributing their bit to the task of nation-building. "With so much lost ground to recover, to advance rapidly the nation needs unity, co-operation in all fields, and a high spirit of endeavour" (Government of India, 1956a: ch. 23, ¶49). There is a notable discursive continuity here with the stirring tenor of participation that characterized the struggle for freedom. The tens of thousands who submitted themselves to state violence, incarceration, and injury in that movement were sustained by their faith in the promise of freedom, however delayed its gratification. Popular participation found expression in the idiom of voluntary sacrifice, driven by the sentiments of nationalism and national duty. The same logic, albeit mobilized and top-down, informed the question of the realization of citizens' rights after independence: now too a sacrifice was demanded, through a similar strategy of the mobilization of people in a common purpose.

> The problem is to create a milieu in which *the small man* who has so far had little opportunity of perceiving and participating in the immense possibilities of growth through organised effort is *enabled to put in his best in the interests of a higher standard of life for himself and increased prosperity for the country. In the process, he rises in economic and social status.* . . . (ibid., ch. 2, ¶3; emphasis added)

While the first fruits of freedom, in the form of civil and political rights, had been realized, the fuller enjoyment of social and economic benefits had to await the enlargement of the social product. Only if everybody cooperated in its enhancement could a better quality of life for all be eventually assured through a trickle-down effect. The duties of work and productive citizenship continued to trump substantive rights.

This was not however a variant of the evolutionist argument in which rights are historically sequenced, with social and economic rights following civil and political ones, for nowhere in this discourse of delayed gratification is welfare conceived as a right. Even as the imperative of combating poverty was recognized as a moral and ideological objective, its progressive realization was to be accomplished not through legal entitlement, but through social policy. Though the long-term goal remained a reduction in inequalities, with a preeminent role for the state, the primary objective of dirigiste economic policies was to facilitate not redistribution but the accumulation of capital and its alignment with productive technologies for higher levels of economic growth, to eventually achieve self-reliance and obviate dependence on foreign capital. This clearly represented the unfinished nationalist agenda, extending the gains of the recently accomplished project of political nationalism to the economic domain. Nehru's hope that increased national wealth would "trickle down" and so reduce inequalities was no revolutionary project of economic transformation. If anything, "there was a tolerance towards income inequality, provided it was not excessive[22] and could be seen to result in a higher rate of growth than would be possible otherwise" (Chakravarty, 1987:

10). The "socialist pattern of society" was neither about rights nor about equality. An ersatz notion of welfare held out the ever-unredeemed promise of social citizenship.

From Charity Disguised as Welfare to Welfare Disguised as Rights

The 1990s initiated a dramatic change in language, a modest change in practice, but arguably little change in the basic philosophy of welfare in India. The earlier expectation that planning for growth and development would eventually trickle down made it necessary to devise poverty alleviation programs—mostly through employment generation works—and special programs of relief for those afflicted by drought or location. None of these strategies aimed to address social inequality per se and the Indian socioeconomic landscape continues today to be characterized by endemic hunger and malnutrition, unacceptably high levels of illiteracy, disease and ill-health, lack of housing, sanitation, drinking water, and above all work.

India's poor performance on human development indicators[23] cohabits uneasily with its impressive performance on economic indicators. The reforms initiated in 1991 led to dramatically higher growth rates, sustained for the last many years at around 9 percent, and giving rise to labels like "India Rising" and "India Shining." Curiously, this time of neoliberal ascendance has also been a period in which many social and economic rights have come to be legislated, and the air is thick with many more such rights signaled in activist slogans as well as judicial pronouncements. At least one of these (education) has made the transition from the Directive Principles of State Policy to the Fundamental Rights, some others have become statutory rights, and yet others have received judicial recognition. Each has been born of an extensive, sustained and widespread mobilization by civil society organizations. In each of these, further, the higher judiciary has played a crucially important role. A new regime of social citizenship is apparently being inaugurated, in an ideological environment and material circumstances that are not generally associated with such concerns.

The first characteristic of the preceding regime of social citizenship was, as we saw, the arguments of underdevelopment and unaffordability offered as an alibi for withholding welfare. In prosperous times, this argument can have little purchase. If anything, the presence of Indian billionaires who figure on the lists of the world's richest individuals,[24] and the aspirations of the nation as a global economic superpower, makes abysmal poverty aesthetically and morally offensive. Despite this, the cost of two of India's most ambitious programs of economic rights—the right to work and the (yet to be legislated) right to food—have been the subject of impassioned contestation, within government and outside it,[25] centered on the question of their affordability. The right to work in the form of an employment guarantee scheme for rural India, initially limited to 200 districts, was subsequently extended to the entire country, while the coverage and costs of the right to food are currently under debate. Even so, the social sector expenditure of the central government—including health, education, water, sanitation, labor, and special programs for disadvantaged groups—has hovered between a mere 0.95 and 1.15 percent of GDP in the period from 1990–1991 to 2000–2001.[26] As the upper and middle classes of Indian society have been less than enthusiastic about these programs,[27] a cynical interpretation of their acceptance might suggest a combination of embarrassment at the spectacle of 250–300 million poor people in an economy marked by unparalleled consumerism, and the imperatives of a global image, particularly one that is frequently subjected to unflattering comparisons with China. Foreign direct investment being a key component of this growth, an attractive shop window for a nation should be one that does not reflect the blemish of poverty.

The second shift registered in the new regime of social citizenship is that from charity to rights. Both before and after economic reform, the political domain has been the home of the idea of formal equality. The contest between the rival doctrines of equality of outcomes and equality of opportunity has been confined to this sphere and expressed somewhat unconventionally in the idiom of caste politics rather than economic opportunity. Over time, mediated by democracy, the political has become a domain in which some widening and deepening of democracy has taken place. The widening of the social base of democracy has occurred through the politics of the backward classes; the deepening has been the result of a constitutional initiative to empower the bodies of local governance. In these somewhat more democratic times, claims to welfare have come to be expressed in the vocabulary of rights. The jurisprudence of welfare uses this language, and the policy response is also strikingly receptive to it. This has been seen as "a victory of sorts" for Indian democracy, showing that "the underprivileged majority is not completely marginalized in this elitist political system" (Dreze, 2010: 511). At the same time, the use of the language of rights in a context marked by the pursuit of unrestrained economic growth, with little evidence of pro-poor policy concern, suggests the plausibility of a class abatement thesis.[28] Rights, especially social rights, with formidable obstacles to their swift realization, can furnish a compelling legitimation of inequality.

The third characteristic of the contemporary regime of social citizenship is that while older categories of beneficiaries endure, they are sometimes sought to be finessed and at other times expanded, with a variety of public goods attaching to them. While the most visible and politically contentious addition was that of the Other Backward Classes (as beneficiaries of reservations policies),[29] the most significant though much less debated such effort entailed the identification of the poor and the sifting of the poor from the nonpoor. This was attempted through the invention, in 1997, of the categories of Below Poverty Line and its awkward obverse, Above Poverty Line. As categories that are conceptually contentious and impossibly difficult to administer in practice, they are a provocative reminder of the undecided question of who is a citizen. They have etched the defining line between those who may, and may not, be entitled to welfare provision, and are central to contemporary debates in social policy, from conditional cash transfers (CCTs) to the right to food which, as we shall see, is most centrally about the virtues of selective targeting.

Finally, the definitive change that has been wrought is that the citizen is now presented as a rights-bearing agent. Released from the duty to produce, her only duty now is to consume,[30] for consumption fuels the economy and makes India grow globally. Rights are for those who cannot afford consumption. Politics itself—the primary arena for the performance of citizenship, even if only through participation in elections—has been transformed into a televised spectacle for consumption, turning citizens into consumers of "media-ted" political messages that are no less synthetic than advertisements.

What is striking is that the moment of the acknowledgment that the nation can afford to help the poor is also the moment when the responsibility for social assistance has already been transferred and diffused among a multiplicity of agencies, not all of which are a part of the state. The practices of the New Public Management—including the commodification of public services and the application of neoliberal principles to the public sector—are an aspect of this phenomenon, as are Public–Private Partnerships, network governance, and the outsourcing of public services to nongovernmental organizations in the name of decentralization.

The post-reform shift thus takes the form of a split between, on the one hand, citizenly rights assertions (such as the right to work or the right to food) and, on the other, the increasing abrogation of the vocabulary of citizenship in favor of the new lexicon of customers, clients, and users. As the language of governance has become less friendly to citizens and their rights, the patois of citizenship has become more rights-oriented. The shift to a self-denying and self-limiting strategy of state action was prefigured fairly early, from the Eighth Five Year Plan (1992–1997) which explicitly sought to reexamine and reorient the role of government and the process of planning. Signaling the global trend of centralized economies disintegrating, it declared that some of the precepts and practices of the past had now outlived their utility (Government of India, 1992, 1.1.6) and that the role of government should be "to facilitate the process of people's involvement in developmental activities" (ibid., 1.4.47). The reinvention of the state as a facilitator and enabler rather than a doer was accompanied by a sudden discovery of "the people"—not as rights-bearing citizens but as members of "a people's movement" for development. Among the institutional models proposed for such officially mandated participation were those managed by users, stakeholders, and beneficiaries. The plan document spoke of user charges on public services as a form of revenue mobilization, and mentioned public utilities such as irrigation, electricity, water, and higher education as examples of such services. This of course was the language of the times—new public management, participation, and decentralization—as the world (and its bank) revisited the issue of the role of the state in a changing world.[31] As the developed world, led by Thatcher and Reagan and inspired by Milton Friedman, turned its back on the decommodification of public goods, developing countries were enjoined to act likewise. In India, the commodifying impulse of the new governance reforms resulted in the franchising of many public services, including in the form of public–private partnerships, and effected a transition from beneficiary to customer and client. Over the last two decades, this has created a more stratified social universe populated by visible and duly labeled beneficiaries, clients, customers, and citizens—and a vast sea of invisible others.

The emergence of a rights discourse at this particular point in historical time is intriguing. In other historical contexts, the explanation for the emergence of the idea of citizenship under capitalism has been that citizenship helps to assuage the tension between capitalism and democracy, with democratic struggle replacing and even precluding the class struggle. On the other hand, citizenship may legitimize, rather than mitigate, the inequalities of social class, as it eliminates social conflict and seeks to incorporate the working class. The deployment of the language of social rights at this point in India's economic history lends itself to similar interpretation, with the language of welfare becoming more strident as the audacity of the state and the rapaciousness of capital grow. The difference is that in India it is the assertion of social and economic rights, rather than the civil and political rights of citizenship, that coincide with capitalist development. Comparatively speaking, the conditions under which social citizenship rights emerged in different countries vary enormously. In the Soviet Union and the other former communist states of eastern Europe, for instance, SERs were never in doubt, and hence the chief objective of civil society mobilization in this region through the 1980s was to reclaim civil and political rights.

The central questions however are about the content of these new social rights. How universal are they, and indeed how realizable? Are the legal or constitutional sanctions they have been given adequate guarantees of their realization? Does the move from the rhetoric of welfare to the rhetoric—and some legislation—of rights indicate that the goal of social policy is now to mitigate social inequality, or merely to alleviate poverty? We approach these questions through the experience of two rights—the right to education, which has already been constitutionalized and legislated; and the right to food, which, while it is yet to find legal expression, has brought to the fore many of the normative concerns that bedevil the question of social citizenship.

A Right to Food?

Two thousand five hundred children die of malnutrition every day in India.[32] Ranked 67 out of 84 countries on the Global Hunger Index 2010, India is home to an astonishing 42 percent of the world's underweight children and 31 percent of its stunted children. Between 1990 and 2008, the prevalence of underweight children and the rate of under-fives mortality fell from 60 to 44 percent and 12 to 7 percent, respectively. However, between 1998–1999 and 2005–2006, the percentage of children under three years who were underweight declined only from 43 percent to 40 percent (International Institute for Population Sciences, 2007: 273). The Global Hunger Index of 1990 characterized India's condition as "extremely alarming." The Index of 2010 shows that a marginal improvement has taken India to the superior category of "alarming," though its ranking still remains lower than Rwanda, Mozambique, Burkina Faso, and Sudan, among others (International Food Policy Research Institute, 2010). "How," asks Lawrence Haddad, "can India move away from the Dr. Jekyll and Mr. Hyde scenario of being an economic powerhouse and nutrition weakling?" (IDS, 2009: 1).

Although chronic hunger and malnutrition, even starvation, have been in the public eye since at least the mid-1980s when there was a famine situation in some districts of the state of Odisha, food security still remains an elusive and contested goal. As the draft food security bill has given up the ghost of universal provision, the search now is for ways of making the targeted version as inclusive as possible. In what follows, I provide a brief background to India's steady, though yet unfulfilled, move in recent years toward a right to food.

India's experiment with publicly funded and provided food security has undergone major policy and discursive shifts in the years since independence. The Public Distribution System (PDS) has its origins in the system of rationing introduced in 1939 in the course of WWII. This was abandoned in 1947, with a new scheme being enacted in 1950 to distribute foodgrains to the people. The PDS is a form of rationing that provides households with selected essential commodities—such as wheat, rice, sugar, and kerosene—at subsidized rates and in specified quantities. In the early days, since domestic production was too low to be able to meet need, this was mostly grain imported from the United States under the PL-480 program. In the 1960s, to contend with food scarcity induced by a terrible drought and price instability, the scope of the PDS was widened to make it near universal. The next decade was one of plentiful production in which the buffer stocks procured by the government were used not only for distribution through the PDS, but also in employment programs for which compensation was offered in kind. This meant that the PDS was effectively incorporated into the larger strategy for poverty alleviation (Swaminathan, 2000: 11).

In the 1990s, the PDS saw a simultaneous increase in stocks and a fall in distribution, as the gap between market prices and those of the PDS narrowed. In 1992, the Revamped PDS was launched primarily for remotely located areas with special needs, such as drought-prone, hill, or tribal areas. It was reinvented in 1997 when an altogether new categorization effected a deuniversalization of public food provisioning, justified by the need to more effectively target the needier sections of the population, an enterprise encouraged by the World Bank. This took the form of using an income poverty criterion to differentiate between those who were above the poverty line (APL) and those below it (BPL). Not only was the PDS then recalibrated to provide a higher quantity of foodgrains at lower prices to BPL households, a third category called Antyodaya was also introduced in 2001 for "the poorest of the poor" or the destitute whose entitlements would be further subsidized. About 40 percent of BPL households got designated as eligible for the Antyodaya Anna Yojana (or the Cereals Scheme for the Poorest of the Poor). Above Poverty Line households would be entitled to a smaller quantity of foodgrains at no subsidy whatever.

In practice, there were egregious errors of wrongful inclusion and exclusion in each of these categories, with large numbers of "ghost BPL cards"—in some states, there were more cards than households. The differential levels of provisioning, as well as the differential pricing and subsidy levels for different categories of the population also proved to be ineffective. The truly needy frequently could not access these for want of formal entitlements and/or resources; the delivery systems were weak and full of leakages and corruption, with a high percentage of food finding its way to the open market; the storage infrastructure in the states was inadequate and unhygienic; the states with the largest number of poor often did not lift their quotas from the central government; and to make matters worse the government actually exported grain, at virtually BPL price levels, instead of using it in the multiple other welfare schemes in existence. The Planning Commission itself estimated that 58 percent of the subsidized foodgrain that left the central pool did not reach those below the poverty line (Government of India, 2005: foreword), but was either siphoned off along the chain of supply or else diverted to APL households (ibid: ii). Essentially, a system meant to keep the rural poor out of acute hunger ended up benefiting the nonpoor in urban areas, and also apparently the cattle of the more developed countries. Thus, the famous Dharavi slum in Mumbai, with a population of over one million, could produce only 141 BPL cards, making their poverty an official fiction (Swaminathan, 2000: 97).

The Saxena Committee Report confirmed earlier research findings that widespread errors had occurred in previous censuses, so that 61 percent of poor households were misclassified as nonpoor (errors of exclusion) while 25 percent of nonpoor households were included in the category of the poor (errors of inclusion), and found to be in possession of BPL or Antyodaya cards (Government of India, 2009.: 20). On the other hand, moneylenders in the poorest districts of eastern India typically had over 400 BPL cards in their custody, as collateral for extortionate loans.[33] The Saxena Committee recommended the "automatic inclusion" of destitute households, designated primitive tribal groups, single women-headed households, households headed by disabled or underage persons, homeless households, and households with any bonded laborer. For the rest, it laid down guidelines for a survey, providing a set of criteria for identifying the poor. Overall, the Committee supported the principle of universalism even as it recognized the importance of correctly identifying the poor.

> We respect the view that all basic entitlements should be universal. We believe that the Directive Principles of State Policy in the Constitution should never be compromised or undermined; instead they need to be realized, strengthened and further taken forward. Food for all, health for all, education for all, work for all—these should be taken as the bottom line. The BPL identification exercise should under no circumstances be used to dilute these principles. In no way should it be used to exclude people from their basic rights and needs. (ibid.: 3)

Prospects for legislation on the subject look bright at this moment, though given its present title—the Draft National Food Security Bill—it is clear that this will not be, like education, a fundamental right. Nor, despite a perfunctory nod in the direction of universalism, will it be universal. The objective of the bill is "to ensure public provisioning of food and related measures to enable assured economic and social access to adequate food with dignity, for all persons in the country, at all times, in pursuance of their fundamental right to be free from hunger, malnutrition and other deprivations associated with the lack of food . . ." (National Advisory Council, 2011: 6). It makes special provision for children of all age groups, and for four additional categories of people: *migrants* (so they can get food wherever they are); *destitute persons* (one freshly cooked nutritious meal per day without any charge); *homeless persons and the urban poor* (community canteens where freshly cooked nutritious meals are available); and *emergency and disaster-affected persons* (open feeding centers, accessible and free of charge, for one year). None of these recommendations has yet engaged with the impact of policies of trade liberalization and of the liberalization and deregulation of agriculture that will inevitably have a deleterious impact on food security for the poor (Birchfield and Corsi, 2010: 734–738). But when enacted, the right to food will represent a happy and unusually successful partnership among three entities that are frequently at loggerheads with each other in democracies—the courts, the government, and civil society.

The International Covenant on Economic, Social and Cultural Rights (ICESCR)[34] makes recognition of the right to food by signatory states binding, whether through constitutional or legal enactment or simply through policy. It is one of those rights that are expected to be progressively realized by states, though this is taken to imply that states may remain inactive on account of and till such time as resource constraints persist. They are obliged to take positive steps—such as set targets, legislate and make policy, monitor progress, establish institutional mechanisms, and so on—toward the full realization of the right. They are also expected to disallow retrogressive measures and protect minimum essential levels of access to food (United Nations High Commissioner for Human Rights, 2010: 21–22).

The "progressive realization" clause in the ICESCR reflects the debate in the late '40s around the justiciability of this right. The right to food, described as a "manifesto right" (O'Neill, 1986: 101) was perceived as being difficult to precisely define, in addition to the difficulties of specifying the nature of states' obligations to provide it and of adjudicating claims that it had been violated. Even so, twenty-three countries explicitly recognize the right to food as a human right of individuals. Some, such as South Africa, directly specify it as a universal stand-alone right; others specify it as a right for specific categories of people, such as children; yet others nest it within a broader right to a dignified standard of living. Thirteen countries—including Sri Lanka, Bangladesh, Brazil, and Ghana—incorporate the right, explicitly or implicitly, as a directive principle of state policy. In the Indian Constitution, the state is asked to regard as one of its primary duties "the raising of the level of nutrition and the standard of living of its people and the improvement of public health" (Article 47). An additional thirty-three countries recognize broader rights—such as the right to well-being or an adequate standard of living or a right to development—which are generally considered to include the right to food. This yields a total of fifty-six constitutions in which the right to food is recognized in one form or another (Knuth and Vidar, 2011: 13–22).

The normative specification of the right itself has been transformed over time to specify more precisely what is encompassed by such a right. In its most recent international articulation, the right covers adequacy (in terms of both quantity and quality), availability, and permanent access to food with dignity and in ways that do not infringe the enjoyment of other human rights (Golay, 2009: 11–12).

The right to have regular, permanent and free access, either directly or by means of financial purchases, to quantitatively and qualitatively adequate and sufficient food corresponding to the cultural traditions of the people to which the consumer belongs, and which ensures a physical and mental, individual and collective, fulfilling and dignified life free of fear. (United Nations Economic and Social Council, 2001: 7)

There is a considerable body of jurisprudence around the right to food across the world, which encompasses the question of defining the legal obligations of states and the relation between executive provision of budgetary outlays and judicial oversight of violations; the justiciability of these obligations and whether they imply respecting the right or protecting the right or indeed fulfilling the right to food; the special protections for detainees and indigenous people; and the availability of legal remedies in different countries. In India, a Supreme Court judgment of 1981 *(Francis Coralie Mullin v. The Administrator)* had interpreted the right to life under Article 21 of the Constitution as including "the right to live with human dignity and all that goes along with it, namely, the bare necessities of life, such as adequate nutrition." Two decades later, the People's Union for Civil Liberties (PUCL) filed a petition in the Supreme Court, asking for a writ of *mandamus* to compel the government to provide food for starving citizens in drought-affected areas who were dying even as the granaries of the state were overflowing. Though *People's Union for Civil Liberties v. Union of India & Ors.* (2001) is yet to be finally decided, it has yielded several interim orders that have paved the way for the imminent enactment of a right to food and contributed to this body of jurisprudence. Initially, the petitioners sought to draw the Court's attention to the breakdown of the Public Distribution System and to the inadequacy of drought-relief works, asking it to direct the government to provide employment in drought-affected rural areas and to provide subsidized foodgrains to all households. Gradually, this was expanded to encompass various other issues beyond the strictly food related: e.g., schemes such as the Integrated Child Development Scheme, the National Old Age Pension Scheme, the National Maternity Benefit Scheme, and the Mid-Day Meal Scheme; starvation deaths; employment; and governance issues such as transparency and accountability. A series of court orders followed, of which three may be singled out for particular mention. The first directed all state governments to implement the Mid-Day Meal Scheme, giving every child in primary school a free cooked meal on every school day, including during vacations in areas affected by drought. Those that tarried got reminders, but by 2008, 120 million schoolchildren had begun to get a cooked meal—of however indifferent a quality—at school every day (Right to Food Campaign Secretariat, 2008: 29) which had the additional positive consequence of raising the enrollment of girl children. Second, in 2006 the Court ordered that the Integrated Child Development Scheme—which provides supplementary nutrition, health care, and preschool education for some 60 million children below the age of six years—be universalized with quality, within a time frame. Finally, though a BPL census had just been completed, the widespread concern about irregularities in it made the Court ask the government to frame clear guidelines for the identification of the BPL families.

Above all, of course, since this was a case about the "right to food," the Court reprimanded the central and state governments for the continuance of starvation deaths.

> The anxiety of the Court is to see that the poor and the destitute and the weaker sections of the society do not suffer from hunger and starvation. The prevention of the same is one of the prime responsibilities of the Government—whether Central or the State. How this is to be ensured would be a matter of policy which is best left to the government. All that the Court has to be satisfied and which it may have to ensure is that the foodgrains which are overflowing in the storage receptacles (. . .), and which are in abundance, should not be wasted by dumping into the sea or eaten by the rats. *Mere schemes without any implementation are of no use. What is important is that the food must reach the hungry.* (Supreme Court Order of August 20, 2001; emphasis added. Right to Food Campaign, 2008)

Even as India inches toward food security through legislation, there is a countermovement—almost a Polanyian "double movement"—at work. Official economic policy makers[35] (Mehrotra, 2010) as well as the World Bank (2011) have argued that the Public Distribution System, with its leakages amounting to between 41 and 58 percent of the total outlay, should be reconsidered altogether, and replaced by cash transfers for food, education, and health on the model of Brazil and Mexico. The assumption that the Latin American experience is replicable ignores the fact that these middle-income countries already had the basic social infrastructure—in public systems of education and health, for instance—to implement such programs,[36] and that cash transfers here have supplemented rather than substituted existing forms of welfare provision. The problem of destitution in Latin America is not of the same magnitude as in India, and the fact that these are largely urbanized societies with smaller populations also makes implementation less challenging. Nevertheless, even in Latin America, CCTs have been criticized for incorporating the poor only as beneficiaries of social programs rather than as citizens deserving of basic income transfers as a right of citizenship (Yanes, 2011). In the field of education too, a cross-national UNESCO study has drawn attention to the quality deficit in CCTs, arguing that while they may have positive effects on school attendance and completion of a certain number of years of schooling, in terms of real educational attainment "there is very limited support for the conclusion that CCTs are effective educational instruments, in particular with regards to their ability to increase learning" (Reimers, da Silva, and Trevino, 2006: 10–11).

With respect to food in particular, cash transfers are subject to inflation in a way that food entitlements are not. Equally importantly, cash is subject to misuse, unequal intrahousehold distribution of food, and various possibilities of commercial exploitation. In general, the expectation that cash transfers will replace public services by sending people off, coins jingling in their pockets, to shop for food, health, and education on the market is tantamount to shrugging off public responsibility because it is administratively cumbersome.[37] Handing out cash where the basic conditions for using it—decent schools and health clinics, for example—simply do not exist is unlikely to be helpful.[38] With low levels of financial inclusion; poor access to banking facilities;[39] scarcity of health centers; the propensity of the delivery system to leak like a sieve; and the continuing challenge of "identifying" the poor, cash transfers do not offer an assurance of providing a satisfactory solution for poverty.

The Right to Education

In 2009, India's Parliament passed the Right of Children to Free and Compulsory Education Act, making the right to education—free and compulsory—a fundamental right for all children from age six to fourteen. This education will be free and compulsory, and conducted in a neighborhood school until such time as a child's elementary education (from grade one to eight) is complete. This Act gives effect to the Eighty-Sixth Constitution Amendment Act of 2002, and came into force on April 1, 2010. Despite the lapse of eight years from the passage of the constitutional amendment to the coming into force of the act, the legislation has been widely celebrated as representing the culmination—though, in the view of many, an unsatisfactory climax—of a long and hard-fought struggle to universalize educational provision in India.

Primary school enrollment in India has historically been low, and though it is now estimated that 95 percent children are enrolled in primary schools,[40] it is officially estimated that as many as 10 million children in the six to fourteen age group are not attending or have dropped out of school. The forward linkages with enrollment in secondary and higher education have therefore been weak, with the Gross Enrolment Ratio at these higher levels being 45.5 percent and 26.7 percent respectively. These figures are unsurprising given that, over the last six decades, public investment in education has been abysmally low, even by the standards of developing countries. Not merely access to education but also the quality of it has been deeply problematic. Even as the Human Development Report for 2010 shows that there has been no decline in literacy[41] and education since the 1970s anywhere in the world, the inequality-adjusted Human Development Index[42] shows that India's loss is 41 percent in education and 31 percent in health (2010: 87). The Census of 2011 reports that literacy rates have gone up to 64.8 percent in the aggregate, with 75.3 percent for men, and 53.7 percent for women. In rural India, the overall literacy rate is lower at 58.7 percent, with men being at 70.7 percent and women at just 46.1 percent (Government of India, 2011e).[43]

The challenge of educating a vast unlettered population was apparently well understood by the founders of the Indian Republic. However, despite animated discussion in the Constituent Assembly about whether it should fall within the competence of the central or state governments in the federation, the Constitution did not recognize education as a fundamental right. The word education occurs no less than ten times in the chapter on Fundamental Rights in the Constitution—but it is largely about the rights of religious minorities to manage or buy property for or operate community educational institutions, or for the state to make special provision for "backward" groups to gain access to educational institutions. Here, education merely formed part of other provisions to respect the cultural rights of minorities or redress disadvantage for particular social groups.

Eventually, like so many other claimants to the status of a right, education too found a home in Article 45 of the Directive Principles of State Policy, which enjoins the state "to provide, within a period of ten years from the commencement of this Constitution, for free and compulsory education for all children until they complete the age of fourteen years." For what it is worth, it should be said that this is the only article in the Directive Principles which specifies a time limit, albeit one unheeded for a full fifty-nine years. It was only in 2009, as we shall see, that education was upgraded from its earlier status as a Directive Principle to its new status as a Fundamental Right. In 1976, a constitutional amendment took education from the state list to the concurrent list[44] with a view to giving the central government a greater role in the area.

The real impetus for a right to education came with a landmark judgment[45] of the Supreme Court, relating to higher education, and emerging from the Public Interest Litigation jurisdiction of the apex court. In the *Unni Krishnan* case, the Court sharply reprimanded the state's neglect of education and of Article 45, whose time limit of ten years had already been exceeded four times over. It referred to earlier judgments that had read the right to live with human dignity (*Francis Mullin,* 1981) and the right to livelihood (*Olga Tellis v. Bombay Municipal Corporation,* 1985) in Article 21 of the Constitution. Now, reading Articles 41,[46] 45,[47] and 46[48] together, reading part 4 of the Constitution as complementary to part 3, and even citing the American case *Brown v. Board of Education* (1954) in its support, the Court pronounced education to be the very basis of democratic citizenship.

> Education means knowledge and "knowledge itself is power." As rightly observed by John Adams, "the preservation of means of knowledge among the lowest ranks is of more importance to the public than all the property of all the rich men in the country." . . . It is the tyrants and bad rulers who are afraid of spread of education and knowledge among the deprived classes. Witness Hitler railing against universal education, he said: "Universal education is the most corroding and disintegrating poison that liberalism has ever invented for its own destruction." . . . A true democracy is one where education is universal, where people understand what is good for them and the nation and know how to govern themselves. (*Unni Krishnan J.P. v. State of Andhra Pradesh,* 1993: 60–61)

The bench castigated the government for spending more money on and giving greater attention to higher education at the cost of primary education, and in particular neglecting the rural areas and the more disadvantaged groups in society. Holding that "a child (citizen) has a fundamental right to free education up to the age of 14 years" (ibid.: 62) it said that "a citizen has a right to call upon the State to provide educational facilities to him within the limits of its economic capacity and development" (ibid.: 64), leaving the question of determining these limits to "the subjective satisfaction of the State" (ibid.).

This judgment made it possible to use a writ of *mandamus* to claim access to education, an opening that was used to good effect by nongovernmental organizations, becoming the launching pad for a coalition of 2,400 such organizations all over India to come together under the banner of the National Alliance for the Fundamental Right to Education (NAFRE). It was this mobilization that led to the enactment of the Ninety-Third Constitutional Amendment Act of 2001, which inserted a new clause, 21A, providing for free and compulsory education to all children between the age of six and fourteen years. Article 45 was simultaneously amended to provide for early childhood care and education for children below the age of six. A new article was also added to the Fundamental Duties, placing the onus of providing education on the parents/guardians of the child. The exclusion of children below the age of six from the ambit of the right was strongly criticized, as was the attempt to shift the burden of obligation to provide education from the state to parents. The proposed financial allocation to make this right real was also half of what education experts had estimated the requirement to be.[49]

Following a change in government in 2004, the process of drafting an acceptable legislation to give effect to the constitutional amendment of 2002 began. The Right to Education Act (RTE) of 2009 is meant to give effect to that amendment of 2002, and despite several drafts being provided by different committees and working groups, the Act retains many of the flaws of its predecessor. These include the restriction of the right to children between six and fourteen, ambiguity about financial provision, placing the responsibility primarily on the states, and a complete neglect of issues of quality. In fact, despite education being designated a justiciable right the Act contains no provision for penalizing or prosecuting any government official if the right is violated. The managements of private schools, which are forced to accept 25 percent of their students from poor backgrounds, have already gone to court in appeal against this. The critics of the Act accuse it of advocating the idea of neighborhood schools while explicitly allowing for private schools to continue and even promoting their growth. It is well known that school fees operate as a hindrance to universalizing primary education (Tomasevski, 2003), and therefore reliance on the private sector for achieving this is unwise. While disbanding such schools is scarcely an option, it is also clear that the middle class, having entirely withdrawn from the public sector in both education and health, is unlikely to support the improvement of quality in public schools. The class divide is accentuated in the government's ambitious new program to engage in skill development for those outside of the formal education system, suggesting skills for the poor and education for real citizens.

As with food security—where proposals for a right to food and for cash transfers are being simultaneously contemplated—the constitutional right to education is also jeopardized by contradictory tendencies. For the next Plan (2012–2017), the government is unequivocal about the need to intensify efforts to develop and operationalize Public–Private Partnerships "in School and Higher Education in accordance with the needs of a fast growing economy" (Government of India, 2011a: 10–11). Given the already considerable number of nongovernmental organizations to which elementary education has been farmed out, it is not entirely clear how government would discharge the obligation that the citizen's right to education entails. Placing the burden of the obligation to provide on the government appears to be at odds with the phenomenon of the pluralization of education providers. The right may be justiciable, but the diffusion of the responsibility points to a new form of class abatement.

Education may now become accessible to the vast majority, but it will be a long time before quality education becomes available and provides citizens with avenues of social mobility. In a rapidly democratizing polity where the vernacular is valorized, Marshall's propagation of education as a means of effecting an "equality of manners" is no longer relevant. Its enduring relevance lies in another direction—that of narrowing the gap between the quality of education available to different classes of citizens. Only when that is achieved will education become an instrument for transcending class differences and advancing the project of citizenship.

The Right to Work and Other New Rights

Estimates of rural poverty in India vary greatly, from the Planning Commission's own figure of 28 percent to the Suresh Tendulkar Committee's figure of 37.2 percent[50] and the N. C. Saxena Committee's estimate of 50 percent. Poverty is clearly linked to the inadequate opportunities for rural men and women to secure employment and earn a livelihood. In 2006, the enactment of the National Rural Employment Guarantee Act (NREGA) inaugurated a public works employment scheme in 200 districts of India, giving a legal guarantee of one hundred days' employment every year to every household in rural India that was willing to do manual labor for the statutory minimum wage. There was a great deal of contestation about the affordability of this program, resulting eventually in a closely fought and hard-won victory. The scope of the Act was subsequently (2008) extended to cover all of India, at a cost of approximately 0.65 percent of the GDP.

The program is theoretically universal, but depends upon self-selection so that only those who are willing to work for the minimum wage will claim it. It has helped protect rural households from hunger and poverty; stemmed distress migration to urban areas; empowered women with independent incomes; and strengthened institutions of local governance. Though it suffers less from problems of mistargeting, there has been evidence of leakages and the inadequacy of the transparency safeguards that were put in place. Much remains to be achieved in terms of realizing several provisions of the Act, including work on demand, unemployment allowance, and worksite facilities. As Jean Dreze wrote, the possibilities of backlash and "quiet sabotage" should not be underestimated (Dreze, 2010: 512). These fears have proved true, as several activists who exposed the embezzlement of program funds by officials, in collusion with contractors, have been killed.

Nevertheless, the fact that this is a legal entitlement gives it enormous potential as a tool that workers can use to organize themselves to demand not only this right, but also other forms of social protection. The actualization of this potential, as a study of an earlier incarnation of this program shows, depends crucially on intermediation by activist organizations. It is only when they mobilize people to claim their rights through, for instance, the law courts, that ordinary citizens benefit from what is already a statutory right.[51] In the context of NREGA, too, a recent survey of the states of northern India shows that this has been particularly successful in Rajasthan, a state which has a history of popular mobilization for the right to information and the right to employment. NREGA has also, in Badwani district in Madhya Pradesh, been described as the "empowerment guarantee act." This success has been due to civil society efforts in building a workers' organization that not only claimed work, but also extracted from a reluctant administration the legally payable unemployment allowance (Khera, 2011: 175–183). Workers in the unorganized sector are now organizing to claim rights, as Rina Agarwala's study of workers in the *bidi* (hand-rolled cigarettes) and construction industries shows. They are organizing to make claims on the state rather than on their employers, demanding attention to their needs of social consumption, and using the language of citizenship rather than the traditional vocabulary of labor rights (Agarwala, 2011).

The guarantee of rural employment for a maximum of a hundred days per family per year is by all reckoning an impressive advance in the face of widespread poverty and destitution. Nevertheless, along with the proposals for cash transfers, it does recall the Poor Laws and Factory Acts of Britain in the nineteenth century. Does the packaging of policies of relief and protection as rights substantively alter their quality, or does it reify exclusion from citizenship, as Marshall had suggested?

The last two years have seen a spate of High Court and Supreme Court judgments creating new social and economic rights, including a right to water and the state's concomitant duty to conduct scientific research on it; a right to "safe education"; the right to shelter and protection against eviction for *jhuggi* (slum) dwellers; the right of displaced tribal people to livelihood and rehabilitation; and, most significantly, a right to health care. In the *All India Lawyers' Union* case, the court invoked the ICESCR to argue that "Health is a fundamental human right indispensable for the exercise of other human rights. Every human being is entitled to the enjoyment of the highest attainable standard of health conducive to living a life in dignity" (paras. 30–31). On the other hand, the Approach Paper to the Twelfth Five Year Plan says that the "role of PPP in secondary and tertiary health care must be explored with greater vigour. Planning Commission needs to evolve appropriate concession models to facilitate this" (Government of India, 2011b: 6).

While the creation of new rights—fundamental and otherwise—is welcome, the experience of the right to education suggests that optimism needs to be tempered with caution. In that case, the court pronouncement was made in 1993, the Constitution was amended in 2002, and the legislation that gave it life was enacted only in 2009. In other words, it took more than a decade and a half from the date of the court judgment deeming education to be a fundamental right and the right actually becoming even formally available to citizens. It is not easy to be sanguine about the prospect of other rights, with similar origins in jurisprudence, getting legislated and becoming justiciable.[52]

Is Social Citizenship Nigh?

This chapter has tried to address the paradox of the recognition of social rights in a time of neoliberal ascendancy. There is a superficial resemblance to the historical experience of many western countries where citizenship struggles coincided with the emergence and consolidation of capitalism. These, however, were struggles for civil and political citizenship, which helped make democracy safe for capitalism,[53] and their successes anticipated and sometimes obviated struggles for social citizenship. In the United States, for instance, Michael Mann has argued that the early attainment of civil and political rights meant that claims to social and economic rights did not follow because "the (white) working class was civilly and politically *inside* the regime, it had little need for the great ideologies of the proletariat excluded from citizenship—socialism and anarchism" (Mann, 1987: 343).

In India the struggle for citizenship was not an autonomous struggle but a concomitant of the nationalist movement for freedom from colonial rule. As the struggle for civil and political citizenship was encompassed by that movement, to be free from colonial rule was also to have exchanged the oppressive status of an imperial subject for the liberating one of citizen of a sovereign state. Today, it is the struggle for social citizenship that coincides with the consolidation of a buccaneering capitalism, which enjoys unprecedented dominion over the state. The acceptance of social rights could be read as indicative of the failure of the state-capital alliance to contain the discontents of poverty or manage the social externalities of capitalism better. One way or another, it is clear that the contradictory tendencies of social citizenship and neoliberalism remain in continuing tension with each other, and in these concluding paragraphs, we return to some of the questions about social citizenship raised at the beginning of this discussion: is the determination of eligibility a mere technical issue in delivering citizens' material entitlements or is it the defining marker of the normative aspiration contained in the idea of citizenship? Does the post-1991 regime of social citizenship represent a substantive or merely a rhetorical advance over the previous regime? What are the solidarity costs of such rights recognition?

Insofar as some social rights are now justiciable, the post-1991 regime of SERs commends itself as offering some protection for the vulnerable against the worst effects of neoliberalism. But even the World Bank has argued that "safety nets in India remain primarily 'nets' rather than 'ropes' or 'ladders' which seek to promote sustained movement out of poverty" (2011: xi). A review of recent debates suggests that not much more than cautious optimism is warranted about the new-generation social rights. The bogey of affordability that has been persistently raised in respect to both the National Rural Employment Guarantee Act and the proposed Food Security Bill is indicative of the rather low levels of support from the better-off and articulate sections of Indian public opinion, which exercise an inordinate influence over public policy quite out of proportion to their numbers. Powerful reformist lobbies have been vociferous in expressing reservations about the extent of public spending that is entailed, even though the projected total expenditure for NREGA is at present less than 1 percent of GDP.

The legislation of each of these rights has occasioned contestation—not so much between government and opposition as intragovernmental disagreements, as well as differences between government and civil society. Each time a right is actually legislated, the objective is achieved with the help of some political bargains within and outside government with the economic rationale being trumped by the prospect of rich political dividends; each time some compromises also have been made on content, so that what is achieved is less than what was sought. The current popularity of cash transfers as the new magic bullet (Hanlon, Barrientos, and Hulme, 2010) and the best alternative to state provision suggests that at best rights are embattled and protecting them requires persistent struggle, and at worst that rights are not being taken seriously but are being used in a sophisticated buy-out of legitimacy instead. The efficacy of justiciable rights is in any case precarious in a policy environment that increasingly emphasizes outsourcing and public–private partnerships as preferred modes of governing. The move from outsourcing to cash transfers proceeds in two steps. The first of these is the diffusion of the responsibility to provide even the most basic public goods through farming these out to the market or nongovernmental organizations. The second, modeled on the actual practices over the last two decades of the middle and upper classes of Indian society, effectively seeks to privatize all public goods and simply give poor citizens some cash to purchase these directly on the market without addressing the myriad difficulties—economic but also social and cultural—this presents.

The new regime of SERs also does not signify a substantial break from the procedures and practices of the old one. As the contest between the rival principles of universalism and targeting in the right to food has been settled in favor of a targeted approach—albeit one that is proposed to be pegged at 70 percent of the population—it necessarily reproduces the reliance on categories of disadvantage and exception ostensibly constructed as categories of inclusion. The pursuit of more effective targeting may refine, but is unlikely to transcend or even dramatically reinvent, categories such as Below

Poverty Line. The deployment of such categories of inclusion will remain a double-edged instrument in relation to citizenship rights. On the one hand, these cultivate the impression of improved access to substantive citizenship for disadvantaged groups. On the other, the severance of particular sets of rights from the civic status entrenches already existing hierarchies of citizenship, through a paradoxical inversion that places those who need or get social rights far below those who do not. This takes on especially pernicious forms in respect of groups disadvantaged by their caste or religious identity (as in the case of special programs for the scheduled castes or the Other Backward Classes or the Muslims), by begetting newer and apparently nondenominational forms of exclusion, even as older ascriptive forms of discrimination are reified. It is not at all clear whether it is the project of equal citizenship that has thereby been advanced, or whether inequality has been further legitimized. Indeed, the principle of universality was intended precisely to prevent targeted services from being seen as "poor services for poor people" (Powell, 2002: 233) and so to advance the goal of integration.

The opposition between universality and selectivity in public provision is not quite the binary it appears to be, for universalism and targeting stand at opposite ends of a continuum that moves from full universality to universally available and free, to universally available but not universally free, to modestly costed and heavily subsidized. We have already discussed the forms of exclusion engendered by antipoverty programs, ostensibly based on categories of inclusion. While antipoverty programs are confined to target populations and available *exclusively* to the poor, there are other forms of public provision that are apparently universal but subsidized in the name of the poor. A curious bifurcation occurs between antipoverty programs and those services—such as water and electricity—that are subsidized in the name of the poor but are effectively available only to the nonpoor and are sometimes almost exclusively appropriated by the well-off. The subsidies for water and electricity are meant to enable access for the poor, but living as they do on the margins of legality, the urban poor are forced to rely on private provision that varies from electricity lines stolen directly from the poles to purchased water and sanitation. At the same time, elites are selective in their appropriation of subsidized public services, quick to appropriate some as they forsake others in favor of private providers. Having turned their backs on public education and health, for instance, they are responsible in no small measure for the decline in the quality of these services, as the classes that have political voice do not have any stake in their improvement, while the classes that are entirely dependent on these services lack the voice to effect such change.

The selective provision of services thus undermines civic solidarity as well as the quality of services; universalism is by definition a better safeguard of both. In the countries of the North, welfare policy has generally been underwritten by a social consensus that no citizen can be allowed to fall below a minimum level of well-being. Where ideological contestation has occurred over welfare policies, it has invoked the principles of contribution and redistribution. Nozickian political theory, based on Friedmanite economic principles, claims that redistribution is illegitimate because it gives some individuals (the noncontributing and undeserving poor) a claim on the wealth, and therefore the labor, of others. Since labor is the Lockean essence of an individual, any redistributive initiative is tantamount, Nozick says, to giving some people ownership in the persons of others (Nozick, 1970). Variants of this argument have found echoes in many countries where welfare—and therefore taxation—policies have figured on electoral platforms. Underlying the attack on the welfare state in Britain in the 1980s, for instance, was a view of "citizenship as a coercive bargain" (Ignatieff, 1995: 55). It finds reflection also in the concern of advocates of social rights that welfare provision may actually make society less cohesive and unified, as some citizens feel burdened by having to contribute to the sustenance of their needy compatriots. India has witnessed a raw demonstration of the solidarity costs of rights in the form of impassioned protests (in 1990 and again in 2006) against quotas for the backward classes, and the next section of this book deals with that question in greater detail.

These are formidable obstacles to the realization of social citizenship. The singular respect in which the new generation of social rights is an unambiguous good is the opportunity provided to appeal to the courts against the violation or nonprovision of these rights. Access to the justice system is far from easy, and the body of public interest jurisprudence shows that people usually need and depend upon the support of civil society organizations to claim their rights. But civil society is a complex concept in contemporary India, one that needs to be seen through a lens that is pluralizing rather than totalizing. There are multiple strands of civil society, at least two of which are relevant for our present concerns. The first of these comprises those who have reaped the benefits of liberalization and whose occupational affiliations are in the new economy of technology and the services sector. In the last few years, these sections have begun to perceive themselves as members of civil society intervening in issues of public concern. This trajectory arguably started with the young professional middle classes agitating and holding candlelight vigils to protest a series of high-profile murders in which the victims and their families were denied justice because of the political or financial clout of the killers. Beginning with vigilantism about the legal and judicial system, these groups have recently rallied behind the anticorruption campaign led by the self-styled Gandhian activist Anna Hazare along with some former civil servants and lawyers. The agenda of these sections of civil society has thus expanded from concerns about the rule of law to broader governance issues such as accountability and transparency. However, nowhere in their media commentary or their interventions on social networking sites is there any talk of poverty or redistribution, much less of equality. This component of civil society is, despite its focus on governance issues, deeply apolitical and perfectly at home in a neoliberal environment. The irony is that, in spite of inhabiting an amiable zone of agreement with the state on neoliberalism, it is at loggerheads with the state on questions of governance.

The other segment of civil society that is relevant from the point of view of social rights is also not political in a partisan sense, but deeply political in its core radical preoccupation with seeking to mitigate the worst exclusionary impacts of neoliberal economic development. It seeks to influence policy in a pro-poor direction, including through participation in quasi-official policy forums.[54] It is cognizant of the limitations of policy implementation, and has championed SERs as the only way of guaranteeing rights and making them justiciable. These members of civil society endeavor to translate policy into rights and thereby bring it closer to the normative objective. It is *this* civil society that Partha Chatterjee's "political society"[55] often depends on to demand rights, participate in policy networks, help formulate laws, and help ordinary citizens to go to court to redeem the promised guarantees of rights. Strangely enough, while these citizens dispute the neoliberal policy orientation of the state, the state is infinitely more receptive to this form of civil society than the other, possibly because demands for accountability cut closer to the bone for the political class than do abstract rights to food or work. In the short to medium term, therefore, the burden of advancing the project of social citizenship rests quite considerably on the shoulders of the latter type of civil society, along with the judiciary.

PART THREE

Identity

7

Genealogies of Mediated Citizenship

In chapter 4, we encountered the colonial view that, as an insufficiently individuated social order divided by language, caste, and religion, Indian society
could scarcely yield a conception of citizenship, much less individuals who
could be citizens. This assumption appears to have enjoyed wide acceptance
as a descriptively accurate understanding of the nature of Indian social diversity, so that the validity of the premise was seldom called into question. Such
questioning of this assumption as occurred in different strands of nationalist thinking was motivated largely by a defensive impulse to establish that
these were, in one way or another, communities that were either essentially
compatible or could be rendered thus. All the argumentative strategies of
nationalists—adducing evidence of historical coexistence and tolerance; char-
acterizing the differences between communities as elite conflicts not reflective
of local realities of living together separately; and asserting the possibility of
constructing a territorially unified nation-state which could accommodate
all these differences in a peaceable fashion—were oriented to countering the
argument that the divisions in Indian society were irretrievably hostile and
irreconcilable, rather than to providing an alternative understanding. This
accounts for the preoccupation, in the political discourse of late colonial

India, with specifying exactly how, on what terms, and to what extent the relationship of the citizen to the state may be mediated by community. The idea that communities possessed political agency found articulation in their negotiations with the colonial state for a greater institutional presence, with political and legislative representation being viewed as the preeminent form that citizenship could take.

Twentieth-century Indian history is replete with examples of such contestations between universal and group-differentiated conceptions of citizenship. There is even a discernible continuity between arguments for the colonial institutional innovation of providing representation for particular social groups and the justifications offered for group-differentiated citizenship a century later. I will argue that the complexity of the Indian experience—both ideational as well as institutional—suggests that this may be, both conceptually and normatively, a false dichotomy. To the extent that a dichotomous view occludes hybridities, it is more helpful to rephrase this as an antinomy rather than a binary of fundamentally opposed conceptions of citizenship. Before I discuss the major contestations of the twentieth century in this frame, let me briefly identify the relevant theoretical issues.

Universal and Group-Differentiated Citizenship: Theoretical Signposts

Differentiated citizenship was obviously not the phrase used to describe the forms of the constitutional accommodation of diversity improvised for early twentieth-century India. This is a more recent term influentially deployed by political theorists to signal their discomfort with universalist notions of citizenship, which entail the recognition of individuals as constitutive units of the polity, and as bearers of equal rights without any consideration of inequalities in their wealth, social status, or identity. But, of course, the presence of inequalities, especially those based in group identity, and marked by the discrimination or disadvantage that attach to belonging to particular social groups, can result in a lack of voice and participation in the polity for members of these groups. In these circumstances, the language of common citizenship renders invisible the many inequalities that lie concealed beneath the mask of formal equality and obfuscates the inadequacies of liberal neutrality as state policy.

The philosophical bases of these rival conceptions of citizenship can be simply stated. A universalist conception of citizenship affirms the equality of all citizens as individuals of equal moral worth. As such, every individual citizen is seen as the bearer of equal rights to, for instance, life, liberty, physical security, freedom of speech, conscience, movement, and association. No gradations of citizenship are recognized, as all enjoy equal rights and all are equal before, and in the eyes of, the law. At least in formal terms, the rights of citizenship attach equally to all citizens of the political community which is the universe in which such rights are available. The assertion of equal rights for all citizens runs the obvious risk of ignoring the need for special protection for such groups of citizens as may be subject to forms of discrimination or exclusion on account of their belonging to a minority culture, such as, for example, racial, religious, or linguistic minorities or indigenous peoples who have an altogether distinctive culture. By adopting color-blind or difference-blind policies, universal conceptions of citizenship fail to provide such groups with guarantees for protective rights such as their right to practice their own culture or speak their own language or worship their own gods. Difference-blind policies that see all citizens as equal and none as especially deserving on account of disadvantage may in fact be clandestine vehicles of dominant cultures, which they serve to reinforce and entrench even as they affect liberal neutrality and perfect equality. As such, cultural difference is the chief source of claims to differentiated citizenship rights, with such rights taking many forms, such as rights to special representation or rights of self-government. In general, differentiated rights of citizenship are rights to symbolic recognition and, arising out of this, to the material and institutional resources of a society.

Group-differentiated citizenship has become a widely accepted strategy to assuage the discomfort with liberal, homogenizing, difference-blind accounts of citizenship. In Iris Marion Young's definitive formulation of the basic principle of differentiated citizenship, "a democratic public, however that is constituted, should provide mechanisms for the effective representation and recognition of the distinct voices and perspectives of those of its constituent groups that are oppressed or disadvantaged within it" (Young, [1989] 1995: 188–189). Young specified oppression as including exploitation, marginalization, powerlessness, cultural imperialism, and vulnerability to violence motivated by hatred and fear. Though she explicitly included poor and working-class people, she also argued that such groups are defined by their "comprehensive identities and ways of life" (ibid.: 199), rather than by any particular position or interest.[1] In keeping with this emphasis, identity-claims have generally been treated as the most suitable candidates for group-differentiated citizenship, so that a religious minority is more likely to make such a claim and have it heard than, say, a group of displaced persons. Differentiated citizenship finds institutional expression in many familiar forms: rights to guaranteed representation in institutions of governance, minority rights, language rights, affirmative action, and of course various modes of symbolic recognition.[2]

Even the most avid advocates of differentiated citizenship do however recognize two types of anxieties associated with it. The first of these has to do with the implications of group-differentiated citizenship (henceforth GDC) for the quality of citizenship in the polity as a whole. To the extent that differentiated citizenship speaks to the dimension of citizenship as status (or "thin" citizenship) rather than citizenship as practice ("thick" citizenship), and the first is logically prior to the second, differentiated citizenship does not provide an account of how status might translate into practice, which arguably requires the recognition of a common and even universal purpose. If "all is particularity," as Ronald Beiner (1995: 10) puts it, where, in the absence of a civic community, might citizenship be located or practiced?

Further, GDC provokes fears of the postponement, perhaps indefinitely, of the possibility of articulating a shared common purpose for the polity as a whole. This is because of its propensity to provide institutional incentives for the entrenchment of identities, and their reinforcement and hardening. High levels of differentiated citizenship are typically associated with anxieties of weakening social cohesion and integration, which may acquire an extreme form in areas where minorities are territorially concentrated, even possibly spawning demands for secession and self-governing states (Kymlicka and Norman, 2000: 39–40). Indeed, the very possibility of differentiated citizenship rights may bring into existence new categories of disadvantaged citizens. Special rights for minorities almost invariably generate apprehensions among members of the majority community, as well as various subgroups within minorities, that they may become second-class citizens. This begets the challenge of designing institutions and policy instruments that would most effectively further the objectives of GDC, while avoiding these pitfalls.

A second class of anxiety is about the proper determination of which groups should receive differentiated citizenship rights. This could imply making judgments not only about which groups are disadvantaged or oppressed, but also about what, in a particular context, qualifies as oppression or disadvantage; distinguishing clearly, in the words of Kymlicka and Norman, "the reality of inequality and the oppression and stigmatization it fosters . . . from the perception of unequal status" (ibid.: 32). Since GDC is assumed not to encompass all inequalities that are morally objectionable but only those rooted in, *pace* Young, comprehensive identities and ways of life, there is a need also to provide reasons for why difference-based inequalities should be redressed through differentiated rights of citizenship while non-difference-based inequalities do not demand similar attention. This is of particular interest in the Indian context where the two types of inequalities—cultural and symbolic, on the one hand, and material, on the other—tend to overlap. For instance, being a poor Dalit or Muslim woman is to be simultaneously disadvantaged on several counts—not merely caste or religious identity, but also gender and class. There are also finally concerns about how to balance competing claims to recognition, and the nitty-gritty of formulating the appropriate criteria to adjudicate competing claims to differentiated citizenship.

Many of the theoretical concerns associated with the dichotomized categories of universal and differentiated citizenship are curiously resonant in contemporary India. The nationalism-communalism binary—the once hegemonic categories that framed the historical understanding of anticolonial Indian thinking, now decisively and deservedly jettisoned—could be viewed as mapping neatly onto these. This would however be too simplistic and reductionist a reading of a field crowded with claims and assertions that defy easy classification. Part of the complication is philosophical, reflected in the profound anxiety about individualism that characterizes Indian thinking from the late nineteenth century onwards, and its discomfort with the idea of the individual as the exclusive basic unit of the political universe, whose membership of the state may be unmediated by community. The centrality of community as possessing legitimate political agency naturally leads to questions about how best political institutions can be tailored to represent its interests, especially where the identity of a community is also linked to claims of disadvantage.

The contention over universal and group-differentiated citizenship in late colonial India was thus substantively about whether or not the relationship of the citizen to the state should be mediated by community. For advocates of GDC, communities possessed primary political agency and mediation by community was the very essence of the citizen–state relationship. The quality of political obligation that followed was, of course, similarly mediated. The universalists, on the other hand, offered the promise of individual political agency, individual rights, and an unmediated relationship between citizen and state, yielding a standard liberal account of political obligation. But both conceptions need to be qualified and internally differentiated. The imitatively liberal—arguably upper class and upper caste—position that yielded the broadly universalist conception of citizenship was modified by a commitment (in varying degrees) to forms of minority rights, which were from the earliest stirrings of nationalist thinking part of the modern Indian politico-intellectual horizon. Communitarian claims also did not emanate exclusively from cultural minorities or otherwise disadvantaged groups. The two preeminent articulations of communitarian identity that fueled political mobilization in late colonial India were those of majority Hindu and minority Muslim identity. As a communitarian identity of privilege rather than disadvantage, the majoritarian community identity obviously did not make claims to differentiated citizenship and indeed sought, this chapter will argue, to construct alternative, even perverse, universalisms. This was clearly a function more of politics than of philosophy or theology.

This chapter surveys the major institutional practices and political arguments for what could be described as GDC before 1947. It seeks to identify and differentiate between the major strands of argument for universal and group-differentiated citizenship in late colonial India. The three preeminent forms of universalism discussed are: (a) the substantive and inclusionary universalism of the Congress contrasted with (b) the descriptive and exclusionary universalism of Hindu nationalism, and (c) the most unequivocally universalist citizenship claim of the women's movement. Three major forms of group-differentiated citizenship are similarly identified. While the mechanisms are different in each case—for example, separate electorates for the Muslims and reserved seats for the Dalits—GDC is in each instance presented as an antidote. In the case of the Muslim League, GDC is an antidote to the prospect of majoritarian rule; in the case of Dalits, it is an antidote to caste oppression and discrimination; and in the case of the tribals and to a lesser degree the Other Backward Classes, whose claims were at this stage largely confined to the provinces, it appears as an antidote to backwardness. This chapter essays a discussion of the three preeminent forms of universalism and of the first two categories of claims to GDC. The normative and political implications of the third, GDC as an antidote to backwardness, and its role in the forging of the constitutional consensus and in the politics of independent India, are the subject of the next chapter.

Colonial Institutional Innovations for
Group-Differentiated Subjecthood

Even before India attained independence and enacted a constitution that sought to balance the universal and the particular, the imperial British government in India had already quite successfully flirted with forms of group-differentiated representation that could—given the colonial context and the rather skeletal and empty forms of legislative opportunities this afforded—only very loosely be described as citizenship. The colonial state had carefully separated out and delinked from each other the principles of differentiation and of citizenship, giving recognition to the first and largely ignoring the second. The structures of governance in the colonial period provided for the articulation of the communitarian interests of the Muslim minority through the institutionalization of separate electorates.[3] But quotas had existed even prior to this. As early as the 1880s, Punjab experimented with separate electorates in local government and communal representation in the bureaucracy, the apparent purpose of these policies being—though eventually unsuccessful—to prevent violence between Hindus and Muslims, and to secure the loyalty and quiescence of what was perceived to be an inconveniently combative Muslim minority (Barrier, 1968). At the national level, however, it was in the Government of India Act of 1909 that the principle of separate electorates for elections to the provincial legislatures was first recognized.

While it would be egregiously anachronistic to claim that quotas or separate electorates were strategies of GDC in the contemporary sense, the rationale for quotas in the colonial period does bear comparison with more recent arguments for them. The chief justification in the colonial period was not so much about disadvantage or oppression as it was about *special interests*. The idea that representation should be differentiated by social groups had been a part of colonial discourse since the late nineteenth century with the phrase "classes, races, and interests" from the Aitchison Commission Report on the Public Services (Wolpert, 1967: 147) enjoying enormous currency. The assumption underlying separate representation was the conviction that the intensity of group differences in India precluded any possibility of commonality, and the task of colonial governance was therefore to "manage" these differences by allowing each group to have its point of view and its interests represented "by the mouth of some member specially acquainted with them," as a government dispatch of 1892 stated.[4]

The crystallization of official discourse on issues of representation was not an uncontested process. There was disputation within the political establishment in Britain and in India on every aspect of institutional reform: the enhancement of nonofficial representation; whether this was to be done through election or nomination; and, most importantly, how different groups were to be represented. Lee-Warner, whom we encountered as the author of *The Citizen of India,* was also, in part, the author of the script of group-differentiated citizenship in India. Along with Theodore Morison, his fellow member in Whitehall's Council of India in Lord Morley's tenure, he supported the creation of electoral colleges based on "race, caste or religion" throughout India, and separate representation for Muslims (Wolpert, 1967: 141). Morley himself hailed the "didactic value" of representative institutions for training Indians in "habits of political responsibility" (ibid.: 159). The 1908 Royal Proclamation drafted by him announced that measures were planned to satisfy the claim of "equality of citizenship, and a greater share in legislation and government" (Ghose, 1921: 238). Minto's famous assurance to the 1906 deputation demanding separate electorates for Muslims, forcefully articulated the position that group representation, rather than individual franchise, was the way forward.[5] The need for separate representation was usually justified with reference to attributes of "backwardness" of the community in question, a category that has endured, as the next chapter shows, in public policy to the present day.

Initially, colonial policies of differentiation did not frame issues of representation as questions of citizenship, but as time wore on, there does appear to have been a clear official recognition of the relationship between citizenship and differential representative entitlements. By the 1920s, there was an explicit recognition, in both official and nationalist circles, of the adverse implications of separate electorates for a common citizenship. The Congress, in its Lahore session of 1909, expressed its strong disapproval of the creation of separate electorates on the basis of religion. Morley's friend Gokhale took a pragmatic view, arguing that only such special treatment and separateness could remove the soreness in the minds of minorities, and was therefore necessary for the realization of a real union (Wolpert, 1967: 196). For Ayesha Jalal, separate electorates were "effectively a class concession advanced in the name of a religious community," as they benefited only the already powerful who no longer had to contest elections against non-Muslims, while being entirely meaningless for the majority of ordinary Muslims who did not have the franchise (2001: 160). Intended thus as an instrument of pragmatic instrumentalism, a calculated investment to obtain support, separate electorates also "put a formal seal of approval on the institutionalized conception of Muslim political identity . . . that (was) profoundly divisive and inherently conflict-oriented" (Hasan, 1996: 193).

In the first official recognition of the Depressed Classes[6] as a distinct and disadvantaged group, the Government of India Act of 1919 chose to give this group representation in the form of nonofficial nominated members in the Central Legislative Assembly as well as the Provincial Legislatures. This strategic colonial imperative was however rhetorically elided in the appeal of the Montagu-Chelmsford report (which resulted in the Act of 1919) to a universalist conception of the citizen–state relationship.

> The history of self-government among the nations who developed it and spread it through the world, is decisively against the admission by the State of any divided allegiance; against the State's arranging its members in any way which encourages them to think of themselves primarily as citizens of any smaller unit than itself. (Government of India, 1918: 148)

Similarly, the Statutory Commission recognized separate electorates to be an obstacle in the way of the growth of "a sense of common citizenship" and looked forward to the day when "a general recognition of the rights of minorities will make such arrangements unnecessary" (Government of India, 1930a: 30). Thus, even as the institutional arrangements for differentiated representation were strengthened and expanded, the rhetoric remained firmly wedded to a universal conception of citizenship.

Arguments for Universal and Group-Differentiated Citizenship before 1947

The two decades before independence are a cornucopia of rival and competing conceptions of citizenship. As we approach these through the two umbrella categories of universal and differentiated citizenship, there is an important caveat: while practically every citizenship claim on the Indian political firmament can be domiciled in one or other of these architectonic categories, the categories themselves allow for significant internal differentiation, often yielding arguments that do not conform to the implicit normativities of these as elaborated in the canon of western political theory.

Three Forms of Universalism

Substantive-Inclusionary Universalism

There would be little dispute about the description of the Congress as articulating a broadly universal conception of citizenship, the first and classic statement of which is arguably to be found in the report of the Motilal Nehru Committee (for the All-Parties Conference) that recommended universal adult franchise and the complete dissociation of state and religion. The Nehru Committee Report also rejected separate electorates but did propose their replacement by reservations for Muslims in provinces in which they were in a minority. Within the Congress, in the years that followed, it was the vision forcefully advanced by the younger Nehru, Jawaharlal, that was consistently universalist, though it has been argued that given the historical absence of an exemplary period of Indian political unity, even a secularist like Nehru found it hard to resist making civilizational claims that assumed a cultural unity that was recognizably Hindu (Sarkar, 2005: 275). While it is true that the Congress accommodated many and very diverse ideological strands from Hindu nationalism to socialism—both the Hindu Mahasabha and the Congress Socialist Party were incubated in, and eventual breakaways from, the Congress—its self-image was unequivocally universalist. A powerful articulation of the universalist position came from Govind Ballabh Pant who, in 1946, referred to

> a morbid tendency which has ripped this country for the last many years. The individual citizen who is really the backbone of the State, the pivot, the cardinal centre of all social activity, and whose happiness and satisfaction should be the goal of every social mechanism, has been lost here in that indiscriminate body known as the community. We have even forgotten that a citizen exists as such. There is the unwholesome, and to some extent a degrading habit of thinking always in terms of communities and never in terms of citizens. (CAD 1: 332)

The Congress Election Manifesto in the same year also emphasized its universalism, qualified only by the need to enable cultural diversity to thrive and social injustice and inequality to be remedied, as an instrument of making the larger universalist goal more robust.

> The Congress has stood for equal rights and opportunities for every citizen of India, man or woman. It has stood for the unity of all communities

and religious groups and for tolerance and goodwill between them. It has stood for full opportunities for the people as a whole to grow and develop according to their own wishes and genius; it has also stood for the freedom of each group and territorial area within the nation to develop its own life and culture within the larger framework, and it has stated that for this purpose such territorial areas or provinces should be constituted, as far as possible, on a linguistic and cultural basis. It has stood for the rights of all those who suffer from social tyranny and injustice and for the removal for them of all barriers to equality. (*Indian Annual Register*, 1946, reproduced in Sarkar, 2007: 269)

The so-called "umbrella" character of the Congress—its ability to not merely reflect but also accommodate the diverse and even conflicting elements of Indian society—was seen as an unambiguous virtue, as a quality of inclusiveness rather than a sign of diffuseness and incoherence. Even though national identity was defined in "national-civic" rather than "national-ethnic" terms (Beiner, 1995: 8), it remained a rather fragile construct, with an ambivalent and ultimately meaningless unity-in-diversity approach. Jawaharlal Nehru's *Discovery of India* was unarguably the *locus classicus* of this approach. In his Marxist understanding of communal conflict between the Hindus and Muslims, poverty, backwardness, caste, region, and religion were all viewed as different faces of the same retrograde phenomenon, which could only be transcended by the alliance of science, reason, and economic development.

In a letter to Lord Lothian, a year after the passage of the Government of India Act of 1935, Nehru systematically repudiated the British argument of the inherent Indian tendency toward division and disunity by religion, race, and language. Hindus and Muslims, he said, were "essentially the same amalgam of races"; linguistic diversity was scarcely a problem as many of the languages were closely allied in their roots; and religious conflict in India, never as bloody as that in Europe in the Middle Ages, was fundamentally "political, economic and middle class" in character (J. Nehru, 2003a: 534). Notwithstanding official claims about the Act of 1935 being symbolic of Indian unity, it was, Nehru said, only a prelude to greater disunity, as it sought to divide India into many compartments, religious and other (ibid.: 535). Though he did not burden Lothian with a treatise on historical materialism, in *An Autobiography* ([1936] 1989) published the same year, Nehru provided a thoroughgoing Marxist analysis of communal politics in India, alleging that the conflict between the two communities was, at least in the Punjab, Sindh, and Bengal, a class conflict between the richer, urban creditors who were Hindu and the poorer, rural, indebted Muslims. He castigated the communalism of the Hindu Mahasabha, contested its claims to an "irreproachable nationalism," and openly accused it of being a camouflage for upper-class Hindu banking interests (ibid.: 466–467). As such, the endless wrangling between Hindus and Muslims over percentages of seats in the legislatures were only a manifestation of the middle-class intelligentsia's obsession with and struggle for scarce jobs. Though the Marxist in Nehru gave little quarter to cultural arguments of group-differentiated citizenship, he accepted the need for special provisions for minorities and disadvantaged groups, with the proviso that these should not be permanent. His reservations on the subject had however less to do with class analysis and more with the aspiration to construct a civic nationalism. His words as he moved the Objectives Resolution in the Constituent Assembly in November 1948 reveal his deeply conflicted feelings on the subject.

> While it is our bounded duty to do everything we can to give full opportunity to every minority or group and to raise every backward group or class, I do not think it will be a right thing to go the way this country has gone in the past by creating barriers and by calling for protection. As a matter of fact nothing can protect such a minority or a group less than a barrier which separates it from the majority. It makes it a permanently isolated group . . . (J. Nehru, 2003b: 77)

Even earlier, in response to a demand from a leader of the Momin sect complaining about the monopolizing of all opportunities by upper-class elites among Muslims, Nehru sympathetically proffered an argument of economic determinism to explain why some groups were left behind. Having done so, he rejected the claim of a subquota for Momins saying that while it would appear initially to be advantageous, it would eventually be injurious to the community itself as it would retard its growth. The superior alternative was education, general and technical, which would go much further in making such communities stronger (Anwar, 2001: 229–231). Nehru's writings make clear that his acknowledgment of the need for state protection for minorities and backward groups did not attenuate his overarching and passionate commitment to the creation of an Indian civic community.

Gandhi's commitment to civic nationalism was no less than Nehru's, though his philosophical perspective on the relationship between the individual and the state was rather different from that of his younger comrade.

Although he attributed the Hindu–Muslim divide to colonial rule, Gandhi increasingly recognized that Hindu intolerance and the patronizing attitude of Hindus toward Muslims was as much to blame for Muslim separatism as Islamic fundamentalism (Hardiman, 2003: 173). His support for separate electorates for the Muslims, as well as for the more controversial Khilafat movement,[7] grew out of his conviction that caste and religious identities were secondary to the primary identity of the Indian and, consistent with this, his expectation that Hindus should respond to Muslim demands in order to gain the latter's trust. Gandhi's critics—including secular Muslims—argued at the time that supporting the Khilafat movement was a retrograde step because it made common cause with reactionary elements in the community and encouraged a dangerous dalliance between politics and religion. Gandhi was also receptive to claims of linguistic diversity, which he considered fully compatible with civic nationalism. It was only on the question of the Dalits' demand for separate electorates that he adopted a position of truculence, going on a famous fast-unto-death, thereby compelling Ambedkar to accept reservations instead. His reluctance to give in to the Dalit demand was in part an outgrowth of his personal revulsion against untouchability, and his intense desire to envelop Dalits within the tight embrace of the Hindu fold even if this meant disregarding their desire to define themselves differently and autonomously. It is another matter that this negated the Dalits' own understanding of their predicament and left behind a legacy of deep animosity that has not yet quite disappeared. Gandhi's insistence on incorporating Dalits under the canopy of the Hindu community, as well as his acknowledgment of linguistic units and of separate electorates for Muslims, signify a broadly universalist vision, even as they signal some of the tensions and contradictions of such a conception.

At the core of Gandhian social philosophy stood the individual, and while this version of individualism bears no more than a faint resemblance to the liberal view, it was nevertheless a startling departure for a society in which individuals were rarely comprehended as moral beings outside of their family, caste, or community identities. Gandhi's individual defied such classifications and could easily belong to an infinite and ever-expanding set of concentric circles that widened but did not ascend and were therefore without hierarchy. Life would be like an oceanic circle at whose center was the individual, ready to perish for the village, and the village itself ready to perish for the circle of villages till "at last the whole becomes one life composed of individuals, never

aggressive in their arrogance but ever humble, sharing the majesty of the oceanic circle of which they are integral units" (*CWMG* 91: 326).

Self-determination seems like a logical derivative of such an individual-
centered philosophy. Gandhi had already asserted in *Hind Swaraj* (1909)
that India was a nation even before the arrival of the British, and the nation
was for him constituted of and by individuals. The importance of the individual citizen in Gandhi's thought is attributable to the place of conscience
in his ideas, the reference point of which cannot be other than the individual. This is also the basis of political dissent, which must therefore ultimately be the decision of the individual dissenter. The *Purna Swaraj* (total
swaraj) Declaration of Independence that Gandhi authored in 1930 carried strong echoes of the French Declaration of Independence, not merely
in its title but also in its reference to the "inalienable rights" of people to
freedom (*CWMG* 48: 261). The relation between the individual and the
collectivity in Gandhi is of particular interest because political mobilization required the bringing together of tens of thousands of persons, each of
whom was presumed to be participating in protest in ways that answered
the moral imperatives of every individual conscience, with all having indi-
vidually accepted the principle of *ahimsa* (nonviolence) and the method of
satyagraha (truth force). For all of these, the touchstone could not but be the
individual. The individual is thus central not only to Gandhi's moral theory
but also to his philosophy of political action, which can only be undertaken
by the satyagrahi in the fullest realization of the motivations, purposes, and
implications of his actions. The prefix *swa* (meaning self) in Gandhi's concepts of *swaraj* (self-rule) and *swadeshi* (economic self-reliance) has strongly
individualist connotations of autonomy, even as it is easily generalizable to
a social or political collectivity.

Although Gandhi was not, like Nehru, an avowed socialist, he was no less
aware of the other important fault lines in Indian society than his Marxist
disciple, only conceptualizing them differently. Perhaps the most compelling example of this is the contrast Gandhi made between what he labeled
"constitutional *swaraj*" and "organic *swaraj*." Apparently based on a distinction between the formal and the substantive, the first could be enacted by
law but would be inadequate to solve the problems of "real *swaraj*" or "the
swaraj of the masses" (*CWMG* 42: 365). The impulse of constitutional *swaraj*
was expressed through the political agency of the intellect, and the coming together of the Moderates, the Extremists, and the Muslim League in

the Lucknow session of the Congress in 1918 was a *swaraj* of this type. As opposed to this, the popular mobilization for civil disobedience in the Bardoli satyagraha of 1921 was an example of "organic *swaraj*," made possible by the faith and through the agency of ordinary unlettered people.[8] On the one hand, this disjunction between the organic and the constitutional represents an acknowledgment and possibly acceptance, by Gandhi, of the existence and different roles played by the elites and the masses of Indian society in the same national endeavor. On the other hand, it reiterates the centrality of both, and the inadequacy of either by itself, to the achievement of the national project.

This complementarity between the constitutional and the organic versions of *swaraj* also illuminates the twin projects of state and society in Gandhi's vision. It has long been assumed that Gandhi was strongly opposed to the state, which he saw as an organ of concentrated monopolistic violence, and a supporter instead of grassroots voluntarism and civil society. This opposition of state and society has been convincingly repudiated in recent Gandhi scholarship, which sees a shift in his position from an initial view of the state as minimalist, protecting the rights of citizens and guarding them against external aggression to a later conception of the state, which would guarantee and protect the rights of the vulnerable sections of society (Parel, 2006: 52–53; Hardiman, 2003: 19). While the limited, constitutional state has a legitimate role to play in protecting its citizens, the citizenry also contributes to the legitimacy of the state by holding in reserve its right to resist. This was why Gandhi famously described the satyagrahi as a friend, and not an enemy, of the state. The legitimacy of the state was underscored by the quotidian obedience accorded to it by citizens. If they decided to embark upon civil disobedience, their acceptance of the punishment levied by the state equally underlined its legitimacy. As Parel writes, "only those who habitually obeyed the law were entitled to disobey it" (2006: 56).

Gandhi's attitude to caste and religious differences in Indian society is marked by a curious, almost personalized, element that finds expression in the representational claims he made both in the case of the Muslims and the Dalits. These were of course repudiations of the representative claims of Jinnah and Ambedkar respectively, and were in turn forcefully rebutted by the latter two leaders. On occasion, Gandhi made the claim on behalf of the Congress,[9] but very often it was made on his own individual behalf. Even as the Congress purported to represent everybody, Jinnah characterized the

Congress as a Hindu organization and Gandhi as its leader. Addressing the AICC session in August 1942, Gandhi reminded its members that

> the members of the All-India Congress Committee are like members of Parliament representing the whole of India. The Congress from its very inception has not been of any particular group or any particular color or caste or of any particular province. It has claimed ever since its birth to represent the whole nation and on your behalf I have made the claim that you represent not only the registered members of the Congress but the entire nation. (*CWMG* 83: 182)

As for himself, he described Jinnah as "utterly wrong. That is absurd. I am a Moslem, a Hindu, a Buddhist, a Christian, a Jew, a Parsi. He does not know me when he says I want Hindu rule. He is not speaking the truth" (quoted in Hardiman, 2003: 173–174). Even as Jinnah accused Gandhi of being the Hindu leader of a Hindu party, the leaders of the Hindu Mahasabha—especially Moonje and Savarkar—questioned the Congress's competence to represent the Hindus because it had banned its members from becoming members of the Mahasabha (*Pioneer,* March 5 1940, reproduced in Panikkar, 2009: 584).

The question of who could and did represent the Hindus and Muslims was thus the subject of many rhetorical claims and counterclaims, but arguably the most intensely contested was Gandhi's claim to represent the Dalits. Gandhi described himself as "an untouchable by adoption" as he had as a twelve year old quarreled with his mother for treating a sweeper in their home as untouchable (Gandhi, 2008: 344). Even as he acknowledged that Ambedkar had been born an untouchable, he nevertheless described as "improper" Ambedkar's claim to speak on behalf of all of India's Untouchables, saying that "I myself in my own person claim to represent the vast mass of the Untouchables" (Hardiman, 2003: 131). At stake in this representational claim, of course, was the tension between universalism and differentiation; the commitment to the universal required the incorporation of the Dalits. His rejection of separate electorates for the Dalits was informed by his fear that saw the potentially numerous divisions of Indian society as fueling endless claims that could only "spell India's ruin" (Gandhi, 2008: 806). While he was willing to countenance quotas for disadvantaged groups, he was anxious that the "protection of neglected classes should not be carried to an extent which will harm them and harm the country" (*CWMG.* 83: 119). His rejection of the two-nation theory was similarly grounded in his insistence that Muslims were related by blood to Hindus and were "children of the same land" (Gandhi, 2008: 602).

In general, Gandhi's universalist citizenship was inclusive of all who inhabited the territorial space of the nation, if insufficiently sensitive to the self-definition of diverse groups. His universalism thus was slightly different than Nehru's. Nehru's commitment to liberal universalism did not preclude recognition of the problems of cultural diversity. Indeed, Nehru was willing to make departures from the principle of strict equality in the short term, in the belief that a civically defined nation would eventually be achieved as the fullest promise of modernity was realized. Gandhi's was a more assimilationist universalism that feared division and difference and strove to overcome it and to stitch different groups and communities together by moral suasion. As a strategy of political mobilization, this talent for creating coalitions was enormously successful; ideologically it often smacked of compromise in the service of transient and fragile unities.

These were clearly not the only two positions within the Congress Party. There was a wide range of opinion on these questions, though the public position of the party supported universalism, even if often less than robustly articulated. In the wider public sphere, too, unconventional arguments had begun to emerge, buttressing the case for universalism. Deploying an argument of efficiency against quotas, *The Tribune* of the Punjab argued editorially that efficiency and complete freedom from religious bias were necessary attributes of public servants. But unconscious biases would inevitably creep in if people were recruited on account of their belonging to one or other community, and this was manifestly undesirable.

> A Government whose servants think of themselves primarily and principally not as citizens but as Hindus, or Muslims, or Christians is, indeed, a Government that is doomed to utter and irretrievable failure. (*Tribune,* June 16, 1939, reproduced in Hasan, 2008a: 102)

Descriptive-Exclusionary Universalism

The conception of citizenship advanced by Hindu nationalist politics may be interpreted as a descriptive, rather than substantive, form of universalism. The proposition that this conception, scripted by the leaders of the Hindu Mahasabha and the Rashtriya Swayamsewak Sangh (henceforth RSS), should be viewed a distinct subcategory of universalist citizenship may seem startling, for Hindu majoritarian ideology would appear to belong, almost self-evidently and even perversely, to the category of GDC, as citizenship is anchored to identity, and the aspiration is to create classes of citizens in which Hindus occupy pride of place. On the other hand, its very majoritarianism pushes it aspirationally in the direction of a proto-universalism, and this is why it is both plausible and useful to think of Hindutva as a distinctive and exclusionary version of the universalist argument. The strategies to achieve this complete synonymy between the nation and the religion vary across the proponents of Hindutva—ranging from the elimination of minorities to their reconversion and assimilation.

Hindu philosophy had already wrestled with its internal theological demons in the form of the doctrine of *adhikari bheda,* which the historian Sumit Sarkar defines as a doctrine of "differential rights, claims, or powers" conveying the idea that "each *jati* (caste) and *sampraday* (sect) has its own rituals and beliefs, in a unified, but hierarchically differentiated structure within which each knows its appropriate place" (Sarkar, 2005: 277). The concept of *adhikari bheda,* Sarkar argues, could be accommodated within a conservative catholic embrace that maintained the norms that corresponded to each group's place in the hierarchy so as to preserve the hierarchy as a whole. However, as people from the lower castes entered political life in late nineteenth-century Bengal, this straitjacket fell into disuse; the political agenda of consolidating a Hindu unity led to its repudiation and eventual disappearance (ibid.: 286). The philosophical doctrine of differentiation, we might infer, made way for a political doctrine of homogenizing communitarianism.

Following its separation from the Congress in the late 1930s,[10] the career of the Hindu Mahasabha registers a perceptible ideological shift. As late as January 1939, its leader B. S. Moonje (president of the Mahasabha from 1927–1937) wrote a letter deploring attacks on the businesses and lives of Muslims in Gaya, and explicitly cast suspicion on the complicity of the police and the magistracy (Letter to Jayakar, January 4, 1939, reproduced in Hasan, 2008b: 1855). The Resolution emanating from its annual session in December 1939 listed a charter of rights that included freedom of conscience; the right to state protection for religion, language, and culture; and the equality of all citizens before the law, irrespective of religion, caste, or gender (ibid.: 1920). Only a year later, however, Moonje was endorsing Jinnah's theory that Hindus and Muslims could not be part of one nation, but must necessarily be divided into a Hindu India and a Muslim India. (speech at Gorakhpur Hindu Mahasabha Conference, September 2, 1940, reproduced in Panikkar, 2009: 97). The break between the Congress and the Mahasabha was complete and hostile: the Congress specifically banned its members from taking membership of the Mahasabha.

It was Savarkar, elected president of the Mahasabha in 1937, who coined the word Hindutva, and defined it in terms of the geographical unity of the Indian nation and its association with territory, race, and culture, with religion being ostensibly only one component of culture. Savarkar cleverly asserted commonality with Muslims in terms of their inheritance of Hindu blood "almost unaffected by an alien adulteration" (Savarkar, 1923: 33). Without explicitly stating that religion trumped all other features of potential belonging, he pointed to the extraterritorial locus of the affiliation of non-Hindus, arguing that they could not be Hindus only because for them their alien Holyland (Punyabhu) was above their Fatherland (Pitribhu).

> Ye, who by race, by blood, by culture, by nationality, possess almost all the essentials of Hindutva and had been forcibly snatched out of our ancestral home by the hand of violence—ye, have only to render whole-hearted love to our common Mother and recognize her not only as Fatherland (Pitribhu) but even as a Holyland (Punyabhu); and ye would be most welcome to the Hindu fold. (ibid.: 43)

The majority of Indian Muslims and Christians, Savarkar claimed, could "come to love *our* land as *their* fatherland" (ibid: 33) as they had "all the essential qualifications of Hindutva but one . . . that they do not look upon India as their Holyland" (ibid: 43; emphasis added). Savarkar's dissimulations—in particular his profession that religious minorities should enjoy equal formal rights of citizenship—were dispensed with by Golwalkar (the second head of the RSS) who argued that non-Hindus who did not respect and revere the Hindu religion and adopt its culture and language could stay in the country in subordination "claiming nothing, deserving no privileges, far less any preferential treatment, not even citizen's rights" (Golwalkar, 1939: 48).

The two versions of the universalist argument discussed so far—viz., the national-civic argument of modernists like Nehru, and the national-ethnic argument of Hindu nationalism, are quite fundamentally opposed to each other. The first form of universalism is identity-neutral, accommodative of difference and appreciative of diversity, though it could be vulnerable to the charge of representing the view of dominant religious and caste groups. Counterposed to this is the rival Hindutva form of universalism that views the "other" as actually a part of the "self"—a part that has been separated (by conversion) and misled into owing allegiance to a holy land beyond the land of the Hindus—that may be readmitted on the condition that it agrees to forsake its otherness. This is an argument that seeks to universalize through homogenization. It projects majoritarianism into universalism, through the systematic elimination or incorporation of difference. Being intolerant of difference, it would have us either absorb or banish diversity. The distinction between the two forms of universalism is that while the first accepts the coexistence of diversity within a pluralist framework, the second wishes to devour or eliminate it in an aspirational mononational and monocultural state. Though Hindutva clearly makes a claim based on a particular identity, it is the claim of a dominant group, and not one based in disadvantage or oppression. If it argues for differentiated citizenship, it does so by marrying this identity with the idea of universalism, such that differentiation creates an exclusion from the Hindu universal.

This projection of the particular as the universal is also evidenced in the views of Hindu organizations toward the claims of lower castes, before as well as after 1947. It has been argued that the upper-caste orientation of Hindu nationalist organizations, and the RSS in particular, stemmed from the latter's Maharashtrian origins and the fear of Dalit assertiveness in that region (T. Basu et al., 1993: 10). The organic vision of the Hindu Rashtra (nation) refuses to recognize the need for special rights for groups. Hindutva differentiates between Hindus and non-Hindus, but will not acknowledge claims of differentiation from other Hindu groups. If it is intolerant of Muslim claims to personal law, it has historically also opposed sectional claims from within the Hindu fold for quotas in public services, though political expediency has encouraged it to make some concessions to these in recent times.

In the 1990s, the RSS, the ideological fountainhead of the Bharatiya Janata Party (BJP), was vocally hostile to the announcement of the implementation of the Mandal Commission Report, even proposing a gradual reduction in the quotas for Scheduled Castes. The BJP initially opposed caste quotas, but eventually capitulated to what it saw as the political necessity of attracting the substantial vote of the Other Backward Classes, and to please its partners in the National Democratic Alliance. In general, however, the approach of the BJP has been to encourage groups like the OBCs to see themselves as

Hindus first. It has viewed itself—vis-à-vis the undifferentiated Hindu community—as an assimilative and absorptive entity, much like the Congress did historically, albeit with a wider and more heterogeneous assemblage of social groups. At least in respect of the claims of the OBCs, there is a discomfiting similarity between these two forms of universalism. Earlier forms of Nehruvian universalism could recognize the interests of disadvantaged caste and tribal groups as deserving (even if temporarily) special provision, but were not equally sympathetic to the claims of the Other Backward Classes.

Impeccable Universalism

A third, quintessentially liberal, assertion of universal citizenship was contained in the claims advanced by women's organizations, in the early years of the twentieth century, for the franchise and equal political status, with a simultaneous rejection of special provisions such as separate electorates or quotas. The first women's delegation to wait upon the secretary of state and the viceroy (Montagu and Chelmsford) in 1917 asked the colonial government to give women the vote, and thereby grant them the status of "people" (Forbes, 2004: 92). The following year, Sarojini Naidu—who had led that delegation—argued eloquently at the Congress session for the rational, scientific, and political soundness of enfranchising women. She simultaneously reassured her audience—which passed the resolution by a resounding three-fourths majority—that this was no transgression of tradition and that women would not, by participating in politics, become less feminine. Her views were echoed by other women leaders, such as Saraladevi Chaudhurani, who defined the sphere of women as including politics and "comradeship with men in the rough and tumble of life" (Forbes, 2004: 94).

In 1925, in her message to the forthcoming Cawnpore Congress of which she was president-elect, Naidu provided a curiously gendered account of the party's programmatic vision:

> Mine, as becomes a woman, is a most modest domestic programme merely to restore to India her true position as the supreme mistress in her own home, the sole guardian of her own vast resources, and the sole dispenser of her own hospitality. As a loyal daughter of Bharata Mata, therefore, it will be my lovely though difficult task, through the coming year, to set my mother's house in order, to reconcile the tragic quarrels that threaten the integrity of her old joint-family life of diverse communities and creeds, and

to find an adequate place and purpose and recognition alike for the lowest and the mightiest of her children, and foster-children, the guests and the strangers within her gates. (Quoted in Sitaramayya, 1935: 490–491)

Through this metaphorical feminization, mainstream political issues—freedom from colonial rule, intercommunity conflict, and the need to address caste disadvantage—were translated into a feminine (rather than protofeminist) vocabulary. These claims were nevertheless accompanied by a strong rejection of any preferential treatment as violative of their demand for absolute political equality. In fact, women's organizations even rejected the prevailing property qualification for the vote and demanded universal adult franchise in joint electorates and on equal terms with men. The language of strident universal citizenship, and resentment at being treated as a "reservable" category rather than as equal, pervades the documents that emanated from women's organizations through the 1930s, the ultimate touchstone of these arguments being the Karachi declaration of the Indian National Congress in 1931.

Women's demands for enfranchisement were strongly influenced by the ideas of the British suffragists, many of whom were in touch with the women's movement in India. Eleanor Rathbone actually disagreed with the Indian women's insistence on universal adult franchise, which she believed would materialize in due course anyhow. She prioritized representation as being more important for social reform, and suggested to Indian women colleagues that they should accept reservations. Eventually, this turned out to be the only concession that women could in fact extract. The denial of the franchise on the grounds that it was "premature" triggered angry activity and depositions before many official committees in England as well as in India. Their claim to speak on behalf of all Indian women was dismissed by British officials who viewed them as elite exceptions to the vast majority of women in India—stereotypically characterized as veiled, uneducated, and ignorant—and therefore representing only their own limited class.

The women's campaign for the franchise was effectively thwarted by both colonial officialdom and the nationalist leadership. The claims of women to universal citizenship were repeatedly rebuffed and indeed treated as deserving of differentiated policy rather than being admitted on terms of political equality. Where women leaders demanded a proportion of 1:5 female to male voters, the White Paper of 1933 recommended an increase from the existing 1:20 to 1:10. In 1933, the All India Women's Conference repudiated both separate electorates and reserved seats thus:

We look upon nominations, reservation of seats, and co-option in any sphere
of activity as a pernicious and humiliating system which must run counter to
all real progress. However impartially carried out it must, by its very nature,
engender an inferiority complex amongst those for whom it caters, a contingency to be avoided at all costs . . . (Quoted in Dhanda, 2008: 5)

The official nationalist position supported the women's demand for enfranchisement no more than did the colonial state. Gandhi himself enjoined women to first join forces with men in the fight against the greatest
common enemy, British rule, the removal of which would bring with it the
right to vote among all other rights. Other prominent nationalists too preferred that women busy themselves with issues of civil rights and franchise
instead of engaging in culturally disloyal discussions on patriarchy and subordination.[11] Indeed, Lord Montagu actually expressed his reluctance to
offend (male) nationalists on religious grounds by conceding the demands
of women (Forbes, 2004: 99). One way or another, women dropped their
political demands out of deference to Gandhi and accepted political quiescence. Coaxed—by the government, the nationalist leadership and their
friends in the British suffragist movement alike—the leaders of the wom-
en's movement eventually accepted reservations as the first step towards
social reform.

In the 1930s, even as Gandhi's opposition to Ambedkar's proposal for
separate electorates for the Scheduled Castes was sustained, women came
to be treated—like Muslims—as a discrete constituency. Both Muslims and
women received the right to vote in separate Muslim-only and women-only
constituencies respectively, with Muslim women finding themselves under
considerable pressure by the Muslim League to support community candidates, and disavow gender affiliations. Sporting a position that was ostensibly
favorable to women's representation, Jinnah said it was absolutely essential to
"give every opportunity to our women to participate in our struggle of life
and death." This participation was apparently to be performed from the safe
confines of their homes, because, said Jinnah, "women can do a great deal
within their homes even under *purdah*" (presidential address at the All India
Muslim League Annual Session at Lahore, March 22, 1940, reproduced in
Panikkar, 2009: 546). The Indian National Congress likewise supported only
those women who contested reserved seats, with even Nehru using nationalism to trump women's demands. In the 1937 elections to the provincial
assemblies, four million women voters were enfranchised, though only a

quarter of them actually voted, and about sixty women contested elections from reserved constituencies (Singer, 2007: 39–45).

Women's claims to universal citizenship were curiously premised on the idea of separate spheres—"separate goals, separate destinies" (Naidu, quoted in Forbes, 2004: 94) —for men and women. While the influence of the public realm on the private sphere of family and household went largely unremarked, citizenship was viewed as belonging to the public sphere to which women would, through their enfranchisement, bring the values and virtues of the private sphere, without in any way threatening men's exercise of their functions and civic duties. The public sphere was presented as a domain where rights were exercised, while the private sphere was represented as a domain of responsibilities, toward families and children, with women's responsibilities in the private sphere also entailing their role as mothers of the nation, imparting civic education to their children. Sacrificing their political demands, thousands of women participated in large numbers in the anticolonial movement, many of them going to jail with infants. The women's movement was effectively swallowed up by the independence movement.

In the Constituent Assembly, as in the years before it, women members opposed reservations for themselves. While the Fundamental Rights were enacted in a way intended to be gender-neutral, social rights were placed in the Directive Principles of State Policy. The visibility of women is therefore greater in this chapter of the Constitution with many articles explicitly mentioning women—e.g., the right to equal pay for equal work, the right to an adequate livelihood, just and humane conditions of work and maternity relief, and, of course, the contentious uniform civil code—being located here, in the only non-justiciable section of the Indian Constitution.

Three Forms of Group-Differentiated Citizenship

GDC as an Antidote to Majoritarianism

The two preeminent claims to group-differentiated citizenship before independence were those of the Muslims and the Dalits. The most radical of these was indisputably that represented by the Muslim League, initially for separate electorates, then for power-sharing arrangements, and eventually culminating in the demand for the separate state of Pakistan. The move from separate electorates to the two-nation theory was not however a linear progression, much less one driven by an ineluctable telos. Muslim society in India was highly differentiated by region, language, and class. Though the politics of the Muslim League were dependent on the construction of a homogeneous Muslim identity, the diversity within Muslim society in India was not merely a matter of sociology but also one of class and politics. The Muslim League was, for instance, the clear object of the ire of the Momins (a Muslim sect), as they complained bitterly in 1939 that despite accounting for nearly half of Indian Muslims, they had been "systematically exploited by Muslim politicians—all of whom belong to the "Shareef" class that is upper class and have demanded and obtained special privileges which they have proceeded to enjoy for themselves" (*Leader,* December 8, 1939, reproduced in Hasan, 2008b: 1415).

The disparate currents of Muslim opinion in the first half of the twentieth century—in the complex ideas of intellectuals like Iqbal, Maulana Azad, Mohammed Ali, and Jinnah—cannot be synthesized into a singular narrative, as their ideas about the relationship between the individual, the community, and the state informed their evolving political projects. Even in the late 1930s, Muslim identity-formation took very different forms in the provincial and national registers: for instance, to be a national minority claiming separate electorates also implied accepting the status of a majority community in Muslim-dominated provinces like the Punjab and granting separate electorates to the Hindu minority at the provincial level. It was complicated even further by the need to negotiate the contrary pulls of colonial subjecthood and Islamic universalist ideas, as when Britain and Turkey were arranged on opposite sides in WWI. Any narrative of the Muslim demand for separate nationhood has to reckon with these complex, multiple, and often discordant sources of the fashioning of a Muslim identity in colonial India, not excluding the response to a developing majoritarian Hindu discourse. This is a history that has been told and retold (Jalal, 2001; Hasan, 1993; Talbot, 1998), interpreted and reinterpreted, and there is little to add here except to affirm that it belongs quite unambiguously to the category of claims to group-differentiated citizenship, a claim that was actualized through the creation of the state of Pakistan.

GDC as an Antidote to Discrimination

The second strong argument for differentiated citizenship, Ambedkar's demand for separate electorates for the Depressed Classes[12] (as Dalits were then labeled), met with strong resistance in multiple quarters, rather like the claim of the women's movement. It was a claim to which the colonial state was less than receptive (Zelliot, 1972: 90). Since these groups represented between 15 and 20 percent of the population, not a proportion to be scoffed at in the electoral arithmetic,[13] it had already generated new fears among the (mostly upper-caste Hindu) nationalists. Gandhi's fierce opposition to this proposal led to the compromise formula arrived at in the Poona Pact to keep Hindus and the Depressed Classes in the same electorates, but reserve a proportion of seats in the assemblies for candidates belonging to the latter group. This was of course an important part of the template provided to the Constituent Assembly.

Even as he advanced claims of group-differentiated citizenship, Ambedkar was a thoroughgoing modernist attached to an individualist view of social organization, inspired by French republicanism. In his incomplete work *India and Communism,* Ambedkar contrasted "The Hindu Social Order" with the two essential principles of a "free social order": that the individual is an end in himself [*sic*] with the object of society being the development and growth of the individual's personality; and that members of society associate with each other on the basis of the principles of liberty, equality, and fraternity. He quoted, approvingly and extensively, from the writings of Jacques Maritain to underscore the "value of the person, his dignity and rights, (which) belong to the order of things naturally sacred" (Ambedkar, 1987, 3: 95–96).

As a modernist and nation-builder, Ambedkar hoped for the annihilation of caste:

> You cannot build anything on the foundations of caste. You cannot build up a nation, you cannot build up a morality. Anything that you will build on the foundations of caste will crack and will never be a whole. (Rodrigues, 2002: 287–288)

But as a Dalit leader, he fought hard for political safeguards for Dalits. In his evidence before the Southborough Committee in 1919, Ambedkar had emphatically announced that the Untouchable was not even a citizen, because the two most important rights of citizenship—the right of representation and the right to hold office under the state—were beyond his reach (Thorat and Kumar, 2008: 75–76). For the Untouchables to be citizens, it was essential for them to be adequately represented in the cabinet, the bureaucracy, and of course the legislatures, with the right to elect their own representatives by adult suffrage, by separate electorates for the first ten years and thereafter by joint electorates and reserved seats.

There are intriguing shifts in Ambedkar's position over time and in response to political imperatives. In the 1920s, for instance, he was far from convinced about the merits of separate electorates, and supported adult franchise as an antidote to these. He recognized that such electorates had the merit of representing the members of a particular group, but he feared their divisive potential and cited the example of many countries[14] in which diversity was accommodated within the framework of a common government (Rodrigues, 2002: 85). On the question of whether there were separate interests that needed to be separately represented, Ambedkar argued that many important issues in the secular domain—such as taxation, education, land tenure, social insurance, the role of the state in the economy, and so on— could hardly be said to be issues that concerned one community alone (ibid.: 83). There can therefore be *special concerns* but not *special interests*. It was this incipient idea of special concerns that found reflection, some decades later, in the deliberations of the Constituent Assembly.

In retrospect, Ambedkar's advocacy of separate representation for the Depressed Classes sits oddly with his declared vision of a society from which caste would be completely abolished.[15] In fact, he oscillated between two quite distinct programmatic visions for the Dalits: on the one hand, emphasizing political organization for the representation of Dalits in public institutions and, on the other, advocating that Dalits convert to non-Hindu religions. Running parallel, there appears to be a tension between them: one, a strategy for claiming rights in public institutions and two, a strategy for opting out— to use Hirschmann's terms, strategies simultaneously of voice and of exit. His attempts at mobilizing labor belonged to a completely distinct third category to which caste was clearly peripheral.

GDC as an Antidote to Backwardness

While the previous two categories of GDC were articulated as political and representative claims by the Muslim League and the Dalits respectively, there was a third category of GDC that did not emerge as a claim, but was imposed by the colonial state on the tribal communities of India, on the grounds of their backwardness. The term backwardness was also being used by the so-called Other Backward Classes, particularly after the more compelling claims of the so-called Depressed Classes had been separated from these. This phrase has been endowed with different meanings at different points in time, with the current meaning having been fixed as recently as 1985. The groups that we identify by the label Other Backward Classes today were recognized in the early 1900s in the princely states of Kolhapur (1902) and Mysore (1920s), as well as in the Bombay and Madras Presidencies, which provided for reservations in public employment and education for "backward communities," defined as all non-Brahmins, and therefore also encompassing the groups that would today be described as Scheduled Castes and Scheduled Tribes. The anti-Brahmin movement of the Justice Party in Madras resulted in the allocation of all public service appointments between various caste and religious groups in a fixed proportion, but the claims of the non-Brahmin castes at this time were not intended so much to reject caste as to usurp caste power from the Brahmins. As such, it was a substantively different project than that of the Dalits, who were fighting discrimination and subordination; and a substantively similar one to that of the Muslim League in that the backward castes were also seeking a share in power, through proportional representation in the legislatures and the administration. The next chapter essays a substantive discussion of the question of the backwardness of tribes and OBCs.

Conclusion

In this chapter, I chose to frame the debate on community, culture, and citizenship using the categories of universal and group-differentiated citizenship that have been central to the political theory of citizenship in recent times. These categories are heuristically useful, and the debate among political theorists on their civic and political implications is particularly instructive. While acknowledging the usefulness of these categories in framing our discussion of conceptions of citizenship in late colonial India, two qualifications are proposed. First, as a dyad of pure types, these categories are excessively dichotomized. The rich and wide range of ideas on the question of citizenship and community in late colonial India—of which only a few strands have been instantiated here—eludes the straitjacket of the binary. The abundance of hybridities encourages us to rearticulate the categories as complex, internally differentiated, and contextually situated. As we saw, the communitarian ideology of Hindutva yielded a perverse and exclusionary universalism rather than a claim to group-differentiated citizenship. Again, the Dalit claim to group-differentiated citizenship was most strongly articulated by Ambedkar, who was an individualist committed to a universal conception of rights.

The colonial resolution of claims to differentiated citizenship was similarly marked by diversity and sometimes even institutional capriciousness. While Muslims were granted religiously differentiated separate electorates, the Dalits (not least because of Gandhi's resistance) were merely granted quotas. On the other hand, the universalist claims of the women's movement were countered with gender-differentiated citizenship on the pattern of separate electorates. It is precisely because neither the claims nor the state responses to them can be neatly classified into one or other category of the binary that we have introduced qualifiers such as substantive-inclusionary and descriptive-exclusionary universalism.

Second, claims to citizenship are typically driven by empirical experiences of oppression or marginalization, and associated with particular policy outcomes or institutional arrangements, such as affirmative action or rights to language, that are seen as fairer or more just. In late colonial India, the three major claims to GDC sought remedies for majoritarianism, discrimination, and backwardness. The aspiration to redress disadvantage through forms of symbolic recognition or affirmative action represented only the exteriority of the problem without offering any resolution of the foundational politico-philosophical issue of whether the citizen can represent herself to the state or whether she needs community mediation for this. The nascent liberal idea of a pure unmediated relationship between citizen and state was buffeted by particular institutional outcomes as it struggled for preeminence against conceptions of citizenship that insisted on mediations by community. Indeed, over time, the primacy accorded to institutional outcomes cast the more fundamental question of how to fashion the relationship between citizen and state into eternal conceptual oblivion. The historically specific character of the evolution of Indian citizenship may lie at the heart of this ambiguity, for the idea of GDC originates in contexts where universalism has already been the default position for a century or more, and claims to GDC are mounted in opposition to it. In India, by contrast, GDC is the default sanctified by the colonial state, and universalist citizenship represents the political agenda of its transformation. The legacy of this unsettled question is apparent in the struggles for quotas and representation even a century on. Markers of community belonging entrench different modes of citizen–state relations, as unmarked (for political purposes) citizens relate to the state quite differently from marked citizens with their reliance on community agency or political parties that proclaim the advancement of community interests.

The major fault lines of the late colonial period—Muslims, Dalits, and women, now seeking GDC—are not dramatically altered after 1947. The most central contemporary challenge of GDC comes from two groups that have either chosen backwardness as self-description or been officially characterized as backward and therefore deserving of GDC. These are the OBCs, whose interests are perceived to have been neglected in the constitutional consensus, and the tribal communities whose recent assertions are prompted by their genuine vulnerability to the consequences of natural resource exploitation, development, and displacement. Given the extraordinary political purchase enjoyed by the idea of backwardness in Indian political discourse, the next chapter is substantially about backwardness as the preeminent basis of group-differentiated citizenship today, and why it might be said to have displaced the canonical concepts—such as oppression, marginalization, and exploitation—that have conventionally justified practices of group-differentiated citizenship.

8

Passages from Backwardness
to Citizenship

In June 1950, a Brahmin woman called Champakam Dorairajan appealed to
the Madras High Court asking for the protection of her fundamental rights
under the Constitution. Her specific plea was for the Court to strike down a
government order by which admissions into medical colleges in Madras were
allocated between different caste groups, implying that she—as a Brahmin—
would not be eligible for admission. The case went on appeal to the Supreme
Court which struck down the communal quota.[1] It was subsequently found
that Dorairajan had not in fact applied for admission. More importantly, this
was the case that led to the enactment of the First Amendment to the Indian
Constitution, allowing for the state to make "special provision for members
of socially and educationally backward classes" without this being in any way
discriminatory.[2]

Backwardness is the unique contribution of Indian political and constitutional discourse to the repertoire of justifications for group-differentiated citizenship.[3] In this chapter, we explore the idea of backwardness as it occurs in
relation to two groups—the tribals and the so-called Other Backward Classes.
Neither of these umbrella labels has any sociological basis; an officially designated tribal person in Nagaland would not perceive any commonality with

an officially designated tribal person in Chhattisgarh. These categories hold no meaning either for the self-description of an individual's identity; they are alien to the lived social experiences of those who are so labeled. They become a part of the self-identification of people only in their occasional interface with government. These are therefore synthetic categories of governance, albeit categories in the perpetuation of which sections of Indian society have an enormous stake. Even as backwardness acquires ever greater validation as a criterion of group-differentiated citizenship, the categories are, as administrative constructs, bedeviled by definitional ambiguities that increasingly fuel contestations and inform conflicts over citizenship. Despite the shared description of backwardness, the forms of group-differentiated citizenship (GDC) offered to the two groups under discussion here were not only different to begin with, but also evolved very differently over time, with vastly different consequences for their citizenship in the present.

Framed as an attribute of communities rather than individuals, backwardness reinforces the idea of citizenship mediated by community. While backwardness generates claims to entitlements in both our cases, in the first, the tribal case, the ascription of backwardness is a *benefaction* of the colonial state persisting into the postcolonial; in the second, it is represented as a *demand* of the Other Backward Classes to GDC. In both, backwardness appears not so much as an innate property of persons as the literal meaning of the word suggests, but as a disadvantage that is largely the product of external social and historical factors,[4] and as such the eminently deserving object of redress. As an externally induced attribute—something that is *done to* one, rather than something that one *is* to start with—backwardness must necessarily be externally remediable.

It is moreover an attribute that attaches not to individuals but to communities. The affirmation of the equal or superior moral worth of communities, rather than the equal moral worth of individuals, fortifies the legitimacy of mediated citizenship. Of course, only particular types of community—demonstrably backward ones—qualify. Since the moral worth of individuals is a derivative of the status of the communities to which they belong, the individual cannot escape the community, her membership of which is simultaneously the source of her predicament as well as the solution to it. Indeed, to become a citizen is to escape the community, but paradoxically the route to becoming an unmarked citizen is only through the community, and on this both the state and the community are of one mind. The advantages of

GDC are conferred upon her by virtue of her community membership, just as the disadvantages that preceded it were a consequence of it. The legitimacy of GDC is then derived, as the very label suggests, from the recognition that communities are rights-bearing political agents in a way that individuals cannot be except in the aggregate, for it is only the claims of communities to equal or higher intercommunity worth that justifies claims to GDC.

As the compelling basis of an entitlement, backwardness is shorn of its literally pejorative and stigmatizing quality. Entitlements generate aspirations to be labeled as backward, with higher degrees of backwardness yielding putatively higher levels of entitlement. Such estimations of relative backwardness are to be found in both administrative[5] as well as political discourse; it is certainly familiar to contemporary Indians as the politics of competitive backwardness. Claims of this kind were commonly made in the constitution-making process, as when the Scheduled Tribes were stated to be "more backward" than the Scheduled Castes (Rao, 1967, 3: 748). Testifying to the Statutory Commission, Dr. Ambedkar made the case that the Depressed Classes needed political representation more than did the Muslims. He even capitulated to prejudice as he endeavored to establish that the untouchable castes were more disadvantaged than the tribals on account of the practice of untouchability.

> The situation is full of humor when one sees members of these Primitive and Criminal Tribes feeling that they would be polluted if they would touch an Untouchable. *They are poor, filthy, superstitious, ignorant, far more than the Untouchables yet they pride themselves as socially superior to the Untouchables.* . . . If the Primitive Tribes have no opportunities for advancement it is because they choose to live in isolation. But once they come out of their forest recesses and take part in civilization, there is nothing that will stand in their way. (Ambedkar, 1989, 5: 143; emphasis added)

As groups vie with each other to obtain rewards from the state, it is not enough for them to establish that they are exploited or marginalized. Their case is strengthened if they are able to establish how much more backward they are as compared to other disadvantaged groups. When backwardness acquires preeminence as a criterion of claims to preferential treatment, the likelihood of other sources of disadvantage—such as marginalization, exploitation, or powerlessness—yielding entitlements diminishes.

The specification of backwardness, as well as the entitlements that follow from it, are of course deeply embedded in context, both historical and political. In what follows, we shall mark the shifts in the career of backward-ness as an idea whose definition varies as it is empirically translated over time but always and invariably appears as a deficiency—sometimes as lack of con-tact with "civilization," at other times as modes of livelihood or practices of cultivation, and often as absence of education. The claim to redress is equally context-specific, as backward groups tend to demand reservations rather than social and economic rights, and the state tends to be correspondingly slow in recognizing such rights. As all self-styled backward groups compete for a share of the same good, there is a disincentive for cross-cutting materially grounded political alliances, such as class coalitions. It is hardly surprising then that the increasing salience of claims to GDC in independent India is accompanied by a gradual eclipse of working class and peasant movements. As the preeminent criterion of entitlements in contemporary India, the idea of backwardness tends also to confine the pursuit of citizenship to the domain of the state or public institutions.

The present of backwardness—its meaning as well as its political pur-chase—is, needless to say, quite different from its past.[6] In the early twen-tieth century, the term Backward Classes was used to denote one or more of the following: the untouchable castes, the aboriginal people, the criminal tribes, and the castes that were not untouchable but belonged to the lower strata. Eventually, the untouchables acquired a distinctive appellation—the Depressed Classes[7]—rendering the category of the Backward Classes simul-taneously residual and ambiguous. As the Constituent Assembly began the drafting of the Constitution, it was tasked with providing "safeguards" for the minorities, the backward and tribal *areas,* the depressed and other back-ward *classes.* Backwardness could thus be an attribute of a place or of a class or community, but definitely not of individuals—except to the extent that they partook of the qualities of the community to which they belonged. The term class was frequently a euphemism for caste, though this was not explicitly stated; it helped that there was considerable ambiguity about which castes could and would be included in this label.

Backwardness as a construct was premised on a prior severance of this concept from that of minority, a separation that occurred in the delibera-tions of the Constituent Assembly. As Bajpai has shown, the Untouchable castes initially claimed to be minorities for purposes of special representa-tion. When, however, many of the privileges attached to minority status were being dismantled, and backwardness held out the promise of reservations, even Muslims began to ground their demands in claims of backwardness rather than minority status (Bajpai, 2011: 163). The progressive diminution of "political safeguards" (such as separate electorates) for minorities was accompanied by a diversion of these in the form of reservations toward the Scheduled Castes and the Scheduled Tribes, designated as Backward. "Cultural safeguards" too were attenuated, though to a lesser degree (ibid.: 53–57). All these were the result of intense contestation in the Assembly, with members of all communities[8] and political and ideological persuasions participating.

Many members of the Assembly were opposed to any special provisions except for the Scheduled Castes and Tribes. Brajeshwar Prasad, who held that there were no minorities and therefore no minority claims worth considering, did acknowledge the existence of backward communities, "people who have been suppressed and oppressed for centuries. It is their claims and their claims alone that shall be taken into consideration" (CAD 10: 238). Attempts to retain separate electorates failed—not even the Scheduled Castes could secure these. Instead, the minorities were provided with cultural rights (such as to practice their religion and establish educational institutions), while the former Untouchables and tribals were given reservations in legislatures, education, and public employment. The only constitutional provision made for the remaining, still undefined and indeterminate, "backward classes" was that empowering the president to appoint a commission "to investigate the conditions of socially and educationally backward classes . . . and the difficulties under which they labour" (Article 340). Other provisions were only added by the First Amendment (1951).[9] These mentions of "socially and educationally backward classes of citizens" are significant, because they clarified, for the first time, which groups were *not* included in this category, even if the question of who *was* included was left wide open. The separate mention of the Scheduled Castes and Tribes, for instance, made it abundantly clear that they are not part of this category. Likewise, the use of the term minority—specified as being based in religion or language—also indicated that these groups were excluded from the ambit of the concept.

The backwardness of the Scheduled Tribes, as we shall see, was conceptualized much as it had been in colonial times; it was also constitutionalized in a way that was not entirely discontinuous with colonial practice. For the Other Backward Classes (OBCs), on the other hand, the idea of backwardness was ambiguous, not least because it was parasitic upon the question of who belonged to this category, which was at this time fairly amorphous and underdefined.

Tribes: From Backwardness of Place to Backwardness of Community

The categories of colonial governmentality in relation to tribal communities[10] were significantly influenced by the perceptions of missionaries as well as of colonial administrator-anthropologists working in the areas where tribals resided. These observers presented tribal communities as backward and primitive noble savages, in need of both protection and moral improvement, an assumption that informed colonial policy for over half a century, and even found some echoes in the constitutional settlement of the question in independent India. Among the flaws of the official sociology that informed the category of Scheduled Tribe was its imposition of a conceptual and administrative uniformity on a socially heterogeneous plurality, mistakenly making similar attributions of backwardness about all the communities encompassed by it.

Although the uniting of large numbers of communities that are extremely diverse—in terms of region, culture, religion, and language—under the singular governmental banner of the Scheduled Tribe[11] is indisputably an artifice, it helpfully signals the exceptions to "normal" forms of governance in all the areas populated by the Scheduled Tribes. The beginnings of such exceptions lie in the Scheduled Districts Act of 1874, which separated these areas from the remit of the new provincial legislatures and from the operation of laws in force in other parts of British India. In the following decades, the colonial state began to distinguish between tribal areas that could be governed more or less directly. The imperative of controlling tribal insurgencies, as well as that of exploiting the mineral wealth of these regions, was undoubtedly an added incentive.

After the passage of the 1874 Act, the determination of the modes of governance appropriate to the tribal areas proceeded through three important moments of colonial deliberation, each of which was underpinned by specific assumptions about civic competence and political representation. The first of these was the Government of India Act of 1919, based on the Montagu-Chelmsford report, which, giving the matter its briefest consideration, regretted that the political reforms planned for the rest of British India could not be implemented in these areas. Their exclusion from the reformed provincial government—which increased marginally the representation of Indians in the Councils—was justified by the argument that "the people are primitive, and there is as yet no material on which to found political institutions" (Government of India, 1918: 129). As such, these "typically backward tracts" (ibid.) would be administered by the head of the province, with the Governor-General-in-Council being given the power to declare any territory of British India to be a "backward tract" and also to declare any law to apply or not apply to such territories (Curtis, 1920: 584). On the basis of this exclusion from provincial government, the Act distinguished between the governance of two types of backward tracts: for those that were completely excluded, only the Governor-General-in-Council could legislate; those that were partially excluded fell within the domain of the "reserved" (or unelected) component of the provincial government, split into what was termed Dyarchy.[12] No questions or discussion on the governance of these areas would be entertained except with the permission of the governor.

In the second moment, the new classification in terms of degrees of exclusion from governance arrangements was formalized when the Indian Statutory Commission renamed the two categories of Backward Tracts as Excluded and Partially Excluded Areas. Despite the change in nomenclature, the language of backwardness persisted. The Commission discussed the Backward Tracts of each province separately: people in the Backward Tracts of Bengal were described as being "as primitive as their agricultural methods" (Government of India, 1930a: 62); those in the Himalayan region were deemed to be administratively unproblematic as their affairs were being "satisfactorily transacted under a patriarchal dispensation" (ibid.: 68); those in Bihar and Orissa were described as "credulous and excitable, and almost as much as ever in need of special protection" (ibid.: 71). The Commission reminded the British Parliament that it was responsible not only for protecting the tribal people from exploitation and for preventing tribal insurgency; its chief duty toward them was "to educate these peoples to stand on their own feet, and this is a process which has scarcely begun" (Government of India, 1930b: 109).[13] Paternalism and protection were, at least partially, seen to be necessitated by the phenomenon of tribal exploitation by moneylenders and by their nontribal neighbors. While protection was entirely compatible with a policy of isolationism, it was not always disinterestedly benign, for it did provide the colonial state with a guarantee of privileged access to the mineral wealth of these regions.

The Government of India Act of 1935 represents the third moment of the incorporation of the Scheduled Tribes in colonial political institutions. In consonance with the official view of the time that those nominated to represent the tribals did not have to be tribal themselves,[14] the 1935 Act provided for modest representation for people from the excluded areas. Once again, their ascribed primitivism provided the justification for indirect representation by "a church or religious organization the heads of which are familiar with their needs and can see that their interests are represented in the Provincial Assembly" (Hansard, quoted in McMillan, 2005: 122). The combination of nominated, indirectly elected, and reserved representatives that ensued was explicitly intended to provide representation *for*, rather than *by*, tribal people. The most prominent leader to emerge at this time was the Oxford-educated Jaipal Singh, who became a member of the Constituent Assembly and contributed to the inclusion of tribal interests in the constitution-making process. The marginality of the so-called backward tracts in colonial discourse in late colonial India is paralleled by the marginality of the tribal question in mainstream nationalist discourse. The constitutional incorporation of the Scheduled Tribes after independence demonstrates some continuity with the colonial discourse of protection, though there was a remarkable ambivalence about how protection should be conceived. Colonial policy had infantilized tribal communities, seeking to isolate them with the stated objective of providing protection from the destructions of "civilization" (Corbridge et al., 2004: 182). The new republic, based on the principle of universal citizenship and equal rights, was confronted with the difficulty of striking a balance between, on the one hand, protecting cultural distinctiveness through autonomy in governance arrangements and, on the other, modernizing through developmental interventions. It did not help that most of those involved in drafting the Constitution had no firsthand familiarity with the regions and peoples for whom they were legislating.[15]

In the search for a modified universalism, the contest between arguments for integration and isolation mirrored the contest between universal and group-differentiated notions of citizenship. Sensitive to this contradiction, Jawaharlal Nehru emphasized the need to find a middle way between the British extreme of treating the tribals as "anthropological specimens to be kept for museum purposes" and another extreme of treating them "like any other citizen." While the latter sounds "democratic and good," he said, it places a great burden on them as they are not suited to compete with the market economy and will only get exploited and oppressed (2003a: 713).[16] Most of Nehru's peers in the Constituent Assembly, however, appear to have shared the prejudices of the colonial state. Even Ambedkar argued against special provision for the Scheduled Tribes, on the grounds that they had not yet developed any political sense, and could easily become instruments in the hands of others (Ambedkar, 1979, 1: 375).[17] More than a decade later, the chroniclers of the Assembly's efforts referred to tribals as "primitive people, simple, unsophisticated and frequently improvident" (Rao, 1968: 569). The two subcommittees on this question[18] agreed that backwardness was a function of the *area* in which tribal people resided, and of the lack of educational facilities, medical aid, and communications (Rao, 1967, 3: 772). The appropriate remedy for their backward condition was development rather than isolation; educational improvement and economic betterment would raise their standard of living and help them assimilate with the rest of the population.

Despite a broad consensus on these recommendations, there were some disagreements about the details.[19] The question of whether backwardness was the property of a place (and its separation or isolation) or of a community was reflected in the principal contention over how the welfare of tribal people not resident in Scheduled Areas (outside Assam) would be governed. Should members of such communities living outside of areas designated as backward be eligible for special provisions just like those living within them? Until this time, the colonial state had used both categories of Scheduled Areas/Backward Tracts and Scheduled Tribes/Backward Tribes more or less interchangeably, glossing over the common though anomalous points where these did not converge on the assumption that (a) backward tribes lived nowhere other than such backward areas and its obverse (b) that only backward tribes lived in backward tracts. This meant that the status of tribals living outside Scheduled Areas was as indeterminate as the status of nontribals living in Scheduled Areas. Some (including Ambedkar) took the position that it was backwardness of area that counted, so that only states with scheduled areas should have Tribal Advisory Councils, and that there was no need to create such councils in states that did not have scheduled areas even if they had scheduled tribespeople living in them. The contrary argument asserted the backwardness of both place and community, and therefore demanded such councils also for millions of people belonging to the scheduled tribes but living outside the scheduled areas.

The needs of the Assam and non-Assam areas were also seen to translate differently into arrangements for democratic governance. The subcommittee on Assam insisted that the idea of democracy was already familiar to the hill people, whose tribal and village councils were based on the principles of general assent or election (Rao, 1967, 3: 690). It was more concerned about protecting the tribal people by controlling the influx of outsiders seeking to expropriate their lands, and giving their local councils a reasonable share in the exploitation of the mineral wealth of their regions. While the other subcommittee (on the excluded and partially excluded areas *other than Assam*) agreed that protection against expropriation of land and being held hostage by moneylenders were most important, it was not as sanguine about the civic competence of tribal citizens in the areas within its purview. The people of the excluded areas had no experience, it said, of modern self-governing institutions, and it would take time to build, from the village up, interest in local government. The general agreement that the tribal people were, through education and external contact, "capable of being brought to the level of the rest of the population" (ibid.: 746) resulted in the consensus on giving them reserved seats in a joint electorate based on adult franchise. The Scheduled Tribes were not, it argued, very different from the Scheduled Castes; if anything, they were "more backward in education and in their economic condition" than the latter (ibid.: 748). The sooner they learned to participate in direct elections, the better it would be.

On the primary form that redress of tribal backwardness should take, there was little disagreement among members of the Constituent Assembly. Apart from the exceptional arrangements for self-governance at the local level, quotas of 7.5 percent (in proportion to their presence in the population) were provided for members of tribal communities in public employment as well as in publicly funded educational institutions, identical to those provided for the Scheduled Castes,[20] except that the latter constituted 15 percent, reflecting their larger proportion in the Indian population. As with the quotas for the Scheduled Castes, these were intended to be transitional mechanisms in force for a period of ten years.[21] The administration of Scheduled Areas in nine Indian states was provided for in the Fifth Schedule, while the Sixth Schedule provided for the administration, through autonomous district councils and the preservation of traditional systems, of tribal areas in the northeastern states. A range of other programs was also provided to enable the development and welfare of the Scheduled Areas and their residents.

More importantly, after the creation of the northeastern states in the 1960s and 1970s, exceptions were made in terms of special constitutional provisions for states with predominantly tribal populations, such as Nagaland, Assam, Manipur, Sikkim, Mizoram and Arunachal Pradesh. For instance, any parliamentary enactment that related to the religious and social practices of the Nagas, or their customary laws, or even civil and criminal justice under such laws, or their lands and natural resources, would not apply to the state of Nagaland unless the state's legislature decided otherwise (Article 371A).[22]

Nevertheless, there remained a tension between integration and isolation, as universalist norms of citizenship were often indistinguishable from an assimilationist orientation[23] toward tribal populations. The integrationist argument appealed to the idea of a civic community bound by ties of fraternity, which autonomous districts could only undermine as they kept "the tribal people perpetually away from the non-tribals and the bond of friendship which we expect to come into being after the attainment of independence" (CAD 9: 1017). In an almost classic illustration of a difference-blind liberal universalist argument underwriting an assimilationist perspective with little room for the distinctiveness of tribal cultures, K. M. Munshi refused to countenance the twinning of the phrases Scheduled Areas and Scheduled Tribes, because the link between community and place should be considered severed once the individual tribal person came to the city and got absorbed in urban life. He was no longer to be "regarded as a different individual from the rest of the community . . . [who] must have a tribal committee to look after him" (CAD 9: 1000). Citizenship, on this account, is appropriately mediated so long as the individual lives within the scheduled area that is coterminous with the scheduled community; once s/he enters society outside this enclave, s/he must become an unmarked citizen, or the exercise would be in vain. The objective was ostensibly the gradual "normalization" of tribal populations and their eventual emancipation from labeled categories of citizenship.[24]

When could this emancipation be reasonably presumed to occur? The Constitution prescribed a ten-year period of reservations for scheduled tribes and scheduled castes, and members of the Assembly were hopeful and even enthusiastic about accomplishing this monumental task in that time. Unlike the present, where the routine and unquestioning extension of this limit every ten years is grudgingly accepted as a special privilege, the ten-year limit was seen, at the time, as an opportunity to "remove the stigma" of having such a large population living in subhuman conditions, and to make "these scheduled tribes and scheduled areas . . . indistinguishable from the rest of the Indian population" (CAD 9: 981). For evidence that the stigma persists, we need only to refer to the website of the National Commission for Scheduled Tribes, which describes these as "primitive, geographically isolated, shy and socially, educationally and economically backwardness [sic]. . . ."[25]

In the case of the tribal people, then, modernity was the remedy for backwardness. The universalist aspect of the constitutional settlement entailed the shepherding of the tribal people into modernity through development. Better communications would make their habitats less remote, and education and reservations would take these communities "forward" on the assumption that once they had successfully escaped backwardness, they would no longer be different or tribal, just unmarked modern citizens. However, the simultaneous recognition of the need for group-differentiated policies arising out of their cultural distinctiveness intervened to soften this modernizing impulse, by guaranteeing a special architecture of governance. The slew of developmental programs initiated in the first few decades after independence—especially the Tribal Sub-Plans of the 1970s—were designed on the premise of difference, but envisaged as leading eventually to a difference-free modern condition. So was the extension, in 1996, of panchayats[26] to these areas populated by tribals. Reports commissioned by the government however repeatedly provided trenchant critiques of state developmental policies that resulted in poverty and deprivation, the denial of tribal rights to land and forests, and development-induced displacement on an unconscionable scale.[27]

Neither the project of modernization through development nor the special architecture of governance succeeded. Many areas populated by tribal people are today in the grip of armed conflict, though the nature of the conflict differs between the northeastern states (especially Nagaland, Manipur, Tripura, Mizoram, and Assam) and those in central, eastern, and southern India (especially Jharkhand, Chhattisgarh, Orissa, and Andhra Pradesh). The former, characterized as insurgencies by the Indian state, represent themselves as movements for national liberation. Their claims to autonomy signify their dissatisfaction with group-differentiated citizenship, as they seek through self-determination to transcend the very boundaries of the Indian nation-state. The latter category has witnessed intense armed conflict between Maoist cadres and the Indian state. In response to claims of the distinctiveness of tribal identity and the developmental neglect of these regions, two new states, Jharkhand and Chhattisgarh, were carved out of the existing states of Bihar and Madhya

Pradesh in November 2000. While the Maoist or Naxalite[28] movement (these terms will be used interchangeably here) currently encompasses many more states, these two lie at the very heart of this tragic challenge.

It is no coincidence that among the sixty-nine most backward districts of India, twenty-one have a tribal population of over 40 percent, while another six have a tribal population of close to 30 percent.[29] Marked by poverty and alienation, the human development indicators of these regions are appalling: there is a significant gap between the literacy rates of tribals in central India and the national average ; their health indicators—including infant mortality, antenatal care, undernutrition, and stunting and wasting—are the worst of all sections of Indian society, which is unsurprising considering the low availability of the most basic health services in these areas, the official excuse for which continues to be their "remoteness." An indicative exercise by the Planning Commission, comparing (in four states) districts where the Maoist movement is active with districts where it is not, reveals an enormous gap on every indicator from literacy and infant mortality to access to banking and roads (Government of India, 2008a: 21). Added to the insult of poor human development indicators of tribal populations is the injury of displacement[30] by development projects that exploit their land, rivers, and other natural resources for the benefit of others. Though the Indian state had appointed itself the protector of these areas, its control over the commanding heights of the economy—to which the public sector program of heavy industrialization was central—made it also the chief perpetrator of exploitative and even predatory forms of development. Tribal rights to land and forest produce were systematically undermined over time.[31] The displacement of tribal people was seldom compensated by adequate resettlement, recalling the concerns expressed in the Constituent Assembly about depriving those tribal people that lived outside the Scheduled Areas of the special rights that attached to tribals living within such areas.

The economic reforms of the early 1990s, India's new links to the global economy, and the unleashing of new consumer appetites gave a further impetus to the depredation of the mineral-rich tribal areas of central India. The state governments of Jharkhand and Chhattisgarh entered into a slew of Memoranda of Understanding with major steel manufacturing companies, providing access to their iron ore, bauxite, and other mineral resources while ignoring the presumptive rights of ownership held by the tribals to the land and resources of these areas and neglecting to obtain the consent of the local

Gram Sabhas (village assemblies).[32] At about the same time, the Maoist movement began to gather strength in these areas, though it would be simplistic to say that the Maoists express the discontent of the poor and dispossessed tribal populations of these areas. The relationships between these citizens, the state, the Maoists, rural elites, and the commercial interests represented by corporations and contractors are infinitely more complex.

While the Maoists have been present in parts of what are today Jharkhand and Chhattisgarh since the 1980s—when they mobilized the people to fight for their water, forests and land *(Jal, Jangal, Jamin)* and even helped them secure higher wages for their labor in the forests—the current phase of Maoist activism can be dated to the 1990s.[33] In 2004, the two Maoist groups active in tribal areas, the People's War Group (PWG) and the Maoist Communist Centre (MCC) merged (voluntarily and in the presence of an international conference of Maoists in Jharkhand) into a new entity, the Communist Party of India (Maoist). In these two states, the basic fundamental relational premise of citizenship has been questioned and even redefined. A state is arguably a minimum necessary condition for citizenship to be possible, but these are regions characterized by the invisibility of the state. With doctors and teachers invariably absent from their clinics and classrooms, and other state officials resisting postings to remote areas, the state has little or no control over vast swathes of territory. The Maoists have stepped into the vacuum created by state personnel, and have demonstrated their willingness to walk miles to meet tribals and listen to their grievances. In Jharkhand, they have effectively replaced the state and created an alternative apparatus that mimics what states typically do: providing education and even paying government schoolteachers to do their job; training tribal youth in basic healthcare provision; mobilizing initiatives for the construction of tanks to harvest water; imparting new practices of cultivation from growing vegetables to planting orchards for the market; and, above all, providing alternative judicial mechanisms for dispute resolution (Mishra and Pandita, 2010: 48–54). The importance of the "People's Courts" is recognized in a recent report from the Planning Commission, which credits this mechanism with the two virtues of speed and effectiveness, but cautions that while disputes arising from exploitation and economic inequality are settled in accordance with norms of justice, disputes in matrimonial matters may be characterized by crudeness and brutality (Government of India, 2008a: 54).

States typically provide welfare in many of these ways and raise taxes in order to do so. The Maoists function through a system of levies on mine owners, industrialists, and contractors in the region and even through a "market in protection" (A. Shah, 2010: 166). These are undoubtedly forms of extortion, and though there are fixed percentages depending on the scale of the commercial activity, they are often arbitrarily enhanced. The state is, on the one hand, effectively replaced by the Maoists and, on the other, uses the presence of Maoists to justify its own absence. Even electoral institutions are subject to their control.

> More than twelve hundred of Jharkhand's four thousand and five hundred panchayats, or village councils, are reportedly under the control of the Maoists. They are in a position to dictate the electoral outcome in more than 30 per cent of the state's assembly constituencies. . . . In as many as 15 districts, large areas have been converted into "liberated zones" . . . where the rebels run a parallel administration. (Mishra and Pandita, 2010: 85)

The price the tribals paid for Maoist governance was recruitment into violent armed struggle. Some citizens of a war zone live in fear and terror; others may—whether voluntarily or by coercion—be mobilized into militias. Historically, and in many countries even today, the duties of citizenship include military service. In central India, the Maoists have created local militias who are provided weapons and military training and are typically deployed against the state, its officials, and its properties, but also against landlords whose lands have been seized and distributed to the landless poor. The otherwise absent state has in turn retaliated with not just the armed might of its police force, but also—in what has been called an "outsourcing" of law and order (Guha, 2007b: 3310)—by sponsoring a rival vigilante army of citizens. The Nagarik Suraksha Samiti (Citizens' Protection Committee) of Jharkhand and the Salwa Judum (Peace Hunt) of Chhattisgarh are such civil militias organized by the state in its war against the "insurgents." The attractions of getting recruited into such militias are not difficult to fathom: a secure salary in a context where bare survival, let alone a proper livelihood, is hard to secure; some education and health care; and weapons that afford a sense of empowerment to those who have thus far experienced only oppression and powerlessness but are now able to speak back to, and even kill, local notables and officials.

Through its sponsorship of the Salwa Judum, and by making itself scarce, the state in Chhattisgarh provided a license to disorder. In civil-war-like conditions, citizens were left to the mercy of the Maoists on the one hand and the vigilante army on the other. Thousands of insecure citizens fled their homes and fields to live in subhuman conditions in refugee camps, and many thousands were forcibly relocated to Salwa Judum camps, which, given their proximity to police stations and camps, made them all the more vulnerable to Naxalite attacks.[34] Members of the Salwa Judum were appointed as Special Police Officers (SPOs) and given firearms and some minimal training in their use. When they were made to fight other local youth enrolled in the Maoist cadres, fratricidal battles resulted; those who were not involved with either group became potential victims of both groups as well as of the security forces of the state (Government of India, 2008a: 76–77). The Planning Commission commented despairingly on the fact that several thousand tribals were shunted out of their homes and habitats and into camps with even worse living conditions than before, and no means of livelihood.

> It delegitimizes politics, dehumanizes people, degenerates those engaged in their "security," and above all represents abdication of the State itself. It should be undone immediately and be replaced by a strategy which positions an empowered task force of specially picked up responsive officials to execute all protection and development programmes for their benefit and redress people's grievances. (ibid.: 77)

In July 2011, the Supreme Court of India pronounced that the Chhattisgarh government's arming of SPOs was unconstitutional. Launching an impassioned broadside against predatory capitalism, the Court rejected the claim of the state government that the SPOs were only being used as guides and sources of intelligence, as there was clear evidence of the SPOs being engaged in combatant roles in counterinsurgency operations. A major concern was the fact that thousands of young men, many having not even passed the fifth grade, and with the merest pretense of legal education and professional training, were being made into cannon fodder.[35]

This brief narrative of state response to the predicament of India's "backward" tribal citizens after independence shows that in the first phase protection became an excuse for developmental neglect by the state; in the second, development became an excuse for large-scale displacement conducted under state auspices; and most recently, security has become an excuse for state repression. Today, while security justifies state (and state-sponsored) violence, and provides an alibi for the lack of development—no matter that this entrenches backwardness—it does not in any way diminish extractive and predatory interventions by the state itself, or by the state in collusion with capital. If human development indicators can be treated as a proxy for backwardness, it is clear that the tribal people of central India remain "backward." Not only did the promise of protection for their cultural distinctiveness prove to be hollow, the developmental policies by which they were to be turned into unmarked citizens failed tragically. Today, these people are subject to exploitation by corporations, contractors, and moneylenders; they live in conditions of extreme vulnerability to violence from the forces of the state as well as the Maoists; and they are, above all, victims of social disarticulation in a society that has been brutalized by the rival arming of their young now pitted against each other.

The Other Backward Classes:
From Residuality to Majority

For the so-called "backward classes," who were neither culturally distinctive nor lived in remote areas, the task of identifying indicators of backwardness was considerably more challenging than that for the Scheduled Tribes. There is no clear or precise answer to what was or is backward about the so-called backward classes, for this has been a description attached to different constellations of social groups at different points in time, with the definition being correspondingly elastic. With the Depressed Classes (later Scheduled Castes) acquiring an autonomous label, the Backward Classes became a residual category. It was also, for a long time, a category that had regional rather than national purchase. Both these limitations were gradually transcended as the category found reinvention as the "Other Backward Classes" which was in fact entirely a conglomeration of caste groups. At the time the Constituent Assembly met, this narrower meaning, from which the Scheduled Castes and Scheduled Tribes had been detached, was yet to be delineated with any degree of clarity.[36] Multiple meanings and connotations bounced back and forth in the debates in the Assembly, leading Ambedkar to finally declare: "a backward community is a community which is backward *in the opinion of the Government*"[37] (CAD 7: 702; emphasis added).

The nomenclatural disputes were, of course, disputes about both social meaning as well as the entitlements that would accompany the designation. When members from the northern provinces assumed the term to be synonymous with the Scheduled Castes, their counterparts from southern India[38] had to explain that the term had a distinctive, almost technical, meaning, which varied from one state to another: in some states only Brahmins were excluded from its ambit while in others it included all the castes between the Brahmins and the Scheduled Castes (Galanter, 1984: 159). There was considerable debate about why castes should be described as classes, as well as some attempts to place everyone who was poor (in economic terms) into this category.

For Nehru and Ambedkar, the civic nation of the dominant consensus had to be a "casteless" society. Academic sociologists like Ghurye denied the very existence of a category such as a Backward Class. For Ghurye, a plural society—such as seemed to be emerging from the hardening of castes and subcastes on an all-India basis—was not merely less desirable than a casteless society, but was also a step away from it (Ghurye, 1993: 451). At this time, the very label OBC concealed the discomfort with using caste officially (except of course for the Scheduled Castes). The claim to backwardness was shrouded in a deliberate misnaming that kept the fiction of a civic nation afloat, even while the law and policy increasingly gave it the lie.[39]

The actual percentage of OBCs in the country's population has always been disputed and remains so to the present day. In the 1950s, various sources, from the census to the Planning Commission, judged it to be approximately 20 percent of the population. It was left to the First Backward Classes Commission, appointed in 1953, to wrestle with the definitional problem, to determine the criteria to be adopted in deciding which groups should be treated as "socially and educationally backward," and to prepare a list in accordance with these criteria. It elected to classify communities chiefly on the basis of their position in the caste hierarchy. Sifting the several thousand claims it received, the Commission drew up a list of 2,399 backward groups, accounting for 32 percent of the population of India, and made proposals for their improvement. The other criteria used to determine backwardness—literacy and educational standards, representation in government and industry, and economic backwardness—were also applied to caste groups and subcastes, rather than to individuals. The idea of backwardness was thus reified as a quality attaching to a group rather than to individual citizens, and as this became the basis of claims to entitlements, it entrenched further the idea of citizenship as a relation between the state and particular communities rather than between the state and its individual citizens. Having produced a landmark report, Kaka Kalelkar, the chairman of the Commission, developed cold feet at the end, and virtually disavowed the report in his covering note. His discomfort was twofold: first, with the determination of disadvantage on the basis of communities rather than individuals and families; and second, with using caste—rather than economic, educational, cultural, and residential criteria—as the primary criterion of backwardness. "It would have been better," he wrote, "if we could determine the criteria of backwardness on principles other than caste" (Government of India, 1956b: xiv).

The government too was not particularly pleased by the excessive emphasis on caste. This was after all the heyday of the nation-building project, with social cohesion and "national integration"[40] being important state objectives. Giving an impetus to caste was viewed as encouraging divisiveness. The Home Minister decried caste as "the greatest hindrance in the way of our progress toward an egalitarian society" and worried that recognizing specific castes as backward could "serve to maintain and perpetuate the existing distinctions on the basis of caste" (ibid.: 172). Leaving it to the states to conduct surveys to determine the numbers of OBCs and make special provisions for them, the Union Cabinet decided in 1961 that no national list of OBCs needed to be drawn up, and announced its own preference for economic criteria rather than caste for purposes of providing assistance to people who needed it for education or technical training. The Commission's report was not discussed in Parliament for a full ten years; and when it was, the government repeated its objection to caste and "communal" criteria as being contrary to the principle of social justice and unfair to the poor.[41]

The issue of backwardness and reservations spawned an enormous volume of litigation, beginning with *Champakam Dorairajan*, mentioned at the beginning of this chapter. In some cases the Supreme Court ruled that while classes need not be only castes, castes definitely qualified as classes.[42] In others, even as it validated caste as a criterion, it was emphatic that caste could not be the sole test of backwardness. The ruling in *Ramakrishna Singh v. State of Mysore* that a person's economic circumstances could be a test of backwardness brought the focus on the individual rather than the community as a criterion. In *M. R. Balaji v. State of Mysore,* similarly, the apex court held that "classes of citizens who are deplorably poor (are) automatically socially backward" and that classifying citizens as socially backward "on the basis of their castes alone is not permissible under Art. 15(4)."

The problem of defining social and educational backwardness remained. The latter came to be increasingly determined by literacy tests—if a high proportion of members of a community was literate, then its claims to backwardness were questionable—on occasion supplemented by a measure of the group's representation in government service. Social backwardness was trickier, and came to be defined entirely by caste-related indicators such as ritual ranking, traditional occupations, untouchability and even popular perceptions of a community's social standing. There was some debate also about whether a community needed to be *both* socially and educationally backward, or whether either one would suffice, and on whether communities could be compared in terms of absolute and relative degrees of backwardness and even "forwardness."

The Report of the Second Commission on Backward Classes, popularly known as the Mandal Commission Report (MCR), sought to provide a definitive settlement of these questions. Castes, it stated, are "the only readily and clearly recognizable and persistent collectivities" (Government of India, 1980: 54). Indeed, poverty being a direct outcome of social and educational backwardness, "the substitution of caste by economic tests will amount to ignoring the genesis of social backwardness in the Indian society" (ibid.: 4). In any case, the economic criterion was difficult to apply and was subject to change. The MCR therefore adopted a weighted ranking, in which a total of 22 points were distributed unequally across factors of social, educational, and economic backwardness, such that indicators of social backwardness (including untouchability, stigma of low occupation, and nomadism) would be statistically weighted three times higher than those of economic backwardness.[43] This was despite the Commission's acknowledgment that the basis for its determination of social backwardness was the data on caste provided by the 1931 Census and also despite the resignation of the chairman of the Technical Committee, the anthropologist B. K. Roy Burman, on account of methodological disagreements about how to determine backwardness. While the Kalelkar Commission had, on this basis, come to the conclusion that one-third of India's population was backward, the Mandal Commission arrived at a proportion of just over half or 52 percent and still counting.[44]

One criterion of backwardness adopted by both commissions was the representation of groups in public services, leading to a curious situation where just one (and that not the most critical) criterion for determining backwardness became the chief and exclusive mechanism to redress it. While the MCR made additional recommendations about the need for structural remedies such as land reform, the report came to be identified with a single criterion, namely caste, and a singular policy instrument, namely reservations. The Commission's recommendation that 27 percent of positions be reserved in public employment and educational institutions for the Other Backward Classes (estimated at 52 percent) entailed a departure from the principle of correspondence—applied in the case of the Scheduled Castes and Tribes—between the quota and a group's proportion in the population. The constraint in the OBC case was the existence of a Supreme Court verdict that imposed a limit of 50 percent for *all* quotas, and also refused to countenance any further differentiation by subgroup.[45]

The announcement of the implementation[46] of the Mandal Commission Report in 1990, as well as the extension of quotas to institutions of higher education in 2006 (popularly known as Mandal-II)[47] triggered a nationwide agitation by young people belonging to the "forward" castes. Both were contested in the Supreme Court, leading to important judicial verdicts, and in both cases a confrontation with Parliament became imminent.[48] The sharp divisions in society were reflected in the judiciary, and in particular in the number of judgments that emanated from many of these cases. The nine-judge Supreme Court bench that decided the first Mandal case (*Indra Sawhney v. Union of India,* 1991) yielded seven different judgments. Three of these were in favor of using purely economic criteria to the exclusion of caste, while the remaining four accepted caste so long as it was not the only criterion to be used. This was the judgment that introduced the idea of excluding "the creamy layer"[49] from eligibility for reservations. The five-judge Supreme Court bench that decided the OBC Education case in 2008 (*Ashoka Kumar Thakur v. Union of India,* 2008) similarly produced four different judgments.

The major contentions—as decided by the courts even if subsequently repudiated by Parliament—have been those relating to issues of detail in everyday administrative practice: the definition of the creamy layer; quotas for promotion and their implication for accelerated seniority;[50] and the carrying forward of unfilled vacancies.[51] On each of these, the Court's ruling has been overturned by Parliament through a constitutional amendment. Thus, the Seventy-Seventh Constitutional Amendment Act of 1995 reversed the Court's injunction against quotas in promotions, by accepting it for OBCs, but restoring such quotas for SCs and STs. Likewise, the Eighty-First Constitutional Amendment Act of 2000 made it possible to carry forward unfilled vacancies to subsequent years in a way that exempted them from the upper limit of 50 percent reservations. Finally, there was the controversy over whether quotas in promotion gave SC and ST officials an artificial seniority over other candidates in allowing them to compete for higher positions by claiming seniority over the latter, even though this seniority had, in the first place, been achieved by quotas in promotions. Here again, the judiciary was overruled by the passage of the Eighty-Fifth Constitutional Amendment of 2001. The contention over the question of whether certain categories of institutions—those not funded by the state or run by minorities—are also obliged to provide reservations was decided by the Ninety-Third Amendment of 2005, exempting minority institutions from this requirement. With the exception of this last, the major contentions over reservations in recent years have been about intrabureaucratic careerist issues, which are obviously of great concern to those who have already accessed differentiated rights, but which could have gate-keeping implications for the admittance of new claimants such as the Most Backward Classes or Dalit Christians.

The entire gamut of policies associated with the MCR, the mass agitation that followed it, and the numerous court verdicts of this time sought to endorse (or rebut) the translation of caste into quotas. By this time, claims arising out of backwardness were rechristened as claims to social justice. The term Other Backward Classes came to be recognized as implicitly equivalent to backward castes, a category of intermediate castes between the upper castes and the untouchables. The concept of social justice in contemporary Indian political discourse has become largely synonymous with the claims of backward and other lower castes and lacks a more general meaning. It is not insignificant that the resurgence of caste in public policy—in the form of contention around the Mandal quotas—coincided with its reinvention in the domain of politics.

The official denial of caste from the Nehruvian period onward had been more programmatic than empirical. Caste and community could be derided at the level of national politics and governance, but they were always relevant to the practice of politics in the states. The election managers of every party, including the Congress, used these categories systematically to mobilize votes. Caste associations, and even federations of these, had skillfully adapted to the demands of modern democratic politics (Rudolph and Rudolph, 1967; Kothari, 1970b). The increasing political assertiveness of these castes was not unrelated to their growing economic power. With all its inadequacies, the land reform program in some states did result in the transfer of land to tenant-cultivators who were generally members of the backward castes. The Green Revolution made them more prosperous and vastly increased their stake in politics, making them participants in the exercise of power at the local and even state levels (Frankel and Rao, 1989). Through the 1960s and 1970s, the Congress had depended on these "middle castes" to win elections and form governments in the states by crafting coalitions among different caste groups. Notwithstanding the linkage between caste and politics, however, the consolidated category of backward castes had little meaning[52] yet in electoral politics; it was too large a category to have any valence at the level of local or even state elections, where one backward caste was often pitted against another, as in Karnataka and Andhra Pradesh. But the politics of backwardness had already become recognizable. In his inaugural address (1967) as vice-president, V. V. Giri said that backwardness had become "a privilege to be fought for and retained to consolidate political power" ([1969] quoted in Ghurye, 1993: 434).

By the 1980s, these groups were resisting co-option and seeking autonomous political identities. The decline of the Congress in the states was thus paralleled by the rise of regional political parties that openly appealed to a coalition of castes and in many cases claimed to represent the specific interests of these sections. Backwardness became a political category of mobilization even as it was being steadily replaced in the policy domain by the idea of social justice. By the 1990s, the entry of the regional backward caste parties into national politics, including as members of ruling coalitions at the Centre, heralded a new phase in the politics of presence. The cabinet of then prime minister, V. P. Singh,[53] was the first to have 20 percent of its members from the backward castes, increasing to 40 percent in the two coalition governments of the United Front in 1996–1998 (Jayal, 2006a: 151–158). Without legislative quotas, and exclusively through the medium of political mobilization, the OBCs now constituted a quarter of the members of the lower house of Parliament,[54] a phenomenon hailed as "the second democratic upsurge" (Yadav, 2000) and the "silent revolution" (Jaffrelot, 2003).

The trajectory of OBC mobilization in the last few decades suggests a process that is more akin to interest group creation than identitarian mobilization. As far back as 1970, Rajni Kothari commented on how politics both divides and unites castes, "fostering new alignments and loyalties, and giving rise to a structure of interests and identifications based on its own standards" (Kothari, 1970b: 94). The paradox of the increasing political salience of caste even as its ritual and social significance decline is now a sociological cliché, and identitarian interest group politics poses both a normative as well as conceptual challenge to theories of group-differentiated citizenship.

In the domains of politics and policy, supported by a progressive judiciary and a reconfiguration of power in the agrarian economy, a once residual category has been decisively reinvented as a political majority. Its unsettling of the fragile constitutional consensus on a civic-national conception of citizenship had two dimensions: first, the inclination to envisage all policy solutions in terms of quotas; and second, the displacement of pan-Indian political parties from the regional political space and the new hegemony of backward caste parties over state politics. The implications of these political developments for the theory and practice of group-differentiated citizenship are the subject of the next chapter.

Conclusion

Working substantially within the received template of colonial constitutionalism, the Constituent Assembly revisited and reshaped the various forms of group-differentiated representation that had been part of colonial discourse since the last decade of the nineteenth century, and given institutional expression since the early years of the twentieth. Even as it repudiated the idea of special interests as being contrary to the principles of a democratic state, it did draw upon the resources of antecedent institutional practices of differentiation, making descriptive representation the most important mechanism for the redress of backwardness.

Backwardness implied low levels of civic competence. This however was an attribute that could not be confined to particular castes but was presumed to characterize much of the unlettered Indian population. Several members of the Constituent Assembly supported an educational qualification for political rights, but both the Sapru Committee and Ambedkar argued forcefully that the suffrage itself would serve as an education, especially for the hitherto excluded untouchables, and therefore no educational or property qualification was acceptable.[55] Together with adult suffrage, the adoption of direct elections and the concomitant rejection of separate electorates or proportional representation were justified by the argument that they made possible the creation of a new national identity superseding the parochial and caste identities of people (Austin, 1966: 46–49).[56]

Caste sentiments were viewed as parochial values that had no place in a modern, civically defined nation. The idea of the nation as a civic community had the support of national political leaders of many persuasions. Since this was also a time when Fabian and Soviet socialisms exercised a profound ideo-logical influence on India's leaders, the only form of backwardness that the nation could reasonably and respectably acknowledge was economic. Uni-versal citizenship based on the political equality of individual citizens was therefore the default position; group-differentiated citizenship was a tempo-rary deviation, justified not by the purpose of giving these groups a voice in legislation, emphatically not for the representation of special interests, but for improving their condition of backwardness. All this had changed by the 1990s. The next chapter surveys the landscape of group-differentiated citizen-ship in the present.

9

The Future of the Civic Community

In a country where the twin forces of democratic politics and a new economic paradigm have mediated a fundamental social transformation, the enduring tension between universal and group-differentiated citizenship appears baffling. The recent challenges to the project of universal citizenship suggest not merely the fragility of the constitutional settlement, but also the ossification of a social and political consensus, beginning in the late nineteenth century, that citizens enter the public sphere preconstituted by their identities, and that mediation by groups so defined constitutes the legitimate form of interaction between citizen and state. The continuities with the colonial era indicate that the fault lines have changed very little.[1] Although the range of institutional forms to which claims are made has become less rather than more varied, the arguments supporting these claims frequently recall the justifications offered for similar claims in the late colonial period.

This chapter has two parts. In the first, I attempt a broad-brush survey of the landscape of the prominent claims to differentiated citizenship in contemporary India, mapping some discursive continuities in the arguments for group-differentiated citizenship spanning a century, and observing the challenges these present to a normative conception of universal citizenship today.

In the second part, I endeavor to bring the empirical discussion (in this and the previous chapter) into conversation with the theoretical anxieties articulated in chapter 7, and propose that the Indian experience of universal and group-differentiated citizenship should be viewed less as a dichotomy and more as an antinomy.

The Thickly Populated Landscape of Group-Differentiated Citizenship

In a triumph of Nehruvian universalism,[2] the citizenship regime inaugurated in 1950 conceptualized the individual as the basic unit of citizenship, whose inclusion in the polity was on terms of equality with every other citizen. Citizenship was defined in "national-civic" rather than "national-ethnic" terms (Beiner, 1995) even as national identity remained a rather fragile construct, a complex and increasingly fraught "national-civic-plural-ethnic" combination.[3] Groups and cultural communities found recognition in the form of special compensatory provisions, but they were not in the first instance viewed as the locus of the primary membership of the individual; nor were they initially recognized as the mandated mediators of group interest vis-à-vis the state. The accommodation of the claims of disadvantaged groups[4] occurred on the grounds, variously, of protection or backwardness or compensation for *historical disadvantage* rather than, as in colonial times, on the presentist grounds that these were *distinctive interests* that deserved special representation in the political system.

In the last sixty-five years, there has been a proliferation of claims to group-differentiated citizenship—largely in the form of quotas—with almost every group and subgroup clamoring for its share. Today, there are claims to quotas not only in public institutions, but also in the private and nongovernmental sectors; these are invariably mediated by the state. The layers of mediation between citizen and state have thus multiplied: the claim of the individual citizen on the state is mediated by community, and the claim of the community on the private sector is in turn mediated by the state.

Across the century, there are also striking continuities in the arguments offered for and against quotas. Caste and religion (and sometimes both these simultaneously) remain the preeminent axes of such claims, with gender being a recent addition. Indeed, caste has emerged as the architectonic category structuring other forms of group-differentiated citizenship. All other claims must either be filtered through caste or else mimic it in the justifications they offer. A bill proposing legislative reservations for women has been blocked for nearly two decades because it does not provide for subquotas on the basis of caste. Similarly, there have long been and remain sharp divisions within the Muslim community with respect to proposals for policies of affirmative action for Muslims based on the inclusion or otherwise of upper castes among them.[5]

The Hindu export of caste, via conversion, to other religions in India— Islam, Christianity, Buddhism, and Sikhism—has meant that lower-caste converts have not succeeded in escaping caste but carry their caste identities with them into their new faiths. This has led to the existence of upper castes, middle castes, and lower castes among all these religious groups, and to continuing discrimination in mosques, churches, and even burial grounds. While Dalit Sikhs and Dalit Buddhists are officially recognized as Scheduled Castes, Dalit Muslims and Dalit Christians are not, on the specious and controversial grounds that caste is a purely Hindu phenomenon, and Sikhism and Buddhism are offshoots of Hinduism.[6] However, since many of the southern states had provided quotas for Muslims in the early twentieth century and the census (from 1901 onward) listed such Muslim groups, both the first and second commissions on Backward Classes also included backward groups among the Muslims.[7] Some states even provide for quotas for backward Christian groups.[8] The proclivity of official policy to cling to historical precedent even at the cost of ridiculous policy inconsistencies has meant that Muslim OBCs are entitled to quotas while Muslim or Christian Dalits are not. In the former case, castes have a legal existence outside of the Hindu fold; in the latter, non-Hindus can definitionally have nothing to do with caste, and conversion implies the renunciation of the special rights that are attached to the unjust discriminatory practices associated with Hindu society.

Quotas for Muslims have been controversial, despite their gross underrepresentation in public institutions. While the OBCs have latterly rephrased their demands in the language of social justice, official documents—such as the Sachar Committee Report (Government of India, 2006) on the social, economic, and educational status of Muslims in India—continue to use the vocabulary of backwardness. The Sachar Committee Report (henceforth Sachar) characterized the Muslims as being only slightly less backward than the Scheduled Castes (SCs) and Scheduled Tribes (STs) and more backward than Hindu-Other Backward Classes (OBCs). It highlighted the "development deficit" among Muslims, and presented data on their exclusion in many spheres: public and private sector employment; their lack of access to bank and microcredit as well as to social and physical infrastructure (in terms of schools, health centers, water, and sanitation); and their poor human development indicators, especially literacy rates, dropout rates, and infant mortality rates. But instead of proposing quotas, it made the case for mainstreaming, more inclusive development, and a systematic effort to enhance educational and employment opportunities for Muslims. It also suggested ways of strengthening Muslim participation in governance through the institution of a "carefully conceived 'nomination' procedure" which could bring them into bodies of local governance to compensate for their lack of effective political agency (Government of India, 2006: 241).

Several state governments—Kerala, Karnataka, Tamil Nadu, and Manipur—already provide quotas for Muslim OBCs. In Andhra Pradesh, a four percent quota for fifteen Muslim backward caste groups was struck down by the High Court[9] of that state in February 2010 and upheld as constitutionally valid by the Supreme Court a month later. Around the same time, the West Bengal government also announced a reservation of 10 percent for Muslims who were economically, socially, and educationally backward. Though it invoked in its support the recommendations of the Ranganath Misra Commission (Government of India, 2007) in advance of the central government's decision on it, the proximity of elections to the state legislature were widely if cynically assumed to be a relevant consideration. The Misra Commission had recommended a quota of 15 percent for minorities in education and employment, of which 10 percent would be reserved for Muslims. It also recommended a subquota of 8.4 percent for minorities within the 27 percent quota for OBCs, with 6 percent being reserved for Muslims and the remaining 2.4 percent for other minorities (Government of India, 2007: 153). In the Uttar Pradesh Assembly elections in early 2012, the issue of Muslim quotas became the focus of competitive electoral populism, with the Congress offering to designate 4.5 percent of the OBC quota for Muslims.

The Jamiat Ulema-i-Hind (JUH), a leading Islamic organization, has been vocally supportive of quotas for Muslims. A National Movement for Muslim Reservation has been formed which endorses the recommendations of the Misra Commission on the inclusion of Muslim and Christian Dalits in the lists of Scheduled Castes, as well as reservations for religion minorities. It also rejects the assumption that the Ashrafs[10] are more privileged (educationally and economically) than the non-Ashrafs, but would give Muslim OBCs the first claim on quotas, with the creamy layer cut-off being set low to offset any advantage the Ashrafs might have.[11] Muslim clerics and reservationists have thus not merely demanded quotas, they have also recognized the centrality of caste as the preeminent principle determining the allocation of these.

The intersectionality of caste and religion also inflects the women's question in India. While the existence of personal laws for women belonging to minority religious groups has been used to obstruct rather than promote gender justice, most famously in the Shah Bano case,[12] caste has had a powerful influence on framing the recent debate on gender quotas. Women had resisted the imposition of reservations by the colonial state; their forced capitulation to these was the price they paid for minimal representation. Only one group in the Constituent Assembly argued strenuously against quotas for itself: its eleven women members. Sharing the dominant consensus on equal universal citizenship, they opposed reservations as "an impediment to our growth and an insult to our very intelligence and capacity" (CAD 1: 669). Today, however, women are demanding reservations for themselves.

The First (Kalelkar) Commission on Backward Classes was apparently intrigued by the question of women who "lived under great social handicaps and must, therefore, as a class be regarded as backward. But since they do not form a separate community it has not been possible for us to list them among the backward classes" (Government of India, 1956b: 31).

A quarter-century after independence, the Committee on the Status of Women in its report *Towards Equality* (1974) considered the option of quotas as special protective measures for women, and then rejected them on the grounds, first, that separate constituencies for women would render their outlook narrow, and second, that women were not a community but a category. We have here not only a presumption of equivalence between caste and community, but also the legitimacy of the idea that community alone constitutes the proper basis of entitlements to quotas. Women, on the other hand, are merely a *category* and hence not entitled to quotas. Two members of the Commission, Lotika Sarkar and Vina Mazumdar, in a legendary note of dissent said that while they had "never been supporters of special representation or class representation in any form" (Sarkar and Mazumdar, [1974] 2008: 11), their interviews with women across India had convinced them that women were underrepresented, and that notwithstanding progressive changes in the law, the conditions in which women lived had not improved. As such, quotas were necessary, not only at the level of local governance—which the Commission recommended—but also in higher legislative bodies.

The Women's Reservation Bill—giving women 33 percent reservation in Parliament and the state legislatures[13]—was introduced two decades later. Its passage has been repeatedly blocked by the leaders of the backward caste parties, some of whom expressed their violent opposition by symbolically tearing it to shreds in Parliament. These leaders continue to insist that the bill must provide subquotas for OBCs and minorities, without which only elite women will enter Parliament on reserved seats.[14] In 2010, fourteen years after it was first introduced, the bill was passed by the upper house; it remains to be passed in the lower house, although this is one of those rare legislations that has been supported by women MPs, cutting across the most hostile of party boundaries. The feminist response has been to emphasize the essential unity of women's interests, which must transcend the divisions of caste and community.

Meanwhile, women have, since 1992, enjoyed 33 percent (upped to 50 percent in some states) reservations in both rural and urban local bodies. In the rural *gram panchayats* (local village councils) alone, this had the effect of bringing one million women to elected office. Despite the predictable resistance of local society to women, the abuse of technicalities by local notables to subvert their functioning, and the exercise of surrogate control by male relatives, the *panchayats* have often proved to be institutional spaces for the effective practice of citizenship. Women *sarpanches* (heads of local councils) have, in the face of intimidation and threats, questioned fraudulent accounts, refused to pay kickbacks, and even, wresting it through a court decision, asserted their right to hoist the national flag on Independence Day. Above all, women's representation has translated into development outcomes that are prioritized by women: hand-pumps for drinking water, smokeless stoves, day-care facilities and schooling for girls. Empowerment outcomes are harder to achieve, but the very recognition of powerlessness, not just outside the home but also within domestic walls, is arguably an important first step toward overcoming it. For elected representatives, and equally for their constituents,[15] the *panchayat* provides an enabling, though by no means uncontested, space for the exercise of the rights of equal citizenship, in a way that transcends, instead of entrenching, particularistic identities (Jayal, 2006b).

Of course, not all forms of gender-discrimination can be resolved simply through quotas or even progressive legislation. An example is the challenge of biological citizenship (Rose and Novas, 2002) presented by sex-selective abortion, a practice that acquired disturbing proportions through the 1980s and 1990s. In 1997, a United Nations Population Fund report estimated India's "missing women" as between 32–48 million (Srinivasan et al., 1997). While "son preference" in Indian society has, for several hundred years, encouraged female infanticide, the recent availability of sophisticated technologies of sex-determination has made female feticide possible. Economic prosperity is no inhibitor of such practices, as the abysmal sex ratios in the prosperous states of Punjab and Haryana have shown.[16] Despite the enactment of the Pre-Conception and Pre-Natal Diagnostics Techniques (Regulation and Prevention of Misuse) Act, banning sex-determination tests and providing for up to three years' imprisonment for offenders, the ban has only driven the tests underground, making them more expensive rather than less common. Meanwhile, female feticide also continues to be practiced in economically prosperous regions more than in backward ones, in urban areas more than rural, and even among the Indian diaspora in the United Kingdom.

The realization that quotas are not an all-encompassing panacea has become obvious not only in the case of women and the Scheduled Tribes (discussed in the previous chapter) but also for that of the Scheduled Castes. While access to education and public employment has undoubtedly improved the opportunities available to members of these groups, the outcomes have been neither as substantive nor as widely distributed as could have been expected. The reports of the National Commission on Scheduled Castes[17] have repeatedly pointed to the fact that the reserved positions in Class III (clerical) and IV (peons and janitors) jobs in government are filled much more easily than the higher-ranking jobs in the Class I and II categories, and that almost half the sweepers recruited by the government continue to be from the Scheduled Castes, thus entrenching the link between caste and traditional occupation. More disturbing, and indicative of the persistence of social prejudice, is the fact that even those Dalits who have, through the reservations, entered the middle class hesitate to describe themselves as such (Sheth, 2002). The intergenerational reproduction of advantage—for second- and third-generation beneficiaries of quotas—is a limitation of the quota-based approach. Though there has been resistance to the idea of introducing a "creamy layer" criterion into the Scheduled Castes and Tribes, Dalits themselves recognize the phenomenon and argue for a better targeting of the quotas toward poorer Dalits in rural India (Deshpande, 2011: 249). Notwithstanding these distortions, it is entry into government that gave an impetus to the political organization of Dalits, and the election of a Dalit woman chief minister in Uttar Pradesh. These political achievements are the work of the Bahujan Samaj Party, whose genealogy lies in the All-India Backward (SC, ST, OBC) and Minority Communities Employees Federation, or BAMCEF, the trade union of government employees belonging to these groups.[18]

No more than a disappointing three or four SCs are elected to Parliament over and above those elected on reserved seats (an increase of a mere 0.5 percent over the quota) as should have been the case six decades after independence. Those that are elected are rarely effective in representing the interests of Dalits, only a few hold important party positions, and their appointment to the cabinet is usually governed by tokenism.[19] The quotas have not proved to be adequately effective instruments of addressing the myriad aspects of exploitation, oppression, and discrimination (including market discrimination, untouchability, and "caste atrocities")[20] experienced by Dalits.

The recognition by Dalit intellectuals that all the quotas in the public sector could not offer adequate opportunities to them, and that the economic reforms process was resulting in the further shrinking of this space, encouraged them to think "beyond reservations," about how the newly unleashed energies of market capitalism could be used in the interest of Dalits and tribals. The market was a closed world to these communities of mostly landless agricultural laborers; no entrepreneurs, industrialists or even contractors had emerged from these groups. Young men who acquired engineering degrees through reservations found themselves discriminated against in the job market, and without the capital and skills to become entrepreneurs. The Bhopal Document sought to make a beginning by holding up the example of American equal opportunity and diversity policies in the private sector—from the media to information technology and automobile manufacture—as well as in the not-for-profit sector. These inspired the recommendation of a diversity policy for all public institutions and corporations,[21] as well as policies of Supplier Diversity and Dealership Diversity in all goods and services (Bhopal Document, 2002: 99). The Supplier Diversity policy was adopted by the Madhya Pradesh government, and the modest success it has registered has been attributed to the fact that it does not generate resentment in the way that reservations or land distribution would (Pai, 2010: 413). The central government has also announced a policy of preferential procurement, according to which 4 percent of its annual purchases will be made from units run by Dalits and tribals (*The Times of India*, September 12, 2011).

Today, Dalit capitalism and Dalit entrepreneurship are buzzwords, engendering optimism about globalization and the possibilities of "economic democracy"[22] it may afford. Thirty-one Dalit billionaires (including one woman) have, despite the manifest difficulties of raising initial investment, built business empires in a range of industries from food and real estate to construction and engineering.[23] The Planning Commission has consulted the Dalit Indian Chamber of Commerce and Industry on what steps can be taken to foster and strengthen Dalit capitalism in the Twelfth Plan (2012–2017).[24] At the same time, there is also skepticism about this neoliberal celebration of "some 100-odd individuals (out of more than 170 million) in businesses, the cumulative value of which may not even be a droplet in the corporate ocean" (Teltumbde, 2011: 10).[25] The cynicism that attends Dalit capitalism has much to do with the reality in the countryside, as the Dalit capitalist encounters resistance even in his native village. Ashok Khade, a Dalit millionaire, bought a hundred acres of farmland but could build a large mansion for his mother only in the Dalit quarter, for the upper castes who inhabit the center of the village would not sell him land.[26]

The vast mass of Dalits are landless agricultural laborers, at the mercy of the largely OBC landlords who replaced the earlier, often Brahmin, landlords after the land reforms and acquired economic power after the coming of capitalist agriculture. The relationship between these communities is fraught with conflict, with the OBCs commonly perceived as the oppressors of the Dalits and perpetrators of caste violence. Dalit intellectuals like Chandra Bhan Prasad oppose political unity between these two groups.

> Shudras play with Dalit sentiments—they will point to the social monster called Brahmans, rob Dalits' support, come to power, and then turn to Dalits to oppress them. Every ruling group looks for subjects. And the Shudras, once in power, treat Dalits as subjects as they cannot treat Brahmans as subjects . . . Dalit-OBC unity is theoretically most undesirable, as the fruits of unity will go to Upper OBCs or Upper Shudras, who tend to practice Brahmanism of the medieval era. The Shudras' aim is to dislodge the Brahmans, and continue with the Chatur-Varna Order, while Dalits want to destroy the Order itself. So, when both the categories have different aims, where is the theoretical basis for unity? (Prasad, 2001)

As different caste groups make rival claims to group-differentiated citizenship, conflicts will and do arise. The conflict between the Dalits and the

OBCs is only one such. Others include conflicts within the broad category of OBC as the ritual distance[27] between the castes at the top and bottom of the OBC scale is much greater than that between the lower OBCs (some of whom are called MBCs or Most Backward Classes) and the Dalits. There are even conflicts over subquotas between segments of Dalits, such as the Malas and Madigas of Andhra Pradesh, who occupy very different positions in the ritual hierarchy.

Two contemporary developments have the potential to unsettle the present equilibrium and recast citizenship and its objectification in the form of caste quotas. The first of these is the new caste census, and the second is the marginal shift in affirmative action policies prefigured in official reports. After much controversy, the government has decided to undertake a caste census, currently underway, and the first of its kind since 1931. Until now, most political parties have extrapolated from the caste data of 1931 to formulate their electoral strategies. As there is simply no way of anticipating what the new data will produce, the 2011 caste census, especially oriented to gathering data on the OBCs, could either reinforce or displace presumptions. Largely centered on the question of OBCs, the contestation over whether or not to count caste reflects the sharp divide between the proponents of universal citizenship and the advocates of GDC. The arguments in favor of counting caste highlight its benefits in terms of fine-tuning the reservation policy. As things stand, OBCs, like SCs and STs, are already recognized in a range of official policies and statutes on reservation, so counting them through a census can only help to target reservations better. The fact that the backward caste parties have been vocal in their support for counting caste of course suggests that they also expect the results to yield political benefits for their constituents.

The contrary universalist case rests on primarily two sets of claims, normative and empirical. The normative argument against counting caste invokes the imperiled project of the Indian nation as a civic community, and the anxiety that it may be rendered permanently hostage to identity politics. The project of an *Indian* citizenship is arguably endangered as individuals are asked to represent and report themselves to the state in terms of caste and subcaste. Secondly and simultaneously, the public provisioning of basic welfare may be seen as the right of every citizen rather than the right of particular groups. Considerations of justice surely require that conditions of backwardness— such as poverty and poor indicators of human development—be addressed for all those who suffer these indignities, regardless of caste classifications.

Justice is diminished rather than enhanced when development is parceled out and distributed by caste in the name of "social justice."

Of the four empirical arguments against the caste census, the first is that with the shrinking of the state, on the one hand, and the unorganized sector of the economy housing ninety percent of India's population, on the other, the state's capacity to offer meaningful opportunities to the people can hardly be anything other than low. Second, by creating incentives for political mobilization, the caste census will only diminish this capacity further. The suspicion of caste data and fears of its politicization are of course a legacy of the historical understanding of the colonial census and its creation of categories, which were similarly deployed. Third, if the backward castes could, as they have done, gain social control in the countryside, become economically prosperous and politically successful, it would appear that the nonrecognition of caste in the census has not hindered their achievements in any way. Conversely, being counted has not in any way reduced the injustice and deprivation that characterizes the condition of the Scheduled Castes and Scheduled Tribes. Finally, there is the challenge of ensuring that the data so collected are in fact reliable. The category of OBC being synthetic and heterogeneous, most people will not, it is argued, be aware of whether their caste is encompassed by the label; and many answers they give will be unrecognizable even to enumerators who will be hard put to classify them correctly.

The second development that may cause current policies of affirmative action to undergo a shift is the construction of a Diversity Index, a more sophisticated and technically superior version of what the Mandal Commission attempted. The Expert Group commissioned by the government recommended that a composite diversity index be worked out by obtaining a weighted average of the three essential indices—religion, caste, and gender—used to incentivize diversity in institutions in the public as well as private sector, in employment as much as in housing and education (Government of India, 2008b). Since the Report of the Expert Group was submitted to the government in 2008, no strategy of implementation has yet been proposed that would liberate the project of social justice from its association with caste and quotas and give it a wider and deeper resonance.

In contemporary political and even popular discourse, the concept of social justice translates into policies for addressing caste inequality or special provisions for particular caste groups. Social justice as a slogan has been appropriated by those parties on the political spectrum that claim to represent the scheduled castes and the backward castes, sometimes in the name of the *bahujan samaj* (the majority of society). Many of these parties trace their genealogy to the intellectual legacy of Ram Manohar Lohia and to the erstwhile Janata Dal's particular brand of populist socialism. The key moment when social justice acquired both its present connotation and was consecrated on the political firmament was marked by then prime minister V. P. Singh's description of his government's decision to implement the MCR as "a momentous decision of social justice."[28] (quoted in Bajpai, 2011: 231). However, Bajpai argues, while "social justice was not a recent semantic acquisition . . . its *prominence* in justifications of preferential treatment marked a new departure" (ibid.: 232; emphasis in original). In her insightful analysis of the parliamentary debate on this decision, Bajpai shows how social justice was endowed with an emphatically *social* meaning, referring to the challenge of inequalities of social status and power, rather than material inequalities of wealth and income (ibid.). As had been argued earlier—in official reports as well as in the law courts—all other forms of inequality, including economic, were asserted as flowing from the ritual inequality of caste status. In a logical culmination of this, social justice soon came to be identified exclusively with the need to guarantee social equality for the OBCs.

The limits of quotas are well known and recognized; but the leaders of the backward caste parties have a particular investment in these, whether or not quotas translate into substantive gains for the communities they represent. Questions of land reform, mentioned even in the Mandal Report, remain off-agenda for not just the state but also political parties. This constrains the institutional imagination of Indian society, which remains focused on mostly extending, and occasionally finessing, caste quotas as the core of the program of social justice.

Theoretical Anxieties Revisited

In chapter 7, I outlined two sets of anxieties that political theorists, including advocates of GDC, have identified, and it is to these that I now return in an assessment of the normative and political implications of the Indian experience of GDC.

One set of anxieties, it may be recalled, was about the proper determination of the basis on which groups may be entitled to differentiated rights.

In the Indian context, as we have seen, backwardness has been a distinctive motif and often the authoritative basis for claiming GDC. It has not been easy to specify the concept of backwardness in a way that presents it as a robust claim to justice, equivalent to the claims of oppression, marginalization, and exploitation. The argument that backwardness must have two components—of disadvantage as well as of discrimination—has not found acceptance, evidently because this would limit the application of the concept to the Scheduled Castes and Tribes only. Logically, backwardness should have to be measured in relation to something that is not backward, but it is not entirely clear how that benchmark may be determined for groups to be designated as backward in relation to it. How further might we distinguish between the perception and the reality of oppression?

The definition of backwardness in the Mandal Commission Report (MCR) was, as we saw, overdetermined by ritual criteria, and based on social and demographic data gathered fifty years before the Commission's deliberations. The MCR itself acknowledged that the social salience of caste had declined as its political consequence has increased, but nevertheless chose to base its understanding of social backwardness on this. Another quarter-century has passed since the Mandal Report was submitted, but it still remains the definitive document on social justice. The wisdom of treating backwardness as a static category with an unchanging content has seldom been questioned, though it is reasonable to expect that the attributes of a community change over time, and so arguably would the benchmarks by which backwardness is measured. In its Mandal decision of 1992, the Supreme Court required a revision based on empirical data, but this recommendation has been ignored.

The uniform solution of reservations for all claims, moreover, suggests that backwardness is assumed to have the same characteristics in every group, such that historical, locational, and social differences do not make for different forms of backwardness. But tribal backwardness is arguably very different from Muslim backwardness and would therefore appear to require rather different types of policy intervention. The arbitration of the competing claims of different groups would also seem to require a greater sensitivity to such variations.

As far as the question of determining the eligibility of particular groups in the most just manner is concerned, the Indian way of constructing GDC could be seen as somewhat inconsistent. Claims to GDC are just that—claims of groups or collectivities rather than individuals. This was part of the reason for disallowing economic criteria which were seen to introduce illegitimate, because individual-centric, considerations. However, the judicial introduction of the idea of the creamy layer has meant that individual/household level criteria have in fact been admitted. This introduces an inconsistency, in that only groups (and not individuals) can make claims to inclusion, while only individuals (not groups) can be excluded.

The economic criterion moreover was unacceptable to the Mandal Commission because it was said to be difficult to measure and apply, and because it was fluid and changeable. Following the SC judgment on the creamy layer, this segment is identified by economic criteria, leading to the piquant situation that a criterion that is unacceptable for determining who should be included in the category of OBCs is also the singular criterion that is acceptable for determining who should be excluded from the same category.

Strategies of GDC are usually designed to capture and address one salient indicator of disadvantage. In India, legal and policy provisions have not adequately accounted for the complex and overlapping nature of social inequalities, and in particular the overlap between inherited cultural disadvantages of caste or religious identity, on the one hand and economic disadvantage, on the other. The way in which Mandal assigned weightings clearly prioritized the social indicator of caste ranking. For the Scheduled Castes, the Scheduled Tribes, and the Muslims, who together account for close to 38 percent of India's population, traditional and historical forms of social inequality coexist with, and are reinforced by, inequalities arising out of the sphere of production and economic activity. There is frequently an overlap between cultural and material inequalities. The data clearly show that levels of deprivation—in terms of poverty and human development—are highest for the Scheduled Castes, followed by the Scheduled Tribes, followed by the Muslims.

As for material inequalities, though the chief source of income for most Scheduled Castes is agriculture, ownership of land is lowest among these groups (47 percent as opposed to 70 percent for Hindus). The literacy rates and health data of the Scheduled Tribes are lower than those of any other group. The Muslim minority has not merely lower literacy rates (including female literacy), a lower work participation rate, and lower per capita incomes (the percentage difference being 18 percent), it also has a higher percentage of people below the poverty line, with 43 percent Muslims as opposed to 39 percent Hindus below the poverty line (in 2000). For all these groups, their economic impoverishment mirrors their social marginalization. Of course, it is obviously not the case that all members of these groups are poor, or that there is no poverty among other groups, but only that there is a high degree of overlap between being poor and belonging to these groups. These are also the groups that generally work in the informal economy, which is heavily inflected by inequalities of caste, religion, and gender as when certain caste groups alone engage in occupations that are considered polluting or dirty by other, higher castes.

Multiple and mutually compounding forms of disadvantage suggest that the groups that need special attention may be those that are doubly disadvantaged—i.e., both culturally, and in terms of their human development indicators. Some—e.g., poor Dalit or Muslim women—may be simultaneously disadvantaged in three ways, by gender, class, and caste/religion/tribe. Building in multiple types of disadvantage is a challenge for theories of GDC, which are typically grounded in a single indicator of disadvantage.

If the category of backwardness has not been sufficiently disaggregated and finessed, the strategy for redressing it has also remained unvarying and uniform, with descriptive representation being the goal, and reservations being the singular policy instrument to achieve it. Feminist scholarship offers a useful distinction between descriptive and substantive representation, to consider the outcomes of quota-based approaches for disadvantaged groups. An empirical study of women's representation in 36 countries came to the rather disturbing conclusion that "descriptive representation is severely limited as an avenue for providing substantive representation" (Weldon, 2002: 1171). Existing evidence about the participation of Dalit parliamentarians in India also suggests that descriptive representation does not invariably translate into substantive representation. There is clearly a need for an ongoing empirical assessment of the actual outcomes of GDC policies.

Apart from being limited in this way, descriptive representation can also encourage unwarranted complacency. While the electoral success of leaders belonging to disadvantaged caste groups generates legitimate euphoria, their tenures in government often produce despondency at the lack of distributive outcomes for ordinary citizens belonging to those very groups. The successful political mobilization of not only Dalits, but also backward castes, over the last two decades has yielded rich results in that backward caste parties have come to power in several states, and their numbers in Parliament have increased fivefold since the 1950s, reflected also in a higher representation in cabinets. However, the concern remains that while symbolic inequalities have begun to be more effectively addressed, the inequalities of poverty have not. Likewise, the contrast between the attentiveness of state agencies to identity-based claims of GDC, on the one hand, and the lack of receptivity to claims of social citizenship, on the other, is striking. It is altogether likely that if the claims of tribals were today articulated in the language of identity, they would perhaps attract the attention of the state in the way demands for reservations do. Despite the convergence between ascriptive citizenship and social citizenship, policies are receptive to the first rather than the second. These contrasting policy responses to convergent problems recall Nancy Fraser's caution—articulated in the context of feminism but with connotations beyond it—that, in neoliberal times, governments often find symbolic political solutions less challenging than policies that call for the redistribution of power and material resources.[29]

The concern that GDC for some groups may adversely impact other groups in society is a core issue. Despite the Mandal Commission's firm refusal to admit any subgroup differentiation, India's experiment with GDC has been an experience of increasing fragmentation and competing claims to limited resources, as the conflict between the Malas and Madigas, who together account for 80 percent of Scheduled Castes in Andhra Pradesh, shows. For decades now, the Madigas have been agitating against the larger share of the scheduled caste quota being appropriated by the Malas, and demanding a separate subquota for themselves.

The concern that GDC may create institutional incentives for the invention of new identities of disadvantage was recognized, in the context of demands for separate electorates, by none other than Ambedkar himself.

> Whenever a community grows powerful and demands certain political advantages, concessions are made to it to win its goodwill. There is no judicious examination of its claims, no judgment on merits. The result is that there are no limits to demands and there are no limits to concessions. A start is made with a demand for separate electorates for a minority. It is granted. It is followed with a demand for a separate electorate for a community irrespective of the fact whether it is a minority or majority. That is granted. A demand is made for separate representation on a population basis. That is conceded. Next, a claim is made for weightage in representation. That is granted. This is followed by a demand for statutory majority over other minorities with the right for the majority to retain separate

electorates. This is granted. This is followed by a demand that the majority rule of another community is intolerable, and therefore without prejudice to its rights to maintain majority rule over other minorities, the majority of the offending community should be reduced to equality. Nothing can be more absurd than this policy of eternal appeasement. It is a policy of limitless demand followed by endless appeasement. (Ambedkar, 1979, 1: 366)

This is also illustrated by the violent agitation by the Gujjars in Rajasthan since 2007, who have laid siege to railway tracks and highways to demand a five percent reservation for themselves and three other Special Backward Classes (SBCs). The Gujjars have long enjoyed OBC status but have felt marginalized by the domination of the creamy layer among the OBCs, and in particular by the inclusion of the powerful Jats in this category. On the other hand, the perception that the Meenas have, by virtue of their Scheduled Tribe status, experienced visible mobility through state employment, has fueled the Gujjars' agitation for what would be a ritual "downgradation," even if a secular "upgradation" to the status of Scheduled Tribe.[30]

Above all, there is the question of whether the idea of group-differentiated citizenship can accommodate the idea of a civic community. Is a civic community an aggregation of social groups, or should it also provide a space for the performance of secular individual citizenship? In spite of recognizing and even expanding the scope of group-differentiated citizenship, India has found it manifestly hard to reconcile claims of cultural communities with the project of creating and nurturing a civic community. The future of the civic project, of an overarching conception of the common good putatively shared by all citizens, or even of a shared space in which such a common good may be determined through public reasoning and debate, remains fragile and uncertain.[31]

In this chapter, we have discussed several anxieties articulated by the advocates of GDC: can differentiated citizenship accommodate multiple and overlapping inequalities; can differentiated citizenship be an effective instrument for addressing inequalities other than cultural and symbolic; and, finally, can the idea of group-differentiated citizenship accommodate the project of a civic community? The principled necessity for differentiated forms of citizenship is however not undermined by these questions. In a diverse and complex world, it is neither possible nor desirable to argue for a relentlessly uniform and universal conception of citizenship. The binary of universal and group-differentiated conceptions of citizenship however is, normatively and substantively, a false dichotomy, as both conceptions possess significance in an ongoing democratic project. The challenge is to identify the criteria by which different types of claims to differentiated citizenship can be arbitrated in a manner that is normatively just and satisfactory, and still leaves room for the practice of citizenship.

Epilogue

A history of ideas in twentieth-century India must be, among other things, the history of a new idea, citizenship. Unlike in western antiquity, the rubric of citizenship, either as performance or as equality, was historically alien to Indian experience. There was no antecedent tradition of citizenship that could be excavated or invoked in the way in which chronicles of a national past were produced in impassioned response to the colonial accusation that Indians lacked a history. Even the invention of a history of local democracy and village republics[1]—*pace* Henry Maine and Karl Marx—was pallid and lacking in conviction. Democratic citizenship could only be an aspiration without a past.

This book has attempted a biography of Indian ideas of citizenship across the twentieth century and into the present. Striving to keep the ideational in conversation with social and political developments, it has provided an account of how conceptions of citizenship came to be fashioned through processes of assertion, legislation, and contestation that are invariably inconclusive. In the margins of this story, it has intermittently essayed comments on the forging of a new world of politics and its relation with the social and on the reconfiguration of the ideas of political obligation and legitimacy that modern politics entail.

Indeed, the quest for citizenship in India has been conducted in tandem with the quest for a democratic modernity. Since 1950, both have been state-sponsored projects that are substantially dependent for their realization on societal affirmation. In the following decades, both have been variously destabilized as India has negotiated the terms of its engagement with modernity, not always in ways that are unquestioned or consistent. This book has taken as its organizing principle the three main analytical dimensions of the citizenship question, with one part of the book devoted to each of these: status (that determines who can be a citizen); rights (the bundle of rights and entitlements that accompany citizenship); and identity (the affective dimension of citizenship as belonging). Each of these parts has tracked some selective but significant contestations over citizenship across the century, emphasizing continuities of both claims and contentions. In the pages that follow, I explore four intertwined themes that straddle these dimensions, resonate across the period of study, and remain important to contemporary practices of Indian citizenship. These relate to the defining of citizens in relation to the state and to each other; the persistently beleaguered attempt to construct a civic community; the contested primacy of politics and civil society as sites of citizenship practices; and the contingency of ideas of political obligation and legitimacy. Mindful of the interrelatedness of these, the discussion that follows braids them into a single narrative, instead of addressing them sequentially and in different compartments.

The unfinished project of creating a civic community has traversed the entire twentieth century, often but not always championed by the privileged. If this was the project that animated Ambedkar's vision of a modern and democratic future, it is also the project that today informs some of the arguments presented by the detractors of quotas. Having defined and classified the subject population, the colonial state accused Indians of being fundamentally unfit for citizenship because they were hopelessly and irretrievably divided in ways that precluded the possibility of a civic community. In the twin responses to this charge lie the origins of the two strands of universal and group-differentiated citizenship that were the subject of the third part of the book. One response countered the colonial allegation by offering to construct a political community that could transcend these divisions. The other concurred with the colonial description, and indeed based its claims to group-differentiated citizenship on it. This had a lasting impact on two core aspects of citizenship: between the individual and the state, citizenship came to be a relationship legitimately mediated by community; between citizen and citizen, it enjoined signification by markers of, variously, disadvantage, discrimination, and backwardness.

Among the dualities that India continues to negotiate (often unsuccessfully) is that between the marked and the unmarked citizen. Citizenship is the privilege of the unmarked, but for those who belong to variously disadvantaged groups, the road to citizenship lies only and paradoxically *through* being marked. In the debates of the Constituent Assembly, terms like "mainstream" and "everybody" were frequently used to denote and validate the unmarked citizen. The contemporary version of this is the peculiar concept of the "General"[2] that characterizes all those proper citizens to whom none of these labels—Below Poverty Line, Scheduled Caste, Scheduled Tribe, or Other Backward Class—apply. The "General" has a superficial resemblance to the idea of the universal as opposed to the particular that is invoked by conceptions of group-differentiated citizenship, but it is actually a shadow category itself. Indeed, its existence as a formal category of the residual non-labeled is now acknowledged even in official parlance, including in university admissions lists and court judgments, where it finds regular mention as the "General Category" or the "Unreserved Category."

In the preceding chapters, we identified two types of markers, secular markers of poverty (such as Below Poverty Line) and ascriptive markers of identity (such as Scheduled Tribes or Other Backward Classes). The lure of these labels lies in their promise of a ticket to citizenship, in the form of recognition and redistribution, from cultural rights to welfare entitlements. The pursuit of the markers of difference—job cards for manual work, caste certificates, quotas in college places, and government jobs—is in effect a search for a difference geared to achieving sameness. However, even as they apparently extend the promise of a fuller, substantive citizenship, they simultaneously diminish the citizenship on offer, precisely by virtue of the markers themselves. The sequestration of these categories of exception, as ways of making particular groups of citizens "legible" to the state, is usually justified by the objective of inclusion. In reality, however, they appear to be exclusions from citizenship masquerading as inclusion because the markers never entirely disappear. It is only through the reification of exceptions that inclusion may overcome exclusion.

The state plays a profoundly important role in defining citizenship and its exclusions. The markers that are acceptable at any given point in time are a pointer to this. Take the official squeamishness about the category of the Muslim, a disagreeable reminder of the history and memory of the Partition.

A proposal by the National Advisory Council for welfare schemes for Muslims, including a scholarship scheme for Muslim girls, was recently rejected by the Ministry of Minority Affairs ostensibly because it explicitly named Muslims as its target beneficiaries, which, the government said, was unconstitutional and open to the charge of being discriminatory[3] (*The Times of India*, August 14, 2011). The preference for a more veiled reference to minorities in general is more plausibly explained by the government's fear of exposing itself to the charge of Muslim "minority appeasement," a form of attack particularly favored by the Hindu right.

In turn, unmarked citizens have a lien on the state in a way that people with labels simply do not. Marked citizens have claims on particular agencies or segments of the state, such as the National Commission on Scheduled Castes or Scheduled Tribes, or on particular welfare programs, while unmarked citizens effectively possess the entire and considerable terrain of the state with all the resources that it commands. Since the convergence between the two types of markers—of recognition and redistribution—is rarely acknowledged in official policy, markers are differently stigmatized. Those that address basic needs carry the stigma of poverty; those that address aspirations for social mobility carry the stigma of caste disadvantage. These stigmas are underlined and even entrenched by the very naming of an individual or group as Below Poverty Line or Scheduled Caste, recalling Marshall's argument that a service intended only for the poor immediately becomes less than citizenship.

Even so, the recognition of the citizenship claims of nonelite groups—variously interpreted as a deepening of democracy or the rise of the plebeians[4]—blurs the boundaries posited by a dyadic view of the two worlds of citizenship and its other. Such a view underpins Dipesh Chakrabarty's distinction between the elite language learned under colonial tutelage of "the project of nation-building . . . the rituals of the state, political representation, citizenship, citizen's rights" and the precolonial language of "relationships of power, authority and hierarchy" in which the lives of the subaltern classes have typically been enmeshed. He acknowledges that mass politics have effected a closer juxtaposition of these two contradictory languages (Chakrabarty, 1985: 374). A similar contrast is signaled in the contemporary context in Partha Chatterjee's distinction between civil society as the home of elite groups of proper citizens, professing the principles of civic freedom, equality, and law, and political society as the sphere in which the politics of

the governed are enacted as they make claims to the developmental atten-
tions of the government, often transgressing the boundaries of legality. Like
Chakrabarty, he too recognizes that there are points where citizenship over-
laps with governmentality through the channels provided by democratic politics (P. Chatterjee, 2004: 40–41).

Our account of the evolution of the idea of citizenship in the twentieth
century has emphasized the imitative quality of citizenship as a core element of the package of democratic modernity that nationalist elites strove to
accomplish. The civic community to which the early nationalists aspired was
undoubtedly limited in class terms, while that crafted by Gandhi was vastly
more inclusive. However, despite this difference, the advocates of universalism—from Surendranath Banerjea to Nehru—sought to construct a political
community that broadly conformed to the liberal-constitutional model of
the west. Encapsulated in the Constitution, this lineage of universalism continues into the present even if with fewer adherents. On the other hand, the
lineages of group-differentiated citizenship experienced a rupture. Neither
Ambedkar nor Jinnah, strong proponents of GDC, spoke a plebeian vernacular. The decisive rupture occurred in the 1980s when the class base and social
composition of the lower-caste parties inaugurated a new discourse of social
justice that had little patience with the sedate chamber-talk of constitutional
morality. Today, claims to group-differentiated citizenship are expressed in
a vernacular register; but, conversely, equivalent championships of ideas of
universal citizenship are not visible on the political landscape, provoking the
question as to whether the civic community is exclusively an elite aspiration.

It is nevertheless through the institutions of formal democracy, and in
particular through the language of political representation, that citizenship
has been translated in a more demotic register, as idea and effect if not as a
self-conscious and named social practice. Even as the nonelite find incorporation at the institutional heart of the modern state, these translations of
citizenship are undoubtedly incomplete and uneven. They occur more visibly
in some domains than others: claims to differentiated political representation, for instance, are articulated with more confidence and a greater expectation of being fulfilled than claims to social and economic rights. However,
as the idea of citizenship is expressed through the politics of representation
and democratic institutions, the expanding consciousness of entitlements
and even on occasion of rights invokes notions of legitimacy that rest on
the fulfillment of such claims. For all its inadequacies and even distortions,

the paraphernalia of formal democracy—from political fixers and brokers to transactional rather than ideologically informed political relationships—has become the bridge between the two languages of elite and subaltern politics and the two worlds of, in Chatterji's usage, civil and political society.

There is however a price to be paid for the audacity of making such claims, even through the entirely legitimate mechanisms of democratic politics. As many of the citizenship claims that emanate from the quest for markers deploy the language of identity and community rather than of individual or class subalternity, they simultaneously reinforce the legitimacy of mediated citizenship. The fruits of modernity are negotiated through the assertion of identities that are not entirely comfortable with modern notions of individuated citizenship. Claims to modern institutional spaces or to modern education using arguments of backwardness seek to validate aspirations to political modernity by histories of premodern deprivations. Community mediations between marked citizens and the state play an important role in defining the relationship between the social and the political, as well as the construction of the political itself.

At the beginning of this book, we noted the anxieties of Indian intellectuals and public figures through the late nineteenth and early twentieth centuries about how to sequence the "reform" of Indian society, and noted the debates about whether social reform should precede political reform or follow it. Discussions about how to tame India's social complexity were, at this time, as much a colonial concern as a nationalist one. For the colonial state, the divisiveness of Indian society provided a rationale for centralized and repressive state power; the dominant nationalist response to this was Gandhi's effective knitting together of diverse segments of Indian society in the hope of constructing a civic community out of these different strands. The Constitution represented a more ambitious attempt at deploying the political to reform the social in the service of a civic ideal: it sought to strike a fine balance between individuated citizenship cohering with the recognition of communities; a secular inclusive social fabric in which minorities could enjoy special rights; and state-led development and modernization within a paradigm informed by ideas of equity and social justice.

In all these ways, the project of citizenship has paralleled the architectonic project of constructing a civic community as an imperative, even a precondition, for modern politics. Over time, however, the political has devoured the civic community itself. Both in its methods and its content, the political is often at cross-purposes with the civic. In the postmendicant phase of the movement for freedom, politics was about protest rather than deliberation. After independence, this idiom found repeated expression not only in the political movements about caste and language, but also in a variety of social movements including the student, peasant, and environmental movements, such as the anti-dam and antinuclear movements. Since the middle of the 1980s, the regionalization of the polity provoked a new idiom of politics, in the form of a revival of the idea of community-mediated citizenship, married to an impulse to capture the state rather than challenge it. The deepening of democracy was to be effected through entering the domain of mainstream electoral and parliamentary politics and compelling it to accommodate the demands of communities, and of course to share the spoils of political power, which accelerated in the 1990s as probusiness policies opened up a new range of opportunities for rent-seeking. With state policy becoming mani-festly more receptive to corporate interests than to the needs of the poor, the embeddedness of the political in the social came to be supplemented by its embeddedness in the economic.

In terms of content, likewise, it is economic reform and globalization that have given impetus to the project of making *individuals* out of the members of this social world. In the economic domain, these are consumer-citizens negotiating a marketplace of multiple choices, acquiring English language skills as an instrument of upward mobility, and chasing aspirations through employment in the business process outsourcing, technology, and services sectors. This energy was particularly palpable in the small towns of India, from which young people are breaking through meritocratic entry-level bar-riers into the diverse and intensely competitive worlds of industry, govern-ment, sports, and the media. Running parallel to the vernacularization of the political is the impetus to devernacularization, or at least a metaphorical bilingualism, created by opportunities in the new economy linked to global capitalism, where upwardly mobile young people, including those belonging to the backward castes, are likely to be located. The gradual expansion in the caste base of industry, at least in southern and western India, also suggests a "democratization of capital" (Damodaran, 2008: 314). The lines between the two language-worlds are increasingly blurred, and people are increasingly coming to position themselves, confidently rather than precariously, on the borders between them.

This new spirit of individualism is somewhat at odds with the customary forms of citizenship in the polity. Community identity has not entirely lost legitimacy as a form of political intermediation, but there is now a possibly creative tension between the rival pulls of individualism born of the market and community as constructed in the sphere of politics. New forms of individuated citizenship are being enabled by civil society activism, the electronic media, and social networking, which offer unusual opportunities for expressive citizenship even if these are largely restricted to the educated middle classes. The affective bases of politics are however far from dead. Individualism in the economic sphere cohabits quite cheerfully with community in the political. Caste continues to have greater political purchase than social; it is a far more potent instrument in the political sphere than the social or ritual. The ties of family too remain strong and resilient, in politics as in the economy. If the largest private corporations in India are family firms, so are the bulk of its political parties family endeavors.[5] The commercial interests of many presidents of political parties—from ownership of educational institutions to media corporations—affirm the ease and fluidity with which economic and political power translate into each other.

The large-scale corruption that has ensued from this traffic between economic and political power has provoked public anger on a massive scale, fueling one of the most symbolically significant interrogations of the political. A recent popular anticorruption mobilization—*India Against Corruption*— presented itself as civil society against a venal state, demanding that Parliament pass, within a specified time period, a "people's"[6] draft of the Lokpal (Ombudsman) Bill.[7] A central claim of the campaign is the priority of citizens over Parliament and the legitimacy of law-making by civil society. Not only does this argument project civil society[8] as inherently virtuous and politics as the repository of evil, it also entails an unauthenticated representational claim on behalf of a presumptively undifferentiated, homogenizing, and totalizing civil society. Echoing the middle-class distrust of the state as inherently undesirable and inefficient, this agenda seeks the curtailment of the state's role in the lives of citizens to the absolute minimum. In its refusal to acknowledge the significance of state intervention for the welfare of the poor, the argument betrayed its origins in the middle class that forms its most substantial constituency and prefers to cast its vote on Facebook and Twitter rather than in the polling booth.

Further, since there is no way of arbitrating the representational claims advanced by particular segments of civil society (however well intentioned), the same argument could be deployed by other sectional groups, not excluding corporate lobbies, as they seek to influence government policy. The grounds on which the claim of civil society (in whatever form) to speak on behalf of the welfare of the people may be privileged over the claim of capital to speak on behalf of the prosperity of the nation are not entirely clear. The principle that the prerogative of formulating the law is transferable—whether to civil society or technocratic experts or business leaders—is inherently dangerous, because it does not provide us with any criteria by which to determine the legitimacy of such competing claims.

These trends complicate the contemporary ambivalence about the political, in particular the question of the boundaries of this sphere and the agents who are active in it. As we have seen, unmarked citizens have long played a preeminent role in circumscribing the sphere of the political and participating in it. In recent decades, one set of ascriptively marked citizens have claimed and gained entry to this sphere, through a combination of the politics of recognition and political mobilization. Clearly, not all citizens marked in this way have succeeded in doing so, and the predicament of the tribal populations of central India is a melancholy reminder of this. Another set of marked citizens—the poor—have however remained on the periphery of this sphere. Theirs is an almost schizophrenic existence vis-à-vis the political: they vote in the political, but could otherwise be said to inhabit a prepolitical condition. As a recent debate on the poverty line[9] as the basis for welfare entitlements illustrates, activists and intellectuals who intervene to speak for the poor invariably speak on their behalf, expressing their claims through a form of nonmandated representation.

Meanwhile, unmarked citizens who have, for more than a century, monopolized the domain of politics, are today turning against it. Among early Indian liberals, there was consensus on the object of the political being to transform the social. The social, in this conception, was the den of tradition, conservatism, custom, and unreason; in contrast to it, the political was constructed as modern, rational, empowering, and emancipatory. The developmental interventions of the Indian state after independence, including attempts to reform Hindu personal law, were informed by such assumptions. Today, as we have seen, a powerful section of civil society seeks to author an inversion of the relationship between the social and political. As the older elite aspiration for a liberal sphere of politics gives way to its current construction of politics and civil society as irrevocably adversarial domains, the relationship between the social and the political is transposed. The debasement of the political is inferred from the perception that politicians are venal and corrupt, providing the justification for an antipolitics program. Politicians and legislatures stand banished from this innovative and even presumptuous script of the political, in which "the people" enact laws. There is however no requirement that the overweening power of corporations be removed from this sphere. The possibility of dissent within civil society is also ruled out by definition. It is deeply ironical that this moment of active citizenship coincides with a denial of the legitimacy of politics.

These recent challenges have thus brought into question not just the legitimacy of the government, but of politics itself. In colonial India, we noted the threat of withholding political obligation from a state that did not provide its subjects with protection for their liberty and property, or give them the right to defend their country by going to war. At the cusp of independence, we saw how notions of allegiance and loyalty were deployed to refuse citizenship to Indians in Africa, and how Muslims returning from Pakistan were considered suspect unless there was an oath sealing the contract between the state and *that* particular group of citizens. Similar arguments have also been made in respect of political rights for nonresident Indians. The idea of citizenship as a contract permeates political discourse in late colonial India, and around the time of independence, there is also a shift in the nature of the contract, from the colonial emphasis on duties to a new priority placed on rights. Today, as the rights regime is being gradually strengthened, the discrediting of politics by none other than citizens who have enjoyed monopolistic and even hegemonic control over it suggests that there are different principles of legitimacy for different social groups. Those who are dependent upon the state for their basic needs have little choice but to cling to it; those who have liberated themselves from the services formerly provided exclusively by the state but now available on the market have disavowed it. The legitimacy deficit to which the anticorruption movement of 2011 drew public attention is also a deficit that calls into question the very basis of the enterprise of politics.

The civic community remains a fragile and unfinished project, reflecting the failure of an earlier tradition of rhetorical social-democracy to channel the affect of community into a more secular sense of social solidarity, and to invent an egalitarian ideology that could address and transcend caste and class differences. As group-identity claims were increasingly presented as claims to substantive equality, their political accommodation swiftly became a proxy for the redress of inequality. By giving disadvantaged groups a greater presence in public institutions, India's affirmative action policies have successfully advanced the project of social inclusion in a diverse democracy, and have also been effective instruments of managing diversity and therefore containing its potential for social conflict. While social conflict has been kept at bay, however, social fragmentation has not, with less than optimal implications for forging solidarity among citizens.

In the many and enduring contestations over Indian citizenship across the twentieth century, one of the bleakest and most telling inversions is that between the *Harijan basti* (Dalit hamlet) and the gated community. In the countryside, the *Harijan basti* has conventionally been located just outside the main village, testifying to practices of untouchability. The ritual purity of caste Hindus is maintained and protected by this spatial separation of polluting citizens who nevertheless continue to provide their ritually pure caste superiors with a variety of services and labor. In the affluent neighborhoods of India's globalized metropolitan cities today, the gated community arguably performs the same role in an inverted fashion. The spatial location of unmarked citizens, behind walls of hidden privilege and at a comfortable distance from the world of marked citizens, is not however an exclusion born of coercion. It is instead a form of self-exclusion from the world of citizenship as solidarity. The inequalities of citizenship are not irremediable if the glue of solidarity is within reach. Neither the absence of solidarity nor the tolerance of inequality bode well for the future of citizenship.

Notes

Introduction

1. While the Indian experience of citizenship reflects many of these tensions and ambivalences, some of these are irrelevant to this project and others lack significance.

2. These appear to be particularly abundant in the American context, beginning with Grover Cleveland's hortatory *Good Citizenship* (1908). More recent studies, as opposed to exhortations, include Michael Schudson, *The Good Citizen* (1999), and David Ricci, *Good Citizenship in America* (2004).

3. Charles Tilly (1999: 255) makes a distinction between top-down claims that cover both rights and obligations and bottom-up claims through which people acquire rights and obligations by mobilizing to make demands upon the state. The first, Tilly argues, regularly generates the second, though most claim-making fails.

4. Cf. Holston, *Citizenship: Disjunctions of Democracy and Modernity in Brazil.* (2008).

5. Most famously, this is the burden of Robert Putnam's argument in *Making Democracy Work* (1993).

6. In his *On the Jewish Question,* Marx argued that while the state abolishes the distinctions of birth, social rank, education, and occupation by declaring that these are nonpolitical distinctions and that "every member of society is an equal partner in popular sovereignty," it nevertheless "allows private property, education, occupation,

to *act* after *their* own fashion . . . and to manifest their *particular* nature" (Marx, 1963: 12). Michael Ignatieff (1995: 64) reads this as suggesting that, for Marx, man's identity as bourgeois was his real identity while his identity as *citoyen* was a false, purely legal, and mythic identity.

7. The Alfred Marshall lectures that were published as *Citizenship and Social Class* in 1950 were delivered at Cambridge in 1949.

8. Cf. the Parekh Report's recommendations for "how a genuinely multicultural Britain urgently needs to reimagine itself." The Runnymede Trust, Commission on the Future of Multi-Ethnic Britain, 2000. http://www.runnymedetrust.org/projects/ meb/reportPartOne.html#rethinking.

9. The use of citizenship tests in the United States is not new. It dates back to the early twentieth century, though literacy and civic knowledge were requirements for naturalization even prior to this. The changes in the civics tests over time reflect the shifts in policy toward particular groups of immigrants. Thus, if the earliest test was meant to discourage immigrants from Eastern Europe, the test adopted in 1952 was designed as a barrier to admission of Asian immigrants and communists, and subsequent tests have responded to immigration challenges from Latin America (Etzioni, 2007: 354–355). The most recent changes inaugurated in 2006 are perceived as being biased against those who have inadequate English language skills.

10. Unveiled in November 2005, this test is based on a report prepared by the political scientist Bernard Crick, which also recommended the introduction of compulsory citizenship education in schools. The book *Life in the UK* contains information about British history, laws, and institutions, but also about multiculturalism, public services, and employment, which potential citizens are expected to be able to answer. British historians pointed out errors in the test, which Crick defended as the result of haste so as not to keep immigrants waiting. A large number of guides to this book have since appeared, though the official one remains *Life in the United Kingdom: A Journey to Citizenship* (Home Office, 2007). http://www.guardian.co.uk/ uk/2006/apr/29/immigration.immigrationpolicy.

11. http://www.timesonline.co.uk/tol/news/uk/article584914.ece. British television channels were rife with spoofs of the test, including jokes about it being outsourced to Bangladesh. As an example, see http://www.youtube.com/watch?v=4do mfg9ea4E.

12. The Australian test has been criticized for its exclusionary potential vis-à-vis disadvantaged sections of applicants, especially those who were illiterate or uneducated or stateless. http://news.theage.com.au/national/citizenship-tests-give-no-fair-go-mp-20070314–2a5.html.

13. Commonwealth of Australia (2008) *Moving Forward . . . Improving Pathways to Citizenship: A Report by the Australian Citizenship Test Review Committee,* August 2008. Accessed on March 24, 2010, at http://www.citizenship.gov.au/_pdf/moving-forward-report.pdf.

14. Cf. http://www.dw-world.de/dw/article/0,,1935900,00.html.

15. http://www.hrw.org/en/node/82373/section/7. Also see http://static.rnw.nl/ migratie/www.radionetherlands.nl/currentaffairs/region/netherlands/080515-dutch -immigration-mc-redirected.

16. This had been effectively delegitimized in the Fundamental Law on Education enacted in 1947 under conditions of American occupation. http://www.news24.com/ Content/World/News/1073/d17aa92311c04347aa86b9foee3de9c0/16-11-2006-04-27/ Japan_passes_patriotism_bill; http://www.wsws.org/articles/2007/jan2007/japa-j03 .shtml; and http://search.japantimes.co.jp/cgi-bin/nn20060429a1.html.

17. The scheme envisages employing young people (between 16 and 25 years of age) at minimum wage standards, to spend six months to a year on projects relating to children, the sick and elderly, the environment and international development (Crabtree and Field, 2009). The benefits are intended to redound to the young people—creating "bridging" social capital and "producing better citizens" (ibid.: 36–37)—with some positive spillover into the wider social realm. A sponsored poll (with a small sample size) showed that 64 percent of adults supported such a program. The idea of a national civic service is finding sympathizers in left-wing circles. Cf. David Lammy's "Time for a Compulsory Civic Service Scheme" in *The New Statesman* blog, August 17, 2011. http://www.newstatesman.com/blogs/the-staggers/ 2011/08/civic-service-young-children.

18. During the Depression of the 1930s, President Franklin Roosevelt initiated a Civilian Conservation Corps which led to more than three million young men planting billions of trees, building almost a thousand parks and fifty thousand bridges (Crabtree and Field, 2009: 39).

19. The Hindi word *Aadhaar* means foundation or basis.

20. The idea of a technology-driven single identity number is also justified in terms of reducing the duplication of "identity silos" and so reducing the costs of multiple forms of verification of identity, and obviating currently widespread malpractices such as individuals holding multiple PAN numbers to evade tax. A networked central database is envisaged in which currently different forms of identification—election card, the tax card, drivers' license, bank account, passport details, photograph, and address—could potentially be amalgamated in a single form of identification. Such convergence of information can be a matter of concern if the data is not confidential and access protocols are not adequately stringent. The proposed networking of databases—of the UID (in the Central Identities Data Repository), the National Population Register (which actually covers only citizens, while the UID covers all residents), and the National Intelligence Grid meant to enable the tracking of people and resources under watch for security reasons—also creates misgivings.

21. The assumption that the principle of jus soli was the principle governing citizenship in France, while Germany followed the jus sanguinis principle, has been

most famously advanced by Rogers Brubaker (1992) and most persuasively countered by Patrick Weil (2008).

22. The concept of the citizenship regime, formulated by Jenson and Phillips in the Canadian context, draws upon neo-institutionalism and political economy to identify patterns of change in the relationship between the state, the market, and communities in that country. In times of economic and political turbulence, such as neoliberal reform, it is argued, citizenship regimes undergo change as the role of the state, the division of labor between the state and the market, and the relationship between state and civil society are fundamentally restructured (1996: 113). In the Latin American context, Deborah Yashar has interpreted the resistance of indigenous movements in five countries of that region to neoliberalism through the concept of a citizenship regime that is a composite of boundaries (who has citizenship), form (of interest intermediation), and content (of rights and practices) (Yashar, 2005: ch. 2).

23. The concept of a citizenship regime is not intended to convey a homogenized or singular conception of citizenship, and the idea of synchronically existent multiple citizenship regimes arguably renders the concept of such a regime irrelevant if not oxymoronic. Nor is it intended to preclude multiple forms of relationship between states and individual citizens (or groups of citizens) which indisputably exist in every polity. While these may occasionally render the citizenship regime inchoate, they are better understood as contradictory elements of particular citizenship regimes, features that may pull the regime in one or other direction, but that form an ineluctable part of the complex whole that is the citizenship regime. Multiple citizenship regimes cannot, by definition, coexist, even as multiple conceptions of citizenship certainly can. It is the relationship of these contending conceptions—advancing rival claims to determine and define the citizenship regime—in relation to the dominant citizenship regime that is of the essence.

1. The Subject-Citizen

1. Perhaps the most famous example of this was the dedication in Nirad Chaudhuri's book *Autobiography of an Unknown Indian* (1951) "To the memory of the / British Empire in India / Which conferred subjecthood on us/But withheld citizenship; / To which yet / every one of us threw out the challenge; /'Civis Britannicus sum' / Because / all that was good and living / within us / was made, shaped and quickened / By the same British rule."

2. Morrison delivered these lectures when he was Alexander Robertson Lecturer at the University of Glasgow in 1904–1905.

3. The Association was started by Gandhi and included several industrialists among its members. Its chief objective was to advocate the cause of the overseas Indians. It was still in existence in May 1948 (cf. Tinker, 1976: 318). Fifteen bulletins of

the Imperial Indian Citizenship Association, running to 700 pages, were published, in 1927, in a volume titled *Indians Abroad,* edited by S. A. Waiz.

4. In the empire, franchise was based on class rather than race, so that Indians in Great Britain could vote there on the same basis as other British subjects, and some were even elected to the House of Commons. However, Indians were excluded from the franchise in Canada and Australia (cf. Tinker, 1976: 39).

5. The phrase in the heading of this section is taken from Edmund Burke's searing critique of Warren Hastings's statement defending himself against impeachment by arguing that the moral qualities of actions in Asia were different from those in Europe. Repudiating this argument, Burke said: "these gentlemen have formed a plan of geographical morality, by which the duties of men in public and in private situations are not to be governed by their relations to the great governor of the universe, or by their relations to men, but by climates, degrees of longitude and latitude . . . as if, when you have crossed the equinoctial line, all the virtues die" (Keith, 1922, 1: 143–144).

6. The comparison was not lost on Indian leaders such as Rash Behari Ghose, the president of the Indian National Congress (1890) who asked rhetorically: "Shall Christian England fall below pagan Rome, who in her best days, conquered only to extend the privileges of citizenship to her subjects, investing them with equal rights and equal laws, equally administered?" (R. B. Ghose, 1917: 18).

7. Lionel Curtis remarked that the work being done for Indians by the British Commonwealth included but encompassed more than "that which Rome did for the peoples of Europe." The beginning made in terms of providing representative institutions would, he said, be advanced depending on the pace at which Indians rose to "a sense of their duty to their fellow-citizens" (Curtis, 1916: 176–177).

8. The ambiguities of citizenship in imperial Britain have led Gorman to describe this, in its content, as a "hybrid citizenship model of *subjecthood,*" in which subjecthood, consisting of the shared dependence on a common law that provided for civil liberties and was encapsulated in the person of the sovereign, was supplemented and affirmed by the bonds of citizenship, comprising a shared cultural identity—of language, history, and so forth (Gorman, 2006: 18). Citizenship as common subjection to a sovereign was the dominant principle; citizenship as national identity was secondary, apart from being a later development.

9. Indeed, it has been argued that the holding of nominal citizenship meant less to the people in Great Britain than to those in its overseas territories, if for no other reason than that the privileges of citizenship in Britain itself were limited to the select few who could own or inherit land, which had for long been the basis of the franchise. Overseas, the idea of common subjecthood had much greater purchase as it helped to legitimize claims to political representation (Karatani, 2003: 6).

10. Territorial control was of many types, including mandate, protectorate, crown colony, suzerainty (cf. Gorman, 2006: 20).

11. In 1899, New Zealand enacted an Immigration Restriction law by which any new arrival who could not pass a literacy test in some European language could be declared a "prohibited immigrant." Royal assent was accorded in 1900 with the law having been deemed to be nondiscriminatory, and Australia and Canada following suit (cf. Tinker, 1976: 22).

12. In lectures delivered in 1926, subsequently published as *The Indian Citizen: His Rights and Duties,* Sastri cited the argument of eminent lawyers in Britain that while Great Britain had laws, and each of the Dominions had laws, there was no law that binds the entire Empire: "there is no such thing as British Empire law and British Empire citizen" (1948: 50).

13. These were of course the aspirations of a limited section of the Indian elite. In the political lexicon of the times, it was only the moderates who cared about citizenship; the extremists in any case rejected it outright.

14. Sir William Wedderburn (quoted in Zacharias, 1933: 103).

15. The Court of Directors' Despatch of 1854 (drawn up by Sir Charles Wood), often referred to as the Charter of Indian education, had recommended the setting up of an education department in every province; the establishment of universities in the big cities; and the setting up of at least one government school in every district and grants-in-aid for private schools. The purpose of this was to promote mass education, including in the vernacular. The Universities of Calcutta, Bombay, and Madras were also established in accordance with these recommendations. Cf. Chamberlain, 1899: 42–46.

16. Henry Maine had in 1886 estimated the number of educated Indians as less than 4,500 (Gopal, 1965: 166). The basis of Maine's calculation is unclear, for in 1864–1865 alone, Indian universities produced 5,000 graduates, and in the early twentieth century, there were already 30,000 Indian graduates (Brown, 1985: 118).

17. Cf. note by Lytton, dated May 30, 1877 (B. D. Basu, 1933: 195).

18. Surendranath Banerjea passed the competitive examination for the Indian Civil Service, but was initially not allowed to join on account of a minor discrepancy between Indian and English forms of calculation in the reporting of his age. Banerjea won his case and was appointed to the civil service, but dismissed fairly quickly over a minor matter.

19. Cf. Ayesha Jalal (2001: 153).

20. This did not imply, Buch reassured his readers in 1938, that Roy was "in the slightest degree indisposed to contemplate the prospect of India as a nation *politically independent*" (Buch, 1938: 93).

21. The most famous case was that against Bal Gangadhar Tilak, a member of the Bombay Legislative Council and editor of the *Kesari,* whose imprisonment for eighteen months energized popular nationalist sentiment and made him a national hero.

22. B. Majumdar argued that the British Indian Association of the Bengal Presidency was the most enduring of such associations, because the zamindars and

landlords—"a body of rich, educated and comparatively leisured class of citizens"—who made up its membership were not present in such large numbers in the other two presidencies (1965: 73).

23. Behramji Malbari (1853-1912) was the premier advocate of social reform as a precondition for political reform; while K. T. Telang (1850-1892)was the most eloquent supporter of the position that political reform was easier to achieve—since it was being negotiated with a civilized and reasonable government—and that, having been achieved, it could be applied to the social domain (Buch, 1938: 115–124).

24. Writing in 1938, Buch depicted the journey of Indian liberalism from the early nineteenth to the early twentieth century as one that began with "religious liberalism" and progressed, through "social liberalism," to the final step in its evolution, "political liberalism," best exemplified in the visions of Surendranath Banerjea, Dadabhai Naoroji, Pherozeshah Mehta, G. K. Gokhale, M. G. Ranade, and other so-called moderates, whether of the Congress or the Indian Liberal Party. C. A. Bayly summarizes the key concepts of early nineteenth-century Indian liberalism as "the mixed constitution incorporating a degree of popular representation, the free press, free exchange and a division of the executive from the judiciary and legislature" (Bayly, 2007: 7).

25. Of Madras, Bombay, Bengal, the United Provinces, Punjab, Bihar and Orissa, the Central Provinces and Assam.

26. Nabagopal Mitra was the editor of the National Paper. He was nicknamed "National" apparently because he was excessively fond of using the word national in everything he wrote. Mitra was not however much of a democrat; he believed India's destiny lay in being Hindu and even favored dictatorial rule.

27. The elective principle, limited to the propertied, professionals, and traders, was first introduced in 1882 for municipal councils and rural boards. The Indian Councils Act of 1892 introduced nonofficial representation in both the Indian Legislative Council as well as provincial councils, but these were to be nominated by certain bodies. Even the 1909 reform envisaged elections which were either indirect or else conducted in separate electorates. In all cases, the franchise was extremely restricted (Chiriyankandath, 2001: 57–58).

28. The Second Congress in Calcutta (1886), for instance, spoke of the need to constitute an electorate of "all persons possessing such qualifications, educational and pecuniary, as may be deemed necessary" (Indian National Congress, 1910, 3: 4).

29. President of the Indian National Congress in 1920, and a well-known Moderate nationalist from southern India.

30. The influence of the ideas of Darwin and Spencer on ideas about race in nineteenth-century Britain is well known. Even socialists, such as the Fabians, were under the sway of ideas of racial supremacy. It was hardly surprising then that British imperialist publicists, such as Arnold White, should hold a vision of imperial citizenship that was explicitly defined by "whiteness" (cf. Gorman, 2006: 26).

31. In this work, community includes both caste and religion, contra Chatterji's emphasis on race, which has earlier been contested by Scott who privileges religion (1995: 197).

32. Secretary of State for India.

33. Sumit Sarkar notes that the introduction of separate electorates in the United Provinces in 1916 witnessed government servants, pensioners, and landlords outnumbering "less reliable groups, like professional men, traders, or *ulama* in the 'Muslim franchise'" (Sarkar, 1983: 140).

2. Legal Citizenship and the Long Shadow of the Partition

1. Three election petitions filed in the Allahabad High Court challenged Sonia Gandhi's election on various grounds, ranging from her ineligibility to be a citizen by naturalization to the unconstitutionality of the Citizenship Act of 1955. *Rashtriya Mukti Morcha v. Union of India* (2006) was one such case in which the Delhi High Court held that domiciliary citizenship is a recognized concept in the Indian constitutional scheme and, based on the debates of the Constituent Assembly, that a domiciled person could not be barred from holding public office.

2. In the United States, for instance, only natural-born citizens are eligible for the positions of president and vice-president. Thus, even Henry Kissinger and Madeleine Albright would have been ineligible for these positions, though governors of American states can be foreign-born and/or dual citizenship holders. Israel does not even permit the holding of dual citizenship by its legislators, who must renounce their non-Israeli citizenship before making their declarations of allegiance to the state and assuming the rights of a member of the Knesset. Haiti-born, and a French national by marriage, Michaëlle Jean was appointed Governor-General of Canada in 2005. On the grounds that this is a largely ceremonial position, the French government decided to not enforce a law that allows it to withdraw French citizenship from those who hold positions in the government or military of another country. However, to keep controversy at bay, Jean voluntarily renounced her French citizenship within two days of assuming office.

3. Sessions of the Indian National Congress—e.g., Ahmedabad 1902, Madras 1903, Benares 1905, Allahabad 1910—frequently passed resolutions demanding, for overseas Indians, the rights and privileges of British citizenship in common with the European subjects of the empire.

4. The gendered quality of citizenship, and even citizenship claims, is echoed in much citizenship discourse of the time. It recurs frequently in the debates discussed in this chapter, and is retained to preserve the flavor of the original discussion.

5. According to the memoirs of the Indian civil servant and diplomat, Y. D. Gundevia, B. N. Rau was initially insistent on the condition of domicile. Gundevia, who had represented India in Burma and was keenly interested in the issue of

overseas Indians, persuaded Nehru and Rau that the Burmese government's condition for giving citizenship to Indian settlers—eight years' residence out of ten in the years immediately preceding independence—was excessive, and an Indian who was refused citizenship by Burma would effectively be rendered a stateless person. This was how B. N. Rau's insistence on domicile as a condition of citizenship was overcome (Gundevia, 2008: 51–60).

6. The British Nationality and Status of Aliens Act 1914 and the Indian Naturalization Act 1926.

7. This was the report of an All-Parties Conference in response to the frequently reiterated British challenge to Indians to formulate a scheme of constitutional reform that would be acceptable to a cross-section of Indian opinion.

8. V. Rodrigues, however, perhaps overstates the inclusive character of these provisions in arguing that these articles had "pronounced features which could be termed secular, understood as non-preference to any and inclusion of members of all relevant communities or groups. . . . The fact of Partition . . . was not allowed to affect the understanding and demarcation of citizenship. . . . Formally, all those who were found in Pakistan could be citizens of India if they made such an option before the relevant provisions were enacted by the Constituent Assembly" (Rodrigues, 2008: 168).

9. It could be argued that the Constitution was legislating citizenship only for the period just after independence, and until the enactment, by Parliament, of the laws of citizenship. In that sense (and the CAD reflect this), the constitutional enactment of citizenship was only meant to have a temporary life. However, the debate over whether Article 7 could trump Article 5 continued to figure in judicial pronouncements for some decades.

10. The Census of India 1951 used the term "non-Muslim refugees" to describe Hindus and Sikhs coming in from Pakistan.

11. Dr. P. S. Deshmukh said that he feared that the article "would make Indian citizenship the cheapest on earth" (CAD 9: 353).

12. Y. D. Gundevia's discussion of the contention over the concept of "domicile" shows that neither long residence, nor ownership of immovable property, were in themselves or even together considered adequate proof of domicile. "There was a consensus on the idea that domicile was, basically, a matter of 'intention'" (Gundevia, 2008: 53).

13. There is no reliable estimate of the numbers of such people. Zamindar reports that figures ranging from 200,000–300,000 are mentioned in contemporary accounts, based on a calculation of 2,000 returnees per day. Delhi alone was said to have 40,000 such refugees, though Zamindar's calculations suggest a figure of 11,900 for Delhi (Zamindar, 2008: 86).

14. Gandhi was in favor of all those who had been uprooted on either side of the border returning to their homes with dignity. Thus, Hindus and Sikhs should be welcomed back to Pakistan, he said, and "we should tell the Muslims who have gone

away that their houses and their land are as they had left behind and that they should come and occupy them. If we get over our madness and behave as gentlemen, things will be all right" (*CWMG,* December 6, 1947, vol. 98, no. 6: 5).

15. Zamindar suggests that the law was named after a similar Israeli legislation targeting the "absentee" properties of Palestinian Arabs (2007: 130). Such institutional arrangements were, of course, familiar in WWII Europe. Britain, for instance, had a Custodian of Enemy Property. The Indian office was also rechristened as the Custodian of Enemy Property after the India-Pakistan war of 1965.

16. The Indian claim, based on its estimation of the value of properties left behind by those leaving Pakistan, was much higher than what Pakistan was either willing to acknowledge or able to pay (Zamindar, 2007: 125–127).

17. Joya Chatterji, "South Asian Histories of Citizenship, 1947–70." Unpublished paper.

18. The shared recognition that it was desirable to prevent the kind of large-scale displacement that had taken place in the Punjab led to the signing of the Nehru-Liaquat Ali Pact of 1950. According to this agreement, both India and Pakistan would protect their minorities, give them freedom of movement, equality of citizenship and an equal opportunity to participate in public institutions.

19. The terrible Nellie massacre, in which over 2,000 people were killed, took place in February 1983 as elections were being conducted using these electoral rolls.

20. The Asom Gana Parishad, a regional political party, was a product of the Assam Accord with the central government. Its Chief Minister (from 1996 to 2001) was Prafulla Kumar Mahanta, who was also the leader of the All Assam Students' Union that had led the movement against "foreigners" from 1979 to 1985.

21. The government of Assam furnished information showing that while it had initiated 310,759 enquiries, and completed a high proportion of these, the total number of people declared to be illegal immigrants was 10,015, of whom only 1,481 had actually been expelled. In a blatant display of religious bias, it stated that the Muslim population of Assam had risen 77.42 percent in 1971–1991, whereas the Hindu population of the state had risen by 41.89 percent during the same period (ibid.: 8).

22. The retention of the masculine gender is deliberate because the case law insisted on treating women (and minors) as exceptions, reinforcing the bias that women's and children's citizenship could only be determined according to the citizenship of men, such as their husbands and fathers.

23. This remained a vexed question for some years because the law governing and defining foreigners was the British Nationality and Status of Aliens Act of 1914, according to which only someone who was not a natural-born British subject was a foreigner. That definition was obviously not helpful for distinguishing between Indian and Pakistani citizens. Subsequently, Section 9 of the Foreigners' Act of 1946 placed the burden of proving that someone is not a foreigner on that individual. This was not always compatible with Section 9.2 of the Citizenship Act under which the executive has overriding power to determine whether or not someone has acquired citizenship

of a foreign country. Thus, in all judgments where the Court was called upon to establish the citizenship of an individual, it would defer to the executive. Recent years have witnessed a shift in the matter of burden of proof (as in the Calcutta High Court judgment in *Md. Elahi v. The State of West Bengal*, 2008) which simply dismissed the petitioner's claim that he is an Indian citizen, wrongly accused of being a Bangladeshi, thereby rendering determination by the central government unnecessary.

24. On Caplan and Torpey's interpretation, from the French Revolution onwards, passports have been "essential to states' monopolization of the legitimate means of movement" (2001: 3).

25. The immediate provocation for this enactment was rather innocuous—a case filed by a man appealing the denial of a passport to him (*Satwant Singh Sawhney v. Union of India*, 1967). The Supreme Court's ruling that the right to travel abroad was a part of an individual's personal liberty, and that the government could not refuse a passport without violating both Articles 14 and 21 of the Constitution, necessitated a law specifying the conditions under which an individual could be refused a passport.

26. In many states in the United States, undocumented aliens are entitled to many rights, such as those pertaining to public schooling, drivers' licenses, and property, making citizenship status rather less important, and also rendering rights and status relatively autonomous (Bosniak, 2006: 89).

27. The Nawab of Junagadh (a princely state under British suzerainty in the Saurashtra region of Gujarat) left for Pakistan without signing the Instrument of Accession to the Government of India. In February 1948, the Government held a referendum, in which the people of Junagadh voted overwhelmingly in favor of accession to India. This transfer of sovereignty led to the dispossession of some people who had been granted lands by the ruler of Junagadh in the mid-nineteenth century. *State of Saurashtra v. Jamadar Mohamad Abdulla and Ors* (1961) was about the grant of lands to the respondents by the ruler of Junagadh in the mid-nineteenth century. A resumption of these grants by the administrator (appointed by the government of India) resulted in their dispossession. To appeal their dispossession, they needed to establish that their right in those properties was justiciable in municipal law. But whether the respondents enjoyed the rights of citizens to appeal for relief in the municipal courts in turn hinged on the question of when the transfer of sovereignty would be dated. The Supreme Court held that even if the respondents became Indian citizens when the Indian government annexed the state, they could only assert such rights in the municipal courts as were recognized by the Indian dominion. The new sovereign did not recognize their claim as grantees of the erstwhile ruler of Junagadh, and hence they could not appeal for the restitution of their properties under municipal law. This was a case in which, even as the respondents became citizens of India through annexation, they were not entitled to the properties granted to them by an anterior law, that of the preceding sovereign.

28. Kumar Rani was the owner of substantial properties of which, in 1946, she created a *wakf* (a charitable trust in Islamic law), appointing herself its *mutawalli*

(manager/caretaker) for life and her three sons jointly as *mutawallis* to succeed her. In 1948, Kumar Rani went to Karachi, ostensibly for treatment, and traveled back and forth a couple of times. In *State of Bihar v. Kumar Amar Singh* (1955), the Supreme Court ruled that Article 7 did not apply in her case as, despite being married to an Indian, she had gone to Pakistan with the intention of permanently living there. This was also the case in *Raushan Ara alias Suraiaya v. State of West Bengal* (1996).

29. The Custodian of Enemy Property is modeled on a British institution of the WWII period, enabling the British government to take over 220,000 properties belonging to citizens of Germany, Bulgaria, and Romania.

30. One of the original trustees of the Mahmudabad estate was Mohammed Ali Jinnah. The father of the present Raja of Mahmudabad refers to a meeting with Jinnah in London in 1933 where they discussed family and property matters. Raja of Mahmudabad (2001: 421).

31. Clause 2 of the Ordinance states: "The enemy property vested in the Custodian shall, notwithstanding that the enemy or the enemy subject or the enemy firm has ceased to be an enemy due to death, extinction, winding up of business or change of nationality, or that the legal heir and successor is a citizen of India or the citizen of a country which is not an enemy, continue to remain vested in the Custodian till it is divested by the Central Government."

32. A moving example of this contingency is the story of one of the greatest Urdu poets, Josh Malihabadi, who migrated to Pakistan in 1958 fearing that the Urdu language would not survive in India after Nehru. Malihabadi has written a poignant account of how he was promised property and business opportunities if he migrated, but lost both and remained a somewhat disillusioned citizen of Pakistan (cf. Josh Malihabadi, 1997). While Malihabadi experienced a sense of belonging to no nation, one of the greats of Hindustani classical music, Bade Ghulam Ali Khan, went to Pakistan but moved back to India and to a successful renewal of his musical career (cf. Gyanendra Pandey, 2001: 70–71).

33. The rival claimant to his property in court was, in fact, the Raja's uncle who was also an Indian citizen.

34. In several court cases, and not just this one, property appears as the glue of citizenship, even possibly at the expense of family relationships. The Mahmudabad family has spent much time living in London, where the former Raja of Mahmudabad died in 1973, after spending barely four years in Pakistan, the country to which he migrated at the time of Partition. This appears to be a distinctive form of the deterritorialization of citizenship usually associated with globalization. Are different citizenships immaterial to family relationships sustained on the soil of a third country?

35. Property even has the power to convey the taint of its former "enemy" ownership: the property purchased by Mullamadakkal Assain of Mallapuram district in Kerala from someone who had migrated to Pakistan is permanently stigmatized as *"Pak bhoomi"* (Pakistani land) *(The Indian Express,* October 24, 2010).

36. Pratiksha Baxi (2009); Urvashi Butalia (1998: ch. 4); Veena Das (2007: ch. 2).

37. There are no reliable numbers though Veena Das endorses the G. D. Khosla Fact-Finding Organization's estimate of approximately 100,000 (Das, 2007: 20).

38. The idea of biological citizenship provides a post-Marshall way of reading the politics of race and nationality, as it has done for the fallouts of Chernobyl and Bhopal. In India, in the 1990s, one challenge of biological citizenship may be seen in the claim that caste discrimination is equivalent to racial discrimination. Another is the example of sex-selective abortion, a practice that acquired disturbing proportions through the 1980s and 1990s (cf. Rose and Novas, 2005).

39. The numbers vary depending on the source. The government informed the Constituent Assembly in December 1949 that 12,000 Muslim women had been recovered in India, and 6,000 Hindu and Sikh women in Pakistan. The Fact-Finding Organization, chaired by G. D. Khosla, claimed that 12,000 Hindu and Sikh women had been recovered in Pakistan, and 8,000 Muslim women in India (Das, 2007: 21).

40. Protocol to the Agreement between the Government of India and the Government of Bangladesh. http://pmindia.nic.in/Final-%20PROTOCOL%20TO%20 LBA.pdf.

41. On the eastern border, Sadiq's "documentary citizens" (2009) implicitly convey the same sentiment through their acquisition, not always through legitimate means, of precisely those official documents that can provide such access.

3. Aspirational Citizenship

1. Thin citizenship refers to citizenship as legal status, while thick citizenship refers to a more active conception of citizenship as belonging and identity and also as performance (Kymlicka and Norman, 1995: 285).

2. In recent times, we have witnessed a burgeoning of scholarly literature in many fields that could be relevant to this case: refugee studies, international refugee law, migration studies, and—in the South Asian context—Partition histories. The political theory of citizenship has only recently brought aliens and nonmembers into its compass; and, notwithstanding this engagement, migrants and refugees still remain about as central to mainstream citizenship theory as their subjects are to quotidian political life. But even the citizenship theorists who lament the normative nationalism of studies of immigration and citizenship, and have administered this corrective, tend to look at the issue exclusively from the perspective of what states should or should not do, or the rights they should or should not grant, rather than from that of claimants to citizenship.

3. See, for instance, Oldfield (1990) and Dagger (1997).

4. This in turn has now been overtaken by the argument that globalization undermines welfare and entails the abandonment of social citizenship as a state project (Sassen, 2006).

5. The 1951 Refugee Convention had emphasized the words "events occurring before 1 January 1951". The Protocol of 1967 removed the requirement that the events causing someone to become a refugee should have occurred before a certain date.

6. Cf. Carens (1995). Though Carens's has been described as "an outlying view" (Bosniak, 2006: 33), scholars are increasingly searching for ways of grounding the rights of even undocumented aliens in moral argument. Cf. Benhabib (2004).

7. Carens argues that as "irregular migrants become more and more settled, their membership in society grows in moral importance, and the fact that they settled without authorization becomes correspondingly less relevant" (Carens, 2009). Ayelet Shachar's principle of jus nexi—or "citizenship by connection to the country" (2009)—reminds us that such connections are double-edged in the claims to citizenship that they yield. On the one hand, they strengthen the claims of resident aliens to citizenship; on the other, as immigrants (legal and illegal alike) forge social connections not only with host populations, but with other immigrants like themselves—sometimes people who come from the same region or ethnic group in their country of origin—they also maintain an alternative circle of social membership, through which their links to the country of their origin are preserved and bonds with it reinforced. Anthropological studies of the diaspora suggest that, in the particular context of avowedly multicultural states, the recognition of cultural difference tends to solidify such difference, giving it a rigid and fixed character rather than something that is being negotiated and reconstructed all the time (Raj, 2003: 188–189).

8. Cf. Walzer, but also Bosniak's argument that "in most legal and political theory, the legitimacy of barriers to territorial entry and to national citizenship is not even on the table" (Bosniak, 2006: 33).

9. Cf. Macedo (2007).

10. India also has refugees from Afghanistan, Bhutan, Iran, and Myanmar.

11. Tibetan refugees who arrived in India after 1979 are not given residence permits. Government grants have also declined. Rolfe argues that the change in the treatment of refugees signals a shift in the official discourse that now constructs Tibetans as internal minorities (Rolfe, 2008: 267).

12. There are other districts of Rajasthan and of Gujarat that have migrant populations of this kind, but this study does not comment on those. Farhana Ibrahim's study of the Dalit Meghwals who migrated to the Kachch region of Gujarat—in the shadow of the war with Pakistan in 1971, when Indian forces occupied Thar Parkar—and were given citizenship, shows how the settlement of large numbers of non-Muslims in a predominantly Muslim area contributed to boundary-formation and, through it, state formation (Ibrahim, 2008: ch. 3).

13. The *Gazetteer* of 1908 mentions a figure of 16,000 Rajputs in what was then called the District of Thar and Parkar. It mentions the "Soda tribe, formerly the dominant race in Thar and Parkar . . . of Rajput origin. . . . The rest are mainly low-caste or wild tribes, such as Dhers, Kolis and Bhils" (*Imperial Gazetteer* 23 [1908]: 310).

14. In some recent incidents, affluent Hindus have been kidnapped and even, on occasion, killed for ransom. The abduction, forced conversion and then abandonment of Dalit women is documented in Shah, 2007.

15. Dhananjay Keer writes that Ambedkar was upset that scheduled castes in Pakistan (and Hyderabad state) were being forcibly converted to Islam, and advised them thus: "I would like to tell the Scheduled Castes who happen today to be impounded inside Pakistan to come over to India by such means as may be available to them" (quoted in Keer, 1971: 399). It is not known whether Dalits in Pakistan were even aware of this sage advice.

16. These include Barmer, Bikaner, Jaisalmer, Jalore, Sri Ganganagar, and Jodhpur, among others. A new organization has also been established for those who have already obtained citizenship. This is the Seemant Lok Sangathan (Border Peoples' Organisation), meant to promote cross-border peace initiatives. The grant of citizenship was accomplished under the region-specific delegation of powers to district collectors for Rajasthan and Gujarat, by the amendment to the rules under the Citizenship Act.

17. The government figures, provided by the Divisional Commissioner of Jodhpur, are 2,828 people (70 Muslims and the remaining Hindus) still awaiting citizenship. They pertain only to the division, which includes the districts of Jodhpur, Jaisalmer, Barmer, Jalore Pali and Sirohi, Personal interview, April 16, 2007).

18. The scale of in-migration in this period may be inferred from Ibrahim's data for population growth during 1971–1981. In this period, she shows that the population of scheduled castes in Kachch increased by close to 40 percent, and that of scheduled tribes by almost 57 percent, while the population growth rate in the rest of the district was barely 24 percent (Ibrahim, 2008: 95).

19. The committee consisted of the state's Home Secretary, Rehabilitation Secretary, Revenue Secretary, and Deputy Home Secretary; the Divisional Commissioner of Jodhpur; and a representative of the Pak Visthapit Sangh.

20. Willem van Schendel's work on the "Enclaves" in India and Bangladesh makes a similar point about the surprisingly moderate response of L. K. Advani of the BJP to the Tin Bigha corridor: "any party may come and go but a government should honour its predecessor's decision, so we have to ensure the corridors functioning smoothly" (2002: 140).

21. This is despite the fact that approximately half of the scheduled castes in Pakistan are agricultural laborers, with others performing domestic labor, or daily wage work in the towns, or menial work that other social groups will not do. Eighty-five percent of them earn less than the official minimum wage of an unskilled worker. Bonded labor is also prevalent, and generally related to caste. Labor market discrimination is reinforced by the practice of untouchability. It is no surprise then that the incidence of poverty is higher among these groups or that two-thirds of the scheduled castes are illiterate (Z. Shah, 2007: sections 3, 5, and 8).

22. "Thappa" translates literally as stamp; but the meaning here is closer to stigma.

23. These people experience the state as *thing* on an everyday basis and in its most unfriendly form, but nevertheless crave to experience it as an *idea* (Rudolph and Jacobsen, 2006: vii).

24. ". . . we should expect a theory of the good citizen to be relatively independent of the legal question of what it is to be a citizen, just as a theory of the good person is distinct from the metaphysical (or legal) question of what it is to be a person" (Kymlicka and Norman, 1995: 285).

25. "Man, it turns out, can lose all so-called Rights of Man without losing his essential quality as man, his human dignity. Only the loss of a polity itself expels him from humanity" (Hannah Arendt, [1951] 1962: 297).

26. This recalls scholarship on Latin America (Yashar, 2005) that shows how social citizenship still has adherents in parts of the world that are struggling against the neoliberal abandonment of public provisioning for the welfare of citizens.

27. Tamil Nadu is the only state that provides for its (Sri Lankan) refugees to be given identity cards by which they can access all welfare schemes. The refugees however complain that the state government is willing to give them driving licenses for cars but not for two-wheeled vehicles.

28. The imperative for official identification and registration has a long history. In Britain, for instance, a parish-based system of national identity registration was in place since 1538 and became the basis for verifying social security claims (Szreter, 2007). However, it was just a century ago that the right of people to enter *only* the country of which they are citizens was consolidated in international law (Caplan and Torpey, 2001: 10).

29. In the United States, the Immigration and Naturalization Act of 1965 encouraged immigration by making conditions of entry less discriminatory on racial grounds.

30. The term diaspora is here being used to denote emigrant populations, and not in its historically specific meaning, indicating a population (originally Jewish) dispersed by forcible expulsion.

31. Non-Resident Indians is the term for those Indians living abroad who retain their Indian citizenship.

32. In the 2000s, remittances—mostly from the Middle East—constituted 3 percent of India's GDP (Kapur, 2010: 112).

33. One of the grounds on which the petitioner, Talat Jamal Siddiqui, contested the rejection in the High Court was because the official notification uses gendered language—words such as "he" and "himself"—enabling her to claim that it did not apply to her (cf. *Talat Jamal Siddiqui v. Union of India and Anr*, 2011).

34. In his address at the tenth Pravasi Bharatiya Divas on January 8, 2012, the prime minister, Manmohan Singh, promised that the government would take steps "to enable Indians resident abroad to participate in our election processes." http://

pmindia.nic.in/speech-details.php?nodeid=1124. Two years earlier, he had said: "I recognize the legitimate desire of Indians living abroad to exercise their franchise and to have a say in who governs India. We are working on this issue and I sincerely hope that they will get a chance to vote by the time of the next regular general elections. In fact, I would go a step further and ask why more overseas Indians should not return home to join politics and public life as they are increasingly doing in business and academia" (http://www.deccanherald.com/content/45653/full-text-pms-speech-pravasi.html).

35. Australia and Canada also have substantial numbers, in the region of 60,000 each, while emigrants in Kenya, New Zealand, and France account for about 15,000 each. These figures are current through August 30, 2010, and were accessed on March 3, 2011, from the website of the Ministry of Overseas Indian Affairs. http://www.moia.gov.in/services.aspx?ID1=41&id=m3&idp=35&mainid=23.

36. On the propensity of the Hindu diaspora to make donations for poverty relief in India to organizations of the Hindu Right, see Nussbaum, 2007: 306–14.

37. Canada and Australia disenfranchise emigrants after five and six years, respectively, of their having moved abroad.

38. http://pbdindia.org/exhibitions.html.

4. Pedagogies of Duty, Protestations of Rights

1. For the definitive survey of the international debate on this question, see Beitz, 2009: 21–26.

2. The International Covenant on Civil and Political Rights and the International Covenant on Economic, Social and Cultural Rights.

3. While C. A. Bayly locates the origin of the modern idea of rights in India in the rights of specific classes of people, such as landholders and tenants or seamen and soldiers (cf. Bayly, 2012: 30–31), our focus here is on the rights that could be said to be of more general, if not universal, application.

4. The term "social citizenship" is used here in the sense in which it appears in T. H. Marshall's *Citizenship and Social Class:* to indicate the incorporation of social and economic rights in the status of citizenship.

5. Not all colonial accounts of course are unmindful of or unsympathetic to Indian opinion and aspirations; and equally many Indian writers identify strongly with the modernist gifts of colonialism. Both, in turn, were internally differentiated, which is scarcely surprising at a time when nationalism was still struggling to find a voice. Indeed, even the apologists of empire were grappling with their own apprehensions. In Niall Ferguson's phrase, at the turn of the century the attitude of the British toward their empire "flipped over from arrogance to anxiety" (Ferguson, 2002: 222). The Boer War was an important contributory factor, apart from existing political and ideological differences between the more radical and socialist critics of imperialism and its conservative defenders.

6. In his correspondence with Lee-Warner in 1883, Maurice Macmillan referred to the *English Citizen* series brought out by his publishing house. See also J. R. Peddie's *The British Citizen: A Book for Young Readers* (1920), J. G. Bourinot's *How Canada is Governed* (1895), and David E. Cloyd's *Civics and Citizenship* in a series called *Teaching in the Elementary Schools* (1916). In the United States, "good citizenship" was also a concern in the public domain, with a (not incumbent) president, Grover Cleveland, himself publishing an address on the subject in 1908, based on a lecture delivered in 1903 (Cleveland, 1908). It is not entirely clear what the purpose of these textbooks in the dominions may have been, though the Australian case suggests that the twin challenges of war and immigration were responsible for the articulation of a particularly conservative and even racist conception of citizenship in the early twentieth century (Davidson, 1997: 79–83).

7. Lee-Warner was also a political agent in Kolhapur, and the author of *The Protected Princes of India* (1893), the second edition of which (1910)—*The Native States of India*—was retitled to make it more "neutral" (Ramusack, 2004: 57).

8. All references to and quotations from letters and official memoranda are from the Private Papers of Sir William Lee-Warner in the British Library's India Office Records. Mss. Eur. F92/9, Correspondence and Papers about *The Citizen of India* (London, 1897).

9. Only a couple of decades earlier, the British government in India had contemplated the publication of a moral textbook. Such a textbook had even been recommended by the Indian Education Commission chaired by W. W. Hunter. Lord Ripon's government rejected the idea chiefly because a moral textbook that would be acceptable to people belonging to different faiths in India seemed an impossibility. The idea surfaced periodically but was always, for one reason or another, shelved (cf. Ballhatchet, 1978).

10. Cotton was apparently a surprising choice, having been a critic of British policy in India. When the government withdrew its offer, Cotton began to speak threateningly of compensation. The fear of a lawsuit prompted the government to offer him the task of writing a quinquennial review of the progress of education in India, which he accepted (Ballhatchet, 1978: 198).

11. Lee-Warner's private papers contain an undated and perplexing document— in his own handwriting—classified as private and titled "Extract from letter of the Viceroy to the Secretary of State," which states "The management of our educational system seems to me to be deficient in central authority or control: for instance, I find to my amazement and disgust that Lee-Warner's excellent manual has not been introduced into any of the Government Schools, because the Text Book Committee, on which there is a majority of Babus and only one Government representative, had declined to admit it." This may be explained by the fact that the Government of India's Resolution on Textbooks (February 1900) had left the ultimate decision to prescribe textbooks with local governments, with the committees having a purely advisory role (A. Basu, 1974: 39).

12. *Views of Local Governments as to the Suitability of Sir W. Lee-Warner's "The Citizen of India" as a Text-book for Indian Schools.* 1902. India Office Records, British Library. Mss. Eur. F92/9.

13. It was reprinted three times each in 1899 and 1900, and again in 1903, 1904, and 1905. The revised edition was published and reprinted in 1906, and reprinted twice in 1907.

14. Lee-Warner was persistent in trying to obtain a viceregal endorsement for the revised edition. Finally, Minto's private secretary wrote to him in April 1906 saying that given the state of public sentiment at the time, the government should not even appear to give official sanction to *The Citizen of India.* Two months later, he wrote again clarifying that the government did not discourage any local government or department from patronizing the book: "Their whole attitude towards it is one of benevolent neutrality. But the Lord & Lady Minto have ordered copies for themselves" (Letters from Private Secretary's Office to Lee-Warner, dated April 27 and June 15, 1906). Private Papers of Sir William Lee-Warner. India Office Records, British Library. Mss.Eur. F92/9.

15. The account of the polity in this, as in several such books, bears a strong imprint of the philosophy of the Oxford Idealist tradition, especially T. H. Green's principle of the mutual interdependence between the individual and society.

16. In the second edition, he actually reminds his readers that the first meaning of the word citizen is "one who lives in a city" (Lee-Warner, 1907: 3).

17. This was despite the fact (cited earlier in the chapter) that as a civil servant Lee-Warner had opposed the expansion of the elective principle to the local bodies.

18. A copy of this book in the India Office collection of the British Library has inscribed below this, on the title page, "B. G. Doraisami Pillai, B.A.", the position of the inscription suggesting authorship rather than ownership of the book. B. G. Doraisami Pillai was a vice-president of the Natal Indian Congress at its formation in 1894 (*CWMG* 1: 178). http://www.gandhiserve.org/cwmg/VOL001.PDF. Since authorship cannot be definitively established, I refer to the author acronymically as AIC.

19. K. T. Telang (1850–1892) was a judge of the Bombay High Court, a lawyer, and public speaker well known for his knowledge of Hindu law and his championship of liberal education and the English language. Telang was the first Indian vice-chancellor of Bombay University.

20. In an article published in *The Journal of the Society of Arts* in 1895, Lee-Warner had endorsed the view of R. P. Karkaria (the author of a tract titled *The Late K. T. Telang and the Present Political Movement in India*) that Indians must address the crying need of moral and social reform instead of chasing "the phantom of premature political advancement" (Karkaria, 1895: 25).

21. R. N. Gilchrist taught at Presidency College, Calcutta, and was the author of political science textbooks that survived into undergraduate syllabi in Indian universities even three decades after independence.

22. Here, Gilchrist is implicitly invoking a conception of the patrie that comes from the republican tradition, especially Rousseau, Montesquieu, and Voltaire, for whom patrie was not represented by language, culture, or ethnicity, but by the rule of law, liberty, and self-government. But the territorial rootedness of patriotism has not historically inured it from associations with blood, honor, and soil, as in Robespierre's justification of the reign of terror as a way of defending the patrie from its internal and external enemies. As such, patriotism has been no less vulnerable to justifications of violence than nationalism. On the supposed contrast between patriotism and nationalism, see Viroli (1995), Nandy (2006), and Jayal (2006c).

23. Shrikrishna Venkatesh Puntambekar, born in 1890, was an Oxford graduate, a barrister-in-law, and professor of history and politics at the Benares Hindu University (1925–1946). He was the author of *An Introduction to Civics and Politics* and of the text cited here, *An Introduction to Indian Citizenship and Civilisation* (1929). The study of civics was inaugurated at the BHU in 1923, at the same time as the study of ancient Indian history and culture. The BHU's particular emphasis in these areas appears to inform Puntambekar's understanding of civics. Puntambekar was most well known for a tract he wrote on hand weaving and hand spinning, which Gandhi frequently cited. He also contributed an essay to a UNESCO project on human rights in 1948, at the time when the United Nations was drafting the Universal Declaration of Human Rights (Puntambekar, 1948).

24. V. S. Srinivasa Sastri was a member of the Servants of India Society and a Liberal politician, who made a remarkable journey from being an educationist and school headmaster to Agent-General in South Africa to Privy Councilor. A contemporary described him as an "unrelenting critic of Congress politics" (Chandrasekharan, 1932: 18). He was certainly well known as a scholar-politician who appreciated the benefits of the British connection for India, and he sought self-government for India through constitutional agitation.

25. Or, indeed, in Gilchrist's statement that "The great war has proved that though an Indian is not an Englishman, he is a member of the British Empire . . . The war has in many ways brought home to India its sense of imperial citizenship" (Gilchrist, 1920: 191–192).

26. The Motilal Nehru Committee Report, finalized only a year earlier, had produced a list of nineteen fundamental rights, thirteen of which were substantively included in the 1950 Constitution (Rajni Kothari, 1970a: 103).

27. This could be contrasted with Australia, where a popular textbook of 1916 presented the citizen as "someone who obeyed the state rather than one who founded the state in active democracy" (Davidson, 1997: 74).

28. This is ironical because, only four years later, the enactment of the Rowlatt Act triggered strong protest across India, but more particularly in the cities and larger towns, including Bombay, Ahmedabad, Delhi, Lahore, and Amritsar (R. Kumar, 1971: 6–7).

29. There was also a view that the education of the citizen should not be restricted to the political domain. M. Visvesvaraya's thoroughgoing modernist developmentalism envisioned a program of "Indianization" in which the project of nation-building would take place not only in the spheres of politics and society, but simultaneously also in the economy. He proposed, among other things, the use of English as a common language, training in civics in school, travel and dining with all classes of people, and the development of skills in some profession or trade (Visvesvaraya, 1920: ch. 15).

30. Social service organizations were another important site. See C. A. Watt (2005).

31. So great was the influence of Herbert Spencer that Vivekananda actually translated Spencer's *Education: Intellectual, Moral and Physical* into Bengali. Spencer's evolutionary view of how education should be designed in accordance with the process of natural growth (such that physical exercise—for growth into a "good animal"—should precede other forms of development) was attractive not only to Vivekananda (Baumfield, 1999: 204–205), but also to the Arya Samaj.

32. The Gurukul Kangri opened in 1902. Its program of study extended over a period of fourteen years, including high school and college.

33. Cf. Fischer-Tiné, 2001.

34. It is notable that Gilchrist disputed Mookerji's claim of the fundamental unity of India by stating that "the whole treatise is compiled from the Hindu point of view" (Gilchrist, 1920: 211). It is unlikely that Mookerji would have quarreled with that description as he himself attributed his "Hindu conception of patriotism" to the *Atharvaveda* and the *Manusmriti*. In fact, in his introductory essay to Narendra Nath Law's work on the ancient Hindu polity, based on Kautilya's then-recently discovered *Arthasastra,* Mookerji wrote that all the administrative problems that were still exercising the British government in India had been dealt with by Kautilya, suggesting an evolutionary continuity of "Indian administration through Hindu, Mahomedan and modern times" (Mookerji, 1914: xlv).

35. This emphasis on the local was implicitly questioned by Sukumar Dutt when he argued that "the actual nidus of politics" and the crucial test of the relationship between the state and society is the relation between the central and local levels of government. In India, local governments may have historically enjoyed great freedom, but now—as in Europe—they cannot function outside or independently of the state itself because this would be inconsistent with state sovereignty (Dutt, 1926: 170).

36. The failure of R. L. Brayne's Gurgaon experiment of "village uplift" in the 1920s has also been attributed to his attempt to teach the sons of farmers about fodder, crops, and ploughing furrows, while their fathers wished them to acquire examination certificates and religious learning (Dewey, 1993: 88). Brayne himself was contemptuous of the Lambardar's son who qualified as a lawyer, on the grounds that his degrees were not helpful for village improvement. As a lawyer, the young man would be in a profession that was useless as well as parasitical (Brayne, 1929: 102–103).

37. Even though Patrick Geddes's lectures and touring exhibition on citizenship in 1915 presented a more inclusive model in terms of classes and social groups, it was limited to the local (Hazareesingh, 2000).

38. This irony recalls Bertrand Russell's definition of Virtue as "submission to the government" in his social and political satire of *The Good Citizen's Alphabet* (1958).

39. Partha Chatterjee notes that Anandachandra, the author of *Byabahar Darsan,* the first Bengali textbook on politics, published in 1878, uses the term subject *(praja)* rather than citizen *(nagarik)* even in his discussion of popular rights and popular sovereignty. Anandachandra, says Chatterjee, did not make a Rousseauian argument about how the citizen must obey the general will because he himself has made it; for him, the general interest of society was the "task of a superior moral sense" (P. Chatterjee, 1995: 109).

5. The Unsocial Compact

1. Somers and Roberts define social and economic rights as including "the collective social entitlements and cultural aspirations (education, health care, and substantive social equality) that require both intervention by the state into the (ideologically) free market and enforcement by the policies and institutions of law, legislation, and nation-states" (2008: 387). These are usually contrasted with civil and political rights that are believed to require only restraint rather than positive intervention by the state. On a conceptual plane, of course, it has been argued that there is nothing distinctively social about social rights. Upendra Baxi's aphorism "rights are . . . *social* or not *at all*" draws attention to the conditions of sociality—social existence, belonging, identity, and solidarity—in which alone rights can be claimed and enjoyed (U. Baxi, 2007: 42).

2. Two major tracts of this genre in colonial India are S. Satyamurthy's *The Rights of Citizens* (1919) and Ram Manohar Lohia's *The Struggle for Civil Liberties* (1936). A more subtle variant was Akshaya Ghose's annotated compilation *Laws Affecting the Rights and Liberties of the Indian People* (1921) with a sympathetic preface by a British barrister, Eardley Norton.

3. The Rowlatt Act of 1919 was a law motivated by the fear of sedition. As such, it sought to make permanent the restrictions on civil liberties that had been introduced during the war, including the system of special courts and preventive detention for two years without trial. Gandhi's first all-India *satyagraha* was against this law.

4. Though the bill got a sympathetic reception in the Commons, the defeat of the British Labour Party shortly after its first reading meant the abandonment of the bill (Rao, 1966, 1: 44).

5. In February 1928, an All Parties Conference was convened by the Congress Working Committee with the object of drafting "a Swaraj Constitution for India." The conference was attended by representatives of all the major political formations

of the time, including the All-India Hindu Mahasabha, the All-India Muslim League, the All-India Liberal Federation, the States' Peoples Conference, the Central Khilafat Committee, the All-India Conference of Indian Christians, and others. At its next meeting in May 1928, the conference decided to appoint a seven-member committee, with Motilal Nehru as its chairman, and including Subhas Bose and Tej Bahadur Sapru as its members. The committee was charged with the task of preparing a draft constitution providing for full responsible government for India, on the lines of the Dominion Status enjoyed by Australia, New Zealand, Canada, and South Africa. The Nehru Report was adopted, with some amendments, in August 1928 at the All Parties Conference in Lucknow.

6. There is a peculiar sense of *déjà vu* about these debates in the context of contemporary Indian politics, with the banner of social rights now being raised by the leadership of the Congress Party and the National Advisory Council, while the first priority of the government is its strong commitment to neoliberal economic reforms.

7. The formation of this committee was an outcome of the breakdown of the Gandhi–Jinnah talks. The Non-Party Conference constituted this committee, consisting of academics like Dr. S. Radhakrishnan, lawyers and judges, and other eminent public men who were not affiliated to any political party, with Gandhi's approval. Dr. Ambedkar declined to send a representative of the Scheduled Castes, and the committee therefore used his speeches and writings, along with memoranda received on the issue of the Scheduled Castes, to discuss remedies for the conditions of bonded labor and landlessness under which these castes labored, and schemes of social security and redistribution of wastelands to enable their advancement, both educational and economic (Sapru Committee Report, 1945: 240–242).

8. The individuals included Sir Mirza M. Ismail, the Dewan (prime minister) of the princely state of Mysore, and S. A. Latif, who outlined an alternative constitution in his correspondence with Dr. Rajendra Prasad (Hasan, 2008: 1816–1823).

9. By the time Manabendra Nath Roy wrote his draft constitution, he had already traveled a long ideological distance from Communism (he was the founder of the Communist Party in both Mexico and India) to a philosophy of his own invention, Radical Humanism.

10. Recent political events in India, in particular the popular mobilization around a Lokpal (Ombudsman) Bill, recall this discussion of the legitimacy of the people as lawmakers.

11. The members of the committee included Jacques Maritain, Harold J. Laski, and E. H. Carr, among others.

12. Eleanor Roosevelt herself was the chair of the drafting committee and a moving spirit of this charter of rights.

13. Apparently, the Indian delegation was unable to answer the Latin American objection to its position, which asked whether it was easier to implement the article on racial discrimination! (Berkes and Bedi, 1958: 148)

14. The distinction was reflected in the notes (September 2, 1946) prepared by the Constitutional Adviser B. N. Rau, which launched the discussion on Fundamental Rights in the Assembly. Rau held up as a useful model the distinction made by Lauterpacht between "rights meant to be enforced by the ordinary courts and . . . rights incapable of or unsuitable for such enforcement" (in Rao, 1967, 2: 33). He also recognized that "in the peculiar circumstances of India, there may well be a demand for a Bill of Rights enforceable in the courts," but cautioned that the drafting of such a bill would need to be done very carefully and "must be reserved for a future occasion" (ibid.: 36).

15. K. T. Shah was a socialist economist, educated at the London School of Economics and Gray's Inn. He was recruited to Mysore University by Visvesvaraya, along with S. Radhakrishnan and Radhakumud Mookherjee. He was also the first professor of economics at Bombay University, the secretary of the National Planning Committee of 1938, and a member of the Constituent Assembly from Bihar. A close friend of Dr. Radhakrishnan and G. S. Ghurye, he visited China (as member of an Indian trade union delegation) and wrote a book about it in 1953.

16. Ambedkar's socialist predisposition was well known. At a press conference in July 1946, he claimed to be "more radically inclined" than the Congress, which he described as "a pseudo-socialist organization" (*Bombay Chronicle,* July 25, 1946; reproduced in Sarkar, 2007: 905).

17. The influence of the lawyers in the Constituent Assembly was clearly disproportionate to their number, which, on Austin's calculation, was barely 12 out of over 300 members (Austin, 1966: 19).

18. Letter dated April 3, 1947, from the SCFR to the Advisory Committee on Fundamental Rights, Minorities and Tribal and Excluded Areas (Rao, 1967, 2: 137).

19. Minutes of the SCFR, April 15, 1947 (ibid.: 168).

20. Dr. Panjabrao Shamrao Deshmukh represented the Central Provinces and Berar in the Constituent Assembly. He was a social activist who had worked with the Satyashodhak Samaj founded by Phule and fought, alongside Ambedkar, for temple entry for the untouchables. After independence, he became Minister for Agriculture in Nehru's first cabinet.

21. Rao, 1968: 328–329.

22. Jean Dreze cites a conversation between Ambedkar and the novelist Mulk Raj Anand in May 1950, in which Anand asked Ambedkar why the Constitution did not make the right to work a fundamental right. "I was only one of the members of the drafting Committee," Ambedkar replied (Dreze, 2010: 510).

23. Jaffrelot writes: "He considered the 'Directive Principles' as 'instructions' but underlined that they 'had no legal value.' Hence Ambedkar accepted an emphatic reference to the village in a section of the Constitution whose articles had no practical implications. In this manner he succeeded in defusing a very strong Gandhian demand that could have questioned the overall framework of his project. In the same

manner he sealed the fate of many other Gandhian propositions" (Jaffrelot, 2005: 112).

24. Some of the articles that generated intense debate expressed a rural, and often Gandhian, sensibility, in their emphasis on panchayats, cottage industries, and agricultural cooperatives. Ambedkar had strong views on panchayats, grounded in a clear understanding of the oppressiveness of local society. Famously describing the village as "a sink of localism, a den of ignorance, narrowmindedness and communalism," Ambedkar had declared himself satisfied that the draft constitution had adopted the individual, rather than the village, as its unit. When the provision relating to panchayats was proposed for incorporation in the Directive Principles, Ambedkar accepted it without comment. Nevertheless, for Mahavir Tyagi and other Gandhians, Gandhi's spirit was missing from the Constitution, which therefore suggested that "the Constitution is dead" (CAD 7: 499).

25. Jaipal Singh opposed the provision on prohibition vociferously, in defense of the religious rights of the tribal people (cf. Guha, 2007a: 116).

26. Letter from Washington, November 11, 1947 (Rao, 1967 , 3: 226).

27. In *Sri Shankari Prasad Singh Deo v. Union of India and State of Bihar* (1951), the Supreme Court had upheld the unfettered power of Parliament to amend the Constitution. This was overturned in the landmark Golak Nath judgment of 1967.

28. The Communist Party of India had officially declared support for the government in Parliament.

29. Maya Ray, Lok Sabha Debate on the Constitution (Forty-Fourth Amendment) Bill, October 27, 1976: 75.

30. However, a public interest petition challenging the inclusion of the word "socialism" in the preamble was recently withdrawn when the Supreme Court deemed the issue to be "highly academic" (*The Indian Express,* July 13, 2010).

6. Social Citizenship in Neoliberal Times

1. This was the central puzzle that T. H. Marshall addressed in his classic *Citizenship and Social Class* (1950). It was also the contradiction that Dr. B. R. Ambedkar signaled in his famous speech of November 25, 1949, in India's Constituent Assembly. Ambedkar offered the gloomy prophesy that if, notwithstanding political equality, we continued to deny social and economic inequality, "those who suffer from inequality will blow up the structure of political democracy." (Rao, 1968. 4: 945)

2. The term welfare state was reputedly coined by Archbishop William Temple in contrast to the "warfare states" of World War II, though the genealogy of the institutional form that goes with the term is generally traced back to Bismarck's innovations in social policy in late nineteenth-century Germany. Bismarck's social legislation—health insurance, accident insurance, and old age and disability insurance—was ironically inspired by his desire to keep the socialists at bay.

3. Marshall's canonical definition of social citizenship defines it as encompassing "the whole range from the right to a modicum of economic welfare and security to the right to share to the full in the social heritage and to live the life of a civilized being according to the standards prevailing in the society" (Marshall, [1950] 1992: 8).

4. These are the rights provided by "de-commodifying welfare states," such as the United Kingdom, where what is minimally entailed is that "citizens can freely, and without potential loss of job, income, or general welfare, opt out of work when they themselves consider it necessary" (Esping-Andersen, 1990: 23). Though the architect of the twentieth-century welfare state was Beveridge, authorship of the first welfare state of the nineteenth century is generally attributed to Bismarck. The Bismarckian system of social insurance was financed through contributions and therefore provided assistance only to those who were employed. The Beveridgian welfare state in Britain represented an advance over the Bismarckian model as it was the first unified and universal system of social security providing, more generously and therefore at a much higher cost, social protection for individual citizens.

5. See, for instance, Atul Kohli (2012: introduction).

6. Atul Kohli has argued that "the Indian state has shifted from a reluctant pro-capitalist state with a socialist ideology to an enthusiastic pro-capitalist state with a neo-liberal ideology. This shift has significant and, on the whole, negative implications for pursuing redistributive policies in India" (Kohli, 2009: 14). Indeed, the Congress Party's official commitment to "inclusive growth" is not always advanced with the same enthusiasm as its simultaneous governmental promotion of capitalist interests.

7. Constitution of the Federative Republic of Brazil 1988, http://www.brazzil .com/carta88.htm.

8. Constitution of the Republic of South Africa, http://www.info.gov.za/ documents/constitution/1996/a108-96.pdf.

9. The idea of "unenumerated rights" refers to rights that are inferred from other legal rights without being expressly specified in the law. The Ninth Amendment of the US Constitution provides protection against the infringement of unenumerated rights. The Fundamental Rights in the Irish Constitution—which also has a section on social and economic policy called the Directive Principles of Social Policy—have been interpreted by the courts to provide unenumerated rights such as the right of the unmarried mother to the custody of her child. For a discussion of unenumerated rights in American constitutional theory, see Michelman (2006).

10. Many Indian leaders (including B. R. Ambedkar, V. K. Krishna Menon, K. R. Narayanan—president of India from 1997–2002—and Jyoti Basu, the longest-serving communist chief minister of an Indian state) had been educated at the London School of Economics, and were enormously influenced by the social-democratic ideas of Harold J. Laski. As early as 1928, Motilal Nehru quoted Laski in support of his Committee's proposal for adult franchise (M. Nehru, 1995, 6: 141).

11. The Planning Commission was established in March 1950 by a Resolution of the Government of India, with the prime minister as its chairman. The First Five Year Plan (for the years 1951–1956) was prepared in July 1951.

12. "The socialist pattern of society is not to be regarded as some fixed or rigid pattern. It is not rooted in any doctrine or dogma. Each country has to develop according to its own genius and traditions. Economic and social policy has to be shaped from time to time in the light of historical circumstances. It is neither necessary nor desirable that the economy should become a monolithic type or organisation offering little play for experimentation either as to forms or as to modes of functioning" (Government of India, 1956a: ch. 2, ¶3).

13. "Essentially, this means that the basic criterion for determining the lines of advance must not be private profit but social gain, and that the pattern of development and the structure of socio-economic relations should be so planned that they result not only in appreciable increases in national income and employment but also in greater equality in incomes and wealth" (Government of India, 1956a: ch. 2, ¶3).

14. For a detailed account of the politics of land reform, see Frankel, 2006 (2nd ed.): ch. 3–5.

15. This is a trifle surprising because impatience with the charity perspective is reflected in a trenchant comment by Jawaharlal Nehru on the popular usage of the term "social welfare." Himself the chairman of the committee that drafted the Second Plan, Nehru had—in a newspaper article fifteen years earlier—criticized the endeavors of "the lady who visits the slums occasionally to relieve her conscience by the performance of good and charitable deeds" (Nehru, 2003b: 37) as patronizing and condescending, because such social work accepted the structure of society and sought only to soften the harshness of its injustices. He argued that social welfare should properly mean "the well-being of society," including the spiritual, cultural, political, economic, and social (ibid.). To the extent that "social workers" saw their endeavors as completely separated from political action and economic theory, they were doomed to fail.

16. Critical legal studies scholars have long argued that needs are likely to be more effective in advancing the project of social justice than rights, which have a tendency—especially when presented as litigation—to be abstract and even extrinsic to the actual material deprivation and hardship of people (cf. Pieterse, 2007: 801). Mark Tushnet's view that the rhetoric of essentially indeterminate rights should be abandoned in favor of a pragmatic strategy of demanding needs (1984: 1363) is disputed by Jeremy Waldron who points out that needs-claims are every bit as indeterminate and contestable as rights-claims, without the benefit of being "straightforwardly *pre*scriptive" (2000: 121; emphasis in original). Waldron is also critical of the passivity of needs-talk, as the language of needs is invariably the language of supplicants (ibid.: 123).

17. The Census of India 1951 calculated the total population as 361 million.

18. The sentiment underlying Marshall's description of citizenship as "the architect of legitimate social inequality" (Marshall, [1950] 1992: 7) can of course be read into Marx and strands of the socialist tradition. In the Indian context, it finds explicit discussion in Chatterjee (2004: 4) and Jayal (1999: 26–27).

19. *Our India* was also prescribed as a textbook. India's economist prime minister, Manmohan Singh, in a newspaper interview, said that it had "a profound impact" on him when he was young, and even sparked his interest in economics. The *Times of India,* February 20, 2011. http://m.timesofindia.com/PDATOI/articleshow/7530553 .cms.

20. This is of course reminiscent of John F. Kennedy's famous exhortation to his fellow citizens on January 20, 1961: "ask not what your country can do for you—ask what you can do for your country."

21. Turkey banned *Mother India* as a communist film, and in a telling detail the hammer-and-sickle insignia of Mehboob Productions was strategically excised from the print sent to the Oscars, where it was an (unsuccessful) entry in the best Foreign Language film category.

22. At this time, of course, income inequalities were less extreme even if poverty was high.

23. See the United Nations Development Program, *Human Development Report, 2010.*

24. In 2011, India entered the annual World Wealth Report (prepared by Merrill-Lynch Wealth Management and Capgemini) for the first time and at twelfth place. It qualified on account of its 153,000 High Net Worth Individuals (HNWIs, defined as people who have more than US$1 million in cash). India's HNWIs showed an increase of 20.8 percent over 2009, helping the Asia-Pacific to overtake Europe as the region with the second highest number of millionaires. http://www.guardian.co.uk/business/interactive/2011/jun/22/world-wealth-report-2011.

25. Cf. Dreze, 2010: 513.

26. Mooij and Dev, 2004: 106.

27. Counting opinion pieces in *The Hindu,* a leading English newspaper, over six months, Jean Dreze found that out of a total of 300 articles in six months, only 30 dealt with education, poverty, gender, human rights, and other social issues put together. Not a single one dealt with health or nutrition (Dreze, 2004: 1724). It is arguable that other national dailies would have even fewer articles.

28. Marshall interpreted the New Poor Law in England after 1834 as a form of "class abatement" because it "treated the claims of the poor, not as an integral part of the rights of the citizen, but as an alternative to them—as claims which could be met only if the claimants ceased to be citizens in any true sense of the word" ([1950] 1992: 15). Until 1918, paupers who were placed in workhouses forfeited their civil liberties and political rights. Similarly, the condition of the enjoyment of protective measures under the Factory Acts deprived citizens of their right to conclude employment contracts freely (ibid.). Today, of course, such exceptions are rarely explicit or formalized in law.

29. A distinctive and anomalous category is that of farmers entitled to subsidized agricultural inputs, including, in many states, free water and electricity. It is well known that these subsidies are disproportionately helpful to the larger and wealthier farmers, rather than to the small or marginal farmers forced to commit suicide in distress when their crops fail and debts cannot be repaid.

30. In Nazi Germany, culturally idealized conceptions of citizenship prevailed not only in the political sphere, but were also reinforced through the marketplace (Wiesen, 2008: 147).

31. *The State in a Changing World* was the subject of the World Bank's World Development Report of 1997.

32. Submission made to the Supreme Court by the counsel for the People's Union for Civil Liberties on May 10, 2011. The petition also stated that the annual number of deaths caused by malnutrition in India exceeded the number of total live births in the United Kingdom and was one-third the number of all newborns in the United States, *Hindustan Times,* May 11, 2011.

33. In a stinging critique, P. Sainath, a member of the committee, described the classification of citizens into APL and BPL as "an exercise in exclusion and abdication of responsibility" (Government of India, 2009: 42). He cited the example of regions with acute poverty where several hundred BPL cards of villagers were kept by the local moneylender as collateral for their borrowings. A universal system would obviate such abuse.

34. Article 11 of the ICESCR 1966 recognizes the right to an adequate standard of living, including adequate food, and the fundamental right to be free from hunger. One-hundred sixty states are signatories to this covenant, and the United States is not one of them.

35. A committee on reform of the PDS, headed by Montek Ahluwalia, the Deputy Chairman of the Planning Commission, has reportedly recommended that a cash subsidy be given to Below Poverty Line families to bridge the difference between the Minimum Support Price (at which grains are procured by the government) and the price at which they are sold in the Public Distribution System ("PDS Reform: Don't Give Grains, Transfer Subsidy to Poor, Says Panel," *The Hindustan Times,* March 24, 2011). The Government of India's *Economic Survey* for 2010–2011 also makes a mention of cash transfers, approvingly citing the example of a scheme inaugurated in 2008 and called Dhanalakshmi. This provides for CCTs to be given to parents of girl-children to pay for their registration at birth, immunization, and school enrollment till the eighth grade (*Economic Survey,* 2011d: 318).

36. Brazil has had social protection policies since the 1930s, including a system of contributory social insurance (Soares, 2011: 55).

37. Even the official advocates of CCTs recognize that successful implementation would require a system of identifying the poor that is not vulnerable to errors of inclusion or exclusion; that there is a foolproof identification system; and that bank/post office accounts are widely available (Mehrotra, 2010: 6–7).

38. In Latin America, CCTs are conditional upon using health and educational facilities provided by the state. CCTs should, Narayanan argues, be demand-side interventions complementing supply-side initiatives (2011: 44–46).

39. One hundred thirty-five million households in India lack access to banking facilities, second only to China in the extent of financial exclusion. See Seeta Prabhu, "Can Conditional Cash Transfers Work in Rural India?" (*The Wall Street Journal*, July 15, 2009).

40. This is in no small measure due to the Sarva Shiksha Abhiyan (Education for All Campaign) started by the government as the chief instrument of implementing the RTE Act. Its mission is to open new schools, construct school buildings and toilets, appoint and train teachers, and provide children with free textbooks.

41. India's most recent census (Government of India, 2011e) shows an improvement in literacy with a 9 percent decrease in illiteracy and women slightly outnumbering men among the newly added literates of the decade.

42. When there is no inequality across people, the Indian HDI will be equal to the HDI. However, as inequality rises, the IHDI falls below the HDI. The difference between the two indicates the "loss" in potential human development on account of inequality (United Nations Development Programme, 2010: 87).

43. http://www.censusindia.gov.in/2011-prov-results/data_files/india/Final%20 PPT%202011_chapter6.pdf.

44. The division of powers between the central (or federal) and the state units of government is specified in Seventh Schedule to the Indian Constitution. This has three lists, a Central List, a State List and a Concurrent List in which both center and states can legislate.

45. *Unni Krishnan J. P. v. State of Andhra Pradesh*, 1993.

46. Article 41: "The State shall, within the limits of its economic capacity and development, make effective provision for securing the right to work, to education and to public assistance in cases of unemployment, old age, sickness and disablement, and in other cases of undeserved want."

47. Article 45: "The State shall endeavour to provide, within a period of ten years from the commencement of this Constitution, for free and compulsory education for all children until they complete the age of fourteen years."

48. Article 46: "The State shall promote with special care the educational and economic interests of the weaker sections of the people, and, in particular, of the Scheduled Castes and the Scheduled Tribes, and shall protect them from social injustice and all forms of exploitation."

49. The Tapas Majumdar Committee had estimated that a sum of US$3 billion (as opposed to the US$2.1 billion that was allocated) would be required over the next ten years to implement the right to education (Sripati and Thiruvengadam, 2004: 155).

50. The High Level Committee headed by Professor Suresh Tendulkar recomputed the rural poverty line, arriving at an estimated total poverty (urban as well as

rural) of 37.2 percent as opposed to the official estimate of 27.5 percent (Government of India, 2011c: 7–8).

51. This was the case of the Maharashtra Employment Guarantee Scheme, which, in response to drought in the 1970s, provided employment on rural works as a matter of legal right (Joshi, 2005).

52. A distinction has been proposed between systemic (as in South Africa) and conditional social rights (as in India). The latter are dependent upon state action, such that the violation of a social right can occur only when the state actually launches a program to fulfill it but fails to implement it properly. This suggests that the recognition, by the apex Indian court, of rights to education or health, has an essentially expressive function. (Khosla, 2010)

53. There is an enormous body of literature to support the view that citizenship struggles replaced the class struggle and helped resolve the tension between political democracy and the capitalist economy. Variations of this argument are offered by Quadagno (1987), Mann (1987), and Dahrendorf (1996).

54. Aruna Roy led the successful campaign for a national right to information legislation; Jean Dreze spearheaded the movement for the right to food; and both were leading campaigners for the right to work. These, and several other activists, have been members of the National Advisory Council through which they have participated in the formulation of draft laws for the consideration of government and parliament.

55. Political society, in Chatterjee's usage, may be defined as poor subaltern populations, subjects of governmentality rather than practitioners of citizenship (Chatterjee, 2004: ch. 2).

7. Genealogies of Mediated Citizenship

1. In the American context, these criteria yielded the following plausible candidates for differentiated citizenship: "women, blacks, Native Americans, Chicanos, Puerto Ricans and other Spanish-speaking Americans, Asian Americans, gay men, lesbians, working-class people, poor people, old people, and mentally and physically disabled people" (Young, [1989] 1995: 195). In a telling example of the inconsistencies and temporalities entailed in such characterizations, Young apparently dropped Asian-Americans from a later republication of this paper (Joppke, 2002: 247).

2. Group-differentiated citizenship may also accommodate some concerns arising out of a communitarian perspective on the individual, which is markedly different from the individual who presides over the core of liberal-individualism—autonomous, rational, deracinated, and aware of not only her preferences but also her reasons for them. Communitarians repudiate this view of the unencumbered individual, showing that individual values, interests, and preferences are substantially shaped by cultural communities to which people belong, and these, in fact,

are fundamentally constitutive of an individual's identity. While communitarianism often forms the basis of claims to GDC, liberal theory too—despite its individualist philosophical core—claims to be able to accommodate these (Kymlicka, 1991). As such, the liberalism-communitarianism binary does not automatically translate into claims to universal and differentiated citizenship in state policy. This is especially so because while disadvantage, oppression, and exploitation provide the basis for claims to GDC, these are not necessary attributes of all community identities. All communitarian identities do not generate claims to GDC, though there can be and often is an overlap between them.

3. In a separate electorate, a particular group is represented by a legislator chosen by an electorate that is composed solely of members of that group. Thus, both the electorate and the candidate belong to the same community. In a reserved or quota seat, by contrast, the candidates must belong to the particular social group, but the electorate is a mix of all the social groups that happen to live within the area of the constituency.

4. In the debate leading to the Indian Councils Act of 1892, a government dispatch claimed that "representation of such a community upon such a scale as the Act permits can only be secured by providing that each important class shall have at least the opportunity of making its views known in the Council *by the mouth of some member specially acquainted with them*" (A. C. Banerjee, 1946: 298; emphasis added).

5. "... any electoral representation in India would be doomed to mischievous failure which aimed at granting a personal enfranchisement, regardless of the beliefs and traditions of the communities composing the population of this continent." (Lord Minto quoted in Wolpert, 1967: 189).

6. Depressed Classes was the name by which the "untouchable" castes were then known. Gandhi subsequently gave them the name "Harijan" (People of God), but both of these usages have now been overridden by the two currently dominant usages: the official category of the Scheduled Castes and the political category of Dalit (the oppressed).

7. The object of the Khilafat movement, led in India by the western-educated Muslim intelligentsia and supported by clerics, was to protect the Caliphate (the Khalifa of Turkey) against perceived British hostility in the war years. The cause was not a particularly robust or progressive one as the British eventually sided with the Khalifa against secular reformists like Kemal Ataturk.

8. "The way to constitutional swaraj may lie through Lucknow, the way to organic swaraj, which is synonymous with Ramarajya lies through Bardoli", Gandhi wrote to B. G. Horniman in August 1928 (*CWMG* 42: 414).

9. In February 1940, Gandhi wrote in *The Harijan,* "The Congress endeavours to represent all communities. It is not by design, but by the accident of Hindus being politically more conscious than the others, that the Congress contains a majority of Hindus. As history proves the Congress is a joint creation of Muslims, Christians, Parsis, Hindus, led by Englishmen. . . . And the Congress . . . retains that character.

At the present moment a Muslim divine is the unquestioned leader of the Congress and for the second time becomes its president" (*Harijan*, February 24, 1940, reproduced in Panikkar, 2009: 608).

10. The Hindu Mahasabha had actually started as a group within the Congress Party, anchored by Lajpat Rai and M. M. Malaviya, who asserted the need for Hindus and Muslims to be on terms of love and goodwill, distanced themselves from talk of a Hindu Raj, and commented on incidents of communal violence in the language of pain and despair rather than of aggression and violence.

11. This coheres with P. Chatterjee's ([1989] 2006) argument, for a somewhat earlier period, that nationalism domesticated the issue of women by confining it to the home, refusing to make it a matter of political negotiation with the state.

12. The term Depressed Classes emerged in the 1920s to differentiate the "untouchables" from the rapidly expanding list of what were, since the 1870s, described as "backward classes." The term Scheduled Castes replaced "Depressed Classes" in the Government of India Act, 1935 (Jaffrelot, 2008: 249–250).

13. This was particularly the case in Bengal and the Punjab, in both of which the Hindu and Muslim populations were fairly evenly balanced in terms of numbers.

14. He specifically mentioned Poland, Latvia, Estonia, Czechoslovakia, and Austria.

15. In a later phase, he was of the view that the "solvent" for caste was intermarriage (Rodrigues, 2002: 289).

8. Passages from Backwardness to Citizenship

1. *State of Madras v. Shrimathi Champakam Dorairajan*, 1950.

2. Article 15 prohibits discrimination on grounds of religion, race, caste, sex, or place of birth. Clause 4 of the article—inserted by the First Amendment—states that nothing in this article or in clause 2 shall "prevent the State from making any special provision for the advancement of any socially and educationally backward classes of citizens or for the Scheduled Castes and the Scheduled Tribes." Similar caveats were applied to Article 19 (granting rights to various freedoms) and Article 29 (dealing with the rights of minorities to establish and administer educational institutions or of other groups to conserve their language, script, or culture).

3. Group-differentiated citizenship has, as the last chapter showed, been canonically justified on grounds of "exploitation, marginalization, powerlessness, cultural imperialism, and vulnerability to violence motivated by hatred and fear" (Young, [1989] 1995).

4. The Report on Excluded Areas to the Constituent Assembly, for instance, described the Mikir tribe as "probably the most backward of all the tribes of the Assam Hills though *their backwardness is probably not their own fault*" (Rao, 1967, 3: 728; emphasis added).

5. The colonial administration also engaged in such rankings of groups in terms of relative backwardness, with the secretary of state for India indicating that areas with a preponderance of aboriginal or "very backward" people should be placed in the category of partially excluded areas (cf. Rao, 1967, 3: 733–734).

6. A nomenclatural history of the term suggests that it originated in the realm of education and in the Madras Presidency in 1872. Apparently under the influence of Christian missionaries, the Education Commission of 1882 identified and made recommendations for the education of the following classes of the population as deserving of special treatment: the Aborigines (tribals), sections of the Muslims, the low (untouchable) castes, and the poor, regardless of caste. The term "backward races" was gradually extended to specify "backward or indigent races or castes" (Radhakrishnan, 1990: 511). Half-fee provisions to enhance the enrollment of children belonging to backward social groups generated competitive claims to be labeled backward, and the department of public instruction would draw up lists of backward groups, which were periodically revised as more and rival petitions were received. The resentment against the Brahmin monopoly over higher education, bureaucracy, and the new professions fueled the anti-Brahmin movement of the backward castes in Madras that started in 1916. In 1921, the progressive and enlightened ruler of Mysore famously launched an initiative to recruit backward communities—defined as all communities other than Brahmins—into the public service of the state.

7. In 1924 the Depressed Classes had included the aboriginal and criminal tribes, as well as nomadic tribes and backward castes. By 1930, when the Starte Committee considered the question, the Depressed Classes signified only the untouchable castes, and the Backward Classes—without the Depressed Classes—encompassed Aboriginals and Hill Tribes and Other Backward Classes (OBCs), including wandering tribes (Galanter, 1984: 156).

8. R. K. Sidhva castigated the practice by which influential groups collected signatures and persuaded the colonial state of its claims to be labeled backward. He condemned the colonial policy by which his own community (the Zoroastrians or Parsis) became the beneficiary of such backwardness when its members were actually highly educated (CAD 10: 245).

9. Article 15 (4) has already been discussed. Article 16, which guarantees equality of opportunity in public employment, is similarly qualified by a clause that allows the state to reserve appointments or posts for "any backward class of citizens which, in the opinion of the State, is not adequately represented in the services under the State" and for the Scheduled Castes and Scheduled Tribes.

10. We use the label "tribal" here despite the fact that some scholars have dismissed the category as a colonial construct that hides the enormous heterogeneity within the groups officially designated as Scheduled Tribes (cf. McMillan, 2005: 110–111, Corbridge et al., 2004: 177). While this is true, the fact remains that this is a policy category and hence cannot be avoided in this discussion. The preferred

political term—analogous to Dalit for the Scheduled Castes—is Adivasi (original inhabitant), but this applies only to the tribals of central India.

11. It is estimated that as many as 500 different endogamous communities are encompassed by this label (Guha, 2007b: 3306).

12. Dyarchy divided the executive powers of each provincial government between reserved subjects (such as policing, justice, and land revenue) that would be governed by ministers nominated by the Crown and transferred subjects (such as education and public health), which would be entrusted to ministers who were chosen by the governor from among those elected to the provincial legislature.

13. The memorandum prepared by the Chota Nagpur Improvement Society of south Bihar had asked, on the one hand, for popular government, representation, the franchise, and modern education; and, on the other, for the protection of local customs, laws, and languages (Prakash, 2001: 59–60). The claims of the memorandum were ignored in favor of protectionism and isolationism.

14. Social workers and missionaries were perfectly acceptable as their representatives, and the Statutory Commission recognized that it was only in two of the nine constituencies with a preponderance of aboriginals that members truly representative of these groups were returned; the other seven were represented "by members of the very classes whom the aboriginals regard as most hostile to them." The Commission observed that the only representative of the entire Backward Tracts of Assam was a nominated Welsh missionary (Government of India, 1930a: 160–61).

15. This is evidenced in the slanging match between the Congressmen who had worked the longest among tribal people, A. V. Thakkar, and Jagpal Singh, acknowledged as the chief spokesman of tribal interests. Thakkar accused Jagpal Singh of not having traveled widely enough in tribal areas, while Singh accused Thakkar of not knowing any tribal languages. As both sought to prove their greater familiarity with tribal issues, it was clear that neither was adequately qualified to speak on behalf of *all* tribals (CAD 9: 989–993).

16. In fact, Nehru recognized that the apparently "primitive" ways of the tribals are in some senses "more advanced" as "they belong to a different type or genre of society" (2003a: 713).

17. There was a hint of self-congratulation in Ambedkar's favorable comparison of the enfranchisement of the tribals with the disenfranchisement of blacks in the United States; suggesting that while the United States had placed the "Red Indians" in "Reservations of Boundaries" outside the purview of American law—"made by white people for white persons and for the purpose of the white civilization"— India had succeeded in providing "cycles of participation," binding the authority of Regional and District Councils with the authority of the provincial government and Parliament (CAD 9: 1027).

18. The Advisory Committee on Fundamental Rights, Minorities and Tribal and Excluded Areas—arguably the most important committee in the constitution-making

process—was charged with making recommendations for constitutional provisions for the Excluded and Partially Excluded Areas, a task that was divided up between two subcommittees, one for the North-East Frontier (Assam) Tribal and Excluded Areas, and the other for the areas other than Assam.

19. In relation to Assam, the chief disagreement was about the division of powers between the District and Regional Councils, on the one hand, and the governor, on the other. While Ambedkar was in favor of greater autonomy and powers for the Councils, Assamese leaders were divided on the question, some wanting to restrict the power of the governor to dissolve the Council, others preferring to retain existing arrangements unchanged.

20. Many other policies were imitatively formulated for both these groups, with the rationale for clubbing them not being entirely clear. The Scheduled Castes and the Scheduled Tribes Prevention of Atrocities Act of 1989 (and its subsequent amendments) apply to both Scheduled Castes and Scheduled Tribes. Likewise, the constitutional provision (Article 338) for a Special Officer for Scheduled Castes and Scheduled Tribes was replaced by a multimember commission, the National Commission for Scheduled Castes and Scheduled Tribes, whose focus was largely on the former group. This body was divided, by the Eighty-Ninth Constitutional Amendment Act, into two separate commissions for the two groups only in 2003.

21. Both the quotas for Scheduled Castes and Scheduled Tribes have been regularly extended every ten years without any debate or contention.

22. The special provisions for Mizoram were similar to those for Nagaland; Manipur, Assam, and Sikkim had other special provisions made for them (Articles 371C, 371F, and 371G) after they became states of the Indian Union.

23. Convergence is not of course the same as identity, as Bajpai points out, noting a similar convergence between modernist arguments of civic nationalism and Hindu nationalist arguments against minority rights (2011: 85).

24. Dr. Ambedkar looked forward to a solution by which the difference between the majority and the minority would be transcended, as they would merge into one (CAD 7: 39).

25. http://ncst.nic.in/writereaddata/mainlinkFile/File415.pdf.

26. The Panchayat Raj Institutions of local self-governance were given constitutional status in 1992. In 1996, a form of these institutions was extended to the Fifth Schedule Areas.

27. These documents span three decades from the 1960s to the 1980s. The first was authored by the distinguished anthropologist Verrier Elwin; the second by U. N. Dhebar; and the third by B. D. Sharma. For details, see Guha, 2007b.

28. The word Naxalite comes from the village Naxalbari in West Bengal from which an earlier generation of Maoists, in the 1970s, launched their violent struggle against the oppression of peasants by rural landlords.

29. This is based on census data (Government of India, 2011e) and Debroy and Bhandari (2003).

30. The Scheduled Tribes account for 8 percent of India's population and 40 percent of the victims of Development-Induced Displacement. Barely a third of those displaced by development have been resettled. The Panchayats (Extension to Scheduled Areas) Act 1996 requires that the consent of the Gram Sabha be obtained before any transfer of land takes place, but this is frequently ignored. Meanwhile, a comprehensive law on resettlement and rehabilitation has been awaited for several decades now, even as the need for such a law has acquired urgency due to the displacement of peasants across India by the creation of Special Economic Zones. It has now been linked to the enactment of legislation on Land Acquisition. The draft law neither privileges the free and informed prior consent of the people, nor provides a guarantee of rehabilitation equivalent or superior to existing practice. (Government of India, 2011f).

31. The passage of legislation for forest conservation—designed to inhibit the diversion of forestland to nonforest purposes—resulted in the evictions of the tribals themselves on the grounds of their illegal occupation of forestland. Simultaneously, industrial forestry continued apace giving privileged access to commercial interests. In 2006, the Forest Rights Act provided a legal guarantee of the rights—of cultivation, usufruct, and protection and conservation—of forest-dwellers, enabling their participation in conservationist initiatives.

32. Cf. *Samatha v. State of Andhra Pradesh and Others*, 1997.

33. The example of communist mobilization in China, as Prasenjit Duara has argued, is instructive. It is in "peripheral geographical spaces" where the state and elite power structures are weak that such mobilizations of grievances occur (Duara, 2011: 35).

34. Nearly 50,000 citizens were already living in these camps in March 2006, and over 100,000 were displaced by Maoist conflict in 2009–2010 alone (Norwegian Refugee Council, 2010: 13).

35. The Court mentioned that while 538 police personnel had been killed in operations against Maoists in Chhattisgarh between 2004–2011, "173 SPOs, i.e., young, and by and large functionally illiterate, tribals, have been killed in the same period" (*Nandini Sundar and Ors. v. State of Chhattisgarh*, 2011: 37).

36. Some members used the phrase to encompass the section between the highest castes and the scheduled castes; some as synonymous with the Scheduled Castes; others to refer to a stratum of non-untouchable Hindu castes; and yet others to refer to "all but Brahmins" (Dhavan, 2008: 211–12).

37. Ambedkar also specified that the task of determining which community was backward would be enrusted to local governments. Between 1947 and 1951, several state governments made special provision for OBCs in higher education, in the form of reservations, scholarships, and fee concessions. The task of determining which castes could be included in the list of Backward Classes would continue to be executed by state governments, a practice that has usefully continued into the present as the same castes are sometimes backward in one state and "forward" or not backward in another.

38. The category of Backward Classes originated, as we noted earlier, in the Madras Presidency and Mysore State, and remained, till the middle of the twentieth century, very much a southern phenomenon.

39. Ghurye speaks dryly of a Maharashtra minister using the term classes "evidently as a cloak for the unconstitutional-looking word 'castes'!" (Ghurye, [1969] 1993: 43).

40. The mandate of the National Integration Council, constituted by Nehru in 1961, was to "combat the evils of communalism, casteism, regionalism, linguism and narrow-mindedness." http://mha.nic.in/pdfs/NICmaterial020707.pdf. Nehru himself disliked the term backward. As he told the Backward Classes Commission, it seemed wrong to call anyone by that name given that 90 percent of Indians were poor and backward (quoted in Galanter, 1984: 168n70).

41. The same year, a Parliamentary Study Group chaired by the socialist leader Jayaprakash Narayan identified the "weaker sections" as being primarily economically backward, with caste being a factor contributing to their backwardness.

42. In *P. Rajendran v. State of Madras* (1968), the Court ruled that a caste is also a class of citizens while in *A. Periakaruppan v. State of Tamil Nadu* (1971), it said that a caste has always been recognized as a class (Beteille, 1981: 9, 26).

43. Among the social indicators, which were assigned a statistical weight of 3 points each, were the following: being considered backward by others; mainly dependent on manual labour for livelihood; the marriage of 25 percent women and 10 percent men at younger than 17 years of age; a female work participation rate of 25 percent above state average. Educational indicators were weighted at 2 points each, and these included the following: the number of children between the ages of 5 and 15 years who never attended school, and the dropout rate in the same age group at 25 percent above the state average and the proportion of matriculates at 25 percent below the state average. Finally, the economic indicators were assigned a statistical weight of 1 point each. These included the average value of family assets; *kuchha* (made of mud, bamboo, etc) housing; drinking water at a distance of more than 0.5 km; and consumption loans of the household. The highest total score was 22, and all castes that secured 11 points or more were listed as socially and educationally backward.

44. The Census of 2011 is currently undergoing a supplementary exercise of gathering data on caste, a proposal that was also intensely debated, but eventually rejected, before the last census (2001).

45. Tamil Nadu recognizes "compartmental reservation." Of the 50 percent quota for OBCs, 20 percent is set apart for the most backward sections while the remaining is for the less backward. These subquotas for the most backward and the less backward are in turn subdivided between caste groups (cf. Srinivas, 1997: xviii).

46. The Commission was appointed in 1979; its report had been submitted in 1980, but had been ignored by the government till 1990.

47. This extended the 27 percent quota to institutions of higher learning that had hitherto been exempted from its purview, such as the Indian Institutes of Technology and the All India Institute of Medical Sciences.

48. It has been argued that—along with the right to property and Parliament's right to amend the Constitution—this proved to be one of three most important sites of conflict between Parliament and the Supreme Court in independent India (Dhavan, 2008).

49. The "creamy layer" refers to the advantaged sections among disadvantaged OBC groups. This is determined by an economic criterion, so an annual income above a certain level disqualifies a backward class family from availing of reservations. The creamy layer exclusion does not yet apply to the Scheduled Castes and Scheduled Tribes though the case is increasingly being made that it should.

50. "Accelerated seniority" refers to the process by which "reserved candidates got promoted through their own reserved channels of promotion and also accessed "merit" promotional posts on the basis of their earlier promotion through reservation of quotas. Once promoted, the reserved candidates also demanded "accelerated seniority" to claim a right to appointment to the promotee reserved seat on the basis that they were SC and ST and to the promotee merit seat on the grounds that having been promoted earlier they were senior to their merit competitors" (Dhavan, 2008: 68).

51. This means that vacancies that are unfilled by OBC candidates cannot be de-reserved, but will be carried forward to the next round.

52. The category also had little social meaning, with a plethora of conflicts between the upper and lower sections of the backward castes. Scarce resources like quotas inevitably mean that such conflicts of ritual and social hierarchies are carried over into the politico-administrative domain.

53. V. P. Singh was the prime minister who announced the implementation of the Mandal Commission's recommendations.

54. In the first general election of 1952, OBCs accounted for only 5 percent of members of Parliament in the Lok Sabha, the directly elected lower house of Parliament. By 1996, they had achieved a representation of 20–25 percent (cf. Jayal, 2006a: ch. 6).

55. The risk of enfranchising the entire adult population, the Sapru Committee stated, should be taken to prevent the concentration of power in the hands of a powerful few. Hence, though the average voter's "judgment may be faulty, his reasoning inaccurate, and his support of a candidate not infrequently determined by considerations removed from a high sense of democracy, he is yet no better or worse than the average voter in many parts of Europe where adult franchise has been in force for some time" (Sapru Committee Report: 168).

56. Three mechanisms of representation were proposed in the Constituent Assembly, any or all of which could qualify as (imperfect) forms of group-differentiated

citizenship. Rochana Bajpai's work shows that separate electorates were opposed on grounds of universal citizenship and political equality, but most strongly on grounds of "national unity" and a common political community. Proportional representation was considered unsuited to an unlettered electorate and even viewed by some as an introduction of separate electorates by the back door. The consensus of the Assembly was on the third alternative, viz., reservation of seats (quotas), and these were couched in the language of transition (Bajpai, 2008: 377).

9. The Future of the Civic Community

1. The number of groups entitled to reserved seats was significantly larger under the Government of India Act of 1935. The electorate, according to Granville Austin, was "split into no less than thirteen communal and functional compartments for whose representatives seats were reserved in the various parliamentary bodies" (Austin, 1966: 144).

2. Nehru recognized well the dilemma of reservations; he would have liked to put an end to them but realized that, in the case of the Scheduled Castes, it would not be desirable. "I try to look upon the problem not in the sense of religious minority but rather in the sense of helping backward groups in the country. I do not look at it from the religious point of view or the caste point of view, but from the point of view that a backward group ought to be helped and I am glad that this reservation will also be limited to ten years" (CAD 8: 331).

3. The idea of a purely civic nationhood is itself a contested one. Rogers Smith, for instance, disagrees with the proposition that "political communities can be sustained by agreement on shared political principles alone" (Smith, 2003: 190). The amorphous quality of the Indian combination of "national-civic-plural-ethnic" may explain its fragility in the face of the first systematic attempt to give concrete shape to the nation, viz. the project of Hindutva.

4. The reserved seats in joint electorates and reservations in public institutions provided for the Scheduled Castes and Scheduled Tribes were not intended as a denial of equality; on the contrary, they were measures designed to promote substantive equality. In respect of religious minorities, though separate electorates were decisively rejected, there was recognition that the principle of equality was an insufficient guarantee for minorities who could, in the presence of a dominant majority, always be insecure in the enjoyment of their cultural rights. This resulted in a range of guarantees for the freedom of religion, including the freedom to practice and propagate it, as well as separate personal laws for members of religious minorities. Both separate personal laws and policies of compensatory discrimination were, moreover, viewed as *interim* measures on the path to a society in which greater social equality and processes of secularization would eventually lead to the universalist norms of citizenship becoming firmly entrenched.

5. The recent contention over the inclusion of upper-caste Syed "Mallicks" in the list of Backward Classes in Bihar recalls the demand, discussed in chapter 7, of the Momins for representation in the civil service and ministries in proportion to their numbers. While some spokesmen of Muslim interests advocate reservations for all Muslims, others do not favor quotas that will only benefit the upper-caste sections, the *ashrafs*.

6. A recent and fundamental disagreement on this question is to be found in the 2007 Report of the National Commission on Religious and Linguistic Minorities (chairperson: Justice Ranganath Misra) in which the member-secretary (the civil servant attached to the Commission) wrote a note of dissent to the Commission's recommendation to include Dalits from other faiths under the provisions of reservation.

7. Hesitant to use caste as a criterion for Islam and Christianity, the Mandal Commission used two criteria: untouchable converts *(arzal)* and occupational communities *(ajlaf)* whose Hindu counterparts have been included in the list of OBCs (Government of India, 2006: 195).

8. Kerala provides 14 percent reservation in government jobs for Hindus, 12 percent for Muslims, 4 percent for Latin Catholics, 10 percent for Scheduled Castes and Scheduled Tribes, and some more for other smaller groups. In engineering and medical colleges, Kerala's 25 percent quota is divided between, among others, Hindus (9 percent), Muslims (8 percent), and Christians (1 percent).

9. *T. Muralidhar Rao and Ors v. The State of Andhra Pradesh and Ors.* (2007).

10. The Ashrafs are the descendants of nobles with foreign blood (typically of Persian or Arabian origin). The *ajlaf* are converts from the ritually low-caste groups, and the *arzal* are converts from the untouchable castes (Government of India, 2006: 192).

11. Statement of the National Meeting of Reservation Activists, 2010, http://www.syedshahabuddin.com/documents.html.

12. While the criminal law applies to all citizens equally, minority communities in India are allowed to follow community-based personal laws in civil matters such as marriage and divorce. In the Shah Bano case, the Supreme Court used a provision against destitution in the criminal law in order to uphold the right of an elderly Muslim woman divorcee to maintenance. In the uproar that ensued, Muslim clerics and other conservative elements among the Muslim political leadership argued that this constituted interference in Muslim personal law. At around this time, the Congress government of Rajiv Gandhi also lost a couple of by-elections in constituencies with substantial Muslim populations. Reading the political signals, the government passed a controversial law undoing the effect of the judgment and creating an exception to the universal application of the criminal law. This was a blow not only to Muslim divorcees, but also to the cause of gender justice and equality (cf. Jayal, 1999: ch. 3).

13. The percentage of women in the Fifteenth Lok Sabha (the directly elected lower house of Parliament) is, at 11 percent, the highest ever, almost double the

average that has varied between 6 and 7 percent. In the Council of Ministers today, we have eight women in a total of eighty-seven ministers (10.8 percent).

14. Ironically, this was the very criticism Lotika Sarkar and Vina Mazumdar offered, in their note of dissent, to buttress the case for quotas.

15. A 23-state survey of the performance of Elected Women Representatives (EWRs) shows that the gender gap in constituents' satisfaction with their leaders is a mere 2 percent (Government of India, 2008c).

16. While recent reports suggest some improvement in Punjab and Haryana, there has long been a correlation between prosperity and sex-selective abortions. An example is the higher availability of clinics providing ultrasound sonography and a lower sex ratio in Maharashtra, where almost 80 percent of these clinics are located in the five richest districts of the state, whose sex ratio also happens to be the lowest (Chandran, 2006).

17. See, for instance, the National Commission for Scheduled Castes and Scheduled Tribes' Fourth Report (1998) and Sixth Report (1999–2000 and 2000–2001).

18. In an uncannily prescient observation, the sociologist G. S. Ghurye had predicted this: ". . . before long we will . . . have a few caste and sub-caste groups turned into political parties in miniature and vested interest for preserving their special spoil of the social cake of the Government jobs. From there accretion of other economic and political interests would not fail to begin and thus to solidify them as exclusivist and separatist communities" (Ghurye, [1969] 1993: 441).

19. The most striking exception here is that of Jagjivan Ram, who was a powerful minister in Indira Gandhi's government. His daughter Meira Kumar is now the Speaker of the Lok Sabha.

20. On market discrimination, see Thorat and Newman (2010) and on the persistence of untouchability, see G. Shah et al. (2006).

21. The political support for quotas in the private sector led the government to ask the Confederation of Indian Industry to assess the diversity base of companies. The CII's "caste census" of its over 8000 member firms showed that in the most industrialized states, there was a huge difference between the proportion of SC/ST persons in the population, and their percentage of the workforce in the private sector ("India's Missing Inc.," *The Indian Express,* January 23, 2011).

22. Chandrabhan Prasad, *The Pioneer,* January 16, 2011.

23. Anuradha Raman "The Other Temple Entry," in *Outlook.* May 2, 2011. Rama Lakshmi "New Millionaires Hope to Serve as Role Models for India's Lower Castes," *Washington Post,* April 15, 2011.

24. "Plan Panel Mulls Ways to Spur Dalit Capitalism," in *Livemint.com,* January 10, 2011.

25. Dalit radicals have some discomfort with parallels with Richard Nixon's black capitalism, which is seen as a largely symbolic attempt to co-opt blacks into a conservative political program.

26. Rama Lakshmi, "New Millionaires."

27. The MBCs are of course closer to the purity-pollution line than the Upper OBCs are.

28. The Federation of OBC Employees' Welfare Associations in Uttar Pradesh celebrate August 7—the day on which in 1990 VP Singh announced 27 percent reservation for OBCs in government services—as Social Justice Day.

29. "The shift to a culturalized politics of recognition occurred at precisely the moment when neoliberalism was staging its spectacular comeback. Throughout this period, academic feminist theory was largely preoccupied with debates about "difference" and ". . . tended to remain on the terrain of recognition, where subordination was construed as a problem of culture and dissociated from political economy. The effect was to leave us defenceless against free-market fundamentalism, which had meanwhile become hegemonic" (Fraser, 2008: 106).

30. This is not an unknown trajectory. A similar move from caste to tribe occurred in the case of the people of the Jaunsar Bawar in north India (cf. Bhatt, 1978).

31. It is possible to hazard a historical explanation for this, such that in nations where a national-civic, as opposed to a national-ethnic, culture was already formed and consolidated, differentiated citizenship may have provided a much-needed, but not socially destabilizing, corrective to the homogenizing and uniformizing definition of universal citizenship. By contrast, in a relatively young nation like India where the project of constructing a national identity went hand-in-hand with the anticolonial struggle, the idea of the national-civic was somewhat more fragile. Rogers M. Smith's proposal for an "ascriptive Americanism" (1997: 504) appears to be an appealing idea worthy of translation.

Epilogue

1. Cf. P. Banerjea (1916: ch. 20); R. C. Majumdar (1922: 132–145).

2. This is the term used in official terminology to indicate all those who have not been appointed to a quota of any kind.

3. The Constitution mentions minorities, but does not make a specific mention of particular groups. The government's position was that since Muslims constitute over 70 percent of all minorities, the largest share of the benefits would in any case go to them.

4. Yadav, 2000; Jaffrelot and Kumar, 2009.

5. The dynastic principle determines, with a few exceptions, succession in both. An astonishing one-third of all members of Parliament come from political families, and this trend is repeated all the way down the line to the institutions of local governance. The leadership of most political parties is tightly controlled by a single individual, and—with the exception of three regional parties headed by single women—the principle of inheritance is beyond question.

6. The bill was actually drafted by a committee consisting of a lawyer, a former civil servant, and a retired police officer.

7. Mimicking Gandhi's fasts, the demand was staged in New Delhi in August 2011, in the form of a fast undertaken by the 74-year-old leader of the campaign, Anna Hazare, and concluded only when some assurances had been extracted from the government.

8. N. Garcia Canclini has argued that the concept of civil society has substituted for a radical questioning of the politics of the representation of the popular. By evading the recognition of the heterogeneity of civil society, we treat it as another totalizing concept and simply reproduce the problems with the concept of the popular (Canclini, 2001: 27–28).

9. In the context of the ongoing discussions about how to determine eligibility for food security (cf. ch. 6), this debate was sparked by an affidavit submitted by the Planning Commission to the Supreme Court. In response to the Court's query as to how the poverty line was calculated, the Commission stated that those spending 32 rupees ($0.65) a day in urban areas and 26 rupees ($0.52) a day in rural areas would not be entitled to welfare schemes, as only people below that poverty line are eligible. The members of the National Advisory Council have been in the forefront of a wider public outrage against the insensitivity of this statement, which the Planning Commission has justified by saying that it was intended only to benchmark the "rock-bottom level of existence" (*The Hindustan Times,* October 4, 2011). The government has also clarified that welfare entitlements would be delinked from poverty-line calculations, and be based instead on the socioeconomic caste census that is currently underway.

References

Government Documents and Reports

Commonwealth of Australia. 2008. *Moving Forward . . . Improving Pathways to Citizenship. A Report by the Australian Citizenship Test Review Committee.* http://www.citizenship.gov.au/_pdf/moving-forward-report.pdf.

Constitution of the Federative Republic of Brazil 1988. http://www.brazzil.com/carta88.htm.

Constitution of the Republic of South Africa. http://www.info.gov.za/documents/constitution/1996/a108–96.pdf.

Government of India. 1918. *Report on Indian Constitutional Reforms.* Calcutta: Superintendent Government Printing, India.

———. 1928. *Reports on the Working of the Reformed Constitution, 1927.* Calcutta: Central Publication Branch.

———. 1930a. *Report of the Indian Statutory Commission.* Vol. 1: *Survey.* London: His Majesty's Stationery Office.

———. 1930b. *Report of the Indian Statutory Commission.* Vol. 2: *Recommendations.* London: His Majesty's Stationery Office.

———. 1932. *Indian Franchise Committee.* Vol. 1. Calcutta: Central Publication Branch.

———. 1951. *First Five Year Plan.* New Delhi: Planning Commission.

————. 1956a. *Second Five Year Plan.* New Delhi: Planning Commission.

————. 1956b. *Report of the Backward Classes Commission.* Vol. 1. New Delhi.

————. 1980. *Report of the Backward Classes Commission: First Part.* Vols. 1–2. New Delhi.

————. 1992 *Eighth Five Year Plan.* New Delhi: Planning Commission.

————. 2001. *Report of the High Level Committee on the Indian Diaspora.* http:// indiandiaspora.nic.in/contents.htm.

————. 2005 *Performance Evaluation of Targeted Public Distribution System (TPDS)* New Delhi: Programme Evaluation Organisation, Planning Commission.

————. 2006. *Social, Economic and Educational Status of the Muslim Community of India: A Report.* Prime Minister's High-Level Committee for Preparation of Report on the Social, Economic and Education Status of the Muslim Community of India. Chairman: Justice Rajindar Sachar. Cabinet Secretariat.

————. 2007. *Report of the National Commission on Religious and Linguistic Minorities.* Chairman: Justice Ranganath Misra. Ministry of Minority Affairs.

————. 2008a. *Development Challenges in Extremist Affected Areas.* Report of an Expert Group to Planning Commission. New Delhi: Planning Commission.

————. 2008b. *Report of the Expert Group to Propose a Diversity Index and Workout [sic] the Modalities of Implementation.* Ministry of Minority Affairs.

————. 2008c *Study on EWRs in Panchayati Raj Institutions.* Ministry of Panchayati Raj.

————. 2009. *Report of the Expert Group to Advise the Ministry of Rural Development on the Methodology for Conducting the Below Poverty Line (BPL) Census for 11th Five Year Plan.* Chairman: N. C. Saxena. New Delhi: Ministry of Rural Development.

————. 2011a. *Issues for Approach to the Twelfth Five Year Plan.* New Delhi: Planning Commission. http://planningcommission.gov.in/plans/planrel/12appdrft/ pc_present.pdf.

————. 2011b. *Issues for Approach to the Twelfth Plan: Presentation by Planning Commission.* New Delhi: Planning Commission. http://planningcommission .gov.in/plans/planrel/12appdrft/issues_pc.pdf.

————. 2011c. *Mid-Term Appraisal Eleventh Five Year Plan, 2007–2012.* New Delhi: Planning Commission and Oxford University Press.

————. 2011d. *Economic Survey, 2010–11.* Ministry of Finance.

————. 2011e. *Census of India, 2011.* http://www.censusindia.gov.in/2011-prov results/data_files/india/Final%20PPT%202011_chapter6.pdf.

————. 2011f. *The Draft National Land Acquisition and Rehabilitation and Resettlement Bill, 2011.* http://www.rural.nic.in/Final.pdf.

Government of the United Kingdom. 2007. *Life in the United Kingdom: A Journey to Citizenship.* Norwich: HMSO.

National Commission for Scheduled Castes and Scheduled Tribes. 1998. *Fourth Report. 1996-97 & 1997-98.* New Delhi.

————. 2001. *Sixth Report.* 1999–2000 and 2000–2001. New Delhi.

Parliamentary Debates

(CAD) Constituent Assembly Debates, Vols. 1–12

Lok Sabha Debates on the Constitution (Forty Fourth Amendment) Bill. October-November 1976.

Private Papers

Sir William Lee-Warner, India Office papers, British Library, London.

Collected Works

(CWMG) *Collected Works of Mahatma Gandhi.* 98 vols. http://www.gandhiserve .org/cwmg/cwmg.html.

Cases Cited

*A. Periakaruppan v. State of Tamil Nadu and Ors.*1971. Supreme Court.

All India Lawyers Union (Delhi Unit) v. Government of NCT of Delhi and Ors. 2009. High Court of Delhi.

Ashoka Kumar Thakur v. Union of India & Ors. 2008. Supreme Court.

Bhanwaroo Khan and Ors. v. Union of India and Ors. 2002. Supreme Court.

Francis Coralie Mullin v. The Administrator, Union Territory of Delhi & Ors. 1981. Supreme Court.

I C. Golak Nath and Ors. v. State of Punjab and Anr. 1967. Supreme Court.

Indra Sawhney v. Union of India. AIR 1991. Supreme Court.

Izhar Ahmad Khan v. Union of India. 1962. Supreme Court.

Kesavananda Bharati v. State of Kerala. 1973. Supreme Court.

*M. R. Balaji v. State of Mysore.*1962 Supreme Court.

Md. Elahi v. The State of West Bengal. 2008. High Court of Calcutta.

Mohammed Ahmed Khan v. Shah Bano Begum and Ors. 1985 Supreme Court.

Motimiya, Rahim Miya and Ors. v. The State of Maharashtra. 2003. Bombay High Court.

Mustt Sarabari Begum and Syera Begum and 2 Ors. vs. State of Assam and Ors. 2008. Gauhati High Court.

*Namgyal Dolkar v. Government of India, Ministry of External Affairs.*2010. High Court of Delhi.

Nandini Sundar and Ors. v. State of Chhattisgarh. 2011. Supreme Court

NHRC v. State of Arunachal Pradesh & Anr. 1996. Supreme Court.

*Olga Tellis v. Bombay Municipal Corporation.*1985. Supreme Court.

Ramakrishna Singh, Ram Singh and Ors. v. State of Mysore. 1959. Karnataka High Court.

P. Rajendran v. State of Madras. 1968. Supreme Court.

People's Union for Civil Liberties v. Union of India & Ors. Writ Petition (Civil) 196 of 2001. (yet to be decided)

Rashtriya Mukti Morcha v. Union of India. 2006. High Court of Delhi.

Raushan Ara alias Suraiaya v. State of West Bengal. 1996. Calcutta High Court.

Razia Begum and Ors. v. Union of India. 2008. High Court of Delhi.

Samatha v. State of Andhra Pradesh and Others. 1997. Supreme Court.

Sarbananda Sonowal v. Union of India and Anr. 2005. Supreme Court.

Satwant Singh Sawhney v. Union of India. 1967. Supreme Court.

Shabbir Hussain v. State of Uttar Pradesh. 1951. Allahabad High Court.

Sri Shankari Prasad Singh Deo v. Union of India and State of Bihar. 1951. Supreme Court.

State of Andhra Pradesh v. Abdul Khader. 1961. Supreme Court.

State of Andhra Pradesh v. Syed Mohd. Khan. 1962. Supreme Court.

State of Assam v. Jilkadar Ali. 1972. Supreme Court.

State of Bihar v. Kumar Amar Singh and Ors. 1955. Supreme Court.

State of Gujarat and Anr. v. Saiyad Aga Mohmed Saiyedm Ohmed. 1978. Gujarat High Court.

State of M.P. v. Pramod Bhartiya. 1992. Supreme Court.

State of Madras v. Shrimathi Champakam Dorairajan. 1950. Madras High Court.

State of Saurashtra v. Jamadar Mohamad Abdulla and Ors. 1961. Supreme Court.

T. Muralidhar Rao and Ors v. The State of Andhra Pradesh and Ors. W.P. Nos. 15267 of 2007. (yet to be decided)

T. A. Mahomed Usman v. State of Madras Represented by Secretary to the Government of Madras (Home Department) and Anr. 1959. Madras High Court.

Talat Jamal Siddiqui v. Union of India and Anr. 2011. High Court of Delhi.

Unni Krishnan J.P. v. State of Andhra Pradesh. 1993 Supreme Court.

Books and Articles

Agarwal, Shriman Narayan. 1946. *Gandhian Constitution for Free India.* Allahabad: Kitabistan.

Agarwala, Rina. 2011. "India's Informal Workers and Social Protection." http://casi.ssc.upenn.edu/iit/agarwala.

Alexopoulos, Golfo. 2003. *Stalin's Outcasts: Aliens, Citizens, and the Soviet State, 1926–1936.* Ithaca and London: Cornell University Press.

All Parties Conference. 1928. *Report of the Committee Appointed by the Conference to Determine the Principles of the Constitution for India.* Chairman: Motilal Nehru. Allahabad: All India Congress Committee.

Alston, Leonard. 1910. *Education and Citizenship in India.* London: Longman, Greens & Co.

Ambedkar, B. R. 1979. *Writings and Speeches.* Vol. 1. Compiled by Vasant Moon. Bombay: Government of Maharashtra.

———. 1987. *Writings and Speeches.* Vol. 3. Compiled by Vasant Moon. Bombay: Government of Maharashtra.

———. 1989. *Writings and Speeches.* Vol. 5. Compiled by Vasant Moon. Bombay: Government of Maharashtra.

An Indian Citizen. 1905. *The Indian Citizen.* Madras: Satakopachari & Co.

Anwar, Ali. 2001. *Masawat ki Jung* (The Battle for Equality) (Hindi). New Delhi: Vani Prakashan.

Archbold, W. A. J. (1926) 1973. *Outlines of Indian Constitutional History (British Period).* London: Curzon Press.

Arendt, Hannah. (1951) 1962. *The Origins of Totalitarianism.* Cleveland and New York: Meridian Books.

Arnold, David. 1979. "Poor Europeans in India, 1750–1947." *Current Anthropology* 20, 2 (June): 454–455.

Austin, Granville. 1966. *The Indian Constitution: Cornerstone of a Nation.* New Delhi: Oxford University Press.

———. 1999. *Working a Democratic Constitution: The Indian Experience.* New Delhi: Oxford University Press.

Bajpai, Rochana. 2008. "Minority Representation and the Making of the Indian Constitution." In *Politics and Ethics of the Indian Constitution,* edited by Rajeev Bhargava. New Delhi: Oxford University Press.

———. 2011. *Debating Difference: Group Rights and Liberal Democracy in India.* New Delhi: Oxford University Press.

Ballhatchet, Kenneth A. 1978. "British Rights and Indian Duties: The Case of Sir William Lee-Warner." In *The Concept of Duty in South Asia,* edited by Wendy Doniger O'Flaherty and J. Duncan M. Derrett. New Delhi: Vikas Publishing House.

Banerjea, Surendranath. 1909. *The Trumpet Voice of India: Speeches of Babu Surendranath Banerjea Delivered in England, 1909.* Madras: Ganesh & Co.

Banerjea, Pramathanath. 1916. *Public Administration in Ancient India.* London: Macmillan & Co.

Banerjee, Anil Chandra, ed. 1946. *Indian Constitutional Documents: 1757–1947.* Calcutta: A. Mukherjee & Co.

Banerjee, Sukanya. 2010. *Becoming Imperial Citizens: Indians in the Late-Victorian Empire.* Durham, NC: Duke University Press.

Banting, Keith, and Will Kymlicka, eds. 2006. *Multiculturalism and The Welfare State: Recognition and Redistribution in Contemporary Democracies.* Oxford: Oxford University Press.

Barrier, N. Gerald. 1968. "The Punjab Government and Communal Politics, 1870–1908." *The Journal of Asian Studies* 27, 3 (May): 523–539.

Barry, Kim. 2006. "Home and Away: The Construction of Citizenship in an Emigration Context." *New York University Public Law and Legal Theory Working Papers.* Paper 23.

Basu, Aparna. 1974. *The Growth of Education and Political Development in India, 1898–1920.* New Delhi: Oxford University Press.

Basu, B. D. 1933. *India under the British Crown.* Calcutta: R. Chatterjee.

Basu, Tapan, Pradip Datta, Sumit Sarkar, Tanika Sarkar, and Sambuddha Sen. 1993. *Khaki Shorts and Saffron Flags: A Critique of the Hindu Right.* Tracts for the Times 1. New Delhi: Orient Longman.

Baumfield, Vivienne. 1999. "Science and Sanskrit: Vivekananda's Views on Education." In *Swami Vivekananda and the Modernisation of Hinduism,* edited by William Radice. SOAS Studies in South Asia. New Delhi: Oxford University Press.

Baxi, Pratiksha. 2009. *Habeas Corpus: Juridical Narratives of Sexual Governance.* Centre for the Study of Law and Governance Working Paper. CSLG/WP/09/02.

Baxi, Upendra. 2007. "Failed Decolonisation and the Future of Social Rights: Some Preliminary Reflections." In *Exploring Social Rights: Between Theory and Practice,* edited by Daphne Barak-Erez and Aeyal M. Gross. Oxford and Portland, OR: Hart Publishing.

———. 2010. "Caste Census and Constitutional Justice." *Economic and Political Weekly* 45(37): 25–29.

Bayly, C. A. 2001. *Origins of Nationality in South Asia: Patriotism and Ethical Government in the Making of Modern India.* New Delhi: Oxford University Press.

———. 2007. "South Asian Thought at the Dawn of the Liberal Age, 1800–1840." Lecture 1: *Liberalism at Large; South Asia and Britain c. 1800–1947.* The Basil Wiles Lectures at Queen's University, Belfast. May 15–18. http://www.s-asian. cam.ac.uk/wiles.html.

———. 2012. *Recovering Liberties: Indian Thought in the Age of Liberalism and Empire.* New Delhi: Cambridge University Press.

Beiner, Ronald, ed. 1995. *Theorizing Citizenship.* Albany: State University of New York Press.

Beitz, Charles R. 2009. *The Idea of Human Rights.* New York: Oxford University Press.

Benhabib, Seyla. 2004. *The Rights of Others: Aliens, Residents and Citizens.* Cambridge: Cambridge University Press.

———. 2006. "The Philosophical Foundations of Cosmopolitan Norms." In *Another Cosmopolitanism,* edited by Seyla Benhabib and Robert Post. New York: Oxford University Press.

Berkes, Ross N., and Mohinder S. Bedi. 1958. *The Diplomacy of India: Indian Foreign Policy in the United Nations.* Stanford, CA: Stanford University Press.

Besant, Annie, ed. 1914. *India and the Empire: A Lecture and Various Papers on Indian Grievances.* London: Theosophical Publishing Society.

Beteille, André. 1981. *The Backward Classes and the New Social Order.* New Delhi: Oxford University Press.

Bhatt G. S. 1978. "From Caste Structure to Tribe: The Case of Jaunsar-Bawar." *Eastern Anthropologist* 31(3): 251–258.

Bhopal Document, The. 2002. http://www.indiarightsonline.com/Sabrang/dalit. nsf/o/d9a393997c065c01e5256c2300577906/$FILE/bhopal-net.pdf.

Birchfield, Lauren, and Jessica Corsi. 2010. "Between Starvation and Globalization: Realizing the Right to Food in India." *Michigan Journal of International Law* 31: 691–763.

Bosniak, Linda. 1998. "The Citizenship of Aliens." *Social Text* 56 (Autumn): 29–35.

———. 2006. *The Citizen and the Alien: Dilemmas of Contemporary Membership.* Princeton, NJ: Princeton University Press.

Bourinot, J. G. 1895. *How Canada is Governed: A Short Account of the Executive, Legislative, Judicial and Municipal Institutions.* Toronto: Copp, Clark Co., Ltd.

Brayne, F. L. 1929. *Socrates in an Indian Village (Dehati Socrat).* Madras: Oxford University Press.

Brown, Judith M. 1985. *Modern India: The Origins of an Asian Democracy.* Delhi: Oxford University Press.

———. 2003. *Nehru: A Political Life.* New Delhi: Oxford University Press.

Brubaker, Rogers. 1992. *Citizenship and Nationhood in France and Germany.* Cambridge, MA: Harvard University Press.

Buch, Maganlal A. 1938. *Rise and Growth of Indian Liberalism: From Ram Mohun Roy to Gokhale.* Baroda.

Butalia, Urvashi. 1998. *The Other Side of Silence: Voices from the Partition of India.* New Delhi: Viking.

Canclini, Néstor García. 2001. *Consumers and Citizens: Globalization and Multicultural Conflicts.* Translated with an introduction by George Yúdice. Minneapolis: University of Minnesota Press.

Caplan, Jane, and John Torpey. 2001. Introduction to *Documenting Individual Identity: The Development of State Practices in the Modern World,* edited by Caplan and Torpey. Princeton, NJ: Princeton University Press.

Carens, Joseph H. 1995. "Aliens and Citizens: The Case for Open Borders." In R. Beiner, *q.v.*

———. 2008. "Who Belongs? Immigration, Democracy and Citizenship." In *Of States, Rights, and Social Closure: Governing Migration and Citizenship,* edited by Oliver Schmidtke and Saime Ozcurumez. New York: Palgrave Macmillan.

———. 2009. "The Case for Amnesty." *The Boston Review.* May/June.

Cashman, Richard I. 1975. *The Myth of the Lokamanya: Tilak and Mass Politics in Maharashtra.* Berkeley and Los Angeles: University of California Press.

Chakrabarty, Dipesh. 1985. "Invitation to a Dialogue." In *Subaltern Studies IV: Writings on South Asian History and Society*, edited by Ranajit Guha. New Delhi: Oxford University Press.

Chakravarty, Sukhamoy. 1987. *Development Planning: The Indian Experience*. New Delhi: Oxford University Press.

Chamberlain, William I. 1899. *Education in India*. New York: Columbia University.

Chandra, Bipan. 1989. *India's Struggle for Independence*. New Delhi: Penguin Books.

Chandran, D. 2006. "The Richer the District, the Poorer the Sex Ratio." http://infochangeindia.org/200601035971/Population/Books-Reports/The-richer-the-district-the-poorer-the-sex-ratio.html

Chandrasekharan, K. 1932. *Persons and Personalities: Sketches*. Madras: Madras Law Journal Press.

Chatterjee, Partha. 1993. "The Colonial State." In *The Nation and Its Fragments: Colonial and Postcolonial Histories,* included in the *Partha Chatterjee Omnibus*. New Delhi: Oxford University Press.

———. 1995. "A Modern Science of Politics for the Colonized." In *Texts of Power: Emerging Disciplines in Colonial Bengal*, edited by Chatterjee. Minneapolis: University of Minnesota Press.

———. 2004. *The Politics of the Governed: Reflections on Popular Politics in Most of the World*. Delhi: Permanent Black.

———. (1989) 2006. "The Nationalist Resolution of the Women's Question." In *Recasting Women: Essays in Colonial History*, edited by Kumkum Sangari and Sudesh Vaid. New Delhi: Zubaan Books.

Chatterji, Joya. 2001. "Right or Charity? The Debate over Relief and Rehabilitation in West Bengal, 1947–50." In *The Partitions of Memory: The Afterlife of the Division of India*, edited by Suvir Kaul. Ranikhet: Permanent Black.

———. 2008. *The Spoils of Partition: Bengal and India, 1947–1967*. New Delhi: Cambridge University Press.

———. unpublished. "South Asian Histories of Citizenship, 1947–70."

Chaudhuri, Nirad C. 1951. *The Autobiography of an Unknown Indian*. London: Hogarth Press.

Chimni, B. S. 2005. "Outside the Bounds of Citizenship: The Status of Aliens, Illegal Migrants and Refugees in India." In *Civil Society, Public Sphere and Citizenship: Dialogues and Perceptions*, edited by Rajeev Bhargava and Helmut Reifeld. New Delhi: Sage Publications.

Chiriyankandath, James. 2000. "'Creating a Secular State in a Religious Country': The Debate in the Indian Constituent Assembly." *Commonwealth and Comparative Politics* 38(2): 1–24.

———. 2001. "'Democracy' Under the Raj: Elections and Separate Representation in British India." In *Democracy in India*, edited by Niraja Gopal Jayal. New Delhi: Oxford University Press.

Cleveland, Grover. 1908. *Good Citizenship.* Philadelphia: Henry Altemus Co.

Cloyd, David E. 1916. *Civics and Citizenship.* Teaching in the Elementary Schools Monograph Series, 1. Des Moines, IA: Author.

Cohn, Bernard. 1996. *An Anthropologist among the Historians and Other Essays.* New Delhi: Oxford University Press.

Collet, Sophia Dobson. 1914. *Life and Letters of Raja Rammohun Roy.* Calcutta.

Corbridge, Stuart, Sarah Jewitt, and Sanjay Kumar. 2004. *Jharkhand: Environment, Development, Ethnicity.* New Delhi: Oxford University Press.

Crabtree, James, and Frank Field. 2009. "Citizenship First: The Case for Compulsory Civic Service." *Prospect,* March.

Curtis, Lionel, ed. 1916. *The Commonwealth of Nations: An Inquiry into the Nature of Citizenship in the British Empire, and into the Mutual Relations of the Several Communities Thereof.* Vol. 1. London: Macmillan & Co.

————, ed. 1920. *Papers Relating to the Application of the Principle of Dyarchy to the Government of India.* Oxford: Clarendon Press.

Dagger, Richard. 1997. *Civic Virtues: Rights, Citizenship and Republican Liberalism.* Oxford: Oxford University Press.

Dahrendorf, Ralf. 1996. "Citizenship and Social Class." In *Citizenship Today: The Contemporary Relevance of T. H. Marshall,* edited by Martin Bulmer and Anthony M. Rees. London: UCL Press.

Damodaran, Harish. 2008. *India's New Capitalists: Caste, Business, and Industry in a Modern Nation.* Ranikhet: Permanent Black.

Das, Veena. 2007. "The Figure of the Abducted Woman: The Citizen as Sexed." In *Life and Words: Violence and the Descent into the Ordinary.* New Delhi: Oxford University Press.

Datta, Nilanjan. 2000. "From Subject to Citizen: Towards a History of the Indian Civil Rights Movement." In *Changing Concepts of Rights and Justice in South Asia,* edited by Michael R. Anderson and Sumit Guha. New Delhi: Oxford University Press.

Davidson, Alastair. 1997. *From Subject to Citizen: Australian Citizenship in the Twentieth Century.* Cambridge: Cambridge University Press.

Debroy, Bibek, and Laveesh Bhandari, eds. 2003. *District-level Deprivation in the New Millennium.* Delhi: Rajiv Gandhi Foundation and Konark Publishers.

Deshpande, Ashwini. 2011. *The Grammar of Caste: Economic Discrimination in Contemporary India.* New Delhi: Oxford University Press.

Dewey, Clive. 1993. *Anglo-Indian Attitudes: The Mind of the Indian Civil Service.* London: Hambledon Press.

Dhanda, Meena, ed. 2008. *Reservations for Women.* New Delhi: Women Unlimited.

Dhavan, Rajeev. 2008. *Reserved! How Parliament Debated Reservations, 1995–2007.* New Delhi: Rupa & Co.

Dreze, Jean. 2004. "Democracy and Right to Food." *Economic and Political Weekly* 39, 17 (April 24–30): 1723–1731.

———. 2010. "Employment Guarantee and the Right to Work." In *The Oxford Companion to Politics in India*, edited by Niraja Gopal Jayal and Pratap Bhanu Mehta. New Delhi: Oxford University Press.

Duara, Prasenjit. 2011. "The Chinese Revolution and Insurgent Maoism in India: A Spatial Analysis." *Economic and Political Weekly* 46, 18 (April 30).

Dutt, Sukumar. 1926. *Problem of Indian Nationality.* Calcutta: University of Calcutta. University Jubilee Research Prize Thesis, 1922.

Esping-Andersen, Gøsta. 1990. *The Three Worlds of Welfare Capitalism.* Princeton, NJ: Princeton University Press.

Etzioni, Amitai. 2007. "Citizenship Tests: A Comparative, Communitarian Perspective." *Political Quarterly* 78, 3 (July–September).

Ferguson, Niall. 2002. *Empire: The Rise and Demise of the British World Order and the Lessons for Global Power.* New York: Basic Books.

Fischer-Tiné, Harald. 2001. "'The Only Hope for Fallen India': The Gurukul Kangri as an Experiment in National Education (1902–1922)." In Georg Berkemer, Tilman Frasch, Hermann Kulke and Jurgen Lutt, eds. *Explorations in the History of South Asia: Essays in Honour of Dietmar Rothermund*, edited by Georg Berkemer, Tilman Frasch, Hermann Kulke, and Jurgen Lutt. New Delhi: Manohar.

Forbes, Geraldine. 2004. *Women in Modern India.* The New Cambridge History of India 4.2. Cambridge: Cambridge University Press.

Foster, Michelle. 2007. *International Refugee Law and Socio-Economic Rights: Refuge from Deprivation.* Cambridge: Cambridge University Press.

Frankel, Francine. 2006. *India's Political Economy, 1947–2004: The Gradual Revolution.* 2nd ed. New Delhi: Oxford University Press.

Frankel, Francine, and M. S. A. Rao. 1989. *Dominance and State Power in Modern India: Decline of a Social Order.* Vol. 1. New Delhi: Oxford University Press.

Fraser, Nancy. 2008. *Scales of Justice: Reimagining Political Space in a Globalizing World.* Cambridge: Polity Press.

Galanter, Marc. 1984. *Competing Equalities: Law and the Backward Classes in India.* Berkeley and Los Angeles: University of California Press.

Gandhi, Gopalkrishna, ed. 2008. *The Oxford India Gandhi: Essential Writings.* New Delhi: Oxford University Press.

Ghose, Akshaya K. 1921. *Laws Affecting the Rights and Liberties of the Indian People (From Early British Rule).* Calcutta: Mohun Brothers.

Ghose, Rash Behari. 1917. *Speeches and Writings of Dr. Sir Rash Behari Ghose.* 2nd ed. Madras: G.A. Natesan & Co.

Ghurye, G. S. (1969) 1993. *Caste and Race in India.* Bombay: Popular Prakashan.

Gilchrist, R. N. 1920. *Indian Nationality.* London: Longmans, Green & Co.

Glendon, Mary Ann. 2003. "The Forgotten Crucible: The Latin American Influence on the Universal Human Rights Idea." *Harvard Human Rights Journal* 16:27–38.

Gokhale, G. K. 1908. *Speeches of the Honourable Mr. G. K. Gokhale*. Madras: G.A. Natesan & Co.

Golay, Christophe. 2009. *The Right to Food and Access to Justice: Examples at the National, Regional and International Levels*. Rome: Food and Agriculture Organization of the United Nations.

Golwalkar, M. S. 1939. *We or Our Nationhood Defined*. Nagpur: Bharat Publications.

Gopal, Sarvepalli. 1965. *British Policy in India: 1858–1905*. Cambridge: Cambridge University Press.

———. 1975. *Jawaharlal Nehru: A Biography*. Vol. 1: *1889–1947*. New Delhi: Oxford University Press.

Gorman, Daniel. 2006. *Imperial Citizenship: Empire and the Question of Belonging*. Manchester and New York: Manchester University Press.

Guha, Ramachandra. 2007a. *India After Gandhi: The History of the World's Largest Democracy*. Picador.

———. 2007b. "Adivasis, Naxalites and Indian Democracy." *Economic and Political Weekly* 42, 32 (August 11): 3305–3312.

Gundevia. Y. D. 2008. *Outside the Archives*. New Delhi: Sangam Books.

Hanlon, Joseph, Armando Barrientos, and David Hulme. 2010. *Just Give Money to the Poor: The Development Revolution from the Global South*. Sterling, VA: Kumarian Press.

Hardiman, David. 2003. *Gandhi: In His Time and Ours*. Delhi: Permanent Black.

Hasan, Mushirul, ed. 1993. *India's Partition: Process, Strategy and Mobilization*. New Delhi: Oxford University Press.

———. 1996. "The Myth of Unity: Colonial and National Narratives." In *Contesting the Nation: Religion, Community, and the Politics of Democracy in India*, edited by David Ludden. Philadelphia: University of Pennsylvania Press.

———, ed. 2008a. *Towards Freedom: Documents on the Movement for Independence in India 1939*. Part 1. New Delhi: Indian Council of Historical Research and Oxford University Press.

———, ed. 2008b. *Towards Freedom: Documents on the Movement for Independence in India 1939*. Part 2. New Delhi: Indian Council of Historical Research and Oxford University Press.

Hazareesingh, Sudhir. 2000. "The Quest for Urban Citizenship: Civic Rights, Public Opinion, and Colonial Resistance in Early Twentieth-Century Bombay." *Modern Asian Studies* 34(4): 797–829.

Holmes, Stephen, and Cass R. Sunstein. 2000. *The Cost of Rights: Why Liberty Depends on Taxes*. New York: W.W. Norton & Co.

Holston, James. 2008. *Insurgent Citizenship: Disjunctions of Democracy and Modernity in Brazil*. Princeton: Princeton University Press.

Human Rights Watch. 2010. *"Trigger Happy": Excessive Use of Force by Indian Troops at the Bangladesh Border.* New York: Human Rights Watch.

Ibrahim, Farhana. 2008. *Settlers, Saints and Sovereigns: An Ethnography of State Formation in Western India.* New Delhi: Routledge.

IDS Bulletin Research Summary. 2009. *Lifting the Curse: Overcoming Persistent Undernutrition in India* 40.4 (July). Sussex: Institute of Development Studies.

Ignatieff, Michael. 1995. "The Myth of Citizenship." In R. Beiner, ed. *q.v. Imperial Gazetteer of India, The.* 1908. Vol. 23. Oxford: Clarendon Press.

Indian National Congress. 1910. *The Indian National Congress Containing An Account of its Origin and Growth, Full Text of all the Presidential Addresses, Reprint of all the Congress Resolutions, Extracts from all the Welcome Addresses, Notable Utterances on the Movement, Portraits of all the Congress Presidents.* Madras: G. A. Natesan & Co.

International Food Policy Research Institute. 2010. *Global Hunger Index. The Challenge of Hunger: Focus on the Crisis of Child Undernutrition.* Bonn, Washington D.C., and Dublin. http://www.ifpri.org/sites/default/files/publications/ghi10.pdf.

International Institute for Population Sciences and Macro International. 2007. *National Family Health Survey (NFHS-3), 2005–06: India.* Vol. 1. Mumbai: IIPS.

Jaffrelot, Christophe. 2003. *India's Silent Revolution: The Rise of the Low Castes in North Indian Politics.* Delhi: Permanent Black.

———. 2005. *Dr. Ambedkar and Untouchability: Analysing and Fighting Caste.* Delhi: Permanent Black.

———. 2008. "Containing the Lower Castes: The Constituent Assembly and the Reservation Policy." In *Politics and Ethics of the Indian Constitution*, edited by Rajeev Bhargava. New Delhi: Oxford University Press.

Jaffrelot, Christophe, and Sanjay Kumar, eds. 2009. *Rise of the Plebeians? The Changing Face of Indian Legislative Assemblies.* New Delhi: Routledge.

Jalal, Ayesha. 2001. *Self and Sovereignty: Individual and Community in South Asian Islam since 1850.* New Delhi: Oxford University Press.

Jayal, Niraja Gopal. 1999. *Democracy and the State: Welfare, Secularism and Development in Contemporary India.* New Delhi: Oxford University Press.

———. 2006a. *Representing India: Ethnic Diversity and the Governance of Public Institutions.* London: Palgrave Macmillan and UNRISD.

———. 2006b. "Engendering Local Democracy: The Impact of Quotas for Women in India's *Panchayats.*" *Democratization* 13, 1 (February): 15–35.

———. 2006c. "Revisiting Nationalism." *Economic and Political Weekly* 41, 42 (October 21–27): 4513–4515.

Jenson, J., and S. D. Phillips. 1996. "Regime Shift: New Citizenship Practices in Canada." *International Journal of Canadian Studies* 14 (Fall): 111–135.

Joppke, Christian. 2002. "Multicultural Citizenship." In *Handbook of Citizenship Studies*, edited by Engin F. Isin and Bryan S. Turner. London: Sage Publications.

Joshi, Anuradha. 2005. "Do Rights Work? Law, Activism and the Employment Guarantee Scheme." Research Summary #13. Sussex: Centre for the Future State, Institute of Development Studies.

Kapur, Devesh. 2010. *Diaspora, Development, and Democracy: The Domestic Impact of International Migration from India*. New Delhi: Oxford University Press.

Karatani, Rieko. 2003. *Defining British Citizenship: Empire, Commonwealth and Modern Britain*. London: Frank Cass.

Karkaria, R. P. 1895. *The Late K. T. Telang and the Present Political Movement in India*. Bombay: Times of India Office.

Keer, Dhananjay. 1971. *Dr. Ambedkar: Life and Mission*. Bombay, Popular Prakashan.

Keith, A. Berriedale. 1922. *Speeches and Documents on Indian Policy, 1750–1921*. Vols. 1 & 2. London: Humphrey Milford, Oxford University Press.

Keyssar, Alexander. 2000. *The Right to Vote: The Contested History of Democracy in the United States*. New York: Basic Books.

Khera, Reetika. 2011. "Empowerment Guarantee Act?" In *The Battle for Employment Guarantee*, edited by Khera. New Delhi: Oxford University Press.

Khosla, Madhav. 2010. "Making Social Rights Conditional: Lessons from India." *International Journal of Constitutional Law*. 8 (4): 739-765.

Kidambi, Prashant. 2007. *The Making of an Indian Metropolis: Colonial Governance and Public Culture in Bombay, 1890–1920*. Hampshire: Ashgate.

King, Desmond, and Jeremy Waldron. 1988. "Citizenship, Social Citizenship and the Defence of Welfare Provision." *British Journal of Political Science* 18(4): 415–443.

Knuth, Lidija, and Margret Vidar. 2011. *Constitutional and Legal Protection of the Right to Food around the World*. Rome: Food and Agriculture Organization of the United Nations.

Kohli, Atul. 2009. *Democracy and Development in India: From Socialism to Pro-Business*. New Delhi: Oxford University Press.

———. 2012. *Poverty Amid Plenty in the New India*. Cambridge: Cambridge University Press.

Kothari, Rajni. 1970a. *Politics in India*. Delhi: Orient Longman.

———, ed. 1970b. *Caste in Indian Politics*. New Delhi: Orient Longman.

Kudaisya, Gyanesh. 2006. "Indian Leadership and the Diaspora." In *Encyclopaedia of the Indian Diaspora*, edited by Brij Vilash Lal. New Delhi: Oxford University Press.

Kumar, R., ed. 1971. *Essays on Gandhian Politics: The Rowlatt Satyagraha of 1919*. Oxford: Clarendon Press.

Kymlicka, Will. 1991. *Liberalism, Community and Culture*. Oxford: Clarendon Press.

————. 2000. "Citizenship in Culturally Diverse Societies: Issues, Contexts, Concepts." In *Citizenship in Diverse Societies*, edited by Kymlicka and Norman. Oxford: Oxford University Press.

Kymlicka, Will, and Wayne Norman. 1995 "Return of the Citizen: A Survey of Recent Work on Citizenship Theory" In *Theorizing Citizenship*, edited by Ronald Beiner. *q.v.*

———— eds. 2000. *Citizenship in Diverse Societies.* Oxford: Oxford University Press.

Lee-Warner, Sir William. 1900. *The Citizen of India.* London: Macmillan & Co.

————. 1907. *The Citizen of India.* Revised Edition. London: Macmillan & Co.

Linklater, Andrew. 1999. "Cosmopolitan Citizenship." In *Cosmopolitan Citizenship*, edited by Kimberley Hutchings and Roland Dannreuther. London: Macmillan Press Ltd.

Lohia, Ram Manohar. 1936. *The Struggle for Civil Liberties.* With a foreword by Jawaharlal Nehru. Allahabad: Foreign Department, All India Congress.

Lopez-Guerra, Claudio. 2005. "Should Expatriates Vote?" *The Journal of Political Philosophy* 13, 2: 216–234.

Lothian, Marquess of. 1932. "India and the Franchise Problem." *International Affairs* 11, 5 (September): 593–617.

Macedo, Stephen. 2007. "The Moral Dilemma of U.S. Immigration Policy: Open Borders Versus Social Justice?" In *Debating Immigration*, edited by Carol M. Swain. Cambridge: Cambridge University Press.

Mahmudabad, Raja of. 2001. "Some Memories." In *India's Partition: Process, Strategy and Mobilization*, edited by Mushirul Hasan. New Delhi: Oxford University Press.

Majumdar, Bimanbehari. 1965. *Indian Political Associations and Reform of Legislature (1818–1917).* Calcutta: Firma K.L. Mukhopadhyay.

————. (1934) 1967. *History of Indian Social and Political Ideas: From Rammohan to Dayananda.* Calcutta: Bookland Private Limited.

Majumdar, Ramesh Chandra. 1922. *Corporate Life in Ancient India.* Poona: The Oriental Book Agency.

Malihabadi, Josh. 1997. "My Ordeal as a Citizen of Pakistan." In *India Partitioned: The Other Face of Freedom.* Vol. 2. Edited by Mushirul Hasan. Delhi: Roli Books.

Mann, Michael. 1987. "Ruling Class Strategies and Citizenship." *Sociology* 21, 3 (August): 339–354.

Marshall, T. H. (1950) 1992. *Citizenship and Social Class.* London: Pluto Press.

Marx, Karl. 1963. *Early Writings.* Translated and edited by T. B. Bottomore. London: C.A. Watts & Co. Ltd.

Masani, Minoo. 1940. *Our India.* Calcutta: Oxford University Press.

McMillan, Alistair. 2005. *Standing at the Margins: Representation and Electoral Reservation in India.* New Delhi: Oxford University Press.

Mehrotra, Santosh. 2010. "Introducing Conditional Cash Transfers in India: A Proposal for Five CCTs." Planning Commission. December 3.

Mehta, Uday Singh. 2010. "Constitutionalism." In *The Oxford Companion to Politics in India*, edited by Niraja Gopal Jayal and Pratap Bhanu Mehta. New Delhi: Oxford University Press.

Michelman, Frank I. 2006. "Unenumerated Rights Under Popular Constitutionalism." *Journal of Constitutional Law* 9, 1 (October).

———. 2007. "The Constitution, Social Rights and Liberal Political Justification." In *Exploring Social Rights: Between Theory and Practice*, edited by Daphne Barak-Erez and Aeyal M. Gross. Oxford and Portland, OR: Hart Publishing.

Mishra, Neelesh, and Rahul Pandita. 2010. *The Absent State: Insurgency as an Excuse for Misgovernance*. New Delhi: Hachette India.

Mooij, Jos, and S. Mahendra Dev. 2004. "Social Sector Priorities: An Analysis of Budgets and Expenditures in India in the 1990s." *Development Policy Review* 22(1): 97–120.

Mookerji, Radha Kumud. 1914. "An Introductory Essay on the Age and Authenticity of the Arthasastra of Kautilya." In *Studies in Ancient Hindu Polity*. Vol. 1. Narendra Nath Law. London: Longmans, Green & Co.

———. 1921. *Nationalism in Hindu Culture*. London: Theosophical Publishing House.

Morrison, Rev. John. 1906. *New Ideas in India During the Nineteenth Century: A Study of Social, Political, and Religious Developments*. Edinburgh: George A. Morton.

Nandy, Ashis. 2006. "Nationalism, Genuine and Spurious: Mourning Two Early Post-Nationalist Strains." *Economic and Political Weekly* 41, 32 (August 12–18): 3500–3504.

Naoroji, Dadabhai. 1917. *Dadabhai Naoroji's Speeches and Writings*. 2nd ed. Madras: G. A. Natesan.

Narayanan, Sudha. 2011. "A Case for Reframing the Cash Transfer Debate in India." *Economic and Political Weekly* 46, 21 (May 21).

National Advisory Council. 2011. *Note on the Draft National Food Security Bill*. New Delhi.

Nehru, Jawaharlal. (1936) 1989. *An Autobiography*. New Delhi: Oxford University Press.

———. 1972a. *Selected Works of Jawaharlal Nehru*. Vol. 1. Edited by S. Gopal. Delhi: Orient Longman.

———. 1972b. *Selected Works of Jawaharlal Nehru*. Vol. 2. Edited by S. Gopal. Delhi: Orient Longman.

———. 2003a. *The Essential Writings of Jawaharlal Nehru*. Vol. 1. Edited by S. Gopal and Uma Iyengar. New Delhi: Oxford University Press.

———. 2003b. *The Essential Writings of Jawaharlal Nehru*. Vol. 2. Edited by S. Gopal and Uma Iyengar. New Delhi: Oxford University Press.

Nehru, Motilal. 1995. *Selected Works of Motilal Nehru*. Vol. 6. Edited by Ravinder Kumar and Hari Dev Sharma. New Delhi: Vikas Publishing House.

Newland, Kathleen, and Erin Patrick. 2004. "Beyond Remittances: The Role of Diaspora in Poverty Reduction in their Countries of Origin." Washington, D.C.: Migration Policy Institute.

Nicolet, C. 1980. *The World of the Citizen in Republican Rome.* Translated by P. S. Falla. Berkeley and Los Angeles: University of California Press.

Norwegian Refugee Council. 2010. *India: National and State Authorities Failing to Protect IDPs: A Profile of the Internal Displacement Situation.* Geneva: Internal Displacement Monitoring Centre.

Nozick, Robert. 1970. *Anarchy, State and Utopia.* New York: Basic Books.

Nussbaum, Martha C. 2007. *The Clash Within: Democracy, Religious Violence and India's Future.* Ranikhet: Permanent Black.

O'Cinneide, Colm. 2009. "Bringing Socio-economic Rights Back into the Mainstream of Human Rights: The Case Law of the European Committee on Social Rights as an Example of Rigorous and Effective Rights Adjudication." Social Science Research Network. http://ssrn.com/abstract=1543127.

Oldfield, Adrian. 1990. *Citizenship and Community: Civic Republicanism and the Modern World.* London: Routledge.

O'Neill, Onora. 1986. *Faces of Hunger: An Essay on Poverty, Development and Justice.* London: Routledge.

Ong, Aihwa. 2007. "Citizenship." In *A Companion to the Anthropology of Politics,* edited by David Nugent and Joan Vincent. Oxford: Blackwell.

Pai, Sudha. 2010. *Developmental State and the Dalit Question in Madhya Pradesh: Congress Response.* New Delhi: Routledge.

Pal, Bipin Chandra. 1932. *Memories of My Life and Times.* Calcutta: Modern Book Agency.

————. 1958. 4th ed. *The Soul of India.* Calcutta: Yugayatri Prakashak Ltd.

Pandey, Gyanendra. 2001. *Remembering Partition: Violence, Nationalism and History in India.* Cambridge: Cambridge University Press.

Panikkar, K. N., ed. 2009. *Towards Freedom: Documents on the Movement for Independence in India, 1940.* New Delhi: Indian Council of Historical Research and Oxford University Press.

Pant, Mandakini. 2005. "The Quest for Inclusion: Nomadic Communities and Citizenship Questions in Rajasthan." In *Inclusive Citizenship: Meanings and Expressions,* edited by Naila Kabeer. London: Zed Books.

Parel, Anthony. 2006. *Gandhi's Philosophy and the Quest for Harmony.* New Delhi: Cambridge University Press.

Peddie, J. R. 1920. *The British Citizen: A Book for Young Readers.* London: Blackie & Son Ltd.

Phillips, Anne. 1995. *The Politics of Presence.* Oxford: Clarendon Press.

Pieterse, Marius. 2007. "Eating Socioeconomic Rights: The Usefulness of Rights Talk in Alleviating Social Hardship Revisited." *Human Rights Quarterly* 29, 3 (August): 796–822.

Pitts, Jennifer. 2005. *A Turn to Empire: The Rise of Imperial Liberalism in Britain and France*. Princeton, NJ: Princeton University Press.

Pogge, Thomas. 2001. "Priorities of Global Justice." *Metaphilosophy* 32, 1/2 (January).

Powell, Martin. 2002. "The Hidden History of Social Citizenship." *Citizenship Studies* 6(3): 229–244

Prakash, Amit. 2001. *Jharkhand: Politics of Development and Identity*. New Delhi: Orient Longman.

Prasad, Chandra Bhan. 2001. Interview with S. Anand of the Dalit Media Network. http://www.ambedkar.org/chandrabhan/interview.htm.

Puntambekar, S. V. 1929. *An Introduction to Indian Citizenship and Civilisation*. Benares: Nand Kishore & Bros.

———. 1948. "Human Freedoms and the Hindu Thinking." In *Human Rights: Comments and Interpretations*, edited by UNESCO. Paris: UNESCO.

Purcell, Nicholas. 1986. "The Arts of Government." In *The Oxford History of the Classical World*, edited by John Boardman, Jasper Griffin, and Oswyn Murray. Oxford: Oxford University Press.

Putnam, Robert. 1993. *Making Democracy Work: Civic Traditions in Modern Italy*. Princeton, NJ: Princeton University Press.

Quadagno, Jill. 1987. "Theories of the Welfare State." *Annual Review of Sociology* 13:109–128.

Radhakrishnan, P. 1990. "Backward Classes in Tamil Nadu: 1872–1988." *Economic and Political Weekly* 25, 10 (March 10): 509–520.

Rai, Lala Lajpat. (1920) 2007. *The Collected Works of Lala Lajpat Rai*. Vol. 9. Chief Editor: B. R. Nanda. Delhi: Manohar Publishers.

Raj, Dhooleka S. 2003. *Where Are You From? Middle-Class Migrants in the Modern World*. Berkeley: University of California Press.

Ramusack, Barbara N. 2004. *The Indian Princes and their States*. The New Cambridge History of India. Vol. 3. Cambridge: Cambridge University Press, 2004.

Rao, B. Shiva. 1966–1968. *The Framing of India's Constitution: Select Documents*. 4 vols. New Delhi: Indian Institute of Public Administration.

———. 1968a. *The Framing of India's Constitution: A Study*. New Delhi: Indian Institute of Public Administration.

Reimers, Fernando, Carol DeShano da Silva, and Ernesto Trevino. 2006. *Where is the "Education" in Conditional Cash Transfers in Education?* Montreal: UNESCO Institute for Statistics.

Rhodes, Sybil, and Harutyunyan, Arus. 2010. "Extending Citizenship to Emigrants: Democratic Contestation and a New Global Norm." *International Political Science Review* 31(4): 470–493.

Ricci, David M. 2004. *Good Citizenship in America*. Cambridge: Cambridge University Press.

Right to Food Campaign. 2008. *Supreme Court Orders on the Right to Food: A Tool for Action*. New Delhi: Right to Food Campaign Secretariat.

Rodrigues, Valerian. 2002. *The Essential Writings of B. R. Ambedkar*. New Delhi: Oxford University Press.

———. 2007. "Good Society: Rights, Democracy and Socialism." In *Ambedkar in Retrospect: Essays on Economic, Politics and Society*, edited by Sukhadeo Thorat and Aryama. Jaipur: Rawat Publications in association with the Indian Institute of Dalit Studies, New Delhi.

———. 2008. "Citizenship and the Indian Constitution." In *Politics and Ethics of the Indian Constitution*, edited by Rajeev Bhargava. New Delhi: Oxford University Press.

Rolfe, Ella. 2008. "Refugee, Minority, Citizen, Threat: Tibetans and the Indian Refugee Script." *South Asia Research* 28(3): 253–283.

Rose, Nikolas, and Carlos Novas. 2005. "Biological Citizenship." In *Global Assemblages: Technology, Politics and Ethics as Anthropological Problems*, edited by Aihwa Ong and Stephen J. Collier. Oxford: Blackwell.

Roy, Anupama. 2010. *Mapping Citizenship in India*. New Delhi: Oxford University Press.

Roy, M. N. 1944. *Constitution of India: A Draft*. The Radical Democratic Party.

Rudolph, Lloyd I., and Susanne Hoeber Rudolph. 1967. *The Modernity of Tradition*. Chicago: University of Chicago Press.

Rudolph, Lloyd I., and John Kurt Jacobsen, eds. 2006. *Experiencing the State*. New Delhi: Oxford University Press.

Runnymede Trust, The. 2000. *Commission on the Future of Multi-Ethnic Britain*. http://www.runnymedetrust.org/projects/meb/reportPartOne.html#rethinking.

Russell, Bertrand. 1958. *The Good Citizen's Alphabet*. New York: The Wisdom Library.

Sadiq, Kamal. 2009. *Paper Citizens: How Illegal Immigrants Acquire Citizenship in Developing Countries*. New York: Oxford University Press.

Sapru Committee Report. 1945. *Constitutional Proposals of the Sapru Committee: Report Compiled by Sir Tej Bahadur Sapru*. Bombay: Padma Publications Ltd.

Sargant, E. B., ed. 1912. *British Citizenship*. London: Longmans, Green & Co.

Sarkar, Lotika, and Vina Mazumdar. (1974) 2008. "Dissenting Voices: Note of Dissent to *Towards Equality*, Report of the Committee on the Status of Women in India." In *Reservations for Women*, edited by Meena Dhanda. New Delhi: Women Unlimited.

Sarkar, Sumit. 1983. *Modern India, 1885–1947*. Delhi: Macmillan India Ltd.

———. 2005. "Indian Nationalism and the Politics of Hindutva." In *Making India Hindu: Religion, Community, and the Politics of Democracy in India*, edited by David Ludden. New Delhi: Oxford University Press.

———, ed. 2007. *Towards Freedom: Documents on the Movement for Independence in India 1946*. Part 1. New Delhi: Indian Council of Historical Research and Oxford University Press.

Sassen, Saskia. 2006. "The Repositioning of Citizenship and Alienage: Emergent Subjects and Spaces for Politics." In *Displacement, Asylum, Migration*, edited by Kate E. Tunstall. The Oxford Amnesty Lectures, 2004. Oxford: Oxford University Press.

Sastri, V. S. Srinivasa. (1926) 1948. *The Indian Citizen: His Rights and Duties*. Kamala Lectures, 1926. Bombay: Hind Kitabs Limited.

Satyamurthy, S. 1919. *The Rights of Citizens*. Madras: Ganesh & Co.

Savarkar, V. D. 1923. *Essentials of Hindutva*. http://www.savarkar.org/content/pdfs/en/essentials_of_hindutva.v001.pdf.

Scheffler, Samuel. 2001. *Boundaries and Allegiances: Problems of Justice and Responsibility in Liberal Thought*. New York: Oxford University Press.

Schendel, Willem van. 2002. "Stateless in South Asia: The Making of the India-Bangladesh Enclaves." *The Journal of Asian Studies* 61(1): 115–147.

Schudson, Michael. 1999. *The Good Citizen: A History of American Civic Life*. New York: Free Press

Scott, David. 1995. "Colonial Governmentality." *Social Text* 43 (Autumn): 191–220.

Shachar, Ayelet. 2009. "Citizenship as a Special Kind of Property Inheritance." *Rorotoko*. Cover interview of August 28, 2009. http://www.rorotoko.com/index.php/single/ayelet_shachar_book_interview_birthright_lottery_citizenship_global_inequal.

Shah, Alpa. 2010. *In the Shadows of the State: Indigenous Politics, Environmentalism, and Insurgency in Jharkhand, India*. New Delhi: Oxford University Press.

Shah, Ghanshyam, Harsh Mander, Sukhadeo Thorat, Satish Deshpande, and Amita Baviskar. 2006. *Untouchability in Rural India*. New Delhi: Sage Publications.

Shani, Ornit. 2010. "Conceptions of Citizenship in India and the 'Muslim Question.'" *Modern Asian Studies* 44(1): 145–173.

Shah, Zulfiqar. 2007. *Long Behind Schedule: A Study on the Plight of Scheduled Caste Hindus in Pakistan*. Karachi: Report for Indian Institute of Dalit Studies and International Dalit Solidarity Network.

Sheth, D. L. 2002. "Caste and Class: Social Reality and Political Representations." In *Caste and Democratic Politics in India*, edited by Ghanshyam Shah. Delhi: Permanent Black.

Shklar, Judith. 1991. *American Citizenship: The Quest for Inclusion*. Cambridge: Harvard University Press.

Shukla, Ravi. 2010. "Reimagining Citizenship: Debating India's Unique Identification Scheme." *Economic and Political Weekly* 45, 2 (January 9): 31–36.

Singer, Wendy. 2007. *"A Constituency Suitable for Ladies" and other Social Histories of Indian Elections*. New Delhi: Oxford University Press.

Singh, Deepak K. 2010. *Stateless in South Asia: The Chakmas between Bangladesh and India*. New Delhi: Sage Publications.

Sitaramayya, Pattabhi. 1935. *The History of the Indian National Congress*. Madras: The Working Committee of the Congress.

Smith, Rogers M. 1997. *Civic Ideals: Conflicting Visions of Citizenship in U.S. History.* New Haven CT: Yale University Press.

―――. 2003. *Stories of Peoplehood: The Politics and Morals of Political Membership.* Cambridge: Cambridge University Press.

Soares, Fabio Veras. 2011. "Brazil's Bolsa Familia: A Review." *Economic and Political Weekly* 46, 21 (May 21).

Socialist Party, The. 1948. *Draft Constitution of Indian Republic.* Bombay.

Somers, Margaret R., and Christopher N. J. Roberts. 2008. "Towards a New Sociology of Rights: A Genealogy of 'Buried Bodies' of Citizenship and Human Rights." *The Annual Review of Law and Social Science* 4:385–425.

Srinivas, M. N. 1997. Introduction to *Caste: Its Twentieth Century Avatar*, edited by M. N. Srinivas. New Delhi: Penguin Books.

Srinivasan, K., A Shariff, W. A. Zaman, and C. Bierring. 1997. *India: Towards Population and Development Goals.* New Delhi: Oxford University Press.

Sripati, Vijayshri, and Arun K. Thiruvengadam. 2004. "India: Constitutional Amendment Making the Right to Education a Fundamental Right." *International Journal of Constitutional Law* 2(1): 148–158.

Sutton, Deborah. 2007. "'Divided and Uncertain Loyalties': Partition, Indian Sovereignty and Contested Citizenship in East Africa, 1948–1955." *Interventions: International Journal of Postcolonial Studies* 9(2): 276–288.

Swaminathan, Madhura. 2000. *Weakening Welfare: The Public Distribution of Food in India.* New Delhi: Leftword Books.

Szreter, Simon. 2007. "The Right of Registration: Development, Identity Registration, and Social Security—A Historical Perspective." *World Development* 35(1): 67–86.

Talbot, Ian. 1998. *Pakistan: A Modern History.* New Delhi: Oxford University Press.

Telang, K. T. 1916. *Select Writings and Speeches.* Bombay: Manoranjan Press.

Teltumbde, Anand. 2011. "Dalit Capitalism and Pseudo Dalitism." *Economic and Political Weekly* 46, 10 (March 5): 10–11.

Thorat, Sukhadeo, and Narender Kumar, eds. 2008. *B. R. Ambedkar: Perspectives in Social Exclusion and Inclusive Policies.* New Delhi: Oxford University Press.

Thorat Sukhadeo, and Katherine Newman, eds. 2010. *Blocked by Caste: Economic Discrimination in Modern India.* New Delhi: Oxford University Press.

Tilly, Charles. 1999. "Conclusion: Why Worry about Citizenship." In *Extending Citizenship, Reconfiguring States,* edited by Michael Hanagan and Charles Tilly. Lanham, MD: Rowman & Littlefield Publishers, Inc.

Tinker, Hugh. 1976. *Separate and Unequal: India and the Indians in the British Commonwealth, 1920–1950.* Delhi: Vikas Publishing House.

Tomasevski, Katarina. 2003. "School Fees as Hindrance to Universalizing Primary Education." Paper commissioned for the EFA Global Monitoring Report 2003/4, The Leap to Equality. UNESCO.

Tomory, Rev. A. 1900. *Authorised Guide to Lee-Warner's Citizen of India.* London: Macmillan & Co. Ltd.

Tushnet, Mark. 1984. "An Essay on Rights." *Texas Law Review* 62, 8 (May).

(UNESCO) United Nations Educational, Scientific and Cultural Organization. 1948. *Human Rights: Comments and Interpretations*. Paris.

United Nations Development Programme. 2010. *Human Development Report, 2010*. New York: Palgrave Macmillan.

United Nations Economic and Social Council. 2001. *Report by the Special Rapporteur on the Right to Food*. Commission on Human Rights. http://www.righttofood.org/new/PDF/ECN4200153.pdf.

United Nations High Commissioner for Human Rights. 2010. *The Right to Adequate Food*. Fact Sheet No. 34. Geneva: OHCHR and FAO.

Viroli, Maurizio. 1995. *For Love of Country: An Essay on Patriotism and Nationalism*. Oxford: Clarendon Press.

Visvesvaraya, Sir M. 1920. *Reconstructing India*. London: P.S. King & Son, Ltd.

Wadia, Sophia. 1940. *Preparation for Citizenship*. Bombay: Theosophy Co.

Waiz, S. A., ed. 1927. *Indians Abroad*. Bombay: The Imperial Indian Citizenship Association.

Waldron, Jeremy. 2000. "The Role of Rights in Practical Reasoning: "Rights' versus "Needs." *Journal of Ethics* 4, (1/2). Rights, Equality, and Liberty Universidad Torcuato Di Tella Law and Philosophy Lectures, 1995–1997. Jan–Mar 2000: 115–135.

Walzer, Michael. 1983. *Spheres of Justice: A Defense of Pluralism and Equality*. New York: Basic Books.

———. 1989. "Citizenship." In *Political Innovation and Conceptual Change*, edited by Terence Ball, James Farr, and Russell L. Hanson. Cambridge: Cambridge University Press.

Watt, Carey Anthony. 1997. "Education for National Efficiency: Constructive Nationalism in North India, 1909–1916." *Modern Asian Studies* 31, 2 (May): 339–374.

——— 1999. "The Promise of 'Character' and the Spectre of Sedition: The Boy Scout Movement and Colonial Consternation in India, 1908-1921." *South Asia*. XII, 2: 37–62.

———. 2005. *Serving the Nation: Cultures of Service, Association and Citizenship*. New Delhi: Oxford University Press.

Webb, Sidney, and Beatrice Webb. 1987. *Indian Diary*. Edited by Niraja Gopal Jayal. New Delhi: Oxford University Press.

Weil, Patrick. 2008. Translated by Catherine Porter. *How to be French: Nationality in the Making since 1789*. Durham, NC: Duke University Press.

Weldon, Laurie S. 2002. "Beyond Bodies: Institutional Sources of Representation for Women in Democratic Policymaking." *The Journal of Politics* 64(4): 1153–1174.

Wiesen, S. Jonathan. 2008. "Creating the Nazi Marketplace: Public Relations and Consumer Citizenship in the Third Reich." In *Citizenship and National Identity in Twentieth-Century Germany*, edited by Geoff Eley and Jan Palmowski. Stanford, CA: Stanford University Press.

Willatt, Col. J. 1946. *Citizenship: The Responsibilities and Privileges of the Indian Citizen*. Bombay: Geoffrey Cumberlege, Oxford University Press.

Wolpert, Stanley. 1967. *Morley and India: 1906–1910*. Berkeley: University of California Press.

World Bank, The. 1997. *The State in a Changing World*. World Development Report. New York: Oxford University Press.

———. 2011. *Social Protection for a Changing India*. Vol. 1. Washington, D.C.: The International Bank for Reconstruction and Development/The World Bank.

Yadav, Yogendra. 2000. "Understanding the Second Democratic Upsurge: Trends of Bahujan Participation in Electoral Politics in the 1990s." In *Transforming India: Social and Political Dynamics of Democracy*, edited by Francine Frankel, Zoya Hasan, Rajeev Bhargava, and Balveer Arora. New Delhi: Oxford University Press.

Yanes, Pablo. 2011. "Mexico's Targeted and Conditional Transfers: Between Oportunidades and Rights." *Economic and Political Weekly* 46, 21 (May 21).

Yashar, Deborah. 2005. *Contesting Citizenship in Latin America: The Rise of Indigenous Movements and the Postliberal Challenge*. Cambridge, MA: Cambridge University Press.

Young, Iris Marion. (1989) 1995. "Polity and Group Difference: A Critique of the Ideal of Universal Citizenship." In R. Beiner, ed. *q.v.*

Younghusband, Sir Francis. 1931. *Dawn in India: British Purpose and Indian Aspiration*. New York: Frederick A. Stokes Co.

Zachariah, Benjamin. 2004. *Nehru*. London: Routledge.

Zacharias, H. C. E. 1933. *Renascent India: From Rammohan Roy to Mohandas Gandhi*. London: George Allen & Unwin.

Zaidi, A. M., ed. 1979. *The Encyclopaedia of the Indian National Congress*. Vol. 7: 1916–1920. New Delhi: S. Chand & Co., under the auspices of the Indian Institute of Applied Political Research.

Zamindar, Vazira Fazila-Yacoobali. 2007. *The Long Partition and the Making of Modern South Asia: Refugees, Boundaries, Histories*. New Delhi: Viking Books.

Zelliot, Eleanor. 1972. "Gandhi and Ambedkar—A Study in Leadrhip." In *The Untouchables in Contemporary India*, edited by J. Michael Mahar. Tucson: The University of Arizona Press.

Zook, Darren C. 2000. "Developing the Rural Citizen: Southern India, 1900–47." *South Asia* 23(1): 65–85.

Acknowledgments

This book is based on my Radhakrishnan Memorial Lectures, which were delivered in November 2009 at the invitation of All Souls College and the Oriental Institute, University of Oxford. I thank the Warden and Fellows of All Souls for their magnificent hospitality. I am especially grateful to the Warden, Professor Sir John Vickers, for his unfailing kindness throughout my stay.

This book was substantially written over a year (2009–2010) spent at Princeton University where, as Visiting Fellow in Democracy and Development, I had the privilege of having as many as three institutional hosts. I am deeply grateful to Atul Kohli and Deborah Yashar of the Democracy and Development Program at the Woodrow Wilson School; Stephen Macedo and Charles Beitz of the University Center for Human Values; and Katherine Newman of the Princeton Institute for International and Regional Studies. For an academic, there can be no greater pleasure than the unimpeded freedom to think, read, and write, and this is exactly what Princeton provided, along with the delights of an open-stack library with prodigious holdings.

The book did not, however, begin in Princeton. A month-long immersion in the Bodleian Library at Oxford, made possible by a Charles Wallace India Trust Fellowship, started me on this journey many years earlier. Subsequently, a Senior Fellowship at the Nehru Memorial Museum and Library—albeit abbreviated midway—enabled an early delineation of the contours of the project, even if this book bears only a faint resemblance to it. Shorter visiting fellowships at the Maison des Sciences de l'Homme, Paris, the University of New South Wales, Sydney, and the University of Melbourne provided library resources and opportunities for conversations with scholars with kindred interests. This peripatetic and rather staccato pursuit of the book's concerns would have been impossible without the incredible generosity of my home institution, the Jawaharlal Nehru University, in giving me leave of absence from time to time. I am grateful to all these institutions for their support.

The Jawaharlal Nehru University also provided me with a supportive environment in which to direct a South Asia–wide research network funded by the Ford Foundation, Dialogue on Democracy and Pluralism in South Asia. I am grateful to the Ford Foundation, for this project helped me to build up a substantial collection of books and materials on democracy and citizenship; entailed fruitful interactions with other South Asian scholars; facilitated my burrowing in the private papers of Sir William Lee-Warner in the India Office Records of the British Library in London; and, above all, funded the fieldwork in Rajasthan that is the subject of Chapter 3 of this book. In Rajasthan, the kind assistance of Kiran Soni Gupta, Divisional Commissioner of Jodhpur, and Hindu Singh Sodha of the Pak Visthapit Sangh are gratefully acknowledged, as is also the warm hospitality of the residents of the refugee camps I visited.

Seminars based on parts of this book have been presented at a number of institutions. I am grateful for these invitations as well as for the indulgence of my audiences at these forums, and for their insightful questions. I thank Janaki Bakhle of Columbia University for the invitation to deliver the Mary Keating Das Memorial Lecture; Deborah Yashar for the seminar at Princeton University; Ira Katznelson and Partha Chatterjee for the opportunity to present a part of this work in the Tocqueville Conference at Harvard University; Devesh Kapur for the invitation to the Centre for the Advanced Study of India at the University of Pennsylvania; Subrata Mitra and Jivanta Schöttli at the Cluster of Excellence on "Asia and Europe in a Global Context" at Heidelberg University; Bhaskar Vira, Philippa Williams, and Deepta Chopra for the opportunity to present a fragment as a keynote at their conference "Experiencing the State" at Cambridge University; Ornit Shani for the invitation to join her and Joya Chatterji—my fellow hikers on the citizenship trail—at a conference hosted by the National Archives of India; and the Law and Social Sciences Research Network at the Centre for the Study of Law and Governance, Jawaharlal Nehru University, for encouraging me to convene two panels on citizenship at its inaugural conference and present my work.

I am profoundly grateful to friends and colleagues who have given generously of their time to read parts of this book and provide critical comments and suggestions. Ramachandra Guha encouraged me to extend the original post-independence focus of this book to encompass the twentieth century as a whole. I cannot thank him enough for the introduction to materials I did not know existed, and for giving me detailed and acute comments on the manuscript as a whole. Several others have carefully read and commented on one or more chapters, and their insights have certainly made the book better than it was. Without however burdening them with any responsibility for the final product, I am grateful to Atul Kohli, Barbara Harriss-White, Neera Chandhoke, Ravindra Karnena, Rogers M. Smith, and Shirin M. Rai. I would also like to thank Susanne H. Rudolph, Lloyd I. Rudolph, and John Keane, with whom I had some of my earliest conversations on this subject.

Ravindra Karnena has, for many years, been a well-read and valued interlocutor. He collected materials, conducted pilot fieldwork in Rajasthan, and provided insightful comments on early drafts. I am grateful for his friendship and shared bibliophilism. I thank Shrimoyee Nandini Ghosh, who compiled the case law on citizenship for me, and Arib Ansari and Chander Paul Negi, who provided able research assistance toward the end. I am grateful to Amar Khoday of McGill University for clarifying an important point of refugee law. Discussing the theoretical debates with students in my citizenship classes in 2011 and 2012 has been engaging, and thanks are due to them as well.

It has been a particular pleasure to work with Sharmila Sen of Harvard University Press, whose engagement with the book has been truly impressive: erudite, witty, and professional. I am grateful also for the very helpful reviews of the two anonymous readers.

I would also like to thank those who have helped me in obtaining permission to draw on previous publications of mine: Frances Stewart, John Harriss, Sanjay Ruparelia, and Nitasha Devasar. These include brief portions of "The Transformation of Citizenship in India in the 1990s and Beyond," in *Understanding India's New Political Economy: A Great Transformation?*, ed. Sanjay Ruparelia, Sanjay Reddy, John Hariss, and Stuart Corbridge (New York: Routledge, 2011), in the Introduction and Chapters 2, 3, 7, and 9; brief portions of "A False Dichotomy? The Unresolved Tension between Universal and Differentiated Citizenship in India," *Oxford Development Studies* 39, 2 (2011), in Chapter 8; and portions of "An Immense and (In)complete Democracy," in *Anxieties of Democracy*, ed. Partha Chatterjee and Ira Katznelson (New York: Oxford University Press, 2012), in Chapters 7 and 9.

The writing of a book is an enterprise necessarily dependent on not just the kindness but even the forbearance of family and friends, including their indulgence toward the unforgivable forgetting of birthdays and anniversaries. I have been very blessed in both my family and friends. Several friends traveled to Oxford, some very long distances, to attend one or other of my Radhakrishnan Lectures. Sujata Mehta's is a hugely cherished friendship, and not only because she traveled from Spain for the first lecture. I thank Shirin Rai, Rochana Bajpai, and Clare and Clive Sutton for their friendly excursions to Oxford; and Nandini Gooptu, who made me very welcome there and was extremely generous with her time.

My year at Princeton was greatly enriched by new friendships that quickly acquired a texture of permanence. The generous and affectionate care of Diane Borden and Lalit Ahluwalia was literally crucial to my survival. They have me in pizza-debt forever. Mary and Peter Katzenstein started off as delightful dinner companions, and became treasured friends. I am grateful also for the many kindnesses of Gayatri Badrinath, Sunanda Nair, and Walter Lippincott.

Back in Delhi, in an act of pure altruism, Neera Chandhoke and Chandrika Grover decided to ignore me in the larger interests of my self-imposed hibernation, and while I am grateful to them I hope this will not have become a habit. I am thankful also to Pratap Bhanu Mehta for a supportive friendship and for his possibly unmerited optimism about this project. My colleagues Amit Prakash, Jaivir Singh, and Pratiksha Baxi have cheerfully borne the often distasteful burdens imposed on them by my creative and even cunning endeavors to carve out time to write. It has been a pleasure to share ideas with them, traversing disciplinary boundaries. I have also relied hugely on Amit's remarkable technological abilities, transiting from computer to computer as I worked on this book. I could not ask for more wonderful coworkers. My thanks finally to Modhumita Lahiri for the introduction to the fantastic resources of the Internet archive.

Three people have helped to make everyday life hassle-free. Ashis Das has been an amazingly competent aide, taking care of photocopying jobs, library chores, and the expert detection of documents buried underneath piles of paper. The Brothers Thapa, Mani Ram and Tan Bahadur, are gifted culinary artists who have provided comfort food and made it possible to entertain friends superbly without eating into my working hours.

I remain puzzled and intrigued by how my family has not only countenanced but been positively encouraging of my preoccupation, which has certainly exceeded any reasonable limits of time. It is a matter of the deepest regret that my father, Madan Gopal, a much more driven and prolific writer than I, did not live to see the publication of this book. My mother, Kanta, has always been a rock of boundless love and support and, over the last couple of difficult and lonely years, has borne my neglect of her with incredible indulgence and stoic self-denial. My brother Sachin traveled from Delhi to attend one of the Radhakrishnan Lectures, and I am grateful to him and Nishi for their generosity and affection. I am grateful also to my sisters-in-law, Madhuri Mathur and Usha Lakhanpal, for being affectionately forgiving of my recent inattention. Usha and Dave Sharma gave me untrammeled rights to the guest room in their beautiful home in New York City along with invitations to plays and concerts. Also in New York, Gaurav Butani provided witty company and an agreeable disposition in putting up with eccentric auntly demands. Soniya Carvalho's genuine interest in my work and well-being was a valuable source of support throughout.

Finally, I simply do not have the words to thank the anchors of my existence, my husband, Rakesh, and our daughter, Gayatri. That they are mine means more than anything else in the world. That they are both exceptional practitioners of citizenship has been an added inspiration in the writing of this book.

Index